ICL
A Business and Technical History

I C L
A Business and Technical History

by

Martin Campbell-Kelly
Department of Computer Science
University of Warwick

Clarendon Press · Oxford
1989

Oxford University Press, Walton Street, Oxford OX2 6DP

Oxford New York Toronto
Delhi Bombay Calcutta Madras Karachi
Petaling Jaya Singapore Hong Kong Tokyo
Nairobi Dar es Salaam Cape Town
Melbourne Auckland
and associated companies in
Berlin Ibadan

Oxford is a trade mark of Oxford University Press

Published in the United States
by Oxford University Press, New York

British Library Cataloguing in Publication Data
Campbell-Kelly, Martin 1945-
ICL: a business and technical history.
1. Great Britain. Computer industries. International
Computers Ltd., history
I. Title
338.7'61004'0941
ISBN 0-19-853918-5

Library of Congress Cataloging in Publication Data
Campbell-Kelly, Martin.
ICL: a business and technical history / by Martin Campbell-Kelly.
1. ICL Limited—History.   2. Computer industry—Great Britain—
History.   I. Title.
HD9696.C641   1989   338.7'61004'0941—dc20   89-16318
ISBN 0-19-853918-5

Set by Downdell Limited, Oxford
Printed in Great Britain by
Bookcraft (Bath) Ltd
Midsomer Norton, Avon

Preface

The origin of this book is as follows. In the summer of 1984 I was invited by David Marwood, the company secretary of ICL, who knew of my professional interest in the history of computing, to inspect the ICL Archives in Putney, London. I believe that this was the first occasion that an historian from outside the company had been allowed access to the archives. What I found there was an Aladdin's Cave of historical material —impressive both in its quantity and its quality. There was ample material to write two histories, both of which interested me: one of the British punched-card machine industry and one of the British computer industry. But such a distinction would have been somewhat artificial, for really both punched-card machines and computers belong to the wider domain of information technology, and the history of one has much bearing on the history of the other. I decided therefore that the most effective way of integrating these two histories would be to write a corporate history of ICL, using the company and its ancestors— notably BTM and ICT—to provide a unifying thread to link the narrative.

David Marwood accepted my proposal to write a history of ICL; and to ensure that I would not find my progress blocked because of some change of corporate policy midway through the project, he prepared a contract guaranteeing me unfettered access to ICL's records and executives. The agreement also provided for a consultancy arrangement between ICL and myself; this helped to fund the research and also legitimized my relationship with ICL. Other than specifying two conditions to safeguard ICL's commercial interests, the company has played no part whatever in planning the book or in specifying its content. The two conditions were: first, that ICL would have the opportunity to read the manuscript before publication, and the right to excise any material it considered commercially damaging; and second, that I would respect the need for commercial confidentiality about events occurring more recently than ten years ago. No changes to the text were made as a result of the first condition. Because of the second, however, I have largely confined myself to describing those events of the last ten years which are already in the public domain; to have gone further would have entailed a selective omission of material, leading to an historical imbalance.

Corporate history is often criticized for the narrowness of its scope. In the case of ICL, however, it is scarcely an exaggeration to say that the history of the company is synonymous with the history of the British computer industry, or at least with the greater part of it. This fact arises from the merger and consolidation activity of the 1960s, by which ICL was created as the single flagship British computer company. The creation of ICL was the direct result of government intervention in response to the increasing dominance of the American computer companies, particularly IBM. In fact, a love-hate relationship had existed between IBM and ICL's forebear BTM since the turn of the century; this relationship features heavily in the first half of this book, covering the period when both companies were making punched-card machines rather than computers. Thus, although the book is primarily addressed to readers with a direct interest in the evolution of the information technology industries, I hope it will also be of interest to people concerned with government–industry relations, and with the problems of competing with American multinational companies.

The title of the book—*ICL: A Business and Technical History*—is intended to convey both what the book is about, and what it is not about. It is primarily about the development of an information technology firm from the business and technical viewpoints. The book thus contains a strong core of product-strategy issues, the concerns of technological change, and the economics of research and development (R&D). Again, although all of these relate to information technology, and will primarily be of interest to computer professionals and those interested in the computer industry, I hope that scholars with wider interests in R&D and the firm will find the book a useful case study. In taking the narrow focus suggested by the title, the book inevitably treats far less deeply other important aspects of ICL: manufacturing, marketing, industrial relations, and much more. This was a conscious decision; and, while some readers may question it, I took the view when planning the book that the real interest in ICL was in its products, and in its relations with the government and other manufacturers, rather than in the strictly operational aspects of the business—which are neither good enough nor bad enough to merit special attention. A particular omission is that the book is in no sense a social or nostalgic history of the company, a fact which may disappoint some readers. In fact, ICL is unusual in having an active 'double majority club' for employees with 42 years of service. It thus goes without saying that the corporate spirit of its elders and retired is exceptionally strong. Perhaps one day someone will write a social history of the company; but this is not a task that would be appropriate for an academic historian.

Acknowledgements

It is a pleasure to put on record the debt I owe to the many people who helped me during the historical research for this book. Unless otherwise stated, these people were employees or former employees of ICL. In some cases they were interviewed in depth about their experiences with ICL, in other cases they wrote me long letters; some loaned papers in their personal possession, and others read through individual chapters of the manuscript:

W.R. Atkinson (ex-DTI), A.G. Bagshaw, B. Bassett, B. Bellringer, R.L. Bird, P.L. Bonfield, J. Bull, K. Crook, G.R. Cross, P.V. Ellis, M.L.N. Forrest, C. Gardner (ex-LFE), T.D. Griffin, A.C.D. Haley, N.F. Hedges, T.C. Hudson, A.L.C. Humphreys, P.M. Hunt, L. Knight, C.C.F. Laidlaw, L. Lightstone, K.H. Macdonald, N. Marshall (ex-RCA), A.T. Maxwell, E.C.H. Organ, V.V. Pasquali, J.M.M. Pinkerton, B.C. Warboys, R.W. Whelan, R.W. Wilmot, C.M. Wilson.

Many more people helped me with specific written inquiries, loan documents or photographs, or facilitated my access to manuscript collections and archives. Although there are too many to name here—and I would in any case not want to risk an omission, thereby causing offence—I offer them all my thanks.

I also acknowledge the valuable help of several people who read and criticized the complete manuscript. J.G. Bates, G. Collinson, A.L.C. Humphreys, D.C.L. Marwood, A.T. Maxwell, and G.J. Morris—all presently or formerly with ICL—made constructive 'internal' criticism and factual corrections. W.F. Aspray and A.L. Norberg (Charles Babbage Institute, University of Minnesota), G. Tweedale (National Archive for the History of Computing, University of Manchester), J. Howlett (editor of the *ICL Technical Journal*) and C.A. Jones (University of Warwick), all provided 'external' criticism as business or computer historians. Although it has become something of a cliché to advise readers that all the shortcomings of a book are the responsibility of the author alone, I still think it needs to be said.

Finally, I would like to give my special thanks to the following people, who encouraged me through the four years I have been writing the book. David Marwood, ICL's company secretary, got the project started, and his successor Gordon Bates, sustained it. Arthur Humphreys CBE, former managing director and deputy chairman of ICL, and now a trustee of the Charles Babbage Institute, gave me constant encouragement and valuable criticism. And the book would never have been written without the support of Sir Christophor Laidlaw, ICL chairman 1981-84, and Peter Bonfield CBE, ICL's current chairman and chief executive.

University of Warwick　　　　　　　　　　　　　　　　　　　M.C.-K.
February 1989

Contents

Part I

Punched-card machines

1

Hollerith and the origins
c.1880–1907

Counting a nation by electricity
After a scrutiny as close and careful as it could be made, it seems only possible to say one thing, namely, that the apparatus works as unerringly as the mills of the Gods, but beats them hollow as to speed.

—T.C. Martin, *The Electrical Engineer*, 1891.[1]

Both IBM and ICL have their origins in the punched-card machines invented by Herman Hollerith in the 1880s. In 1896 Hollerith incorporated a small business, the Tabulating Machine Company (TMC), to manufacture and market his machines in the United States. In 1904 a British operation, The Tabulator Ltd, was formed to develop the punched-card business in Britain; this firm was re-incorporated in 1907 as the British Tabulating Machine Company (BTM). It was from these two firms, TMC and BTM, that IBM and ICL were to evolve.

The tabulating-machine companies were, however, part of a wider industrial phenomenon: the emergence of the office-machine industry, which was really the forerunner of today's computer and information-systems industries.

The office-machine industry

Although the computer is a post-Second-World War invention, and the computer business only became a large-scale activity in the 1960s, the data-processing industry has its origins in the office-machine industry that emerged in the closing decades of the nineteenth century. As Table 1.1 shows, no less than three of the top-ten information-systems firms of today were leading office-machine suppliers at the turn of the century.

When office machinery was invented, it bore the same relationship to the office as machine tools had to the factory, or agricultural machinery had to the farm. However, while the histories of machine tools and agricultural machinery have been extensively researched, very little indeed has been written on office machinery.[2] The reason for this omission appears to be that it is only quite recently that we have begun to see office machines and computers as belonging to a much wider domain

Table 1.1 Early office-machine and computer firms

Office-machine firm	Early products	Computer firm	Rank (1988)
Tabulating Machine Company	Tabulating machines (1896)	IBM	1
Remington Typewriter	Typewriters (1873)	Unisys	3
Burroughs Adding Machine	Adder-listers (1895)	Unisys	3
National Cash Register	Cash registers (1885)	NCR	8
British Tabulating Machine Company	Tabulating machines (1907)	STC-ICL	20

Source
Ranking in EDP revenues: 'The Datamation 100', *Datamation*, 15 June 1988, p. 29.

of 'information technology' (or 'information systems' in the United States). Historians have not yet caught up.

There can be no doubt, however, that the office-machine industry was led by the United States, where many of the leading firms came into existence before the First World War. Virtually all of the well-known manufacturers and machines were American: Comptometer, Burroughs, Remington, Dictaphone, Kalamazoo, National Cash Register, Addressograph; and, of course, the Hollerith system itself. The use of office machines in the United States was not only several years ahead of Europe in terms of technology—it was also far more widespread there, owing to cultural differences and to the fact that clerical labour was twice as expensive there as in Britain.

Another development that evolved in parallel with office machinery was that of the cash register, which set many important precedents for the office-machine industry. Pre-eminent amongst the cash-register manufacturers was National Cash Register (NCR). NCR was founded by John H. Patterson in 1884, and it grew meteorically: in 1885 the firm sold just 64 cash registers; in 1887 there were 5400 in operation, and in 1890 there were 16 400.[3] Two factors helped to secure NCR's dominance of the cash-register market: first, the mechanical perfection of the product and its low cost; and second, the way in which it was marketed. The mechanical perfection of the NCR cash register arose from the way in which the product was systematically and constantly enhanced to improve its performance for the user; and its low cost was brought about by mechanical simplification, which reduced manufacturing costs. The selling of NCR cash registers was consciously modelled on the successful sales operation originated for Singer sewing machines. The sales force was highly motivated and trained, and paid on commission, and marketing was an integrated and costly part of the whole enterprise. NCR was the training ground of Thomas J. Watson Sr, who was to become president of IBM; Watson's sales-oriented business values learned at NCR, when absorbed by IBM, created major cultural and operational differences between the American and British punched-card machine operations.

According to an anonymous historian of Remington Rand, as late as 1890 most American offices were unmechanized: 'The typical office of the early Nineties was a cluttered place, busy with clerks endlessly thumbing through ledgers or picking through dusty letters in search for needed information.'[4] Three inventions were to transform the nature of the American office over a period of about twenty years, roughly from 1890 to 1910. These three key inventions were the typewriter, the calculating machine, and the accounting/punched-card machine.

The typewriter was the most important and pervasive of the office machines, eventually accounting for a half of all office-machine sales by value. The typewriter was an evolutionary invention: some of the earliest patents date from the 1820s, but the typewriter needed much mechanical perfection before it was ready for the mass market; it also needed a selling operation to market it. The key mechanical development was due to the inventor Christopher Sholes, who introduced the modern (QWERTY) keyboard, which eliminated the problem of type-bar collision, in 1873. The Sholes patents were acquired by the small-arms manufacturer E. Remington and Sons, who launched the Remington No. 1 typewriter in 1873. It took several more years to perfect the 'visible' typewriter, that allowed the operator to see the copy as it was typed, and to supply upper- and lower-case fonts.[5] According to a contemporary Remington advertisement, the company had sold a total of only 1000 machines by 1880; but by 1885 it was selling 5000 a year, and by 1890 sales had risen to 20 000 a year.[6]

The calculating machine had a similar pattern of evolutionary development to the typewriter. The origins of calculating machines go back at least as far as Blaise Pascal (1623-1662). The first manufactured machine, the Thomas Arithmometer, dated from 1820; and this was followed by better designed, mass-produced machines of the Baldwin/Odhner pattern in the 1870s.[7] These early calculating machines, although adequate for scientific and engineering calculations, were 'lever-set', and too slow for routine accounting operations. The first 'key-set' adding machine, which had a typewriter-style keyboard, was the Comptometer, introduced by the Felt and Tarrant Manufacturing Co. of Chicago in about 1887. The Comptometer was highly successful; hundreds of thousands, and eventually millions, were sold; and it led to the famous

Comptometer training schools set up in major cities where they were marketed (there were several schools in Britain). The Comptometer was not, however, suitable for many commercial users—especially banks—as it did not produce a printed record of the calculation. Another American entrepreneur, William Seward Burroughs (1855-98), patented his 'adder-lister'—an adding machine which printed its results on a tally roll—in 1888. Again, the machine took several years to perfect: the first sales began in 1895, when 284 machines were sold; in 1900 some 1500 machines were sold; and in 1903 nearly 4500 were sold.[8] In 1907, 13 314 machines were sold, and there were 58 different styles—'One Built for Every Line of Business'.[9] Banks were quick to adopt the Burroughs adder-lister, and the same banks later became important customers for Burroughs computers.

By 1900, American suppliers dominated the world's office-machine industry for three reasons: first, the widespread diffusion of office machines in America; second, the superior machine designs and manufacturing technology; and third, the selling operations.

The diffusion of office machines in the United States around the turn of the century was phenomenal. If contemporary typewriter advertisements are to be believed, Remington alone had sold upwards of a quarter of a million machines by 1900. And Remington, although the largest, was only one of many manufacturers; other well-known firms included Royal, Smith Premier, and Underwood, as well as dozens of smaller concerns. The contrast with the state of the British office machinery scene in the early 1900s is remarkable. Even large concerns used very traditional methods. For example, in the Prudential Assurance Company in the early years of the century:

> . . . clerical work continued to be carried on by methods not essentially different from those of thirty or forty years earlier. Records were still compiled by hand. Into ledgers almost too heavy for a junior clerk to lift, were carefully copied details of agents' accounts and every policy-movement. Industrial assurance policies were written by young ladies, while in the basement junior clerks numbered these policies on machines worked by foot. There were few internal telephones. Valuations, although the work was assisted by arithmometers, continued to involve great physical labour.[10]

And one should note that the Prudential was a comparatively innovative organization. Again, in Stewart and Lloyds—one of Britain's fifty largest firms—it was stated that in 1903:

> The only piece of modern equipment was the telephone, with a private line to the Glasgow office. . . . But there was no other office machinery of any kind—no typewriters, adding machines, comptometers, pay-roll listing machines, etc. There were no women in the office. Everything was handwritten and the only

duplication was by letterpress copying. . . . No one trained in a modern office can have any idea of the crudity of office methods and organization at that time.[11]

In the absence of a significant home market, there was little opportunity for a British office-machine industry to become established. But in any case, the American machines were heavily patented, and were so far in advance of anything available from European manufacturers (with some notable exceptions in Germany) that it would have been impossible to compete in terms of product quality. The American manufacturers also had the advantage of large-scale manufacturing. The American factories of Remington and Burroughs, for example, were vast, highly-integrated operations that enabled them to achieve economies of scale that could never have been approached by European firms. Britain's deficiency in manufactures, compared with America, was only too well understood at the time:

Lord Rosebery told a group of British manufacturers in 1901 that it was not military conflicts for which the British should prepare, but rather an economic struggle. The United States was feared, 'because of her unmatched ability to manufacture and her unlimited power to produce.' Pointing to the invasion of American goods in Britian, Lord Rosebery noted that the typewriting machine used in preparing his address, as well as thousands, 'nay, hundreds of thousands of other machines throughout the world' were made in America. The same applied to the table on which the machine stood, his office furniture, bookcases, and chairs. 'All these,' he added, 'can not be made anywhere in Europe so practical, so convenient, or at a similar cost as in the United States.'[12]

It was not generally until after the First World War that American firms began to assemble, and then manufacture, their office machines in European factories.

Compared with the United States' manufacturing advantage, the role of its sales operations in achieving dominance of the office-machine industry seems to have gone almost unnoticed by contemporary observers. In fact, it was generally the case that the most successful of the American capital goods manufacturers were those who made the forward integration into sales; and the leading American office-machine manufacturers quickly established their own sales forces.[13] Early sales efforts for cash registers, typewriters, and calculating machines through conventional retailers had not been successful. Office machines were complex capital goods: they needed a sales force skilled in their operation to sell them, customers needed training in their use, and an after-sales service was needed for repair and maintenance. The most successful of the early office-machine suppliers, such as NCR, Remington, and Burroughs, established integrated manufacturing and selling operations, 'and dominated their markets from the beginning'.[14] Remington had originally built a sales force only for its domestic market, and had hoped to use the Singer Company for overseas sales. When Singer refused, the first London sales office was opened in 1886; and by 1890 distribution channels covered the whole of Europe. In each country, as Remington sales offices were opened, schools were established to train typists and to teach shorthand.[15] The sophisticated selling and training operations of the American manufacturers made it very difficult for British suppliers to compete, even as mere importers of office machines.

This, then, is the office-machine industry backdrop against which the accounting and punched-card machines were marketed. They were, however, later to develop than the typewriter and calculating machines, and were still in embryonic form in the 1880s.

The Hollerith Electric Tabulating System

Punched-card machines have their origins in the electric tabulating system which was invented by Herman Hollerith for the tabulation of the 1890 US population census. This was an operation that was almost industrial in its scale—far larger than the clerical operations of even the largest businesses; and ordinary office machines would have made little impact on the task.

The first United States decennial population census took place in 1790, when the recorded population was a little under four million. The early censuses were comparatively simple affairs: only a few inquiries were made of the head of each family, and the published census reports were modest in scope. By the middle of the nineteenth century, however, the population had increased severalfold, and many more inquiries were being made of every citizen; furthermore, the number of tabulations, as measured by the size of published reports (1605 pages in 1850, for example), had grown considerably.[16] The problem grew worse in the following decades. The census tabulation was largely unmechanized, and the 1880 census took about seven years to process. Given the influx of immigrants that was then occurring—it was expected that the population of America would perhaps double in the next decade—it was evident that in the 1890 census either the scope of the inquiry would have to be curtailed, or a method of mechanical tabulation would need to be introduced.

Herman Hollerith (1860-1929), freshly graduated from the Columbia School of Mines, New York, had joined the Bureau of the Census in the autumn of 1879 to work on industrial statistics.[17] It was there that he learned of the census problem, and also found his vocation as a mechanical inventor. In 1882, he resigned from the Census Bureau, spending a year as an instructor in mechanical engineering at MIT, followed by a short period as an examiner in the US Patent Office, after which he became an

independent patent agent. During these years he worked on both a tabulating system and railway braking systems. A patent application was made
in 1884 for an early form of tabulating system based on a punched paper
tape, and patents for the card-based system were filed in 1887. Conflicting
accounts of the origin of the idea of using a punched-card medium appear
in the literature. The idea may have been suggested by a senior member of
the Bureau staff, J.S. Billings; alternatively Hollerith may have derived
the idea from the Jacquard loom, or the method of punching a physical
description of a railway passenger in his ticket (Hollerith in fact used a
conductor's punch to perforate cards in early trials of the system). In any
event, the development of the idea was entirely due to Hollerith.

From 1887 a number of trials of the Hollerith system were made, compiling mortality and medical statistics. (Hollerith was also entering com-
petitions for braking systems at about the same time, but soon committed
all his efforts to the tabulating system.) The major trial for the tabulating
system came in 1889, when the Director of the Census, Robert P. Porter,
organized a competition to select a tabulating system for the 1890 census.
Three competitors, including Hollerith, submitted entries. Both of the
systems of Hollerith's rivals involved the transcription of schedule entries
on to paper slips or cards, which were then repeatedly sorted and counted
by hand, quick identification being facilitated by colour coding. The
Hollerith system, however, was a convincing winner: his recording of
data was significantly faster than that of either of his rivals, and tabulation
was up to ten times as fast.[18] The reason for the speed of the Hollerith
system was that, unlike the other systems, once a card had been punched,
all manual tallying and sorting was eliminated. Having chosen the
Hollerith system for the 1890 census, the Director of the Census, Robert
Porter, was to become a great proselytizer for the Hollerith tabulating
system, and eventually its promoter in Britain.

The tabulation of the census using the Hollerith Electric Tabulating
System involved three distinct processes: the *recording*, *tabulation*, and
sorting of data. All these processes are shown in the evocative engraving
of Fig. 1.1, which appeared as the cover of *Scientific American* on
30 August 1890, when the census operation was just getting into full
swing.

Each schedule returned in the census contained the information for a
complete family. From this schedule one card was punched for each
person. Data items were recorded in a number of fields on the card (Fig.
1.2a). One field, for example, recorded the gender of the subject. Another
field recorded the age group. Another field recorded 'conjugal condition'
(divorced, unmarried, widowed, etc.). And so on.

The census machine consisted of two parts: the tabulating machine,
and the sorting box. The tabulating machine was used to count the

Fig. 1.1 Cover of the *Scientific American*, 30 August 1890. *Bottom of picture*: the incoming completed schedules are received and assembled for onward processing. *Top right*: schedules are punched on to cards using the pantograph punch. *Top left*: using the census machine, the cards for an enumeration district are tabulated and deposited one-by-one into the sorting box. *Centre*: using a special keyboard, family headcounts are entered for the rough count.

number of holes, in selected positions and in selected combinations, of a batch of cards passed through it. The machine contained a maximum of 40 clock-like counters, each capable of registering up to 9999. Cards were sensed by a hand-operated press which bore a matrix of spring-loaded pins: when the 'pin-box' was brought down on to a card a pin encountering a hole would pass through, and dip into a mercury cup, which would complete an electrical circuit; but if the pin met solid card it would simply be pressed back, and no circuit would be completed. A counter included in the circuit would thus be incremented by one, or not, depending on the presence or absence of a hole. The simplest operation the tabulating machine could perform was to count the number of holes in selected positions in a batch of cards. Thus, in principle, if one counter was wired up to register males, and another to register females, then the effect of passing a batch of cards through the machine would be to obtain the total numbers of males and females recorded on the batch of cards. Invariably, actual counts were much more complex. A counting operation would begin by resetting all the counters, and then reading the cards for an enumeration district one-by-one with the press. When all the cards had been passed through the machine, a supervisor would record the totals, reset the counters, and the operator would begin the next batch of cards. Impressively fast speeds could be obtained by a skilful operator, and even an average operator managed eight to ten thousand cards a day. The sorting box consisted of approximately two dozen compartments, each having an electrically operated lid, normally kept closed. By an appropriate relay circuit, a combination of holes could be used to select a compartment whose lid would fly open when a card of the right type was sensed. The operator would drop the card into the offered compartment and close the lid. The fact that only one lid opened eliminated the possibility of the operator's placing the card in the wrong compartment; closing the lid with a deft tap took almost no time.

The Hollerith tabulating system achieved its superiority over the competing manual systems in a number of ways. First, it enabled as many as forty complex combinations to be counted in a single handling of the cards; this was far more than was possible in a manual system, and was the most decisive advantage of the census machine. Second, the Hollerith system eliminated a great deal of the physical sorting and counting of records of a manual system; thus the sorting box was always used alongside the tabulating machine, pre-sorting cards for a subsequent count with the minimum cost in time and handling. Third, the Hollerith system was inherently more accurate than a manual system, because the possibilities of incorrectly sorting and counting were greatly reduced.

The tabulation of the 1890 census was a technical and financial triumph for Hollerith, and it was enthusiastically reported in the press.

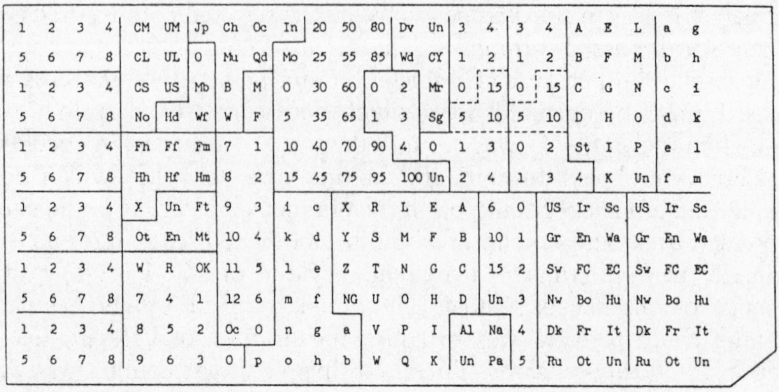

1	2	3	4	CM	UM	Jp	Ch	Oc	In	20	50	80	Dv	Un	3	4.	3	4	A	E	L	a	g
5	6	7	8	CL	UL	O	Mu	Qd	Mo	25	55	85	Wd	CY	1	2	1	2	B	F	M	b	h
1	2	3	4	CS	US	Mb	B	M	O	30	60	O	2	Mr	0	15	0	15	C	G	N	c	i
5	6	7	8	No	Hd	Wf	W	F	5	35	65	1	3	Sg	5	10	5	10	D	H	O	d	k
1	2	3	4	Fh	Ff	Fm	7	1	10	40	70	90	4	O	1	3	O	2	St	I	P	e	l
5	6	7	8	Hh	Hf	Hm	8	2	15	45	75	95	100	Un	2	4	1	3	4	K	Un	f	m
1	2	3	4	X	Un	Ft	9	3	i	c	X	R	L	E	A	6	O	US	Ir	Sc	US	Ir	Sc
5	6	7	8	Ot	En	Mt	10	4	k	d	Y	S	M	F	B	10	1	Gr	En	Wa	Gr	En	Wa
1	2	3	4	W	R	OK	11	5	l	e	Z	T	N	G	C	15	2	Sw	FC	EC	Sw	FC	EC
5	6	7	8	7	4	1	12	6	m	f	NG	U	O	H	D	Un	3	Nw	Bo	Hu	Nw	Bo	Hu
1	2	3	4	8	5	2	Oc	O	n	g	a	V	P	I	Al	Na	4	Dk	Fr	It	Dk	Fr	It
5	6	7	8	9	6	3	O	p	o	h	b	W	Q	K	Un	Pa	5	Ru	Ot	Un	Ru	Ot	Un

[Shown 60 per cent of actual size, $6\frac{5}{8} \times 3\frac{1}{4}$ inches]
(a) form of the 1890 census card

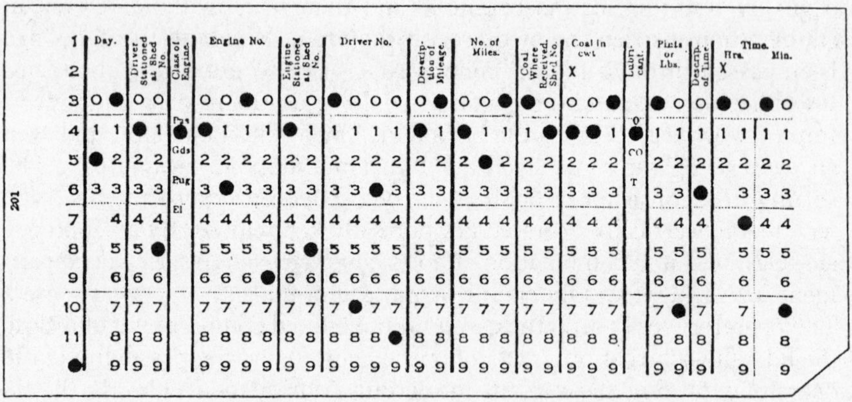

[Shown 60 per cent of actual size, $7\frac{3}{8} \times 3\frac{1}{4}$ inches]
(b) 34-column card, c.1906

Fig. 1.2 Early punched cards

Within six weeks of the start of the census, the 'rough count' of the population was complete (total 62 622 250 citizens). This achievement was only a partial vindication of the Hollerith system, because the rough count was produced not by using punched cards but by registering family counts directly into the tabulating machines using a simple keyboard. After the rough count, the detailed tabulations began, for which nearly 63 million cards had to be prepared, one for each citizen. Altogether seven counts were made, involving several hundred million card-passages through the census machines. The census was completed in a little over two years, a great improvement on the previous census, and much more complex and refined tabulations were produced (the published reports of 10 220 pages were nearly twice the length of those produced for the previous census). Altogether approximately one hundred census machines were used, and several hundred 'pantograph' punches, all of which were maintained by Hollerith and his assistants. The machines evidently needed regular repair and maintenance; but it is possible that the faults were not entirely mechanical:

Herman Hollerith used to visit the premises frequently. . . . Mechanics were there frequently too, to get the ailing machines back in operation. The trouble was usually that somebody had extracted the mercury from one of the little cups with an eye-dropper and squirted it into a spittoon, just to get some un-needed rest.[19]

Hollerith rented, rather than sold, the census machines to the Bureau of the Census, since their use for the equipment was periodical rather than permanent. Hollerith was therefore naturally anxious to redeploy the machines as much as possible to other census authorities—across the Atlantic if necessary. While the preparations for the 1890 census were under way, Hollerith received several inquiries from European countries, as a result of which the system was adopted for the 1890 censuses of Austria and Norway, and also for Canada nearer to home. Hollerith made several trips to Europe during the mid-1890s, consolidating the system's use in European censuses. His reputation was quickly established both in the United States and in Europe, where he was awarded several honours and academic distinctions.

The Tabulating Machine Company

Following completion of the 1890 census, Hollerith traded as *The Hollerith Electric Tabulating System*, operating in a comparatively small way on two fronts. First, census machinery was supplied to the US Bureau of the Census and to the census organizations of other countries. Second, an attempt was made to supply tabulating machinery for commercial use.

Although the census machines had been taken up by Austria and Norway, and were being actively explored by Russia and France, Hollerith had less success in Britain. Hollerith's patron, Robert Porter, although a naturalized United States citizen, was British by birth, and he tried to find backers for the system in Britain. Porter had some scientific standing, both as an industrial pundit and as director of the 1890 census, and he used the platform of the Royal Statistical Society to launch Hollerith on scientific London. Porter and Hollerith gave a joint presentation to the Society in December 1894. Porter spoke on the 1890 census, and Hollerith followed with a formal paper, which he illustrated with magic-lantern slides, describing the workings of the tabulating system.[20] Hollerith was subsequently elected a member of the Royal Statistical Society, which was another distinction to add to his growing list of honours.

In August 1895, Hollerith used an introduction from Porter to Sir John Puleston, a British industrialist with an American business background, to try to persuade him to back the system, but without success. The following year, Hollerith entered into an agreement with the London branch of the Library Bureau to act as a selling agent, but again without apparent success. In the event, nothing was to get started in Britain until Porter moved there permanently.

Meanwhile, in the United States Hollerith began to look to commercial uses for his machines. The cyclical nature of the census business—censuses were taken in the first or second years of the decade almost everywhere—meant that Hollerith would inevitably look for other, non-cyclical, uses for his tabulating machines in order to stabilize the revenues of his business. In 1895 he achieved an important breakthrough by getting the New York Central Railroad to take his machines on trial. The railroad processed four million freight waybills a year, which was a huge clerical operation that threatened to overwhelm the organization. Hollerith aimed not only to reduce clerical labour costs, but also to summarize freight revenues on a weekly basis, instead of the current monthly basis, to help improve financial control.

Unlike the census, which involved mainly non-numerical data (such as marital status, occupation, etc.), the railway operation required the tabulating system to handle numerical quantities—weights, distances, dollar amounts, etc. To meet this new need, Hollerith redesigned the punched card and the tabulating machine. The new card, instead of having the irregular shaped fields of the old census card, was ruled off into a number of vertical columns, with each column able to hold a single digit in the range 0–9. A field of adjacent columns could then be used to represent a numerical value (Fig. 1.2b, p. 12). The new tabulator looked quite different from the old census machine tabulator (see Plates). In place of the clock-like counters, there were four adding mechanisms. Hollerith called the new machine the 'integrating', or adding, tabulator; but it was later known as the 'pin-box' tabulator, on account of the card-reading mechanism, which was much the same as in the original census machine. On the new machine, closing the pin-box over a card caused up to four numbers to be simultaneously added on to four running totals.*

On 28 September 1896, Hollerith's machine passed its acceptance trials at New York Central, and he leased them about five machines,

---

* These inventions were, in fact, based on earlier census developments, and on much trial and further development in between. The developments are well described elsewhere.[21]

which did the work of about twenty clerks, on a permanent basis. Encouraged by the New York Central contract, and the fact that contracts with the Russian and French census authorities were about to be signed, Hollerith decided to form the Tabulating Machine Company. The company was incorporated on 3 December 1896, with an authorized capital of $100 000, to manufacture and rent tabulating machines, and to sell punches and cards. The cards, which sold at about $1 a thousand, were to prove very lucrative, and they accounted for not far short of half TMC's revenues in the early years.[22] The tabulators, however, like the census machines, were rented. This was an important characteristic of the business, since it called for large initial capital outlays, but had the effect of stabilizing revenues by generating a constant rental income that was largely independent of any single year's business.

Following the incorporation of TMC, Hollerith began to plan for the coming 1900 US census. The 1900 population census relied for the most part on the census machines used for the 1890 census, although their number was increased considerably. An apparently simple improvement, the automatic feeding of cards, which eliminated the hand-feeding of cards and the manual closing of the press, was made to some of the tabulators. Although automatic feed was used only to a limited extent in the 1900 population census, where it was used it made a severalfold improvement in the speed with which cards could be processed. Automatic card-feeding was eventually provided in all punched-card machines. Another significant change of punched-card machine use in the 1900 census occurred with the tabulation of the census of agriculture, which required the accumulation of quantities (such as the number of bushels of wheat produced on each farm). Hollerith was able to make use of the new card format and the integrating tabulator that was then in use with the New York Central. A new punching machine, the key punch, was introduced for the punching of the agricultural census cards. This device was a great improvement on the pantograph punch, since cards could be punched far more rapidly using a calculator-style key pad. The key punch was manufactured in essentially the same form for more than half a century (see Plates). The 1900 agricultural census also saw the introduction of another important advance, the electric sorting machine. The electric sorting machine enabled sorting to be carried out as an independent operation, and not merely as a by-product of regular tabulation with the census machine.

Once again the census, completed in approximately two and a half years, was a technical and financial success for Hollerith. Altogether the Tabulating Machine Company supplied over 300 tabulating machines and more than 1600 pantograph and key punches.

As the US census operation wound down, Hollerith turned seriously to commercial applications. Hollerith had pinned his hopes on the railroads, which were America's largest business concerns; but apart from the New York Central—which had built up to an installation of about fifteen tabulators—the remainder of the railroads were slow to adopt them. He did, however, succeed in introducing the machines in Taft-Pierce—a small engineering company which TMC had acquired in 1901 to manufacture the Hollerith machines. During the next two years a few more companies began to use the machines, including the manufacturing company Yale and Towne, the chemical company Niles-Bement-Pond, and Pennsylvania Steel. In 1903 a second railroad, the Long Island, installed the system.

The Tabulator Limited

Robert Porter (1852-1917) was a very capable individual, moving with equal facility in the worlds of diplomacy and politics, industrial economics, and journalism. Following the completion of the 1890 census in 1893, he became a Special Fiscal Advisor and Tariff Commissioner for Cuba and Puerto Rica for President McKinley, in which capacity, among other things, he negotiated the disbandment of the Cuban army. Simultaneously, he was a founding director of the New York Press, and wrote several books on industrial topics—free trade, and Japanese and Cuban industry—as well as a biography of President McKinley.[23] In 1901 President McKinley was assassinated; Porter's political career in the United States came to an abrupt end, and he returned to full-time journalism. Although retaining his American citizenship, he decided to return to England to become the first editor of *The Times* Engineering Supplement. And the idea of setting up a British outlet for the Hollerith machines was perhaps never far from his mind.

According to C.A. Everard Greene, the first general manager of BTM, on arriving in England Porter began a search for an office close to *The Times* in Fleet Street.[24] The search led him to the British Westinghouse building at 2 Norfolk Street, just off the Strand, where he secured a lease from the company secretary, Ralegh Phillpotts. In the course of conversation, Porter told Phillpotts of his background with the US Census Bureau, and of his desire to set up a British company to exploit the Hollerith inventions. It seems that this was just the opportunity that Phillpotts was looking for.

Ralegh Phillpotts (1871-1950), then aged about thirty, was some twenty years the junior of Porter, and had not yet established a real career for himself. Phillpotts was the grandson of a famous Bishop of Exeter, Henry Phillpotts (1778-1869), and he retained strong family connections with Devon.[25] He studied law at Balliol College, Oxford, and after being called to the Bar in 1894 he decided to specialize in commercial law. He was assistant editor of White and Tudor's *Leading Equity Cases* (1901), and then served as company secretary of British Westinghouse until 1904. Subsequently, from 1904 to 1907, he was company secretary of the Speyer Brothers merchant bank. The Phillpotts family was well connected, with members in the church, the law, politics, and the military establishment. There was also a connection by marriage to the Surtees family, well known in the law; and in 1907 Phillpotts became a partner in the legal firm of Surtees, Phillpotts, and Company (later amalgamated with Linklater and Paines). Of Ralegh's generation probably the best known were to be Eden Phillpotts (1862-1960), the novelist, and Dame Bertha Surtees Phillpotts (1877-1932), the educationist.

Phillpotts agreed that he would act as general manager of the British Hollerith operation, with Porter as chairman. In early 1902 Porter obtained an exclusive option from TMC to organize a British company. This agreement, dated 24 February 1902, called for Porter to raise £20 000 capital—the same amount that Hollerith had raised for TMC in the United States—of which one half would be paid to the US company for assignment of patents, and the remainder would be used to establish the UK business, and to import machines at cost plus ten per cent.[26] Although Phillpotts could handle the legal and financial side of the business on a part-time basis, he was not in the least mechanically minded, so before the operation could begin it was necessary to appoint and train a full-time joint general manager to get the business going in an operational sense. In January 1903 Phillpotts offered the position to his young friend C.A. Everard Greene—whom he knew as Kit, but who was later known in the company as Everard.

Not much is known of Everard Greene's background. He was evidently a family friend of Phillpotts, and a number of Greenes are listed as shareholders. Christian Augustine Everard Greene (*c*.1878-1965), was then in his mid-twenties and in search of a career. He had recently graduated in engineering from Cambridge University; had briefly considered, and rejected, enlisting for the Boer War; and was on the point of taking up an overseas appointment with a cable company in Madeira when Phillpotts offered him the chance to take on the British Hollerith business.[27]

Everard Greene accepted. His first task was concerned with what today we would call 'technology transfer', but was then simply called 'learning the business'. For this, he had to go to the source of the Hollerith invention, and he soon found himself aboard the steamship *Minnehaha* bound for New York, and thence by rail to the TMC headquarters at 1054, 31st Street, Washington DC. Hollerith put Everard Greene on the TMC payroll, which must have eased the cash position for the British backers considerably, and he was set to work in the Washington machine shops:

My training consisted of getting an insight into the manufacturing of parts, the assembly and wiring of machines, the making, planning and drawing up of cards for jobs, the investigation and organising necessary for installing and operating machines on the job.[28]

At that time, TMC was working on the Philippines census, which Everard Greene briefly looked in on. He was, however, more interested in the commercial machines. Having become experienced with the mechanics of the machines, he was moved on to learn about the 'systems investigation'—the setting up of a complete installation, and its integration into the accounting department of a business. For this, Hollerith sent him first to the New York Central Railroad. This experience was to stand him in good stead for business with the British railway companies later. Another period was spent working under Gershom Smith at the Pennsylvania Steel Company, another major user. (Gershom Smith was later to be a general manager of TMC, and not much of a friend of the British company.)

Altogether, Everard Greene spent about eighteen months with TMC in the United States. During this time, back in England, Porter and Phillpotts were trying to bring together a syndicate of backers for the new company. These were to be mostly friends and family of Porter and Phillpotts: they included the publisher Sir Gerald Chadwyck-Healey, and the Brownes and Greenes, all of which were to become well-known names in the company. Raising money must have proved very difficult, since only £2000 was raised instead of the £20 000 specified by the 1902 agreement. On 23 April 1904, a new agreement was made between Porter and TMC.[29] No copy of this agreement has been found, but it probably substituted for the large front-end £10 000 payment several smaller payments to be made over a longer period of time.

The new company, The Tabulator Limited, was incorporated on 14 June 1904 with an authorized capital of £5000. Its registered offices were at the British Westinghouse building, 2 Norfolk Street, Strand. At this time, Phillpotts was honorary joint manager, and Everard Greene was joint manager and secretary, and was the sole paid employee, having been on the payroll since 1 April 1904 at an annual salary of £200. In addition to Porter, who was chairman, there were two non-executive directors— Montague Craddock (a director of British Westinghouse and Metropolitan Vickers) and J.L. Hunter (of whom little is known, other than that he was a friend of Phillpotts from Devon).

The board minutes of The Tabulator Limited (which are almost the only surviving record) show that formal board meetings were held at a frequency of three or four times a year, and the impression given is that Everard Greene was left to build up the business as best he could, mainly by following up prospects suggested by his directors and other shareholders. During 1904-5 Everard Greene tried to persuade a number of industrial firms and railways to take the machines on trial, and also prospected the Registrar General at Somerset House to take some machines in readiness for the 1911 British census. Two mechanics were taken on to assist Everard Greene during 1904, and a store-room was rented at Thomas Kesnor, a small engineering company in Fulham, London.

The first organization to give the machines a trial was the Woolwich Arsenal, a prospect that was secured 'through the good offices of Captain F.E. Dyke-Ackland'—a shareholder of The Tabulator.[30] Everard Greene set up a complete system for payroll and production costs; but unfortunately the operation was the victim of an attack of Luddism:

It was not unusual for Machine Operators to find that the machine would not run due to the failure of the electricity supply to the Machine Room. It was not long before it was realised that the supply cable passed through the room where the staff was working, with the result that wires were cut and the Hollerith machine disconnected from time to time and this, of course, considerably upset results and hampered efforts. This went on for a long time, over a period of several months, and eventually it became difficult to make any progress at all. . . . In due course the machines were dismantled, packed and removed and, during their conveyance through the offices, the staff whistled the Dead March![31]

Also in 1905, a second trial took place at the River Don Works of Vickers, Sons and Maxims, in Sheffield. It seems to have been only at this point that it was realized that the Hollerith machines, with decimal counters, could not handle sterling currency. Everard Greene was sent back to Washington to get some machines modified to handle shillings and pence, and ship them back to England. It was nine months before the machines were accepted by Vickers, and a rental income started to flow.

The slow build-up of business was a heavy personal financial drain for the directors and shareholders, as more and more shares were called up. On 2 November 1905, Phillpotts was authorized to renegotiate the agreement with TMC once again. A subsequent board minute states:

Resolved that a Modification of the Existing Agreement be Suggested to the American Co. on a Royalty Basis.[32]

This suggestion was accepted by Hollerith; but it was to prove the worst decision that Phillpotts ever made for the company. Perhaps Phillpotts had no choice, but instead of a once-and-for-all payment of £10 000 for the Hollerith patents, the company would have a permanent millstone round its neck, in the form of an onerous royalty payment which would frustrate its development indefinitely.

During 1905 Porter used his friendship with the general manager of the Lancashire and North Yorkshire Railway (LNYR) to get him to take a set of machines on trial. This resulted in the acceptance of a system using five tabulators and many key punches; even by later standards, this was a substantial installation. Buoyed up by the success of the Vickers and LNYR installations, an order for a further six tabulators was placed with TMC in April 1906.

During the next few months, another machine trial was started with the Great Northern Railway, and the new royalty agreement with Hollerith was settled. Business was, in fact, going so well that buying more machines for rental would soon exhaust the authorized capital of £5000. With two major installations in place it would now be much easier to attract shareholders, and it was decided to refloat the company as the British Tabulating Machine Company, with an authorized capital of £50 000. Once again friends and family were prevailed upon to subscribe to shares. The Tabulator Limited held its final meeting on 29 October 1907, and immediately reopened for business as the British Tabulating Machine Company.

The automatic machines

Although Hollerith's machines had proved themselves indispensable for census work, and had been supplied to a few commercial firms, they had not yet made themselves wholly practical for business applications for two reasons. First, there was the lack of a mechanical sorter, so that sorting was slow and tedious. Second, the tabulators were hand-fed with cards, which was inconveniently slow, and big installations needed a battery of five or more machines to cope with what was not a large volume of trans-actions in terms of large-scale enterprise.

Sorting for commercial applications was initially achieved by the use of a blunt needle. This was a tedious process, although early films show it was accomplished with amazing dexterity:

Sorting by any given field is accomplished very rapidly by drawing off the cards with a knitting needle, and the accuracy of the grouping is indicated at once by the fact that it is possible to see through the hole or holes by which the sorting has been made.[33]

Hollerith had, in fact, developed an automatic sorting machine for the 1901 agricultural census, and some machines had been supplied to the New York Central. This sorting machine automatically read through a stack of cards and deposited them one-by-one into eleven receiving pockets according to the hole punched in a particular column—there was one pocket for each possible digit, and an eleventh pocket for unpunched cards. In the early design, the receiving pockets were arranged horizont-ally, but customers complained that the machine took up too much space, so Hollerith redesigned the machine as the vertical sorter. The new design took up a floor area of only three or four square feet, but in the United States the machine became known as the 'backbreaker', because 'it was difficult for women operators in tight-laced corsets to unload the bottom or nine pocket'.[34] The new machine had a sorting speed of 250–275 cards a minute, which must have been an order of magnitude faster than needle-sorting.

The replacement of the hand-feeding of cards by an automatic feeding mechanism was a vital improvement. Using hand-feeding, a very good tabulator operator could achieve a speed of perhaps 2000 cards an hour, but probably an average operator would only have managed half that. In 1902 Hollerith introduced the semi-automatic tabulator. In this machine, which looked very much like the original pin-box tabulator, cards were mechanically fed into a reading mechanism: 'from 400 to 500 cards could be placed in a hopper and automatically sent down one at a time at the rate of 150 c.p.m.'[35] A speed of 150 cards per minute was equivalent to 9000 cards per hour, which, like the sorter, was an order of magnitude improvement over hand-fed machines. At the most only one or two of the semi-automatics found their way to Britain.

Between 1902 and 1906, Hollerith continued development on the tabulator, turning it into what was to become known as the automatic tabulator. The most important change was to introduce reading brushes instead of the pin-box, which allowed the card to be read while in motion, enabling a much smoother and less mechanically-demanding reading mechanism. In appearance, the automatic tabulator was transformed, although beneath the covers the mechanical changes were less dramatic (see Plates). In place of the crude wooden frame and exposed counters, the new machine was enclosed in a modern metal case—complete with a 'joggling plate' on which to straighten the packs of cards before placing them in the reading hopper. The new automatic machines used a new 37-column card of size 7⅜ by 3¼ inches. This card size was to become the industry standard, although the number of columns later increased first to 45, and then to 80.

The automatic tabulator was introduced in the United States in 1906. According to Hollerith's biographer, this slow gestation of four years displayed a 'curious mixture of cautious engineer and bold entrepreneur'.[36] An alternative explanation might be that Hollerith was simply holding the machines back from the market until the hand-fed machines in the field had repaid their manufacturing cost. This problem, of the introduction of a new machine precipitating a flood of returns of old machines, was to prove endemic to the punched-card machine business, and later to the computer industry.

Once the automatic machines became available in quantity, the American Hollerith business raced ahead. By 1908 Hollerith had thirty customers, and during the next two years revenues doubled and doubled again, and the number of installations comfortably passed the one hundred mark. In America, the Hollerith machines had been swept along by the tide of the booming office-machine market. In Britain, growth was to be much slower, reflecting the slow acceptance of office machinery. In later years, IBM was to constantly criticize BTM for its slow growth. That the growth rates of the two companies were dramatically different is a fact. Table 1.2 shows the revenue and profit progression of the two companies, in ten-year intervals from 1915 to 1985. Except for 1915, when BTM was still very small, and 1945, when its turnover was distorted by war production, the revenues of IBM exceeded those of the British company by a factor of 20 or 30 with remarkable consistency. This was in spite of the fact that IBM and BTM were selling identical products, and that, until 1949, they were selling in mutually-exclusive markets—IBM having two-thirds of the world, and BTM one-third.

Table 1.2   IBM and ICL financial statistics, 1915–1985

	C-T-R/IBM		BTM/ICT/ICL		Ratio of
	Revenues	Net income	Revenues	Pre-tax profits	revenues
1915	$4.5m	$0.7m	£6k	£0.9k	
1925	$15.5m	$2.8m	£122k	£20.9k	32:1
1935	$21.9m	$7.1m	c.£170k	£33.8k	32:1
1945	$141.7m	$10.9m		£101.3k	
1955	$563.3m	$55.9m	£5419k	£891.0k	37:1
1965	$2.5b	$0.3b	£55m	£0.5m loss	16:1
1975	$14.4b	$2.6b	£240m	£16.2m	25:1
1985	$50.1b	$6.6b	£1038m	£53.8m	38:1

Notes
Early CTR/IBM figures are for US and Canada only. Net income is tax-paid.
Revenue ratios are computed using the following currency conversion rates: 1925–45, £1 = $4.00; 1955–65, £1 = $2.80; 1975, £1 = $2.40; 1985, £1 = $1.28.

Sources
For IBM: 1915–25, S. Englebourg, *International Business Machines: A Business History*, Arno Press, New York, 1976; 1935–65, R. Sobel, *IBM: Colossus in Transition*, Times Books, New York, 1981; 1975–85, *Datamation*. For ICL: Annual Reports and internal sources.

IBM took the view that the British company's poor performance was due to managerial incompetence, and the failure to develop an effective selling organization. The BTM view was that its growth was frustrated by the onerous royalties exacted by IBM. The truth lies between these two views, but readers will no doubt judge for themselves.

2

The British Tabulating Machine Company

1907-1919

> The Company, owing to its slow growth, has always had to be financed in a piecemeal kind of way; it has never really had sufficient working capital to deal with the growing business. . . . This being the position the Directors were forced some three or four years back to adopt the policy of limiting new business taken by introducing a limit of only aiming at installing 20 sets of new machines a year, a set being reckoned as a Tabulator and a Sorter. This, you will understand, was a limitation made necessary by the exigencies of finance. If we had had the money available, we could have done very much more business.
>
> —R.B. Phillpotts in a letter to T.J. Watson, 28 August 1918.[1]

The period from 1907 up to the end of the First World War saw BTM grow from a very small business, employing a handful of people importing a few machines from the United States, to a medium-sized business with some manufacturing facilities and employing in the region of a hundred people. Probably the best measure of BTM's progress are its assets and number of personnel (Table 2.1). The assets represented both conventional fixed assets (buildings and machinery), and also a constantly increasing proportion of tabulating machinery on hire. BTM's growth can be seen as taking place in three phases. First, the period 1907-1911 saw the company tackling the two main problems of entering the office-machinery market: the slow acceptance of office machines in Britain, and the need to raise capital for leasing. The second phase of company growth began with its securing a contract to supply tabulating machines for the British census of 1911. This contract transformed the business outlook of the company, and during the remaining years leading up to the First World War the customer base built up to about thirty installations. This growth rate was, however, small compared with that in the United States, where sales of punched-card office machinery were greatly increased as a result of a business merger in 1911 involving Hollerith's Tabulating Machine Company, which laid the foundations for what was later to become International Business Machines. The same year also saw the development of a

Table 2.1   BTM financial statistics 1908–1919

	Assets (£s)	Pre-tax profits (£s)	Personnel
1908	9800	− 607	
1909	13458	− 562	
1910	17657	− 275	5
1911	21042	3325[a]	
1912	25221	1107	
1913	24284	1026	
1914	26402	898	45
1915	26538	909	
1916	31869	2399	
1917	39322	3933	
1918	64352	9000	
1919	80861	10805	*c.*100

Note
[a] The high profits of 1911 were due to fulfilling the census contract.

Source
BTM Annual Reports, 1908–19.

rival American punched-card system by the Powers Accounting Machine Company of New York. The third phase of BTM's early growth was the war period 1914–1919. The trading difficulties of the war were amply offset by an increased demand for the machines in war service and in munitions manufacture. The war period also saw the establishment of the rival Powers Accounting Machine Company in Great Britain, which quickly grew to a size comparable with BTM. The end of the decade thus saw two medium-sized punched-card machine businesses established in Britain.

BTM: early development

BTM began operations with an authorized share capital of £50 000. This was a small sum compared with large-scale enterprises. For example the issued share capital of Western Electric (the forebear of STC) was around a £½ million at this time. None the less, it was a large sum for such a tiny concern, and it was no easy matter for BTM to place its stock. A little short of £10 000 share capital was issued at the time of incorporation. This consisted of £5000 transferred from The Tabulator Limited, and about the same amount of new capital, mainly subscribed by the directors and friends.

The board of the new company, which was essentially similar to that of The Tabulator Ltd, consisted of Ralegh Phillpotts, Robert Porter, and John L. Hunter. C.A. Everard Greene was appointed general manager, and a newcomer, W.G. Dunstall, was made company secretary. The board held its first meeting towards the end of 1907, when the major item of business was the licensing arrangement with Hollerith's Tabulating Machine Company. At this time Robert Porter was based in Washington as North American correspondent for *The Times*, so that he was able to conduct with Hollerith in person the negotiations between the two companies. The resulting agreement took effect on the 31 March 1908. This agreement would eventually assume critical importance for BTM, so that it has been reproduced in this book in Appendix 1.

In summary, the agreement gave BTM the right to market all present and future Hollerith machines in Great Britain and the Empire (excluding Canada) on the following terms:

- TMC would transfer all know-how and patents to BTM. Machines and parts would be supplied at cost plus 10 per cent.
- BTM would use its best efforts to develop a profitable business in its territories.
- BTM would rent tabulators and sorters, and sell punches and cards, at identical prices to the American company, using an exchange rate of 5 dollars to the pound.
- BTM would pay a royalty of 25 per cent of revenues to the American company.
- BTM would pay TMC £2100 immediately as an advance on royalties, with two further instalments of £2000 at the beginning of 1909 and 1910; a total of £6100.
- The agreement would terminate if BTM failed to honour any of the particulars of the agreement.

It seems likely that neither party gave a great deal of thought to the terms of the agreement. In particular, no time limit was put on the agreement, so that it would remain in force until it was dissolved by mutual consent. (In time, the American company would wish to develop the British territories more energetically than had BTM: unable to revoke the agreement, it would enforce it in the letter rather than the spirit, in order to try to force the British company's hand.)

The formation of BTM coincided with the production by Hollerith of the new range of automatic machines, the original hand-fed machines no longer being manufactured. BTM continued to make use of the small engineering firm Thomas Kesnor to modify the American machines for the British market, and in early 1908 a representative of Kesnor's visited the United States to gain experience of the new machines, and also to investigate the feasibility of assembling them and manufacturing the cards in Britain. A high demand for the new automatic machines in America, however, meant that only one set of automatic machines could be spared for Britain during 1908. BTM thus ended the year still with only two customers, Vickers and the Lancashire and Yorkshire Railway, both using hand machines. The new machines began to arrive in early 1909, and arrangements were quickly set in hand for assembly and card manufacture at Kesnor's workshops in Fulham. The company also took on a few additional people to cope with the increased workload. These included A. Cranfield and C.H. Courtney, involved in administration and sales at Norfolk Street, and H. Waters, the company's first maintenance engineer. (These early employees derived no little benefit from being in at an early stage: Cranfield rose to become company secretary and a director, Courtney later headed the South African operation, and Waters became the first works manager.)

By early 1910, automatic machines were installed on trial in five organizations: the Great Western Railway in Swindon; the Co-operative Wholesale Society, the Calico Printers Association, and the Great Central Railway, all based in Manchester; and the General Register Office, Somerset House. In 1911 a set of machines was leased in South Africa, the company's first overseas venture. BTM also had several other requests for machines which it was unable to fulfil, owing to lack of leasing capital. An attempt to increase the issued share capital to £20 000 met with indifferent results, only a little over £3000 being subscribed. This shortage of capital to purchase machines for leasing was to prove BTM's greatest single problem during the next twenty or thirty years. The immediate cash problems of the firm were made worse by the overdue second and third advance royalty payments, each of £2000, owed to TMC. Fortunately Porter was able to intercede with his old friend Hollerith, and the American company agreed to accept payment of the £4000 in debentures.

Although the British company had now been trading for seven years since 1904, it was still experiencing problems raising capital. In part, this is because it was typical of the majority of British manufacturing firms of the period, which were owned and controlled by single families or by partnerships.[2] The shares of medium-sized companies were generally not publicly quoted until the 1930s, so the only way BTM could grow was by ploughing back what profits remained after paying the 25 per cent royalty to TMC, and issuing shares to friends or family who could afford them. BTM's obligations to lease rather than sell machines meant that for a company of its size it needed very large amounts of working capital. The pay-back period for a tabulating machine or sorter was of the order of 2 to 3 years, and if the business was to grow rapidly there would be a negative cash-flow indefinitely. BTM could have grown much faster if it could have obtained low-cost finance secured on the asset value of the punched-card machines. There is no evidence that such an avenue was explored, but Phillpotts was secretary of Speyer Brothers merchant bank, and no doubt if he could have obtained funds this way he would have done so. It is probable that the asset value of the punched-card machines would not have been seen as offering adequate security, because office machinery had still not been seriously accepted in Britain. A BTM punched-card machine was all too often regarded with suspicion as a 'Yankee sewing machine',[3] and potential customers invariably required a three-month trial period before signing a long-term rental contract.

The British census, 1911

Against this background of day to day operations and machine trials at various firms, the greatest prize the company sought was to supply machines for the 1911 British census. Apart from the revenue generated, a big census contract would do more than anything to give the machines an official seal of approval and to raise their credibility among potential users of office machinery. Surprisingly, for an advanced industrial nation, the British Census Office had at no time adopted the Hollerith system, unlike several of its counterparts in European countries. Since about 1904 Everard Greene had persisted in trying to interest the authorities; persistence eventually paid off, and in 1908 BTM was asked to provide estimates and trial machines. Everard Greene approached Hollerith for the supply of census machines, only to receive the reply that TMC had withdrawn from census work altogether, and could not supply them.[4]

The census contract was of such importance, however, that it could not be let slip, and it was decided to develop a counting-sorting machine especially for the British census. The development was undertaken by Kesnor's engineers, but the machine did not perform satisfactorily, and had to be abandoned in the summer of 1910 after several months' development and trials by the Census Office. After the trials the Census Office in any case came to the conclusion that a somewhat different machine was called for, one based on a tabulator equipped with 36 counters. In spite of what was now to be an uncomfortably short development time it was decided to proceed with the new development; but on the advice of G.E. Chadwyck-Healey (a friend of Phillpotts and a BTM shareholder) a consulting engineer, G.H. Baillie, was appointed to monitor progress. Baillie was a consulting electrical engineer with an international reputation; this was to be the first of many such assignments for BTM, and he was elected a director shortly afterwards.

The acquisition of the census machines was formally the responsibility of His Majesty's Stationery Office, not the Census Office. By the time the Stationery Office became involved, however, the decision to use Hollerith machines had passed the point of no return, and much to his chagrin the Controller of the Stationery Office, Rowland Bailey, found that BTM had the upper hand in the negotiations over the price of the contract. The Controller was particularly aggrieved over the cost of the cards, for which BTM quoted 3/6d per thousand for the first million, and 3/- thereafter. Bailey's inquiries suggested that the Stationery Office could have them made for 1/8d per thousand. Everard Greene was, however, adamant that the price quoted should stand:

Our Board regret that they are unable to adopt your suggestion in view of the difficulties which have to be contended with in the manufacture of these cards (of which we have had ample experience) and the heavy risks that would be run in the event of the cards supplied being unsuitable. As we think you already appreciate, our object in devoting so much time and expense to this census work during the past has been not so much the profit that we hope to derive as the publicity which would probably be given to our machines in this country, and should any hitch occur in the matter of the cards a perfectly erroneous impression would be created with regard to the machines themselves.[5]

Of course, while it was true that the machine would not work satisfactorily with inferior cards, this did not mean that BTM's cards were not over-priced. Failing to reach a compromise with BTM, Bailey decided to exploit the government's immunity from the Patent Acts and approached Vickers to make copies of the Hollerith machines in their possession. He was advised that this would take two years and be prohibitively expensive. On the 29 November 1910 Bailey summoned Phillpotts and Everard Greene to an interview and advised them that the Stationery Office had awarded them the census contract on BTM's terms. Bailey reported to his superiors: 'We have been absolutely beaten by the Company in dealing with them over the Census Office mainly, I believe, because the Office let them know beforehand that they considered the machines quite indispensable.'[6] It is not stated in the record, of course, but one senses that the Stationery Office would not be kindly disposed to BTM in the future. In 1915, when the Stationery Office sought punched-card machines for stores accounting, it adopted the machines of the rival Powers company.

In December 1910 the BTM board approved the draft contract for the supply of census machines and cards to the Census Office. It was by far the largest order the company had received, and in fact exceeded its total business to that date. To finance the contract a bank loan of £3000 was arranged on the personal security of the directors and friends. The census took place in April 1911, and Chadwyck-Healey, who was publisher of *The Engineer*, gave the company a little free publicity by printing a description of the Hollerith machines in a series of articles.[7] The articles boasted of the size of the census contract, which called for the rental of 8 counting machines, 15 sorters, and 60 punches, and for the sale of 45 million cards. The census contract accounted for most of the London business of the company, so it made sense to locate the service engineers at Millbank, close to the Census Office. A number of new engineering staff were taken on for the contract, including Charles Campbell, later chief engineer of the company, and H.H. Keen, later the doyen of British punched-card machine inventors.

In May 1911, as processing of the census got under way, it was found that the machines were not operating reliably under heavy use. A meeting of the BTM board was called, which was also attended by Chadwyck-Healey, who understood the census machines well, and Everard Greene. The board faced a real dilemma. If BTM continued with the census, but failed to complete it, then the adverse publicity would probably finish the company for good. On the other hand, if it told the government that it could not fulfil its obligations, and withdrew from the census, then the anticlimax, after all the publicity that had already appeared in the press, would be almost as damaging. It was decided there was no alternative other than to press ahead with the census contract, and Baillie was sent as an emissary to the Census Office to see what immediate steps could be taken to rescue the situation.

The census operation lasted for about two years, 1911-1913; the early problems with the machines were evidently cured, and there are no contemporary reports suggesting that they were a major cause of trouble. In fact the greatest problem was caused by the Stationery Office's attempt to use cheap cards made of British paper, which did not have the precise qualities of those made from American card-stock. Following the success of the British census, censuses for several other countries were subsequently negotiated by BTM. These included the 1911 Scottish census, Egypt in 1917, and Australia in 1921. In 1913 negotiations were also begun to supply British census machines to the German Hollerith company (Deutsche Hollerith Maschinen Gmbh—or Dehomag).

The year 1911 saw the revenues of BTM increase dramatically as a result of the census contract. This was, however, but one contract. The following two years, although seeing no significant increase in revenues, saw the one-off census contract gradually wind down, to be replaced by regular business. Thus, while the end of 1912 saw the total rental business of the company consisting of 64 machines, of which 29 were hired to the census, by the end of 1913 the census accounted for only 4 machines out of a total of 54.[8] As the census business declined it was no longer convenient to house the maintenance operation at Millbank. At the same time, the scale of operation of the company (now with about 45 staff) was becoming sufficient to justify its own assembly shop and card works, instead of sub-contracting to Kesnor's. After some investigations by Baillie and Chadwyck-Healey, suitable premises were acquired in Verulam Street, Fulham, in 1913, and H. Waters was promoted to the position of works manager.

As ever, the main brake on company growth was the lack of working capital to purchase machines from the United States for rental. In the early days there had been difficulty in getting business, mainly because of the novelty of the machines. This situation had been transformed by the census contract, which had greatly increased the visibility of Hollerith machines in Britain. There was now more demand for punched-card machines than BTM could satisfy. Even so, it proved impossible to raise additional money with ease. For example an offer of £20 000 preference shares made in the summer of 1912 met with a very disappointing initial response. Under these circumstances there was little incentive to develop the riskier and less profitable overseas business, and a policy decision was taken not to expand the South African branch beyond the scale of the existing half-dozen machines.

American developments: C-T-R

During the years 1908-1914, in which BTM had made relatively slow growth, the punched-card machine business in America had grown by leaps and bounds. In 1908, Hollerith's Tabulating Machine Company had had about thirty customers and very modest revenues. It had, however, experienced far fewer problems in raising cash for expansion— for example $100 000 preference stock issued in 1908 had been taken up, evidently without any difficulty. During the next few years the company maintained a growth rate in excess of 20 per cent a half-year; and by 1911 it had revenues of $372 294 (about £75 000) a year.[9] A contemporary American report captured exactly the booming American punched card-business:

The system is used in factories of all sorts, in steel mills, by insurance companies, by electric light and traction and telephone companies, by wholesale merchandise establishments and department stores, by textile mills, automobile companies, numerous railroads, municipalities and state governments. It is used for compiling labor costs, efficiency records, distribution of sales, internal requisitions for supplies and materials, production statistics, day and piece work. It is used for analysing risks in life, fire and casualty insurance, for plant expenditures and sales of service, by public service corporations, for distributing sales and cost figures as to salesmen, department, customer, location, commodity, method of sale, and in numerous other ways. The cards besides furnishing the basis for regular current reports, provide also for all special reports and make it possible to obtain them in a mere fraction of the time otherwise required.[10]

By contrast the revenues of BTM in 1913—its most successful year to date—were a mere £4568. This performance was, however, only marginally worse than that of the German Hollerith company, established in Berlin in 1910, and operating under licensing terms similar to BTM.[11] The poor European performance partly reflected the comparatively weak development of the office-machine market and business finance in Europe compared with their progress in the United States.

Business finance and merger activity in the United States were far more advanced than in Europe. For about twenty years, the United States had been experiencing a wave of business consolidations and mergers; and in 1911 Hollerith's Tabulating Machine Company became caught up in a typical business merger of the period. As a result of the merger, the Tabulating Machine Company became a part of the Computing-Tabulating-Recording Company, which was later renamed International Business Machines. The business promoter responsible for the merger was the financier C.R. Flint.* Hollerith personally owned over half the stock of TMC, and had for some years resisted attempted acquisition of his company. He was, however, now 51 years old, and in failing health. Flint bought the company for $2.3 million, of which Hollerith received $1.2 million. A very wealthy man, Hollerith went into semi-retirement, although he remained a consulting engineer to the company, and continued to play a role in the technical development of the machines. He died in 1929.[12]

To form the Computing-Tabulating-Recording Company (C-T-R) Flint brought together three principal companies, each of which contributed one word to the name of the new enterprise: the Computing Scale Company, the Tabulating Machine Company, and the International Time Recording Company. The Computing Scale Company manufactured weighing machines and other machines for retail stores. The International Time Recording Company manufactured automatic time recorders, and had already established subsidiaries in Europe. The C-T-R merger was to some extent a horizontal integration, although sufficiently unusual to be described by one commentator as 'neither horizontal, nor vertical, nor circular. In fact it was so uncommon as to almost justify the description *sui generis*, in a class by itself'.[13] The merger consequently did not have one rationale, but several. First, all three businesses were selling capital goods in broadly similar environments, which promised an economy to be obtained by consolidating the marketing operations. Second, there were economies to be obtained in manufacturing, making for less sub-contracting and some standardization of parts. Thirdly, the combination would be

* Although Flint has never been a well-known name in Britain, he occupies a prominent place in the annals of American business history, being behind such business promotions as the United States Rubber Company and the American Woolen Company.

less vulnerable to economic downturns. In fact, whatever the rationales, the consolidation was spectacularly successful. In his autobiography Flint recorded that C-T-R was not his largest consolidation, but it was his most successful.[14] It is, however, the case that the dramatic growth of IBM between the two World Wars was built on the tabulating-machine operation, rather than the other sectors of the business.

C-T-R formally began operations in July 1911, but, C-T-R being a holding company, the constituent companies continued to trade under their original names. Hollerith's second in command at TMC, Gershom Smith, replaced him as general manager, and his protégé Otto Braitmeyer became assistant general manager. From this point on, the special relationship between Hollerith and Robert Porter of BTM no longer obtained, and the relations between BTM and its American parent changed in character completely.

The new management of TMC immediately set about rationalizing the domestic and overseas business. It was quickly discovered that BTM was £5000 in arrears with its advance royalty payments, Porter and Hollerith having agreed in 1910 that BTM would issue debentures in lieu. This arrangement had not, unfortunately, been sealed at the time of the C-T-R merger, and Gershom Smith did not propose to honour it. This was a very considerable sum for BTM, and it was raised by issuing a circular to shareholders for fresh capital; this enabled the company to remit £3000 in partial payment in July 1912. Gershom Smith, however, insisted on a full cash settlement from BTM. In January 1913 he despatched a stern letter:

We have endeavoured to be fair and liberal with you in every way, but your positive refusal and neglect to comply with the terms of the contract places you in default and places us in a position which makes it necessary for us to (and we hereby do) make formal demand upon you for the amounts now due to us . . . Unless these amounts are paid here in New York or in Washington on or before Feb. 20 1913, you will please take notice that we shall then consider and treat the contract and the license under which you and your customers are operating as terminated and shall proceed accordingly.

In the meantime, and in view of your breaches of the contract, we shall not proceed with any further orders from you.[15]

The BTM board was furious at Smith's intransigence. But in view of the threat to turn off the supply of machines the company had no alternative other than to pay up. Phillpotts' reply remitting the money made his views on Smith's attitude perfectly plain:

I do not in the least want to enter legal discussions. I should have thought you would have known by now, as you are entirely familiar with the personnel of our Company, that we pay up all our obligations just as soon as we can, and if I may say so, it should be more your object to assist in developing our business than to assume in any way a sort of hostile attitude towards us. We are doing all we can in the face of a great many difficulties.[16]

This exchange was in fact just the beginning of a relationship with the American company that was to become increasingly strained, year upon year. In 1914, Thomas J. Watson was appointed President of C-T-R. Watson was one of the great American business leaders of the twentieth century, and during the 1920s and 1930s he turned IBM into one of America's outstanding commercial success stories. Whatever were to be the achievements of the BTM management in the coming years, they could never have matched up to Watson's vision or achievement.

American developments: Powers Accounting Machines

Another development in America, which was to have as nearly as big an impact on BTM as the C-T-R merger, was the formation of another punched-card machine venture, the Powers Accounting Machine Company. The promoter of this company was a man by the name of James Powers, an inventor-entrepreneur very much in the mould of Hollerith, although far less well known.

Powers' initiation into punched-card machinery had occurred in 1905, when Hollerith had made a break with the Bureau of the Census, largely over the price of rentals, and the director of the census had employed Powers as a technical expert in Hollerith's place to improve the census machines in time for the 1911 census. Very little is known of Powers' background, and there appear to be only two extant photographs of him. According to the records of the Bureau of the Census,[17] James Powers was born in Odessa, Russia, in 1871. He was educated at the Technical School of Odessa, and was afterwards employed making scientific instruments. He emigrated to America in 1899, and was employed in turn by several manufacturing companies, including Western Electric. In his letter of application to the census he claimed to have done experimental work on cash registers, typewriters, and adding machines, and to have several patents in his name. In his service with the Bureau of the Census, Powers made improvements to the census card-sorter, and developed an electrically operated card-punch which was lighter and faster in operation than the Hollerith punch. The most important improvement, however, was the incorporation of a printing mechanism in the tabulating machines: this device entirely eliminated the manual transcription from counters that had formerly been necessary, with consequent improvements in throughput and accuracy.[18]

In April 1911 Powers left the Bureau of the Census, and incorporated the Powers Accounting Machine Company to develop punched-card machines for commercial use. The Powers machines used the same sized cards as the Hollerith system, but made use of a mechanical hole-sensing method, rather than the electrical sensing of Hollerith. This had some advantages: it was more reliable than electrical sensing, and was also unaffected by any electrically conductive impurities in the cards. Despite these differences the Powers machines inevitably infringed the basic Hollerith patents, which still had several years to run. Before C-T-R had time to act, an infringement suit had been successfully fought by Dehomag in Germany in 1913. The German court, however, obliged Dehomag to grant Powers a licence to use the Hollerith patents on a royalty basis. C-T-R arrived at a similar arrangement with Powers in the United States.

During the first two years of the existence of the Powers company, 1911-1913, Powers and his assistant W.W. Lasker developed a range of machines suited to the commercial market. The Powers range consisted of three basic machines.[19] First, the 'slide punch', derived from Powers' census punch. Second, a horizontal sorter which was functionally identical to the Hollerith vertical sorter, except that the operator did not have to stoop to remove the cards. The third machine was the printing tabulator (see Plates). The Powers tabulator had a number of improvements over the Hollerith machine, the two most important of which were the ability to print its results, and the 'connection box'. It was the printing feature which had caused Powers to use the phrase 'accounting machine' in the name of his company. Hollerith machines were statistical machines, and they were admirably suited to the processing of statistical data; but because they produced no printed record they had not penetrated the vast market for bookkeeping machines enjoyed by companies such as Burroughs Accounting Machines. The Hollerith tabulator was also inherently inflexible, in that to change from tabulating one card format to another it was necessary to rewire the machine, which was a slow and awkward job. In the Powers machine it was possible to switch from one application to another simply by changing the connection box; this took only a few seconds, which was a considerable attraction in a busy accounting office. The Power's Accounting Machine Company was thus poised to enter the commercial bookkeeping market, in addition to the market for statistical machines opened up by the Tabulating Machine Company.

While the Powers machines were being developed, the Hollerith machines had also been undergoing improvement. For example, around 1912 Hollerith's original counters were replaced by the more reliable 'relayless' type, and the 37-column card was replaced by one with 45 columns, a standard also adopted by Powers (Fig. 2.1). The arrival of the Powers machines, however, created a competitive environment in which the machines evolved much more rapidly than would otherwise have been the case. In 1914 Watson established an 'experimental department' within TMC which began to systematically improve the

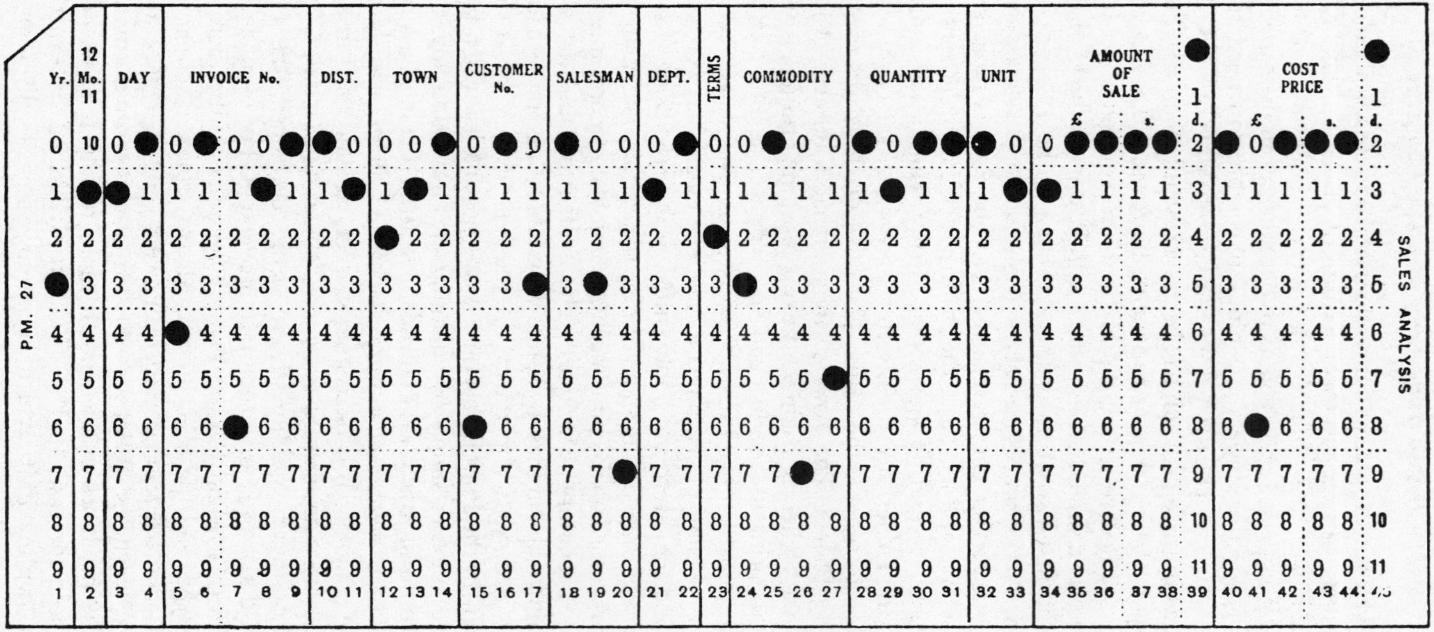

[Shown actual size, 7⅜ × 3¼ inches]

Fig. 2.1   The 45-column punched card

machines.[20] One of the first improvements was a plug-board for the tabulator, in answer to the Powers connection box. Similarly, Powers was forced to abandon its slide punch in the face of the far more effective Hollerith hand punch, and produced an automatic key punch with power operation in 1916; this in its turn was answered by the Hollerith electric punch announced the same year. And so it went on.*

While Powers was developing his machines, and before they were actually placed on the market, he actively promoted them, much as Hollerith had done with his machines a few years previously. In autumn 1913 he made a trip to Europe with a set of demonstration machines, in the hope of establishing overseas agencies. The demonstration machines were installed in the first European Powers agency in Potsdamstrasse 75, Berlin. The Powers Accounting Machine Company paid for three British organizations to send representatives to spend a few days working with the machines in December 1913. These included two members of the Stationery Office, a representative of the National Health Insurance Committee, and Joseph Burn, actuary of the Prudential. The report of the Stationery Office people was enthusiastic:

The general impression we have acquired is, that the inventor has striven to produce not merely an efficient rival or variant of the Hollerith system, but has attempted to extend the scope beyond that of the older (Hollerith) apparatus, and by elimination or combination of certain operations to reduce the work involved to a minimum.[21]

In the course of 1914 and 1915 all three organizations became users of Powers machines.

The minutes of BTM show that reports of the Powers machines began to filter through in mid-1914. Evidently the arrival of a competitor caused little alarm, since BTM had all the business it could handle and more. In fact the board was in a bullish mood: sufficient of BTM's preference stock had been placed not only to settle the debts with the American company, but to leave an ample margin for a considerable increase of business. For a rare few months lack of capital was not uppermost in the company's mind. In 1914, for the first time, the company took an advertisement in *The Times* to have its sixth annual general meeting reported in the 'Company Meetings' pages.[22] Phillpotts announced the payment of a

---

* There were also many minor improvements. The development of punched-card machines was very evolutionary. Although the dozen or so major innovations are well known, there were literally hundreds of small improvements, protected by hundreds of patents. The patent literature gives no hint as to which patents were actually taken up, which were not subsequently developed, and which were merely defensive. It is also the case that innovations often did not make their way into marketable products until several years after the original patent application.

dividend to ordinary shareholders for the first time, and spoke with exuberant confidence for the future.

The First World War

Britain declared war on Germany on 4 August 1914. As soon as war broke out Ralegh Phillpotts enlisted in the Devonshire Yeomanry, holding the rank of Captain for the duration; and Robert Porter took over as acting chairman. A month or so later the board of BTM lost a second director, J.L. Hunter, who also enlisted. Further down in the company there was a steady attrition of staff leaving for active service.

The war cast a gloom over BTM's immediate prospects. The first casualty was its negotiations with Dehomag to supply British census machines for the German census. Another problem to be faced was the continuity of supplies of machines and card stock from America. To guard against shipping losses, the company began to increase paper stocks by importing additional supplies. After the first few uncertain months of the war, however, the gloom lifted, and it became clear that the war was going to do the company a lot more good than ill. Early 1915 saw a general improvement in business outlook in the country. For BTM in particular, the increase in rail traffic, the administration of the armed forces, and the government munitions and aeroplane factories all produced orders for machines and cards. The general labour shortage, and the need to retain existing employees, called for BTM to pay higher wages and war bonuses; but it proved easy to pass these increases on, in the general inflationary climate, in increased card prices and machine rentals. These increases were, however, in flat breach of the agreement with TMC, which required that machines and cards should be rented or sold at identical prices to those charged in the United States.

It seems that fears of shipping losses had been unfounded, and there are no records of any serious difficulty in the supply of machines or paper. In fact the main problem appears to have been obtaining the necessary government licence to import paper—the quota having been reduced to two-thirds of the 1914 level. Incidentally, a point frequently overlooked in the history of the punched-card machine is that the technological problems of making the right quality cards were in many ways as formidable as the problems of making the machines themselves. For example, when the Stationery Office had insisted on experimenting with British manufactured cards for the 1911 census, millions of them had to be repulped. Phillpotts later made the point at length, in his slightly schoolmasterish manner:

The keynote of this machine is to be able to get cards of the proper substance and purity of manufacture. People think that these little manilla 7-inch cards are easy things to make. All we can say is that during the war we found that no English papermakers either could or, anyhow, would make them at all, and therefore we had to face all the difficulties of shipping troubles and delays in order to keep our business going. The accurate and pure manufacture of these cards is an extremely important thing. . . . I have rather emphasized that point, because people, when they first used our machines and we stipulated that they must buy the cards from us or we would not undertake to keep the machines in order, sometimes objected to buy them from us, but as a general rule they did not object long.[23]

The uncertainties of the first year of the war naturally put paid to immediate plans for extending manufacture in the UK. There was also very little technical development of any kind. The main developments at BTM were concerned with making use of cards of low-grade paper. British cards made in the smoky atmosphere of the North of England tended to contain electrically conductive carbon particles, which could cause a false input when sensed by the reading brushes of a tabulator or sorter. One device was a 'speck detector' attached to the card-cutting machines, which could detect bad cards before they went out into the field. Another BTM invention, the 'set-back revolving contact', made the reading stations of tabulators and sorters less sensitive to the conducting impurities.[24] Everard Greene wrote to Gershom Smith, general manager of TMC, to tell him about the set-back rolling contact, and asked 'whether you wish to acquire it, and if so, how you would propose to remunerate us for turning it over to you.' The description of the invention was shown to Hollerith, who commented 'As far as I am concerned, my idea would be to throw the papers in the waste basket and tell the British company to go to.' This comment pretty well summed up the TMC's attitude in general to BTM.[25]

In the autumn of 1914 the first Powers machines had begun to arrive in England. Although reports very favourable to the Powers machines reached BTM, there appears still to have been little concern at the competition. The fact is that BTM had all the business it could handle. Although almost no documents from BTM's early days—other than the statutory board minutes—have survived, there is one fragment which shows financial projections based on the number of new machines BTM introduced each year.[26] As a result of this study it was decided in August 1916 to limit business to the introduction of twenty sets of new machines a year. This was certainly less than the market could have stood. Even so, it entailed a steady raising of capital to finance the increasing business, which could only partly be met out of revenues. To raise the additional capital Phillpotts and Dunstall—who had been elected a director in 1916— approached a number of sources. Owing to government war-time restrictions it was not permitted to advertise capital issues, so that approaches had to be made on a personal basis, and it proved possible to place only a small number of preference shares.

Notwithstanding these financial difficulties, the war years were a comparatively confident and prosperous period for the company, which had built up to a total of fifty installations. In 1917 the BTM works moved to larger premises in Belvedere Road, Fulham. Fig. 2.2 shows a drawing of the BTM works, which illustrates clearly the scale of the business at that time. The ground floor of the factory was mainly given over to despatch and the manufacture of cards. The paper for the cards was delivered in massive reels, which first had to be slit into 3¼-inch wide reels of card stock, the same width as the cards. From these reels of card stock, cards were then printed and guillotined by a number of card-printing presses, and packed in wooden cases for despatch. The punched-card machines themselves were assembled on the second floor from parts imported from TMC. In general tabulators were assembled to the particular requirements of each customer, since the particular application determined the number of counters that needed to be fitted to the machine, and that in turn determined the rental. So far as can be determined sorting machines and punches were imported fully assembled. On the first floor machines were tested prior to despatch, and special attachments for British machines were made in the machine shop. The Belvedere Road works was also headquarters for the maintenance engineers.

Activities at head office in Norfolk Street had also expanded and become more structured with an influx of new people. Everard Greene now had a second in command, the ebullient Max G. Browne, later a major figure in the company. Whereas in the early days of the company most employees put their hand to most tasks, the company had now taken on an embryonic functional structure. There was for example a separate department for accounts, with appropriate professional specialists; and the selling operation was handled by the Systems Department, which in addition to its sales function did all the systems and technical work for the customer, and handled publicity.

Relations with TMC

During 1916 BTM's original £6100 advance on royalties to TMC ran out, and the company quickly fell into arrears with its royalty account. In the summer of 1917 a letter, familiar in tone, arrived from Braitmeyer, assistant general manager of TMC, requesting prompt settlement. All BTM's capital was tied up in machines, and no contingency had been made to pay TMC the royalties it was owed. This was rather lax accounting, but no doubt if royalties had been paid on time BTM would have grown even more slowly than it had. Everard Greene wrote back, asking for more time to pay in view of the war situation. He also raised a much more serious point. The original BTM-TMC agreement of 1908 had

1917–1921

WORKS OF THE BRITISH TABULATING
MACHINE COMPANY LTD

Belvedere Road, Lambeth, S.E.1

(5500 Square Feet)

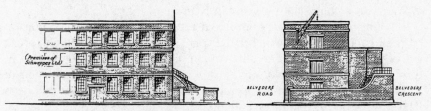

BELVEDERE ROAD

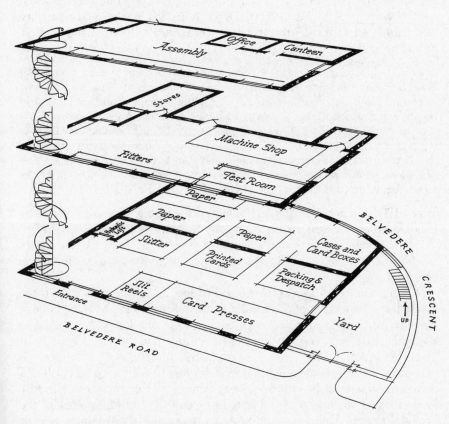

Fig. 2.2 The BTM works, 1917–21

specified that the 25 per cent royalty was to be paid net, without deductions of any kind. At that time income tax was 6d in the·pound, and did not materially affect the agreement. During the war, however, income tax had risen to 6/- in the pound. To pay royalties without deduction now meant that the 25 per cent royalty was equivalent to 33 per cent of BTM's revenues. Everard Greene's appeal to Braitmeyer was entirely without success, and Phillpotts was left to take up the matter directly with Watson, on a chairman-to-chairman basis.

In a long and detailed letter in August 1918, Phillpotts briefed Watson on the history of BTM, which he saw as never having been able to break out of the cycle of lack of leasing capital, leading to failure to expand, in turn leading to a lack of profits to buy machines. Phillpotts went on to show that in its ten years of operation, BTM's total net profit had been £10 773, whereas royalties and tax amounted to £11 836. Since all profits were being ploughed back, the company's growth rate had been effectively halved by the royalty burden. In addition, Phillpotts pointed out the inequity of having to carry the additional tax burden, an eventuality never foreseen in the 1908 agreement. Finally, Phillpotts made an offer which he saw as essential to the ability of BTM to carry on:

It would help us very much if we could say that you were, to some extent, not only the Parent Company but partners with us. Could you therefore see your way to taking fully paid Preference Stock ... for the amount of money £7,000 in round figures which we are at present owing you as above stated: and would you agree to modify the 1908 Agreement so that the royalties payable to you are at the rate of 12½ per cent. of the rentals received by us from customers instead of the 25 per cent. as the agreement now stands. But to offset this, we suggest that you should continue to supply us with machinery as under the present Agreement, but on terms of 20 per cent. instead of 10 per cent.[27]

Watson did not himself reply to Phillpotts' letter, but passed it down to be handled, in due course, by his European manager A.R. Jennings. (In fact Watson operated in a very presidential manner, and there are few letters in the ICL Archives from Watson other than those of a diplomatic character.)

When peace conditions returned to Europe, TMC began to press more firmly for a settlement of the royalty debt. In May 1919, Everard Greene was invited to dine with Jennings. Everard Greene led with a recital of the usual catalogue of problems, but Jennings had clearly already been given his orders by the American company, and had not really come to negotiate. Jennings explained that Watson was unwilling to accept BTM preference shares in lieu of royalty payments, and that moreover the only kind of BTM stock he was interested in was a controlling interest of the ordinary shares. Phillpotts would never under any circumstances, now or in the future, relinquish his personal control or British ownership of the company. There was thus no alternative but to pay up in full, and promptly. Fortunately BTM was, for a rare moment, in a position to meet its obligations; following the relaxation of wartime investment controls, the remaining £8000 of BTM preference stock had been placed, bringing the total paid-up share capital of the company to its maximum authorized £50 000. The proceeds of the issue were almost entirely absorbed in liquidating the TMC royalty debt.

In retrospect, the agreement between TMC and BTM was quite extraordinary. The royalty rate of 25 per cent was iniquitous, and the fact that TMC was only levying a royalty of 5 per cent on the Powers Accounting Machine Company to use the same patents in America ought to have been grounds for a revision. And the fact that TMC determined rentals, and that there was a territorial marketing agreement, were surely both violations of the Sherman Antitrust Act, which forbade price-fixing cartels and the allocation of markets. There is no satisfactory explanation as to why BTM put up with the arrangement until it finally broke with the American company in 1949. It seems BTM just could not find the means to alter the situation.

The Acc and Tab

A British agency for Powers Accounting Machines in Britain had been established in 1915, for which a patent agent named J.E. Evans-Jackson acted both as import agent and British-patent agent. The first two installations in Britain were for the Stationery Office and the Prudential. The latter installation was quite enormous in extent, consisting of forty slide punches, seven sorters and seven tabulating machines. This mechanization was introduced to cope specifically with the high volume of low-premium insurance policies resulting from the 1914 Approved Societies Act. At the time it was said to be—outside of census activities—the largest order ever placed for a punched-card installation in the world.[28]

In November 1915, the Powers agency became a wholly-owned subsidiary of the American company, and was incorporated in Britain as the Accounting and Tabulating Machine Company of Great Britain Limited, with Evans-Jackson as chairman. The company quickly became known by the less ponderous title of the 'Acc and Tab'. The business, based on the import of American-built machines and American-made cards, grew quite rapidly, so that by late 1916 there were about a dozen customers. These included several government installations and some well-known names, such as Cadbury's and Coleman's; another small installation was acquired by Morland and Impey, the British licensees of the Kalamazoo loose-leaf ledger system. As well as statistical applica-

tions of the kind provided by BTM, there were also several full-blown
accounting operations.

The Acc and Tab was established at a time when office machinery was
just coming of age in Britain, so that it had far less difficulty gaining
acceptance than BTM had experienced a decade or so earlier. The greater
use of office machines owed much to the increased tempo of war-time
manufacturing, combined with a loss of clerical labour to the fighting
forces. If one had to single out the point at which office machines 'took
off' in Britain, it would have to be the years 1916–1917. Probably the
most reliable barometer of the acceptance of office machines, at this
distance in time, is the pages of *The Accountant*, the main voice of the
accounting profession in Britain. Up to 1914, there was not a single
article on office machines, other than typewriters and loose-leaf ledgers.
The British office-machine industry mirrored this lack of development;
although there was some manufacturing of loose-leaf ledgers (for example
Morland and Impey had a Kalamazoo factory in Northfield, Birmingham)
there was no typewriter industry to speak of, and no calculating machine
industry at all. In fact as late as 1914 an editorial in *The Accountant*, in
response to an American report, stated: 'We shall be glad if any of our
readers can give us particulars of the Hollerith machine, and state what it
is supposed to do, and exactly how it does it'.[29] After about 1915,
however, articles appeared quite regularly, describing the Hollerith system,
Burroughs machines, Dictaphones, Addressographs, and so on. In 1917
the Office Machinery Users Association was formed, with Professor L.R.
Dicksee as its Chairman and R.M. Holland-Martin of Martin's Bank as its
President.[30] Lawrence Dicksee, who was Professor of Accounting at the
London School of Economics, was the leading British authority on office
machinery, and in 1917 he published the first edition of his book *Office
Machines and Appliances*; the book had the unmistakable tone of a mis-
sionary talking to cannibals; but the ascendancy of office mechanization
was firmly set at that point.[31]

In the improved climate for office machinery the Acc and Tab developed
rapidly after its incorporation in 1915, so that by 1918 revenues for sales
and rentals were about £7000, a figure very much on a par with BTM's
revenues. The Prudential's Powers installation had proved a great success
in compiling the statistical records of the Approved Societies, and the
Prudential actuary, Joseph Burn, was keen to make wider use of the
machines to reduced administrative costs further, and so gain greater
competitive advantage in the insurance industry. There was, however,
considerable anxiety in the Prudential over the assurance of supply of the
American-made machines, and the lack of control over the price of
rentals. Before making the business irreversibly dependent on punched-
card machines, the Prudential decided in 1918 to acquire the British

manufacturing and selling rights for the machines from the American company. The negotiations were conducted on behalf of the Prudential by Francis Impey of Morland and Impey, who as the British Kalamazoo licensees had experience in such matters. No copy of the Prudential–Powers agreement has been found, but it appears to have been a straight cash settlement in the region of £20 000 for the manufacturing and selling rights in Britain and the Empire, no further royalties being payable to the American company nor any restriction being placed on selling or rental prices.[32] Despite the high original payment, this was an arrangement that in the long term was vastly preferable to the agreement between BTM and its American parent.

It is pertinent to ask why the Prudential should have become involved in an office-machine company. The official Prudential history does not record any other instance of its creation or ownership of a subsidiary, so it is clear that it was not set up simply as a money-making venture.[33] In any case, with assets of £113 million, the minute Powers operation was simply not in the same league. Why, for example, did it not simply buy its machines from BTM, which was a reliable British supplier? To this the answer appears to be that BTM tabulators did not print their results, a feature which was essential to the Prudential's operation.[34] The Powers machines themselves, however, apart from the introduction of the automatic key punch in 1916, had not developed significantly during the war years. Furthermore, the American Powers company seemed to have become rather sleepy and showed little sign of making improvements to the machines.

Indeed, the principal mechanical development that had taken place in the war years had been underwritten by Prudential itself. This development, which had been started in 1915 at the suggestion of the Prudential's Powers-machine manager F.P. Symmons, was to design a tabulator that would print letters of the alphabet. A suitable mechanism was invented by the chief British Powers mechanic Charles Foster, and patented in 1916, but had been put to one side for the duration.[35] Joseph Burn saw this development as one which was crucial to his long-term plans to decentralize and reduce the cost of insurance policy administration. It would be a costly development, but one with vast potential for the Prudential business, allowing the complete accounting operation to be done by one system, and thus enabling them to dispense with their batteries of Addressograph and bookkeeping machines. Since it was unlikely that Powers would undertake this development of its own volition, the plan was for the Prudential to do the development, and recoup the cost by supplying machines to other insurance companies. Burn was a great proselytizer of insurance-office mechanization, both in the Prudential and in the insurance industry generally; it seems altogether plausible that his sense of mission was sufficient to carry the day with the Prudential board. (Incidentally, in 1955 Lyons Limited started its subsidiary Leo Computers Limited in a very similar way.)

The board of the British-owned Accounting and Tabulating Machine Company of Great Britain held its first meeting on 13 January 1919. It was a high-powered board indeed. The chairman was A.C. Thompson, general manager of the Prudential; the deputy chairman was Joseph (Sir Joseph in 1920) Burn; the general manager and secretary was F.P. Symmons (later actuary of the Prudential); and the remaining directors were also highly-placed Prudential officers (Appendix 2b).

There is little definite evidence of the reaction of BTM to this higher profile of Powers in Britain. In his May 1919 speech at the BTM annual general meeting Phillpotts went on record as saying:

> We have, I am glad to say, some competition. I say 'I am glad to say,' because in a business of this kind, which is introducing a system into this country, and which was at one time, as I said, a struggle, it is a very good thing to have other people who are also helping education.[36]

Under the circumstances there was probably little else Phillpotts could say in public, other than to make the best of the situation. In fact the Acc and Tab was in an extraordinarily advantageous position compared with BTM. First, it was not saddled with an onerous royalty agreement, as was BTM, and it was free to rent or sell machines as it saw fit. Second, and most important, it had massive resources for working capital. The British Powers operation began operations with £50 000 in paid-up ordinary shares, and £100 000 debentures.[37] By contrast, it had taken BTM more than ten years to place its authorized capital of £50 000. Whatever the Acc and Tab's problems were to be in the future, while it was owned by the Prudential, shortage of working capital would not be among them.

3

Manufacturing at home

the 1920s

When we remember that a quarter of a century ago many of the
Office Appliances now in daily use by thousands upon thousands
of businesses were not even invented, it is evident that this industry
has done well to have so firmly established itself in all the civilised
countries of the world; but seeing that we have barely touched the
fringe of the possible business awaiting us, there is everything to
encourage us to forge ahead, and that spirit permeates the whole of
our Trade as we know it.

—International Export Review, 1927.[1]

Both BTM and the Acc and Tab began the 1920s by starting up manufacturing operations in the UK: this was a crucial step in the process of
becoming manufacturers, instead of mere importers, of office machines.
The British punched-card machine manufacturers were representative of
many companies which sprang into prominence during the rise of the
office-appliance trades in the 1920s; this chapter examines BTM and the
Acc and Tab in their national and international context in the office-
machine industry.

Manufacturing and early machine developments

The reasons for beginning domestic manufacturing operations can be
divided into the psychological and the strategic. The most important
psychological reason was the economic boom of 1919-20: the immediate
post-war period was a time of great business optimism, and the mood of
the times was very favourable to expansion.[2] There were three principal
strategic reasons for manufacturing at home. First, to obviate the risk of
being wholly dependent on an American source of supply. Second, in the
long term it would be more profitable to manufacture than to buy,
especially since sterling had declined in value against the dollar since the
end of the First World War. Third, British manufactured goods generally
had a competitive advantage over imported ones: other things being
equal, a patriotic buyer would almost invariably prefer to buy British.

Acc and Tab had, since its acquisition by the Prudential in 1919,
operated from cramped premises in Southampton Buildings, near Chancery

Lane, London. With a rudimentary workshop in the basement, the premises were equipped for distribution and servicing rather than manufacture. In 1919 the board and managers of the Acc and Tab, whose backgrounds were largely in insurance, had neither interest nor experience in manufacturing office machines. The initial plan was to sub-contract manufacture, and the general manager of Acc and Tab, F.P. Symmons, approached a number of mechanical engineering firms, including Vickers, and Boulton and Paul, to make the punched-card machines for the company.[3] There was at this time no indigenous calculating machine industry in Britain, and therefore no experience on which to cost the work; this was true even of the most experienced manufacturers, who offered to do the manufacturing only on a 'cost plus' basis. Symmons saw this as unacceptable, since it would merely put the company at the mercy of a British supplier instead of an American one; the decision was therefore taken to build a factory.

In January 1920 the Acc and Tab put itself in the hands of a small-time engineering manufacturer, A.L. Pailthorpe, who was engaged to equip, construct, and manage a factory. This was not without risk, because Pailthorpe had no experience of this kind of engineering.[4] Moreover, there was almost no infrastructure for supplying calculating-machine components in Britain of the kind there was in America, so that the Acc and Tab factory would have to be an exceptionally integrated operation; much more integrated than, for example, the burgeoning motor-car or electrical industries. Land was bought on the Mitcham Park Estate in Croydon, South London, and a factory constructed at a modest cost of a little over £8000. The factory began operations in the second half of 1920. In December 1920 the Acc and Tab board received the news that Powers company in America had gone into liquidation the previous month; this created some uncertainty over the continuation of supplies, and gave the best possible incentive to keep up the momentum.

Almost as soon as he had become involved with punched-card machines, the general manager of the Acc and Tab, F.P. Symmons, had asked his engineers to design improvements to make the machines more useful for accounting (as opposed to statistical) work—'alphabetical printing, automatic totaling, subtraction and other features on the tabulator, for a good hand punch, and a reproducing punch.[5]' The factory would of course take several years to gear itself up to produce the entire range of existing and projected machines. The first manufacturing project was an alphabetical printing attachment to fit on to the American-made tabulator. Based on the design of Charles Foster, a prototype was shown at the Business Efficiency Exhibition of October 1920, and it went into full production in 1922.[6] The machine was the only alphabetical printing tabulator in the world at the time, and it opened up a range of new commercial accounting possibilities. The Foster invention was the only really significant British contribution to punched-card machine technology that was taken up on a world scale. Alongside the alphabetic printing development, a census machine was also developed for the 1921 English census, the contract for which had been awarded to the Acc and Tab in 1920.

Starting up the Acc and Tab factory had been a remarkable achievement for Pailthorpe, but he evidently over-stepped the mark in some serious but unrecorded way, and after an interview with the deputy chairman, Sir Gerald May, his contract was terminated in early 1922. In fact Pailthorpe's success probably owed a good deal to his works manager and to other workers who rapidly rose to fill the senior positions. Perhaps the most remarkable of these young men was L.E. Brougham, then in the inspection department, who rapidly rose through a succession of posts to become Chief Engineer, and eventually an executive director. On the machine-design side, three names stand out: A. Thomas, J.E. Last, and C. Foster. Arthur Thomas was appointed in 1920 and visited the American Powers plant in that year to seek out manufacturing and design know-how for the British factory; he was not a particularly prolific inventor, and his strength lay in harnessing the inventive talents of others. He was appointed Technical Superintendent in 1925, and was head of research under various titles until his retirement in 1952. The chief design engineer in the early 1920s was Jimmy Last: his most ambitious early project was a complete redesign of the original Powers sorter; but the 'Croydon sorter' proved a good deal more troublesome than the American machine, and eventually had to be abandoned. Last left the company shortly afterwards, but the lesson was not lost on Thomas: he became aware of the 'not-invented-here' syndrome, and over the next few years progress was made by evolutionary improvement of the proven American models, rather than by drastic redesign. Charles Foster, after making his extraordinary invention of the alphabetic attachment, never made any further important contribution to the development of punched-card machines; he remained with the company as head of the inspection department until his retirement in 1955, in which year he was awarded an MBE for his lifetime of service in the industry.

The Acc and Tab manufacturing operation gradually increased in tempo during 1922-24. After successfully manufacturing attachments for the imported machines, the simpler machines such as the automatic key punch were completely made in Croydon. The last and most complex machine, the tabulator, went into production in 1923 or 1924. From that point on, the Acc and Tab was entirely independent of the American company. The Acc and Tab works was something of a model factory; in 1926 a motion film of the factory was made, and in 1927 an extensive illustrated account appeared in the European edition of *American Machinist*.[7] At first the factory had sub-contracted special trades such as sheet-metal work for the casings and spring-making; but with a workforce of 300 it soon became an operation with an unusually high degree of integration:

The whole organization is as completely as possible self-contained. Apart from raw material in the form of bars, castings, and the like, everything necessary to complete the machine is manufactured on the premises. Thus the firm make their own bolts and screws, springs and ball races, produce their own cards, and even prepare their own illustrated catalogues. This somewhat unusual policy is the result of experience, and it is asserted that no suitable purchased product obtained on ordinary competitive lines can compare even in price with work done under the firm's own control and experience.[8]

Machine drawings of the tabulator, the most complex machine, still exist: it consisted of several thousand parts of several hundred types. The capital investment that the Prudential made in the Acc and Tab plant is not recorded, but it was probably not far short of £500 000—a very substantial investment in British terms.

In parallel with (though quite independently of) the Acc and Tab, the BTM board also decided to build a factory to take over from its assembly operation in Belvedere Road, Fulham, which it had begun to outgrow. The board had its own engineering expertise in the form of directors Baillie and Chadwyck-Healey, and the Fulham factory had experienced personnel, so that the company felt confident enough to construct and equip a factory without outside help. A site was selected in the progressive new town of Letchworth, thirty-four miles north of London, and building started in July 1920. The factory was built at a cost of £14 000, financed by bank loans and a mortgage. It was a handsome building, befitting its Garden City site, and—much extended from its original 20 000 square feet of floorspace—it served as one of ICL's principal factories until the early 1980s. The factory was opened in the summer of 1921, and 60 staff were taken on, including transferees from the Belvedere Road factory. On the administrative side Max G. Browne and A. Cranfield transferred from Norfolk Street to become the factory controllers, and H. Waters took over as works manager in 1922. On the design side, Charles Campbell continued as chief engineer, working closely with his assistant H.H. Keen. Apart from converting machines for sterling, very little technical development took place in BTM during the 1920s, and all the important developments, such as the printing tabulator, came from the United States. Thus Campbell's main technical contribution was in effecting the transfer of know-how on machine developments and machine tools from the United States and Europe, and the patenting of new developments. Keen and his technical staff were mainly involved in assembling non-standard machines for users with unconventional requirements.

Throughout the 1920s the Letchworth factory grew at a much more gentle pace than the Acc and Tab's Croydon factory. The reason for this was that the companies faced different business problems: Acc and Tab had no shortage of capital, but it was uncertain of its source of supply, and a factory was therefore essential to eliminate this risk; BTM had relatively little capital and little uncertainty of supply, but each step it took towards home manufacture represented a further reduction in the cost of acquiring machines. The Letchworth factory thus carried on operations much as at Belvedere Road: machines were first assembled from American parts, and then the simpler parts such as casings and mouldings were made locally. It was not until well into the 1930s that large-scale manufacturing was achieved, and the company developed some of its own machine designs. As late as 1930 the BTM factory had only 160 personnel, compared with about 300 in Acc and Tab's Croydon factory in 1927.[9]

Sales and competition

Although the manufacturing operations of BTM and Acc and Tab differed considerably in size, in terms of revenues they were very much on a par. The data in Table 3.1 give a picture of BTM's financial development during the 1920s. During this period BTM's assets increased from

Table 3.1 BTM financial statistics 1920–1929

	Assets (£000s)	Pre-tax profits (£000s)	Personnel
1920	105	14.2	
1921	122	18.6	
1922	139	14.8	132
1923	143	17.3	
1924	145	18.9	
1925	137[a]	20.9	
1926	144	24.4	
1927	152	[b]	
1928	163	[b]	250
1929	176	28.8	326

Notes
[a] Write down of obsolete tabulating machinery.
[b] No profit figures published.

Source
BTM Annual Reports, 1920–29.

£105 000 to £176 000, and its revenues grew from about £90 000 to £200 000.* Issued share capital was increased only from £44 000 to £80 000 over the decade, so that growth was achieved largely by retained profits; even so dividends on ordinary shares never fell below 10 per cent. Thus BTM was providing an excellent return to its shareholders, and its shares were trading at a healthy premium. Its annual growth rate, however, was well under 10 per cent. Although BTM was a little too small for a public quotation, there is no doubt that, had it chosen to, the company could have expanded much more rapidly than it did.[10] There is little extant data on Acc and Tab's financial development, but the little data that survives in the board minutes suggests that its machine population and revenues were similar to those of BTM—probably within 20 per cent either way.

Both companies grew slowly in the 1920s, much slower than their American parents. One of the main reasons for this was their failure to develop effective selling operations. Selling was actually a more difficult problem than manufacturing; in the 1920s Britain was an accomplished manufacturing nation, but marketing was generally conducted on amateurish lines, and there was very little indigenous experience to draw upon. Creating an aggressive, motivated sales force in the British culture was no simple matter, and the general managers of the BTM and Acc and Tab were not well qualified for the task. Even sales commissions, for example, were viewed as ungentlemanly—they were never used in BTM, and only adopted in Acc and Tab in 1930. Probably the single most important factor that accounts for the relative disparities in BTM's and IBM's growth rates between the two World Wars was the competence of their sales operations.

During the first half of the 1920s both British punched-card companies developed sales and service operations. In addition to its head office in London, BTM had had a Manchester service operation from the earliest days, when a good deal of its business was with Manchester manufacturers. In 1923 the sales and service operation was put on a more formal footing with the formation of a Sales Department in London, and a second regional office was established in Birmingham. The salesmen—'investigators' as BTM called them—were generally from an accounting or similar background, and trained in punched-card methods by a form of apprenticeship, or occasionally enticed from users; their background was thus rather gentlemanly, and was technical rather than sales-oriented. This was very different to Thomas Watson's ethos at TMC in the United States: there the salesman was king, and many of them became very rich indeed on their commissions and stock options.

* BTM Annual Reports did not include revenue figures; the figures cited are interpolated from data in the board minutes.

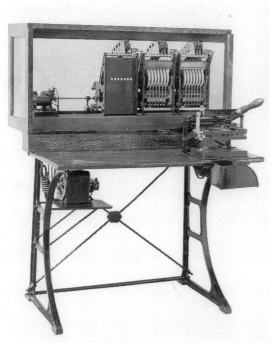

Early punched-card machines

In 1904 The Tabulator Limited (later BTM) obtained the British marketing rights for the punched-card machines developed in the United States by Herman Hollerith. The two principal machines were the pin-box tabulator (*left*) and the key punch (*overleaf*).

The photograph below shows the equipment in use at the Lancashire and North Yorkshire Railway in 1906. This is probably the earliest extant photograph of a British punched-card machine installation. The installation included about five pin-box tabulators (*at rear*) and many more key punches (two of which are shown on the table).

Hollerith pin-box tabulator, *c*.1904

LNYR punched-card machine installation, 1906

Hollerith key punch
Introduced in the United States in 1901, when it cost $75 (about £15), the key punch remained in use in essentially the same form for over half a century.

Hollerith Type 1 tabulator

Hollerith vertical sorter

Hollerith automatic machines
The automatic tabulator (*above, left*) was introduced in the United States in 1906, and in Britain in 1907. It operated at a speed of 150 cards per minute and rented for upwards of £10 a month. The vertical sorter was introduced at about the same time; it operated at 250–275 cards per minute and rented for £4 a month. The vertical design of the sorter was intended to minimize the floor space occupied by the machine, but it earned the machine the sobriquet 'the back-breaker' because operators had to stoop to remove cards from the lower receiving pockets.

Typical Hollerith installation, *c.*1920
A small punched-card machine installation showing a vertical sorter (*left of picture*), a tabulator (*rear of picture*), and two key-punches in use (*on the table*).

BTM census machine, 1911
The census machine was specially designed for the 1911 British census. The census contract was a turning point for BTM, and altogether some 8 census machines, 15 sorters, 60 key punches, and 45 million cards were supplied. (Note the operator on the left performing a 'needle' sort.)

Powers printing tabulator *c*.1913

Connection box

Powers Accounting Machines

In 1911 the Powers Accounting Machine Company of New York began to market punched-card machines in competition with those of Hollerith's Tabulating Machine Company. The Powers printing tabulator (*above, left*) was a major improvement over the Hollerith machine, which did not print its results. The printing feature made the Powers punched-card machines much more useful for insurance companies and banks. Another feature, the connection box, enabled the machine to be reconfigured in seconds for a new application. (A connection box, to approximately the same scale, is shown *above, right*.)

In 1915 a British subsidiary was established, The Accounting and Tabulating Corporation of Great Britain Limited—known as the 'Acc and Tab' for short. The Acc and Tab was always more aggressive in its advertising than BTM, and immediately on starting operations in Britain it began to circulate publicity material citing testimonials from satisfied American users (*facing page*). In 1919 the Prudential Assurance Company, which was the first and by far the largest user of Powers machines outside of America, took over the British company, which was later renamed Powers-Samas.

"From original data to final printed records by Automatic Machines."

Extracting sorted cards

BY APPLYING

POWERS MACHINES

TO WAGES, MATERIAL,

AND LABOUR COSTS,

A POWERS USER

SAVES OVER £1,000

PER ANNUM.

Mr. F. L. Nisbet, *Cost Accountant of the Zenith Carburetor Co., Detroit, says :*

" Powers Accounting Machines are almost superhuman in their ability to turn out accurate and highly diversified data of an invaluable nature at a tremendous saving in money over any other method with which we are familiar.

"We use the Powers equipment on labor and material cost distribution—and through its use we get by mechanical methods the exact cost for labor and material on any one of the 2,000 parts for the various models of carburetors which we make. When working to capacity approximately 1,000 labor job cards and 500 material cards come through the cost department daily. The labor cards are punched on a Powers machine according to the man's payroll number, number of the piece, hours, amount charged and account charged. The material cards are punched according to part number, quantity, amount, account charged, and account credited. Then it is only necessary to run the various cards through the sorting and printing machines—and automatically they are classified and tabulated according to the various items we may want.

"We also keep a check on our payroll by running these cards through the sorting and tabulating machines—even to the correct amount due each man.

"Formerly we required 12 people in our cost and payroll departments, while now with the Powers Accounting machines we get more accurate amd more complete information with only 5 people—which means that we are making a wage saving alone, after deducting the charge for the machines, of $500 every month."

Why not give us the opportunity of showing you how Powers Machines may be profitably applied to your own work ?

THE
ACCOUNTING & TABULATING CORPORATION OF GREAT BRITAIN, LTD.
57/58, CHANCERY LANE, LONDON, W.C.2.

An advertising flier for Powers machines, *c.*1915

BTM Works, *c*.1948

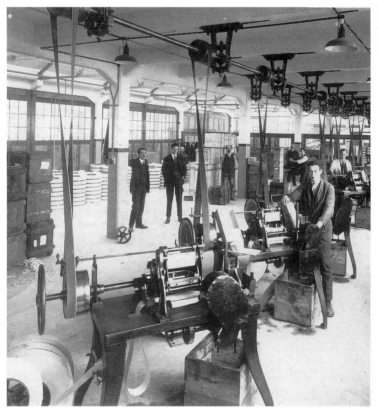

BTM card
production,
1922

BTM Works, Letchworth
The BTM Letchworth factory was opened in 1921, and was expanded frequently
during the boom period of the 1930s. In the photograph of the factory taken about
1948 (*top*), the original works of 1921 is shown in the white box. The interior view
(*above*) shows card-cutting machines in 1922, shortly after the factory was opened.
The photograph on the facing page shows the assembly of tabulators, from
American-made components, in 1927.

BTM tabulator
assembly, 1927

Hollerith Type 3 tabulator

Hollerith horizontal sorter

Hollerith alphabetical punch

Standard Hollerith punched-card machines

Up to the mid-1930s, all of BTM's punched-card machines were based entirely on IBM designs. These illustrations show the three principal machines used by virtually every installation—the tabulator, sorter, and punch. The Type 3 printing tabulator (*top*) was introduced in the United States in 1920, although it was not marketed by BTM in Britain until 1924. The 400 cards per minute horizontal sorter was launched in 1926 (*centre*). In 1928 IBM introduced the 80-column card in the United States, which was taken up by BTM in Britain the following year; the first 'alphabetical' machines—which used the new 80-column card—were introduced by IBM in the United States in 1931, and in the UK a couple of years later. The bottom photograph shows an alphabetical model of the Hollerith key punch.

Powers Four installation at United Co-operative Laundries, Manchester, 1935

Powers-Samas small-card sorter

Powers-Samas small-card machines

The introduction of the BTM 80-column card posed a major competitive threat to British Powers. In order to differentiate its equipment from the Hollerith line, in 1932 it introduced the Powers Four range of low-cost, small-card machines. The new range made punched-card accounting economic for a new class of users, such as the co-operative societies (*above*), that handled a large volume of low-value transactions. Powers Four was a major product success and the small-card machines continued to be sold as late as the early 1970s.

In 1936 an even smaller and cheaper range of small-card machines was introduced—Powers One. The photograph at left shows a small-card sorter, which was small enough to fit onto a cabinet top.

BTM Rolling Total Tabulator, 1935
The Rolling Total Tabulator was BTM's biggest pre-war development project. The British-designed tabulator substituted for imports from IBM in the United States, and produced a significant reduction in royalty payments.

Powers-Samas sterling multiplying punch, 1938

Ancillary machines
In the 1930s several new punched-card machines were designed to augment the basic trio of punch, sorter, and tabulator. These machines included the interpolator (or collator), the interpreter, the cross-adding punch, and the multiplying punch. The sterling multiplying punch (*left*) was one of the last and most complex Powers developments to be completed prior to the outbreak of the Second World War.

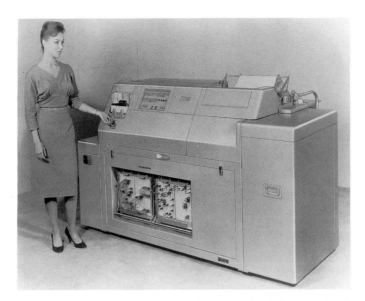

BTM 902 tabulator, *c*.1956

BTM 900 series tabulators
BTM's post-war replacement for the Rolling Total Tabulator was the 900 series of tabulators. Following the break with IBM in 1949, this development became an urgent priority within BTM. The first 900-series machines were put on the market in 1955.

Powers-Samas' American venture, 1950–57
Following the break with Remington Rand in 1950, Powers-Samas decided to sell its small-card machines in America under the trade name 'Samas'. The photograph shows a batch of sorters awaiting export. The American market unfortunately never took to the small-card machines, and the venture was a commercial disappointment.

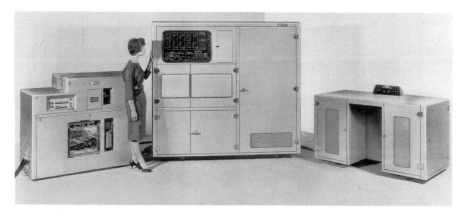

BTM 555 calculator, *c*.1957

BTM electronic calculators

In the 1950s electronics began to be incorporated into punched-card machines. BTM's first electronic calculator, the model 541 multiplier was announced in 1952, and this was quickly followed by the models 542, 550, and 555. The model 555 (*above*) was capable of processing 100 cards per minute, could be plug-programmed with up to 150 instructions, and had a small drum-store for 105 numbers.

Castlereagh factory, *c*.1949

BTM Castlereagh factory

In 1949, in readiness for its post-war expansion programme, BTM acquired a 'distressed area' factory in Castlereagh, Northern Ireland (*above*). The interior view (*facing page*) shows the BTM 555 calculator assembly line in the factory in 1961. The Castlereagh plant was a source of some of ICL's worst industrial relations problems, and it was closed down in 1971.

BTM 555 calculator production, Castlereagh, 1961

Samastronic
prototype,
c.1956

Samastronic
production
model, 1958

The Samastronic tabulator
The Samastronic tabulator was Powers-Samas' most ambitious post-war development project (although in spite of its name, the tabulator contained no electronics
whatever). The two pictures show (*top*) an awesomely complex prototype under
development, and (*bottom*) a production model in 1950s-style 'round-corner'
covers, specified by external design consultants. Because of reliability problems,
the Samastronic was a major product failure and only a few machines were ever
delivered. The Samastronic débâcle was one of the main contributing factors to
the financial crisis that led to Powers-Samas' merger with BTM to form ICT in
1959.

Milk Marketing Board tabulator installation, 1962

Latter-days of the tabulator

After about 1960, the tabulator was increasingly under threat from the computer. The photograph (*above*) is one of a series taken in 1962 showing a bank of 900-series tabulators at the Milk Marketing Board, one of ICT's biggest customers. A contemporary note from ICT's publicity manager accompanying the photographs states 'we should be careful in the use of these as they show such a bank of Tabulators that this could well be a natural for an attack by Computers'. The collapse of the tabulating-machine market began in 1961–62, although many established punched-card machine installations remained in existence until the late 1960s and early 1970s.

ICT 40 range, *c*.1968

The ICT 40 punched-card machines
The ICT 40 range of small-card machines continued to be marketed as late as 1971. Encased in computer-look covers, the ICT 40 range was a re-styled version of the Powers Forty small-card machines launched in 1950, which were themselves based on the Powers Four introduced in 1932.

ICT 1004, *c*.1963

The ICT 1004 calculating tabulator
The ICT 1004 calculating tabulator was ICT's last major punched-card machine introduction. The machine was imported directly from Sperry Rand in the United States, where it was marketed as the Univac 1004. The calculating tabulator was a transitionary machine between the old-style tabulator and the new stored-program computer. Between 1963 and 1966, some 500 machines were sold by ICT, which sustained its revenues until the 1900-series computers could be delivered in quantity.

Not a great deal is known of the Acc and Tab's early selling operation, but all that is known suggests it was even less professional than BTM's. At first the company concentrated on the insurance market: this it did through a network based around the Prudential in London, and the Wesley and General Assurance Company in Birmingham. As the insurance market became exhausted, efforts were made to move into commerce and local authorities. In 1923 sales offices were opened in Glasgow, Cardiff, and Manchester. The Acc and Tab's sales operation was never a real success, and in 1925 it decided to hand over the whole operation to Morland and Impey, who ran a Powers agency alongside their Kalamazoo loose-leaf binder business.

It is interesting that BTM and Acc and Tab, until their merger in 1959, grew at a very similar pace, and at no time did one company become markedly larger than the other. Without any doubt the reason for this situation was the dynamics created by the competition between the companies. Probably the first wind of competition arose with the loss by BTM of the contract for the 1921 English census to Acc and Tab. To judge by Everard Greene's off-hand correspondence with the Stationery Office, he had completely misjudged the mood of the Controller, who was still smarting over his failure to get BTM to negotiate on price for the 1911 census.[11] Phillpotts reported to shareholders at the 1920 AGM:

... no doubt many of you have seen that we are not doing the English Census which is now to proceed, although we did the one that was taken 10 years ago. As a matter of fact we deliberately did not make any very serious effort to get the contract for the Census this year. We came to that decision after careful considera- tion, because we thought that the utilization of material and the concentration of the staff on that one large work might have impeded the growing commercial business we were getting, and we thought that on the whole it was better to stick to what might be business of a continuing nature than to take on what would undoubtedly be a good contract but only a temporary one. ... The Powers Company very rightly made a good deal of the fact that they have got the Census contract, but I repeat what I have said before—that I rather welcome some competition in our business.[12]

It is not on record whether anyone, even Phillpotts himself, was convinced by this statement. The fact is that the loss of the census contract was a blow to the credibility and the finances of the company. It meant that the census machines, carefully husbanded since the completion of the 1911 census, would continue to gather dust; and some accounting ingenuity was required to maintain the revenues for 1921-22.[13] The decision to use the Powers census machines (which were not actually developed when the contract was awarded) was plainly taken on political rather than technical or financial grounds. In this connection, it is interesting that the Registrar General for Scotland insisted on having

Hollerith machines: he was well aware of the reputation for unreliability of the early Powers machines, and, in the absence of a local maintenance operation, put his trust in the far more reliable Hollerith machines.[14] As well as Scotland, BTM was also called upon to supply the census machines for the contemporary South African and Australian censuses, perhaps from similar considerations of reliability.

In the general market-place the companies competed in terms of price, the specification of machines, and their sales and maintenance operations. Price-competition existed in the cost of cards and rentals of machines. Competition kept prices remarkably similar, and they rarely varied by as much as 20 per cent for equivalent items. Whenever one company reduced its prices, the other had perforce to follow quickly. The 1920s were of course a deflationary period, and prices could be expected to drop of their own accord; the minute books of both companies, however, show that many of the price reductions were taken in response to the competitor. In terms of product specification, the advantage lay with the Acc and Tab, its printing tabulators giving it access to the 'accounting machine' market for which BTM could not compete until the arrival of its Type 3 printing and listing tabulator in 1924. There is no evidence that this unduly worried BTM, which still enjoyed a buoyant market for its statistical machines. So far as sales and service were concerned, neither company had the advantage, nor even thought very much in terms of using its sales force to secure competitive advantage.

Relations with the American companies

Both of the British punched-card firms operated under agreements with the American companies, and this had a considerable effect on their long-term operation. Until the companies severed the agreements with their American parents in 1949 and 1950, there were regular disputes about royalties, patent rights, supplies of cards and machines, and sales territories. Whatever the legal position—and international legal disputes were not something that could be resolved in the short term—the American companies were usually in a position to take sanctions against the British companies when they wished to have their own way; sanctions usually took the form of a refusal to supply card stock or machines.

In the case of the Acc and Tab, relations first turned sour following the financial problems of the American Powers company in autumn 1920. The American company was reconstructed in summer 1922, when it was acquired by the Wales Adding Machine Company of Pennsylvania,[15] and the new management sought to renegotiate the territories specified in the Impey Agreement of 1918. It was the vulnerability to a hostile American supplier that had lain behind the Prudential's acquisition of the British rights and the building of a factory; their judgement of the dangers of this situation had proved completely accurate. Fortunately, by this time the Acc and Tab was manufacturing all its own machines at home. To force the Acc and Tab to negotiate, the American company instructed its printing ribbon supplier and its supplier of card stock to cease supplying the British company.[16] The ribbons were easily replaced, but obtaining card stock entailed L.E. Brougham in a grand European tour, bringing back paper samples from Germany and Czechoslovakia.[17] By making some modifications to the card-reading mechanisms use was made of inferior card stock until relations with the American company improved.

The Acc and Tab's relations with its American parent were fraught but not life-threatening. BTM's relations with its American parent, however, were altogether more serious. BTM still operated under the terms of the 1908 agreement: this specified that the company had to pay TMC a 25 per cent royalty on gross revenues, and had to charge the same rentals as in America, assuming an exchange rate of $5 to the pound sterling. Since the war, however, there had been major economic changes: income tax now stood at a rate of 30 per cent, and an excess profits tax had been imposed, which hit BTM quite heavily; the dollar exchange-rate had gradually drifted downwards to $4.80 in 1919, sunk to a low point of $3.60 in 1920, and in 1921 stood at $4.40. In fact, whatever the terms of the 1908 agreement, BTM had had constantly to adjust its prices, first upwards in line with the rising dollar and general inflation, and then downwards in response to the Acc and Tab competition and general deflation.

In early 1922 matters came to a head, when Otto Braitmeyer, general manager of TMC, wrote to BTM claiming that the goods supplied by the American company did not tally with the royalties remitted from England, and demanded detailed royalty statements.[18] These were prepared and sent to the American company in May 1922. Braitmeyer replied that he was unable to check the figures, and made it quite plain that he did not believe them either. The royalty statements are no longer extant, but the course of events suggests that the figures had indeed been slightly cooked; in fact, BTM could scarcely have remained in business if it had stuck to the letter of the 1908 agreement. The 1908 agreement, however, expressly stipulated that the agreement with TMC could be terminated by the American company if BTM failed to honour any particular of it. The British company immediately sought legal advice on whether, if the worst came to the worst and the agreement was terminated, it could continue working the Hollerith patents, and whether TMC would be able to set up in competition in BTM's territories. The legal view was that while BTM could continue to work the patents it had taken out in its own name, the company could do nothing to stop TMC opening up in direct competition. This was not the advice the company had hoped for; a second opinion was sought, and then a third; but the opinion was the same.

BTM was in trouble. During August 1922 Phillpotts, Everard Greene, and Hunter met for a council of war at the Rougement Hotel, Exeter, near Phillpotts' country retreat. It was decided to go over the head of Braitmeyer, and seek an interview with Thomas Watson himself during his forthcoming European tour. The interview was conducted by Hunter, but Watson was unwilling to intervene, preferring to leave the matter in the hands of his TMC executives. In November 1922, Everard Greene sailed to New York to try to negotiate a settlement. The BTM board had empowered him to offer TMC £20 000 of BTM ordinary shares and the Australian rights, in exchange for a royalty reduction from 25 per cent to 15 per cent. The board had evidently misjudged the situation: Braitmeyer was not in the mood to renegotiate royalty rates until BTM had explained the inconsistencies in its royalty accounts. Everard Greene was taken aback by the hostility, and four days before Christmas 1922 cabled back to England that he could do no more. Relations between the companies had reached a low point.

Phillpotts decided that the best tactic under the circumstances was to make a clean breast of the affair, and he cabled directly to Thomas Watson in New York admitting that the royalty accounts had been unintentionally misleading. Early in the new year, 1923, Everard Greene was given an interview with Watson. In the course of the interview Watson made it clear that he wished to secure control of the British company, and was not too concerned at how he achieved this:

. . . Mr. Watson made the statement to me that I was in the position to acquire shares in the Company from those shareholders desirous of selling them, and if I would acquire them for the American Company, there would be a suitable reward for me. So far as I, personally, was concerned, I certainly think this is a very serious matter, for it shows they will not hesitate to take any means at their disposal to attain their object.[19]

Everard Greene was outraged at this affront to his English sense of fair play, but he returned to England having finally made real progress. The American company conceded that there was a case for drawing up a supplementary agreement to bring the 1908 agreement into line with the economic conditions of 1923. On his part Everard Greene agreed to allow the American company to send in its accountants to audit the royalty account.

The supplementary agreement was drawn up during the next few months. In May 1923 the TMC accountants reported on the BTM royalty account, which they found to be deficient to the order of $40 000.

As a condition of making the supplementary agreement, the American company required this money to be repaid, although the lesser sum of £4000 was accepted in view of the 'extenuating circumstances' occasioned by the fall in the value of the pound. The supplementary agreement, which is reproduced in Appendix 1, included the following key points:

- BTM could charge such rentals as it pleased, provided that a royalty of 25 per cent of gross revenues was paid to the American company.
- BTM would not pay royalties on its own attachments.
- BTM could increase card prices as it saw fit, but would pay a royalty of one sixth of such increases.

The question of paying royalties net of tax was left unresolved, to surface another day. The supplementary agreement was signed on 25 September 1923.

For Phillpotts, who was 'a very very old English type of man',[20] the fact that BTM was caught out in what amounted to false accounting was very hard to take. A few days after the signing of the supplementary agreement, he offered the board his resignation. The offer was unanimously rejected.

The office-appliance industry in Britain

By the mid-1920s both BTM and the Acc and Tab had developed into medium-sized companies with annual turnovers in the region of £100 000. They were, however, part of a much larger movement which had grown up around them—the office-appliance industry. The British office-appliance industry consisted of several dozen firms that had sprung up to satisfy (and to stimulate) the need for office mechanization in the 1920s. It is against this larger background that the British punched-card firms need to be seen, in order to get an objective view of their performance during the 1920s. Of course, the British office-appliance industry operated in a still larger international market-place, dominated by American giants such as Burroughs, Remington, Comptometer, and C-T-R. (In 1924 C-T-R was renamed International Business Machines (IBM), a name chosen by Watson as befitting his expansionary plans.) The international office-appliance scene is described later in this chapter.

The office-appliance industry—like the machine-tool industry and later the computer industry—was a barometer of the economy: in a boom period sales would expand ahead of those of general manufacturing, and in a slump capital spending on office-machines would be the first to suffer. Thus BTM and Acc and Tab were subject to similar economic forces to the rest of the office-machine industry during the difficult 1920s, but with two important differences. First, because machines were rented rather than sold outright, there was a smoothing effect on the most violent economic oscillations: in a downturn, while new customers were hard to find, existing customers rarely disposed of their installations. Although BTM had found it harder to develop a business leasing machines instead of selling them, there can be no doubt that the fact that it had done so helped it to survive and prosper during the 1920s. A second advantage the punched-card machine manufacturers had over the other office-machine manufacturers was that they belonged to a special class of business:

. . . a type that might be called 'refill' businesses. The use of its machines is followed more or less automatically and continually by the sale of cards. This type of business also has good precedents: in the Eastman Kodak Co., which sells films to camera owners; in General Motors, whose AC spark plugs are sold to motor-car owners; in Radio Corp., whose tubes are bought by radio owners; in Gillette Razor Co., whose blades are bought by razor users.

In the case of razor blades and spark plugs (somewhat less in the cases of photographic film and radio tubes), manufacturers must compete with one another for the refill market. I.B.M., however, has so far found itself secure in the market of tabulator cards for its machines, because the cards must be made with great accuracy on a special paper stock which, so far, at least, has not been successfully imitated.[21]

In the case of IBM, card sales accounted for 30–40 per cent of total revenues.[22] There are no surviving records in the ICL Archives, but the ratio of card sales to rentals in England was probably about the same.* Sales of cards tended to be little affected by difficult economic conditions, and indeed it was even argued that the pressure for increased efficiency boosted card sales.[24]

The British office-appliance industry was represented by the Office Appliance Trades Association (OATA). The development of the OATA mirrors to some extent the development of the industry itself.[25] It was founded in 1911 by J. Halsby, the British representative of the American Protectograph cheque-writing machine, with about 30 members. The organization petered out during the First World War and was revived again in 1920, this time with 60 members; by 1925 there were 90 members. For a period of twenty years, until the Second World War, the OATA staged the major national trade fairs—the Business Efficiency Exhibitions. Two exhibitions were held each year—one in London and one in the provinces (Manchester, Birmingham, Glasgow, or Cardiff). The 'BEEs' were tremendously popular events, very much the fore-runners of present-day computer fairs, at which the vendors would

---

* According to the *American Machinist*, the Acc and Tab sold 2½ to 3 million cards per week in 1927.[23] This would have given an annual sales value of about £25 000, which was roughly 30 per cent of revenues.

announce their latest machine developments. Even the provincial BEEs would attract in the region of 20 000 visitors. The OATA was also represented by a monthly trade journal, the *International Export Review*—although it must be said that the use of the word 'export' in the title represented an aspiration rather than an actuality, for the UK had a very large balance-of-trade deficit in office machinery.

Although BTM and Acc and Tab joined the OATA in 1920 and exhibited at the early BEEs, it was not until the mid-1920s that punched-card machines had become a part of the office-machine environment and no longer a novelty. In 1924 Sidney C. Downes, assistant general manager of the Acc and Tab, became a member of the executive committee of the OATA, and then became its chairman in 1928. The Acc and Tab in fact played a very prominent role in the OATA, while BTM appears to have taken no active part at all until after the Second World War.

It is worth stepping back at this point to try to assess the position of the British punched-card machine manufacturers in their national context. If we examine the membership of the OATA in 1925 (say) we see that it had about 90 members, which represented perhaps 90 per cent of the industry. In terms of size, BTM and Acc and Tab were in the second rank of British companies: a good deal smaller than the handful of large organizations such as Imperial Typewriter, but on a par with companies like Kalamazoo or British Oliver Typewriter. Even the largest British companies, however, were dwarfed by the big American concerns.

Table 3.2 lists some representative companies contemporary with BTM and Acc and Tab. The companies have been listed in order of the technical sophistication of their products, from filing systems at the simplest end of the technological spectrum to punched-card machines at the most complex end. Filling the middle ground are time-recorders, typewriters, and calculating machines. (These categories are representative rather than exhaustive: also in the middle ground would be addressing machines, dictation machines, duplicators, and many others.) Perhaps the most striking feature of Table 3.2 is that in the more technologically difficult areas, typewriters and calculating machines, the biggest and most successful companies tended to be American-owned importers of American-made machines. Only in the technologically simple areas, such as loose-leaf filing systems, was there a strong British manufacturing base; but even here it is significant that Morland and Impey's main product line was the Kalamazoo loose-leaf filing system, made under licence from the American Kalamazoo Company; again the Rand Kardex system, widely used in banks, was the product of an American company.

Britain was well represented in the manufacture of time-recorders, although the leader worldwide was the International Time Recording Company (ITR), a division of IBM. ITR, incidentally, had its head office in

Table 3.2 Representative office-appliance firms in Britain, *c.*1925

Product category	Representative companies	Ownership and nature of operation
Filing systems	British Loose Leaf Manufacturers	UK-owned manufacturer
	Morland and Impey	UK-owned licensee and manufacturer
	Rand Kardex	US-owned importer
Time recorders	Blick Time Recorders	UK-owned manufacturer
	Gledhill-Brook Time Recorders	UK-owned manufacturer
	International Time Recording Co.	US-owned importer
Typewriters	Remington Typewriter Co.	US-owned importer
	Corona Typewriter Co.	US-owned importer
	Imperial Typewriter Co.	UK-owned manufacturer
	Bar-Lock	UK-owned manufacturer
Calculating machines	Burroughs Adding Machine	US-owned manufacturer and importer
	Brunsviga Calculator Co.	UK-owned importer
	Monroe Calculating Machine Co.	US-owned importer
Punched-card machines	British Tabulating Machine Co.	UK-owned importer and licensee
	Accounting and Tabulating Co.	UK-owned manufacturer and licensee

the Strand, with 'International Business Machines' boldly displayed over the shop front.[26] This would have been an ideal outlet for IBM's punched-card equipment had BTM not been the licensee for Britain. ITR had similar outposts in the British Empire, where again IBM was unable to pursue the punched-card business. Under these circumstances, the desire of IBM to terminate BTM's licence was very understandable.

Typewriters dominated the office-machine business, accounting for over half of the sales, and the typewriter manufacturers and importers were represented by their own organization, The Typewriter Trades Federation. In Britain there was one very large company, the Imperial Typewriter Company, and some medium-sized ones such as Bar-Lock and British Oliver; all of these manufactured in Britain, and had evolved their own designs. The bulk of the market, however, was supplied by subsidiaries of the big American manufacturers: Remington, Royal, Smith-Corona, and Underwood. So far as can be determined, none of the American subsidiaries had manufacturing operations in the UK, although there was some assembly work. The smaller American manufacturers, and continental manufacturers such as Mercedes in Germany, were generally represented by UK agents; these were importers pure and simple, and included firms such as the Parker-Drake Company in London and the Watson Typewriter Company in Glasgow.

Moving on to calculating and bookkeeping machines, the great majority of the big names were American companies: Burroughs, Comptometer, Elliot-Fisher, Muldivo, Monroe, NCR, and others. All these companies had model and well-publicized manufacturing plants in the United States, but so far as can be determined only Burroughs had a small factory in the UK (in Nottingham). The calculating machine manufacturers thus operated largely as American-owned importers, much like the typewriter manufacturers. After America, the most successful nation at manufacturing calculating machines was Germany: the best-known machine was the very successful Brunsviga, and there were several other makes, such as Mercedes, Madas, Euclid, and Thales. Britain, in the whole range of office machinery, was least well developed in manufacturing calculating machines: so far as is known, there was exactly one indigenous manufacturer, and a very small one at that—Guy's Calculating Machine Company.

Set against the very under-developed condition of the British calculating machine industry, the achievements of the British punched-card machine manufacturers, and the Acc and Tab in particular, were quite remarkable. The difficulties of achieving technology transfer into a vacuum are well known; but perhaps even more remarkable was the fact that the British Powers machines were acknowledged to be very much better engineered than those made by the American company.[27] The credit for this excellence lay partly in the matter-of-fact way in which the Prudential management had let Acc and Tab have its head—the manufacturing operation was very expensive, and not without risk—and the high standard of the engineering, manufacturing, and inspection achieved by people like L.E. Brougham, A. Thomas, and C. Foster. (Foster, incidentally, was probably the only senior Acc and Tab person who had had previous experience in the calculating machine industry.)[28]

Against the Acc and Tab's record of achievement, that of BTM inevitably lacks lustre, since it was still essentially manufacturing from American-made parts, which made its operation more akin to that of typewriter assembly. It has to be borne in mind, however, that BTM's capital resources—generated from retained profits, and therefore slow-growing—were far more limited. Moreover the American machines were probably better engineered than any BTM could have made: the IBM machines were already achieving their legendary reputation for reliability, and were considered far better than the American Powers machines (and, to judge by the anecdotal evidence, better than the British Powers machines, too). BTM in the mid-1920s was in fact in a period of transition to large-scale UK manufacture; but it would not achieve a 70 per cent level of home manufacture until well into the 1930s.

Machine developments

The surviving documentation from which to draw a comprehensive picture of the punched-card machines of the 1920s is somewhat fragmentary. In the 1920s BTM sold machines identical to IBM's, and did very little of its own development. Consequently, to a first approximation, BTM sold the same as IBM, though lagging behind by a year or two.

Table 3.3 gives what is believed to be a complete list of the range of the standard machines sold by BTM in 1926 (and therefore excludes census machines and other non-standard machines made to special order). The key new machines of the 1920s were the duplicating key punch, the horizontal sorter, and the Type 3 printing-and-listing tabulator. The original machines dating from the first decade of the century—the hand punch, the vertical sorter, and the Type 1 tabulator—continued to be offered in 1926 and for some years to come, although there had been a good deal of evolutionary improvement under the covers during the passing years. The electric key punch had been introduced in the United States in 1916, and was sold in Britain from about 1920; this was followed by the verifier and the duplicating punch, although the dates of their introduction in the UK are uncertain. In 1926, the new quieter and faster

Table 3.3 BTM 45-column punched-card machines, *c*.1926

Machine	Date	Speed
Card punches		
Hand punch	1904	
Electric punch	*c*.1920	
Hand verifier	*c*.1920	
Duplicating punch	*c*.1920	
Sorters		
Vertical sorter	1907	250-275 cpm
Horizontal sorter	1926	350-400 cpm
Tabulators		
Type 1	1907	150 cpm
Type 2 (automatic control)	1924	150 cpm
Type 3 (automatic control and printing)	1924	75/150 cpm[a]

Note
[a] Speeds for listing/totalling.

Source
Production Costs by the Hollerith Electrical Tabulating Method, BTM, London, *c*.1926
(ICL Historical Collection).

horizontal sorter was produced—this was the long awaited replacement for the much maligned 'backbreaker' vertical sorter.

Of all these machines, the most important development was the Type 3 printing tabulator. When Thomas Watson had created his experimental department at Endicott, New York, in 1914, one of his first objectives had been to produce a printing tabulator in response to the Powers printing machine. By 1916, Watson had set up a competitive research environment in which there were no less than four models of a printing tabulator under development.[29] The approved design was that of Clair D. Lake, one of IBM's most prolific inventors. According to legend, when the machine was announced at the 1919 annual sales conference 'the salesmen stood on their chairs and cheered'.[30]

It remains something of a puzzle as to why it should have taken TMC so long to develop and then to market the printing tabulator. There was no special technical difficulty, as Powers had already proved, and in any case machines such as the Burroughs adder-lister had been in existence since the turn of the century. It seems likely, however, that the printing tabulator was held back from the market for a year or two, since it would tend to make the existing non-printing model obsolete. TMC maximized its profits by having its machines in the field for at least five years. Throughout the history of the punched-card and computer industries, the need to preserve the existing rental base has always been a major factor in introducing new products.

The printing tabulator was rented in America from 1920. The first BTM heard of the development was in 1921; and then it had to write to ask the American company for details. Machines were not sent to England until 1924, perhaps because the American company preferred to unload its stocks of the old-style tabulators on the British company, but also no doubt as part of the hostile action during the dispute over royalties. Two new tabulators were introduced at this date, the Type 2 non-printing model, and the Type 3 printing and listing version. The two new machines were such an advance over the existing Type 1 tabulators that the rentals of the old machines had to be reduced, and their asset value written down, in 1925.

The new tabulators introduced one of the most crucial improvements in their development—automatic control. Automatic control enabled sub-totals to be produced automatically whenever the value in a chosen card field changed—typically a salesman's number or a customer account number. Prior to automatic control, it had been necessary to insert special 'stop' or 'total' cards at each point in the card-deck where a sub-total was required; automatic control eliminated this process. A rather interesting situation occurred in connection with automatic control in Britain. A patent for the elimination of total cards had in fact been taken out by James Powers in 1915, but was never exploited. It was unclear whether the Hollerith patent infringed that of Powers.[31] The matter had never been resolved in America, for the reason that it was a matter of no more than academic interest: TMC already had the right to use the Powers patents, as a condition of Powers having the right to use the early Hollerith patents. No such arrangement existed in Britain, and as soon as the Acc and Tab caught wind of the situation the advice of patent experts was sought to determine whether an action for infringement would be likely to be successful. In parallel BTM took advice to determine what defensive or offensive action might be called for. Eventually a truce was called and, although there is no record of the discussions between the companies (which probably took place between Charles Campbell of BTM and L.E. Brougham of Acc and Tab at a technical level, and between the managing directors Everard Greene and Symmons) the outcome was an 'unwritten agreement . . . that we would not attack any of their patents and they would not attack any of ours'.[32] This in no way affected commercial competition of course.

Table 3.4 Acc and Tab 45-column punched-card machines, *c*.1928

Machine	Date	Speed
Card punches		
Automatic Key Punch (AKP)	1916	
Printing punch (model A)[b]	*c*.1925	
Hand punch (model D)[b]	1928	
Sorters		
Horizontal sorter	*c*.1915	400 cpm
Tabulators		
Non-printing	1915	150 cpm
Numerical printing	1915	75/150 cpm[a]
Alphabetical printing[b]	1923	75/150 cpm[a]

Notes
[a] Speeds for listing/totalling.
[b] British developments.

Source
A. Thomas, 'Powers Samas Accounting Machines: Thirty Years of Progress', 1952 (ICL Historical Collection).

As with BTM, there is no systematic record available of Acc and Tab machine developments during the 1920s. Table 3.4, compiled from a number of sources, lists what is believed to be the range of standard machines supplied in the late 1920s. The original machines supplied from 1915 continued to be the mainstays of the company: these were the automatic key punch, the sorter, and the printing tabulator. Of the original machines, the slide punch fell out of use very quickly, and was never manufactured in Britain. The original American tabulator remained in production, although with a number of incremental improvements over the years, partly to improve its reliability.[33] In addition some functional improvements were made. The most important of these was alphabetic printing, which was put on the market in 1923. In 1927 the Automatic Total Attachment was introduced, which was the Powers equivalent of automatic control. In 1929 the 'long paper feed' attachment was introduced; this apparently simple improvement enabled standard-sized continuous forms to be used with the tabulator, instead of inserting pre-printed stationery a sheet at a time. In fact, the mechanics of paper-handling were every bit as formidable as the arithmetic parts of the machine, a fact often overlooked in the history of information technology.

An altogether new machine, the reproducing punch, was introduced in 1927, long before such a device was offered by IBM. In 1928 the inexpensive Model D hand punch was introduced, with a similar specification to the Hollerith hand punch. A printing punch was also introduced, but did not stay in the range for long.

In spite of this considerable volume of development—there were as many machines as IBM produced, and with greater functionality—these developments were generally technology-led rather than market-led, and there was little concept of a product strategy. The Acc and Tab range was, for example, completely deficient in any kind of verifying machine, which was really a very fundamental requirement. This failure to match development to market requirements is perhaps best illustrated by the case of the Cryptograph Machine. In 1926 the company acquired the patent rights from an inventor, Sidney Hole, for a machine very like the Enigma ciphering machine used on the continent.[34] Two prototype machines were constructed, and displayed with some fanfare at the 1928 Business Efficiency Exhibition; but there proved to be an absence of any demand whatever for the machine, and it was quietly dropped. The crucial point, however, was that within weeks of starting out on the project the sales arm of the company had reported to the board that there was an 'urgent need' for a verifier.[35] This lesson, and others like it, were not lost on the board. In spring 1927 a Sales Committee was formed, which soon took up the whole subject of 'commercial research'—later known as 'product planning'.

Exports and the international office-machine trade

The United States was pre-eminently the world's leading manufacturer and exporter of office machinery. Table 3.5 lists the revenues and profits

Table 3.5   Financial statistics of US office-machine companies, 1928

	Revenues ($millions)	Earnings ($millions)
Burroughs	32.1	8.3
IBM	19.7	5.3
NCR	49.0	7.8
Remington Rand	59.6	6.0
Underwood Elliott Fisher	19.0	4.9

Source
Moody's Industrial Manual, 1930; as quoted in R. Sobel, *IBM: Colossus in Transition*, Times Books, New York, 1981, p. 75.

of the major American office-machine companies in 1928; with revenues of tens of millions of dollars, and profits of millions of dollars, there was no British office-appliance manufacturer that was in the same league. Although the UK was a heavy user of office machinery, it achieved this only at the cost of a considerable balance-of-trade deficit. The United States accounted for about 80 per cent of UK imports (most of the rest coming from Germany). Table 3.6 shows the total US office-machine exports, and the exports to its three largest markets, Britain, Germany, and France. Although UK imports ran at a similar level to those of Germany, there was an important difference, in that Germany had an export trade several times the size of its imports. Thus Britain should more properly be classed with France, which ran an equally serious balance-of-trade deficit.

Table 3.6 US office-machine exports to UK, Germany, and France, 1922–27

	Total ($millions)	UK ($millions)	Germany ($millions)	France ($millions)
1922	17.4	3.9	0.2	2.0
1923	21.7	4.2	0.6	2.8
1924	26.4	4.7	2.5	2.7
1925	33.8	5.3	4.8	3.4
1926	36.3	5.8	3.3	3.8
1927	44.1	7.0	5.2	3.6

Source
Commerce Reports; as quoted in *International Export Review*, May 1928, p. 10.

During the 1920s world consumption of American office machinery grew very rapidly. During the five-year period 1922 to 1927, American typewriter exports approximately doubled from $11.6 million to $20.8 million, and calculating-machine exports increased no less than five-fold, from $2.0 million to $11.5 million. The available data indicates that exports from Germany were about 20 per cent of the value of American exports, which made it the only European country which was a significant force in the world office-machine trade. It is perhaps symptomatic that the only office-machine export figures published by the British Board of Trade were for typewriters and typewriter parts (measured in tons!); presumably exports of calculating machines were too insignificant to warrant tabulation. The value of British typewriter exports was perhaps one-tenth that of Germany, and a fiftieth that of the United States.

There is very little surviving data on the scale of the early overseas operations of the British punched-card machine companies, and certainly no hard financial data. By the early 1920s BTM had a toe-hold, though no more, in the traditional markets of the British Empire: it had had installations in South Africa since before the war, it had a couple of installations with Indian railway concerns, the Egyptian and Australian census contracts, and a single installation with the Central Argentinian Railway Company. During 1923–25 Everard Greene made overseas tours to consolidate existing contracts and to attract new business. By 1926 BTM had replaced its agency agreements with its own branches in the principal cities of its best markets: South Africa (Johannesburg), India (Bombay and Calcutta), Australia (Melbourne), and Egypt (Cairo). From about this point BTM developed its export trade very actively, no doubt spurred on by the very bad home trading conditions during 1926–27. Several senior staff made world tours, and technical people followed the machines to study their operation in hostile climates. In his 1928 Annual Report Phillpotts claimed that the overseas business accounted for approximately a quarter of total revenues.[36] In 1928 Phillpotts himself undertook an overseas tour to stimulate business, and by 1929 exports had risen to a third of total revenues.

The Prudential management of the Acc and Tab had no more confidence in stimulating overseas trade than it did in its home trade, and it therefore put itself in the hands of Morland and Impey. Morland and Impey already had overseas operations in the traditional British Markets for its Kalamazoo business, and it established Powers operations in Australia, South Africa, and India; there is no surviving data to indicate the scale of these operations, but during the second half of the 1920s probably none of them amounted to more than a dozen installations. There was, however, a much larger and more interesting operation in France. At the time that the Impey Agreement had been negotiated in 1918 on behalf of the Prudential, Morland and Impey acquired the rights to market the American machines in France, as the company already had an extensive Kalamazoo operation there. The French business prospered, and was incorporated in 1922 as the Société Anonyme des Machines à Statistiques—SAMAS—from which the trade name 'Samas' later derived. In 1923, however, the American company cancelled the French agency and established its own branch; Morland and Impey therefore arranged to sell the British-made Powers machine instead.[37] During the 1920s and 1930s France was the biggest Acc and Tab overseas market.

Remington Rand and IBM

Up to about 1927, apart from the occasional skirmish, the Acc and Tab had been relatively unaffected by an aggressive American parent; if anything the British company had been more dynamic and forceful. This situation changed dramatically in 1927 with the formation of Remington Rand.

In 1927 America business was in expansive mood, and in the grip of one of its periodic merger waves. For its founder, James Rand Jr (1886–1968), Remington Rand was the culmination of several years of merger and acquisition activity.[38] James Rand was the elder son of James Rand Sr, the inventor of a visible record system widely used in American banks, and the proprietor of the Rand Ledger Company. In 1915 Rand Jr had broken away from his father and incorporated the American Kardex Company. In a friendly family rivalry the two companies rapidly became the two major suppliers of visible-record systems. In 1925 the two companies merged to form Rand Kardex, with father and son as chairman and president respectively. From this point on, Rand Jr made a vigorous series of mergers and acquisitions, culminating with the merger with the Remington Typewriter Company in May 1927. Although not a huge company by the standards of the multi-nationals like Ford or General Electric, the new company Remington Rand immediately became one of the dominant players in the office-machine industry (Table 3.5, p. 66). With assets on formation of $73 million it was about twice the size of IBM. Remington Rand acted as a holding company, in which its subsidiaries operated independently, but with close co-operation in sales and manufacturing.[39] One of the companies acquired in the run-up to the formation of Remington Rand was the Powers Accounting Machine Company; James Powers retired, and the company now became the Tabulating Machine Division of Remington Rand.[40]

Remington Rand quickly breathed new life into the Powers company; and with its vast network of sales and service operations throughout the world began to look at overseas markets more seriously than ever before. Like IBM, Remington Rand found itself inconvenienced by a small British company which it felt had no place in its expansionary plans. Within a few weeks of starting operations, the chairman of Remington Rand interviewed the Acc and Tab's legal representative in New York.[41] The course of the interview is not on record, but the Acc and Tab representative would certainly have pointed out that the British company was not a licensee of Remington Rand: it had *bought* the British and Empire rights to the Powers machines in 1919, and it intended to keep them. There followed the by now almost time-honoured tactic of withholding supplies. The tactic was without effect: all Acc and Tab's machines were made in Britain, and the refusal to supply card stock was a nuisance, but nothing more. Late in 1927 a cable was received from the Acc and Tab's Indian representative reporting that Remington Rand had started to sell Powers machines there. This was plainly against the terms of the Impey Agreement: the Acc and Tab's American legal representative was instructed to take action, and Remington Rand immediately withdrew.

Morland and Impey, unfortunately, were not so well placed. They did operate under a licence, renewable at the discretion of the American company. Remington Rand cancelled the agreement; and when SAMAS continued to sell the British machines a lawsuit was filed for patent infringement. The American company lost the action, so that both American and British Powers machines continued to be sold in open competition in France, as well as the Hollerith machines of the IBM's French subsidiary. Relations with Remington Rand remained frosty for several years, and did not thaw until about 1931, when the American company withdrew from its unprofitable French operation.

Perhaps the key to understanding the relations between the British companies and their American parents, is that at all times and with considerable justification IBM and Remington Rand felt that the British companies failed to make the most of their business opportunities, and that they could do better themselves. A crude but quantitative justification for this assertion can be gathered by comparing the financial statistics of BTM and IBM (Table 3.7). In 1925, a typical enough year, the assets,

Table 3.7   IBM and BTM financial statistics for 1925

	Assets	Revenues	Pre-tax profits	Personnel
IBM	$31.9m	$15.5m	$3.2m	*c.*3900
BTM	£137,000	£122,000	£20,900	*c.*150
Ratio	58:1	32:1	38:1	26:1

Note
£1 = $4.00

Sources
S. Englebourg, *International Business Machines: A Business History*, Arno Press, New York, 1976. BTM Annual Reports.

revenues, and profits of IBM were all massively greater than those of BTM. Probably the key figure was the revenues—which were over thirty times greater—since the small size of BTM's profits reflected the royalties it paid to IBM, and BTM's assets were much smaller, since it had relatively little plant compared with IBM. Beyond the raw financial data, the only comparative records available of machine population indicate that in 1930 the total number of tabulators and sorters rented by BTM was 296 and 246 respectively; it was estimated in the same year that IBM had 3500 tabulators and 3000 sorters in the United States alone.[42] All the statistics indicate the same fact: that the difference in size between IBM and BTM was not a matter of degree, but of two degrees. The relative sizes of IBM and BTM changed relatively little during the next 25 years. But it must be noted that when IBM criticized BTM for its slow growth, the fact of which was unquestionable, it never took into account the millstone of the iniquitous royalty rate, nor the fact that the British office-machine market was much less well-developed than that of the United States.

It is not possible to make a comparative quantitative assessment of Acc and Tab and Remington Rand, owing to a lack of financial data. However, although as a business Remington Rand was of a comparable size to IBM, its Tabulating Machine Division was a much smaller operation. In 1930 it had installed in America 695 tabulators and 620 sorters, about a fifth of the machine population of IBM.[43] Thus Remington Rand's punched-card machine operation was perhaps two or three times bigger than the Acc and Tab's, but certainly no more. This fact perhaps explains why, although relations between Acc and Tab and Remington Rand were often delicate, they never took on the life-threatening quality of the relations between BTM and IBM.

4

Heyday of the punched-card machine industry

the 1930s

This Exhibition might be described as representing the triumph of the Punched Hole, and signalises the dawn of an era in which all classifiable information and all computations, whether for account-ancy or statistical purposes, may be controlled by a hole punched in a card smaller than an ordinary postcard. . . . There is no system of book-keeping, and no method of costings which they cannot carry out with unexampled speed, efficiency and economy.

—Sir Herbert Austin, at the launch of the Powers Four range,
April 1932.[1]

During the 1930s in Britain the traditional industries of shipbuilding, iron and steel, and coal fell into a decline from which they did not recover until the start of the Second World War. The social consequences of the 1930s economic depression, particularly in the North of England, have left an image of the 1930s in Britain that is in some ways misleading. For set against these declining industries there were, particularly in the South of England, bright new industries that recovered very rapidly from the 1929-1932 economic crisis, and during the second half of the 1930s grew at a prodigious rate. Typical of these expanding industries were chemicals, motor cars, and electrical machinery and appliances.[2] The punched card machine industry belonged to this prosperous sector of modern manufactured goods.

During the 1929–32 economic crisis, the British punched-card machine industry not so much declined as failed to expand. Thereafter its growth was rapid, in part fuelled by the increasing demand for its products from progressive industry; for example Sir Herbert Austin's punched-card installation at his Longbridge car plant increased in line with the expansion of the motor trade. Another important factor contributing to growth was the remarkable technical improvement of the punched-card machines themselves, which made the equipment of the second half of the 1930s altogether more attractive and useful. The boom period of 1936-39 was the heyday of the punched-card-machine industry: it experi-enced undreamed-of prosperity, expansion, and technological advancement. By the outbreak of the Second World War it was in every sense a mature industry.

Sales American-style: Powers-Samas Accounting Machines Limited

In 1925 the Acc and Tab had entrusted all its home and overseas sales to Morland and Impey. Unfortunately Morland and Impey's attempt to combine the selling of punched-card machines with its main business of selling Kalamazoo loose-leaf binders had not proved a success, and orders had been lost to BTM. It was clear that the Acc and Tab needed to develop an integrated sales force in the American mould, and in 1929 the board called for a review of its entire selling operation. As a result of this review, conducted by a sales consultant and Arthur Impey, it was decided to set up a dedicated sales company. The new company was named Powers-Samas Accounting Machines Limited. (The trademark 'Samas' had been registered for the machines in France after American Powers refused to allow the French company to use the trademark 'Powers'.) Although the selling company, with about 60 staff, was only about a tenth of the size of the manufacturing company, the Acc and Tab, it immediately became the visible face of the company in all the markets it operated; 'Powers-Samas' became the name by which the product and the company was known.

Powers-Samas was owned jointly by the Acc and Tab and Morland and Impey. Punched-card machines were supplied to the sales company at a discount of about 30–40 per cent of the world sales price, and after deducting selling expenses the resulting profits would accrue to the owning companies. Integration between the manufacturing and sales companies was mainly achieved by product planning and development committees. This arrangement seems to have worked well, although the concept of two separate companies, in which the smaller company acted effectively as an operating division of the larger, was confusing to the outsider. After the Second World War the sales company was absorbed as the sales division of the manufacturing company.

Having created the new sales company, it was decided to bring in a person with American sales know-how to organize it. In July 1929, an American, Harold R. Russell, was appointed the first general manager of Powers-Samas. Russell had been engaged in office machinery sales since 1910; in 1919 he had joined Powers of America, and following the reorganization of the company in 1923 he became its general sales manager.[3] Russell was an engaging and dynamic man, and had been active in the Office Equipment Institute, the American office-appliance trade organization. It is not recorded how Russell came to be appointed: it may be that he was seconded by Remington Rand (the relations with the

American company being much improved by this date); it is also likely that he was well-acquainted with S.C. Downes through the International Union of Office Appliance Trades Associations. Whatever Russell's standing in the United States (and it was clearly not inconsiderable), he must have been an almost uniquely good catch for Powers-Samas.

No records of the selling organization exist prior to Russell's arrival, but it was evidently *ad hoc* and ramshackle—Brougham described it as a 'flop'.[4] In his period of two and a half years with the company, Russell set up the skeleton of a sales organization which had only 65 staff when he left at the end of 1931, but which was to grow more than twenty-fold in the next thirty years. The surviving records from Russell's period give us the first detailed glimpse of one of the British punched-card machine selling organizations.[5]

The heart of the sales operation was at the Head Office, Aldwych House, in the Aldwych, London. The head-office staff included about twenty sales people, and rather more support and service staff. On his arrival, besides introducing selling on commission, Russell created several new departments: publicity, sales-promotion, technical studies, and government sales; at the beginning the departments consisted of just one or two people, but later they were much larger. The publicity department began to place advertisements for Powers-Samas machines in the accountancy journals—it is extraordinary to relate that prior to Russell's arrival there does not appear to have ever been a single advertisement for Powers machines (or for those of BTM). A magazine *Powers-Samas Punch*[6] was also produced, very much along the lines of *Remington Rand World* or IBM's *THINK*—common in America at the time, but less so in Britain. The aim of the sales-promotion department was to co-ordinate the national sales effort by collating data on selected application areas and working with the publicity department in producing brochures with titles such as *Sales Accounting: Powers-Samas Punched Card Methods*, or *Powers Accounting for Management Control*.[7] A reporting system was also developed for the five district offices in Birmingham, Manchester, Leeds, Glasgow, and Dublin. By means of this system 'no prospect is allowed to be dropped or forgotten because of the personal whim of any member of staff'.[8] The technical studies department provided national support on the full range of applications for the district offices, which were staffed by one or at most two sales people, and so could not be expected to have expertise in more than a very few application areas. (In the mid-1950s, as the technology changed, the technical studies department formed one of the first programming groups of the early computer industry.) The government sales department actively targeted central government and local authorities, one of the largest potential markets, and could be called upon by the district sales offices. Russell also set up a bureau service. There had always been a set of machines at head office for demonstration purposes, but now a staff of about ten machine operators was taken on to process outside work, generating some revenue, and sometimes leading to sales. Service bureaux became an important operation for the punched-card machine manufacturers during the 1930s, both IBM in America and BTM in Britain setting up bureaux in 1932-33.

It has been said of the American office-machine industry that the 1920s was the period of the overseas agency, and the 1930s was the period of the subsidiary company.[9] This may have been true of the American industry, but Britain's was to remain in the age of the agency until after the Second World War. With the exception of SAMAS in France (and BTM's much smaller South African subsidiary, formed in 1930) overseas sales would remain in the hands of agencies or branch sales offices. Indeed, even after the war, apart from SAMAS and one or two card plants, the British companies had no overseas manufacturing operations. By contrast, both Remington Rand and IBM were genuine multinationals by the 1930s, with plants in several European countries. Although British office-machine companies were generally much less active overseas than their American counterparts, there were some important exceptions—such as Gestetner and Roneo Vickers, which were both major exporters of dupli-cating machines.[10] By comparison with these, during the 1930s both of the British punched-card machine manufacturers failed to make the most of their export opportunities; and this was to undermine their performance in the post-war period.

With a domestic sales force of only 65 people, and overseas operations on an even smaller scale, Russell was in no position to think of overseas marketing operations on the American scale. The most important Powers overseas operation by far was SAMAS in France, in which the Acc and Tab had bought a controlling interest from Morland and Impey in 1929. In 1932 Remington Rand, having found its French punched-card opera-tion unprofitable, merged it with SAMAS. Morland and Impey continued to operate its Powers agencies in Australia and India. The South African agency was awarded to Matheson and Ashley, well known as one of the country's major importers of all types of office machinery. In addition to these major agencies, Russell set up standard dealership agreements in Spain, Portugal, Argentina, Denmark, Sweden, and Norway. These were all very small-scale, and none of them amounted to more than a few machines a year, although the Norwegian operation had a better footing than IBM, which had not yet established a strong base in Scandinavia.[11]

At the end of 1931 Russell returned to the United States to become general manager of the Powers Division of Remington Rand. Another outside appointment was made for his successor. The new general manager, Walter Desborough, was a surprising choice, but an outstandingly success-ful one, and he remained in office until his retirement in 1952. Aged about forty at the time of his appointment, Desborough was an unusual choice because he was a career civil servant without any commercial or selling experience whatever. He had, however, been instrumental in bringing office mechanization into the British civil service, and was head of the 'Investigation Department' of H.M. Treasury (later the Organization and Methods Division). Desborough was second only to Professor L.R. Dicksee as a proselytizer of office mechanization in Britain: in 1921 he had written one of the first textbooks on office machinery, and he was a prolific writer of articles on the subject, and was in constant demand as a lecturer.[12] Desborough was an almost perfect follow-up to Russell. Russell had put a selling infrastructure into being, which Desborough could probably never have done; and indeed there is no evidence that the business of selling *per se* interested him at all. But Desborough probably had a firmer grasp of the strategic direction of office machinery than anyone in Britain: as general manager of Powers-Samas he showed an almost infallible instinct for the demands of the market-place, and thus ultimately for the products that the Acc and Tab manufactured.

Although we have a good picture of the Powers sales operation, rather less is known of BTM's sales organization in the early 1930s. According to surviving personnel, however, it was similar in structure to that of Powers-Samas: for example, there were branch offices in Britain and overseas, and a head office in London with a systems investigation department and a specialist department for government and railways sales.[13] In the ICL Historical Collection there is a considerable number of brochures dating from this period aimed at specialist markets such as local authorities, cost-accounting in manufacture, and so on. The BTM sales organization evolved more gradually and systematically than did that of the Acc and Tab, and there are no records of drastic reorganizations or bringing in Americans. The sales manager in 1933—who would have been Desborough's opposite number—was H. Victor Stammers. Stammers, who was eventually to become managing director, had grown up through the firm, having been taken on to run the Birmingham district office in 1926. The likely reason for this more gentle evolution of the sales operation is that several of the directors of BTM were familiar with the nature of selling capital goods: Phillpotts had been company secretary of British Westinghouse, G.H. Baillie was a consulting engineer, and G.E. Chadwyck-Healey had great knowledge across the spectrum of engineering. By contrast, the board of the Acc and Tab consisted entirely of actuaries and accountants.

The economic crisis, 1929–1932

The mileposts of the 1929–32 world economic crisis are well known. The period 1927–28 had been a period of business expansion and optimism, and financial speculation. The end of the boom came with the Wall Street crash of October 1929; this event heralded an economic decline that spread across the world, which did not fully recover until the Second World War. An immediate effect of the economic crisis was experienced by the Acc and Tab two months after the crash, in December 1929, when the French Government cancelled an order for 100 sets of tabulating machines—by far the biggest order ever received by SAMAS. The Acc and Tab immediately had to lay off some of its factory workforce.

In Britain generally, the consequences of the economic crisis were appalling: during 1930-31 unemployment rose from 1½ million to 2½ million. Sir Gerald E. May, deputy chairman of the Acc and Tab and secretary of the Prudential, was chairman of the notorious May Committee, established to resolve the financial crisis caused by the explosion of unemployment benefits. The May Committee recommendation, delivered in the summer of 1931, was for a wholesale reduction of benefits. The recommendation was unacceptable to the Labour Government, which resigned and was replaced by the coalition National Government. At this time May, who was aged about sixty, retired from both the Prudential and the Acc and Tab; but he continued in public service by becoming chairman of Neville Chamberlain's Import Duties Advisory Committee.

Office-machine consumption declined alarmingly during the crisis years, world production dropping by 60 per cent. The decline was rapid, but the recovery was also swift. For example, British typewriter exports dropped from £150 000 in 1930 to £105 000 the following year, but had recovered to £153 000 by 1933.[14] By 1936 all the world's office-machine industry had fully recovered, and moved into a phase of rapid growth.

It is instructive to compare this general pattern, of a heavy decline in 1929-33 followed by swift recovery, with the performance of BTM and the Acc and Tab. Table 4.1 shows BTM's financial statistics for the 1930s. There are no figures available for BTM's revenues, but they would have been proportional to the asset value of 'tabulating machinery on hire'. What we see is not a decline in 1929-33, but rather a period of no growth; so far as is known no BTM personnel lost their jobs during this period. After about 1933, there was unbroken growth for the rest of the 1930s. Once again, it was the policy of leasing rather than selling machines that had smoothed out the troughs and peaks experienced by the rest of the office-appliance industry. The value of the rental policy in the 1929-32 economic crisis has nowhere been better described than in the 1932 *Fortune* article about IBM:

In this type of business, manufacturing costs are not deducted from sales to show a profit. The value of machines made is an asset which in effect cancels their cost. The company's revenue consists not of sales but of rentals. From this income it must deduct the cost of servicing and repairing the machines which it has rented

Table 4.1 BTM financial statistics, 1930-1939

	Assets (£000s)		Pre-tax profits (£000s)	Personnel
	Total	Tabulating machinery on hire		
1930	199	72	20	360
1931	209	72	28	
1932	223	69	19	519
1933	272	72	27	643
1934	315	98	38	
1935	376	125	34	
1936	388	145	38	
1937	506	185	40	
1938	628	260	43	
1939	730	320	51	1225

Note
Figures for 1930 are for 9 months only, owing to a change of financial year.

Source
BTM Annual Reports, 1930-39.

out. It must also deduct enough average annual depreciation so that by the time its rented machines wear out they will no longer be carried as assets on its books. After these two deductions . . . the remainder of the rentals received is profit.

Consequently the profit from any one machine is divided and spread over as many years as the machine is rented. Provided the number of machines rented does not change, a company's profits remain just the same during a depression as during a boom.[15]

The only pre-war data available for Acc and Tab during the 1930s is its factory output, shown in Table 4.2. But here again, the pattern is remarkably similar to BTM's: a period of treading water during the crisis years, followed by sustained growth. Incidentally, IBM is often stated to have uniquely 'bucked the depression'; but in fact all the punched-card manufacturers seem to have survived the 1930s very successfully.[16]

The steadiness of BTM's financial statistics conceals the fact that it survived a series of formidable business problems during the crisis years. These problems were the abandonment of the Gold Standard, protectionism, and the 'Buy British' movement.

Britain went off Gold in September 1931. It was 'a turning point in modern economic history', and the pound immediately fell from its par value of $4.86 to $3.80, and reached a low point of $3.30.[17] BTM,

Table 4.2 British Powers production, 1929-39

Year of production	Factory output (£000s)
1929	170
1930	158
1931	158
1932	156
1933	178
1934	245
1935	287
1936	372
1937	571
1938	443
1939	482

Source Powers-Samas Deputy Chairman's Conference Papers, 24 October 1946.

naturally enough, remitted its royalties to IBM at the prevailing rate of exchange. IBM, long used to receiving its royalties at the old higher rate, objected. To judge by Phillpott's comments at the 1932 Annual General Meeting, IBM's attitude must have been almost the last straw in an extremely trying year:

. . . the American Company's attitude to us is, I fear, somewhat like the Congressmen of the Middle West on the Debt problems. They appear desirous of getting all the European money they can and they don't hesitate to try to press us to pay them more, as and when they can. They launched the idea during this past year that we were bound to pay them Royalties, not on a sterling basis but on a dollar basis. Well, not only is this quite contrary to the terms of the agreement between us, as we read them, but also, in fact, absolutely contrary to the actual course of business between our two Companies during many years past. Our Lawyers replied to that effect and up till now we have heard no more about the matter, but I only indicate that as a disturbing factor in the sort of attitude that the American Company takes towards us, namely, that in these times of difficulty all over the World instead of lending us a hand they seem to wish to press us.[18]

BTM continued to pay royalties at the prevailing exchange rate, and IBM did not press the matter again. Although leaving the Gold Standard did not affect BTM's royalty payments, American-made machines did of course have to be paid for in dollars, and this added considerably to their cost.

During the crisis years protective barriers sprang up in almost every country. In Britain the tariffs were recommended by Sir Gerald May's Import Duties Advisory Committee with 'the declared policy of using the grant of protection, not as a cloak for inefficiency and high prices, but a shield behind which British industry could reorganize and re-equip itself to face competition both home and abroad'.[19] The import duties began to take effect in 1932. The effect on the office-appliance trade, half of whose members were still largely importers, was very serious:

Certain of our members have been hit fairly severely by the tariff of 50 per cent. *ad valorem*, which had been imposed on a wide range of specified imports. Combined with the 30 per cent. loss on exchange this practically represents an embargo on the goods affected, and it is naturally a very serious problem.[20]

The duty on adding and calculating machines (including punched-card machines) was 25 per cent, which added considerably to the cost of imported IBM machines and parts. Fortunately, by 1932 BTM was making about 70 per cent of its new equipment in Britain, otherwise the position would have been unsustainable. An import duty also applied to card stock, which was still largely imported from America. For twenty years both BTM and the Acc and Tab had tried to find a really satisfactory long-term substitute without success. The new duty, and the huge volume of cards now being used, caused them to renew their efforts, and jointly they worked to find a British manufacturer who could supply both quality and volume. At last a permanent solution was found with the British paper manufacturers Wiggins Teape; their chemists analysed the American cards, and came up with a substitute that served the British companies for many years.

In July 1932, the Ottawa Agreement established imperial preference, by which the Commonwealth countries maintained favourable tariffs and quotas between one another. This was excellent news for the British typewriter manufacturers, who faced stiff competition from American and German manufacturers in the dominions. Unfortunately, imperial preference was wholly irrelevant to the British punched-card manufacturers, since their territories already excluded the American manufacturers IBM and Remington Rand; the only competition they faced in the Empire markets was from each other.

In addition to the difficulties of international finance, there was a national hostility to non-British manufactures that made BTM's position as an importer and manufacturer of IBM machines increasingly unattractive. This patriotic fervour found its expression in the 'Buy British' campaigns of newspapers such as the *Daily Mail*. It seems likely that the awarding of the 1931 census to Powers-Samas rather than BTM was at least partially influenced by this mood. During 1930 and 1931 the advertisements of British manufacturers began to sprout Union Jacks and slogans like 'All-British'. Powers-Samas was inclined to lay its publicity on fairly thick: '. . . Powers-Samas machines are manufactured throughout of British material, with skilled British labour and backed entirely by British Capital'.[21]

BTM machines were not of 100 per cent British manufacture, but they were about 70 per cent, and that proportion was increasing. But none the less it could not yet describe itself, like Powers-Samas, as 'All-British'. The leading voice of the 'Buy British' movement was the maverick Tory politician Leo Amery, who had 'advocated imperial preference with a zeal that amounted to bigotry'.[22] By a stroke of good fortune Phillpotts and Amery were well acquainted: they had been at Oxford together, and were friends of long-standing. Phillpotts invited Amery to form his own judgement:

I said: "Come and look at the circumstances of the Company and its Factory and see what it does in the way of English Manufacture and what it is planning to do further, and if you agree that it is a legitimate British Concern will you, as being the protagonist of the 'Buy British' campaign, show your appreciation of what we are doing by coming on the Board?" And I am glad to say that . . . the Rt. Hon. L.S. Amery has joined the Board. . . . This appointment, I think, is a distinct advantage to the Company.[23]

After Amery's appointment to the Board in mid-1932, the fact that BTM salesmen could point to him on the board must have rescued many a government and railway contract.

The pressures on BTM to move towards 100 per cent British manufacture were now inexorable: the currency situation, the import duties, the 'Buy British' campaign, and now Amery's position on the board. During the crisis years the Letchworth factory was vigorously expanded. Financing the expansion was not a problem: there was a considerable cash reserve following a share issue in 1929, and in this period of cheap money servicing bank loans at moderate interest was not difficult. Between 1930 and 1933 the number of factory employees rose from 160 to 364, and the factory area rose from 40 000 to 66 000 square feet.[24] Although the operation was still only half the size of the Acc and Tab's, by 1934 it could be truthfully said that BTM machines were 'now almost entirely made in this country'.[25]

Powers developments: Powers Four and Campos

At its second board meeting in November 1929, Powers-Samas had recommended the establishment of a Development Committee to co-ordinate new technical developments from the viewpoints of the manufacturing and selling companies. The Development Committee held its first meeting in January 1930, and met regularly at approximately monthly intervals for the next 15 years. The Development Committee was one of the key factors that ensured Powers-Samas' strong competitive position in the 1930s. After the Second World War the Development Committee was replaced by a much more complex research and development committee structure.

The Powers-Samas Development Committee was, in fact, established at a critical moment in the competition between the Hollerith and Powers lines. In 1928 IBM had introduced the 80-column card. The new card replaced the old 45-column card, which had been the industry standard until then, and offered almost twice the capacity (Fig. 4.1a). The 80-column card was adopted by BTM from 1929, making its new machines far more competitive than those of Powers-Samas, and demanded a response. There were essentially two ways of competing with the 80-column machines: first, by introducing a card of equivalent or higher capacity, or second, by selling machines of lower specification at a lower price.

In America, Remington Rand opted for the first strategy, and introduced a 90-column card in 1930 (Fig. 4.1b). Based on a German development of 1926, the Remington Rand card used two rows of 45 columns on a single card.[26] Although a few 90-column machines were sold by Powers-Samas, the 90-column card was unattractive because it required an awkward decoding mechanism and different timing arrangements that would have needed a costly development program to produce the full range of machines. By contrast, the IBM 80-column range used identical timing to the old 45-column machines, and in fact the new machines could be used with either the old or the new cards. This was therefore much the preferred option for British Powers: unfortunately the 'slotted hole' arrangement that was possible using IBM's electrical brush-sensing could not be used with the Powers mechanical pin-sensing. It seemed possible to squeeze 60 columns on the card, however, and the development of a 60-column range was set in hand with a development budget not exceeding £25 000.

Clearly, 60-column machines would not be fully competitive with the new BTM machines, so Desborough recommended that Powers-Samas should develop an entirely new range of low-cost machines.* As well as

---

* The idea of a low-cost range was not unprecedented, and was certainly anticipated by the Bull punched-card machines. The Bull machines were originally developed by a Norwegian, Frederik Rosing Bull, around 1922. Bull died prematurely and the patents were acquired in 1927 by the Elgi company, the Swiss manufacturer of the Madas and Millionaire calculating machines.[27] The Bull machines were manufactured in France, and a separate company Compagnie des Machines Bull was established in 1933. The Bull machines were first shown at the 1930 Paris business-machine exhibition, where they were examined with interest by the established punched-card machine companies. The outstanding feature of the Bull machines was that they were functionally quite simple, but were correspondingly reliable and inexpensive. It is said that Thomas Watson of IBM saw the machines, and that this was the origin of the IBM '50' low-cost 45-column machines that sold in America alongside the new 80-column machines from 1930.[28] The Bull machines were advertised in Britain from 1932, and, although no machines were probably sold in Britain, their existence must have exerted a considerable pressure on Powers in Britain and SAMAS in France.

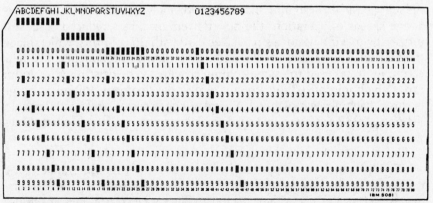

(a) IBM/BTM 80-column card, 1928

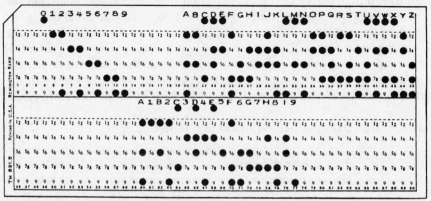

(b) Remington Rand 90-column card, 1930

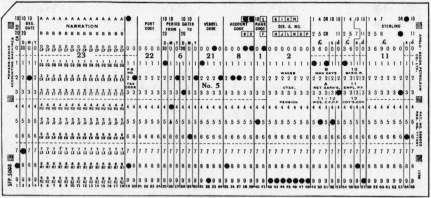

(c) Powers-Samas 65-column card, 1936

[All cards shown 60 per cent of actual size, 7⅜ × 3¼ inches]

Fig. 4.1 Large-card formats, 1928–36

reducing costs by designing machines with a low specification and conservative speeds of operation, the new Powers machines reduced costs still further by making use of a small-sized card with 26 columns, which made the machines physically smaller and used far fewer components. The new card (Fig. 4.2a) used the same column spacing as the existing 45-column card, which minimized the amount of new development. Initially a range of three machines was planned, a hand punch, a sorter, and a tabulator. In February 1932 a substantial initial production run of 100 sets of machines was approved.

The new machines were announced as the 'Powers Four' in April 1932. The launch was supported by an extensive (for the time) advertising campaign in the trade press and an exhibition of machines at Powers-Samas' head office in Aldwych House. The prices of the new machines are shown in Table 4.3. The new machines were generally about half the cost of the large-card machines. When one notes that the rental of a BTM 80-column tabulator was about £500 a year, the cost of £1100 for the outright purchase of a Powers Four tabulator (with a seven-year guarantee) must have seemed extraordinarily good value for those who were content with the limited specification. Another cost-saving advantage was that the cards, at about 2/- per thousand, were half the price of the standard cards.

Table 4.3 Machine selling prices and rentals, 1933

	Powers-Samas 45-column (£)	Powers Four 26-column (£)	BTM 80-column (£)
Tabulator	2000	1100	45 (rental)[a]
Sorter	450	270	9 (rental)[a]
Hand punch	23	18	23

Note
[a] BTM prices are monthly rentals; multiply by about 60 for comparable selling price.

Source
L.J. Comrie, *The Hollerith and Powers Tabulating Machines*, Transactions of the Office Machinery Users Association, London, 1933, pp. 47-8.

The Powers Four range was an instant success, the most successful development the company was ever to make. During 1932 and 1933 the level of interest convinced Desborough that the specification of the machines should be improved in order to attract yet more sales. Thus an automatic key punch was produced, an automatic total attachment, an alphabetic tabulator, and eventually the full range of ancillary machines.

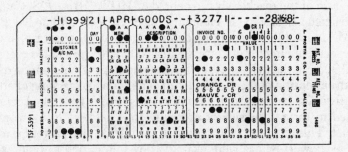

(a) 'Powers Four' 26-column card, 1932

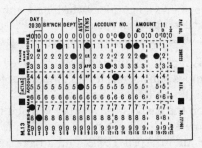

(b) 'Powers Four' 36-column card, 1936

(c) 'Powers One' 21-column card, 1936

[All cards shown 70 per cent of actual size: Powers Four, 4¾ × 2 inches; Powers One, 2¾ × 2 inches]

Fig. 4.2   Powers-Samas small-cards formats

Although the Powers Four was a great success in the long run, the immediate effect on the overall profitability on British Powers was less beneficial. In May 1933 fears were being expressed that the small machines were impacting on the sales of 45-column machines to such an extent that they were becoming the main product of the company. The higher volume of small machines only partly off-set their lower profitability, and the small cards were much less profitable. It was therefore decided to press ahead with all speed on the 60-column development, to restore the competitive position of the big machines.

The 26-column and 60-column ranges were the main Powers punched-card machine developments of the first half of the 1930s. There was, however, a further development that must be described: this is the Campos bookkeeping and accounting machine.

The Campos machine was invented by a Spaniard, F.P. Campos, and an early form of the machine was patented in 1923.[29] By 1928, Campos had constructed a prototype in Hamburg, where it was examined by Professor F.R.M. de Paula—a leading British authority on accounting, and later a non-executive director of Powers-Samas. He wrote a detailed report, dated July 1928, on the machine for Morland and Impey, which in turn brought it to the attention of the Acc and Tab. The Campos machine offered a real breakthrough in the art of machine accounting, and the Acc and Tab decided to form a subsidiary company to develop it into a commercial product. This took about two years. In early 1931 two prototype machines built by Powers-Samas were examined by a Remington Rand executive, whose report to his board was ecstatic:

For the first time in the history of mechanical bookkeeping machines there has been successfully developed in the Campos what one can really call a Control Machine. The Campos links up functions which have hitherto been performed by a series of separate and independent operations in bookkeeping machines. Among its outstanding features are [several] absolutely unique features in the art.[30]

On the basis of this report Remington Rand resolved to take a 20 per cent holding in the Campos subsidiary, for an amount not exceeding £10 000, to secure selling rights in its territories.

In May 1931, on the basis of the prototype machines, it was decided to manufacture and market the machine in quantity. It was launched alongside the Powers Four in April 1932, and advertised in the trade press. The Campos machine was one of the really remarkable developments of its period. To explain what the machine did, it would be difficult to improve on the description offered in 1933 by the distinguished French mathematician and authority on calculating machines Louis Couffignal:

An adding machine with a thousand registers has just been constructed. This is the Campos machine.

It falls into the category of adding and listing machines as far as the calculating mechanism is concerned . . . But the important innovation is that, by specifying an index number, the corresponding register sends the number which it holds to the accumulator or stores the number which was held in the accumulator. . . .

The Campos machine can be compared with the Babbage machine by the fact of its having 1000 registers. But its objective is different and its mechanism is very different.[31]

Thus, although the machine was designed for bookkeeping, its large storage space offered very exciting possibilities for mathematical computation, that immediately called to mind Babbage's famous but unbuilt Analytical Engine of the previous century.

By 1935, however, the Powers-Samas Campos machine appears to have vanished almost without trace. The fact was that the machine could not be made to operate reliably when manufactured in quantity, and deliveries had to be held back. In late 1935 Brougham and A.E. Impey examined the machines under construction on behalf of the Development Committee.[32] They were appalled by the unreliability of the machines, and the obvious impossibility of making them ever work satisfactorily. The Development Committee accepted their recommendation to scrap the whole project. So far as can be determined fewer than 10 machines were built, although at least three of the machines went into commercial use and of these one remained in service, in Paris, until 1947.

In assessing the Campos one can say that as a concept it was truly remarkable, but technologically it was too ambitious for a company with the resources of the Acc and Tab. The idea of holding a large number of accounts permanently in a stand-alone machine really only became practical with the micro-computers of the 1970s. It is fascinating, though quite idle, to speculate on how the Campos, had it been made to work reliably, would have affected the development of mathematical computation in the 1930s and the development of computers. *

Minor developments and patent squabbles

During the early 1930s the punched-card machine industry, especially with the entry of Remington Rand and Machines Bull, was becoming increasingly competitive in Europe.

As might be expected, the leading manufacturing country in Continental Europe was Germany, whose punched-card machine industry was at least on a par with if not larger than that of Britain. The German Hollerith machines were made by Dehomag, which had developed a large manufac-

---

* The Campos machine was revived again, in France and independently of Powers, by its inventor after the Second World War. The post-war machine, sold as the Logabax accounting machine, was much less ambitious, with only 18–200 registers.[33]

turing plant in Villigen. In 1922, a 90 per cent holding in Dehomag had
been acquired by IBM, although Dehomag continued to develop many of
its own patents and machines over the years. There was also a German
company, Powers GmbH, which had developed Powers machines
independently of the American company, much as the Acc and Tab had
done in Britain. The Hollerith and Powers companies of Britain and
Germany were on friendly terms, and communicated technical information from time to time, but otherwise operated quite independently.
France also had a small but growing punched-card machine industry: IBM
operated a subsidiary company and had a plant in Vincennes, and Machines
Bull (with over 70 installations by 1935) had built a factory in St Denis,
Paris. To add to the competitive situation Powers-Samas had opened
several continental agencies in 1930 and 1931, and Remington Rand was
also selling its American-made Powers machines. By 1935 IBM had
opened another plant in Milan, and had subsidiary companies (not
agencies) in over ten European countries. Although Europe accounted for
less than 20 per cent of IBM's volume, it was seen as an area of great
potential, and defended vigorously.[34]

In this competitive climate the punched-card machines of the 1930s
developed very rapidly, and by the late 1930s they had become mature
products built on a highly developed technological foundation. The IBM
80-column machines, and in Britain the Powers small-card machines,
were typical of the few major developments which are well known. Underlying these very visible developments, however, there were literally
hundreds of minor and heavily patented improvements. For example
during 1930–33 British Powers introduced over twenty minor improvements, with names such as 'major-and-minor control', the 'E.J. carriage',
the 'locked pin-box', the 'pence-to-pounds carry-over', and so on.[35] Each
improvement was covered by one or more patents. It was this accretion of
tiny improvements, incorporated in the machines with little fanfare as
they became available, that makes the description 'product evolution'
particularly appropriate.

The competitive position between the manufacturers was defended very
strongly by the filing of patents—many of which were merely defensive—
and the acquisition of patented inventions developed by others. IBM was
particularly active in the latter respect, buying the patents of Royden
Pierce in the United States in 1922 and the Bull patents from the Swiss
Elgi company in 1932.[36] It also had many patents developed by
Dehomag. Over the years there were several patent actions, few of which
proved straightforward either in terms of execution or outcome, for two
reasons. First, the validity of a patent, however thoroughly examined
prior to filing, could in the last analysis only be determined by a court of
the country in which it was being defended. Second, countries varied in

their attitude to the monopoly of an invention, and might, even with a successful action, force a compulsory licence to be granted to the defendant. The complexity of the legal and technical arguments was thus quite formidable.

Probably the best-documented patent dispute arose in connection with the group-control patent. It will be recalled that in 1924 the new-style BTM (that is, IBM) tabulators were equipped with automatic control. Although British Powers introduced its Automatic Total Attachment (ATA) in 1927, this had a different and lower specification to the IBM automatic control, and was supported by its own patents. In 1931, however, a new ATA was introduced with 'major-and-minor control', which enabled it to perform sub-totals and grand-totals, giving it a power equal to IBM's automatic control. According to one source (and the details may well be slightly muddled) there was a prior patent, due to a man named Lorant, developed for German Powers. IBM ultimately bought the patent from Lorant:

> ... legal actions started in 1932 after German Powers and Dehomag had sought without success to compose their difference resulting from IBM's acquisition of the Lorant patents used in the Powers machines. Patent matters became a really grave concern when Powers commenced action at the end of 1932 against Dehomag for infringement of the group control patent. Thereafter, each instituted patent suits aimed at the heart of the other's business in Germany. The important patents on which German Powers and Dehomag commenced legal action in 1932 numbered ten, of which three were owned by Powers and seven by Dehomag.[37]

Now in Britain the Acc and Tab had developed its ATA entirely independently of German Powers, although it inevitably infringed at least the IBM group-control patent, and presumably several others.[38] For several years BTM and the Acc and Tab had had a co-operative arrangement regarding patents, never attacking one another's, no doubt on the grounds that there was enough competition from outside the country without the British companies falling out between themselves. In June 1932, Phillpotts therefore offered the Acc and Tab a licence to use the IBM group-control patent. IBM, however, would not sanction this pusillanimous line, and requested BTM to withdraw its offer; the Acc and Tab board minutes also noted a rumour that IBM proposed to attack Remington Rand by first picking off the British company. Everard Greene was asked to attend a New York patent conference in April 1933 at IBM's expense, and it subsequently offered to bear half of the cost of an infringement action in Britain. From that point on there is no further reference to the matter in the extant records of either British company, but so far as is known no infringement action resulted, nor is there record of a licensing agreement. We do know, however, that Powers-Samas did not withdraw its new ATA from the market. Very likely the British companies quietly got on with the business of making and selling machines, while the German action ground on somewhat inconclusively until 1937.

So much for the automatic control patent. This in fact is the best documented of the patent squabbles. It would probably be possible, given access to the IBM archives and with appropriate legal and patent research in Germany and the United States, to chronicle the group-control dispute more fully and accurately. This would, however, be a somewhat pointless exercise at this distance in time. The reason that the story has been told here at all is that it illustrates the crucial importance of patent protection to the companies on the one hand, and the sheer competitive necessity of overcoming those patents on the other. With 'foundation' patents, such as the 1901 Hollerith patents themselves, an infringement was beyond dispute, and could be settled out of court: this was the spirit in which a licence was granted to American Powers by the Tabulating Machine Company in 1914. With the countless minor improvements, each almost trivial in itself, but vital in the aggregate, an action was not worth the trouble of pursuing. But in the middle ground there were a handful of key improvements that consumed nearly all the litigious effort on patents. *

BTM: the Rolling Total Tabulator, and relations with IBM

In 1933 BTM embarked on its first major development of an entirely new machine, the Rolling Total Tabulator (RTT).[39] This was a formidable undertaking, for BTM had nothing like the development experience or resources of the Acc and Tab. Over the years it had made improvements such as the 'pence translators' for sterling currency in the tabulator, and even one or two complete machines, such as a high-speed gang punch. But the Rolling Total Tabular was on an altogether different scale.

The rationales for BTM's decision to take on the design of its own tabulator have become muddied with time, but three reasons can be identified. The first was financial. Since the 1923 supplementary agreement with IBM, BTM inventions had been royalty-free. The tabulator rented for the most money, and consequently would generate the most additional revenue if no royalty had to be paid. Second, the BTM tabulator had already begun to depart slightly from IBM's by using its own counters, which incorporated the pence translators. When IBM introduced its direct

---

* It is interesting to note that after the war, when computers came on to the scene, patent actions were much less common. This is because the computer manufacturers generally sought competitive advantage not so much by innovation *per se*, but by superior exploitation. For example, all core-memory manufacturers paid royalties to the original inventors, but achieved their market positions by competing in terms of price and performance.

subtraction tabulator in the United States in 1928, BTM had such a large stock of its own counters that it introduced a technique of 'rolling subtraction' that used the existing stock.* Third, the development would be all-British; it would be hard to overestimate the importance of this factor—one can well imagine that Leo Amery would have backed the idea on these grounds, even had it had no other merits.

The leader of BTM's development department was Harold H. 'Doc' Keen. Keen was affectionately known as 'Doc' on account of the repairman's tools he always carried in a black leather holdall, similar to a doctor's bag of the period. He had joined the company in 1912 as a young repairman; his inventive flair was quickly recognized, and he was made head of the Experimental Department when it was formed in 1923. Doc Keen became the most celebrated and successful of British punched-card-machine inventors, and his work would have to be compared with IBM's great inventors such as Lake, Bryce, and Pierce. Like them, he was trained by the school of experience, and had no formal qualifications. After the war, as research and development became professionalized, he was to become isolated as one of the older generation. But in the 1930s Keen was in his prime, and was one of BTM's best assets.[40]

The RTT development proceeded very quickly, and the first machine was delivered to the corporation of the city of Hull in 1933. In BTM's enthusiasm the machine was rushed into production before all the teething problems had been resolved, with the consequence that the first batch of machines were none too profitable, as a result of a high level of modification in the field.[41] Once the machine was proven, however, it became the standard product, and the original IBM-designed tabulator was dropped altogether.

In retrospect, the decision to develop its own tabulator cannot be seen as an altogether fortunate one for BTM: it may have been profitable in the short term, but in the long term the company had burned its bridges, and would not subsequently be in a position to take advantage of IBM's tabulator developments. As luck would have it, more or less in parallel with the RTT development, IBM had developed its own 400-series tabulating machines. Announced in 1931, the 400 series was IBM's most successful pre-war development. Its launch was marked by the dropping of the name 'tabulator' in favour of 'electric accounting machine', or EAM (a term never adopted in Britain). For IBM it marked the end of its transition from statistical applications to full-blown electric accounting. In 1932 IBM announced, at long last, an alphabetical machine, the model

---

* The term 'rolling' came from the way in which to perform a subtraction one number was rolled into an auxiliary counter, and the complement of the other number was added to it; finally the result was rolled back into the original counter. Prior to the subtraction machines, tabulators could only add.

405. Sales were meteoric, and reached 1500 machines in the first year of manufacture, making it IBM's most profitable product up to that date.[42] (Quite why IBM had waited so many years to launch an alphabetic machine can only be guessed at. The most plausible explanation is that with the 45-column card the advantages were marginal, since the most text that the unit record could accommodate was a few characters for product descriptions, etc. With the greater capacity of the 80-column card, however, it would be possible to include names and addresses, eliminating the use of other manufacturers' equipment in addressing-machine hook-ups.)

At all events, BTM's Rolling Total Tabulator was not an alphabetic machine. Indeed it could still be argued that it was a statistical machine rather than a true accounting machine; the pressure to make it alphabetic became irresistible. With extraordinary speed, Keen came up with a suitable alphabetic printing mechanism, based on a modification of his counters. A fan-fold stationery-feeding device was also developed, so that printed statements acceptable to commerce could be produced. The Senior Rolling Total Tabulator was to be BTM's principal tabulator product for the next 20 years, just as IBM's 400 series was to live on into the 1960s. The evidence is that IBM's was the better machine; this was particularly true after the Second World War, when the IBM 407 and other models were announced.

At the time, however, the relative technical merits of the two machines were perhaps a secondary issue, since the main objective of the RTT had been to reduce royalty payments. But even this proved to be less than straightforward. As the tabulator royalty payments to IBM declined, the American company scrutinized the British patent situation very carefully. The essence of BTM's claim for reduced royalty payments hinged on the three Keen patents: for rolling totals, alphabetic printing, and fan-fold paper feeding.[43] The patent situation was typically complex, and was not resolved by IBM until 1938, when it found that all of Keen's patents incorporated inventions previously filed by itself. For example the rolling-total patent was substantially covered by an IBM multiplying-machine patent (which had apparently never been communicated to BTM). IBM thus offered BTM no more than a 'proportionate' reduction in royalties for the Keen inventions they deemed to be novel.

Running in parallel with the RTT royalty problem, was the question of tax on royalties, which had lain unresolved since the time of the 1923 supplementary agreement. The issue had begun to simmer again during the economic crisis of 1929–1932. Although little correspondence from the period survives, it is clear from the minute books that various letters were sent, and visits made by Everard Greene and others, in unsuccessful attempts to persuade IBM to accept royalties net of tax. In 1933 an effort was made to persuade IBM to apply for a tax rebate to the American tax authorities, presumably on the basis of double taxation (which was something of an international issue at the time). After about eighteen months the attempt was abandoned, in the light of a decision of the US Board of Appeals which had upheld a verdict made on a similar case by another company.[44]

In 1935, another ingenious approach was tried, which was probably cooked up by the BTM accountant Arthur Haworth in association with Sir Gerald Chadwyck-Healey. The idea was to persuade IBM to accept not royalties, but payment for 'services rendered' (that is, patents, know-how, machine tools, etc.). BTM could then legitimately claim this as a working expense, and claim full tax-relief. The proposal was formally put to Watson in a letter from Chadwyck-Healey at the end of 1935. As had happened on more than one previous occasion, Watson refused to discuss the matter, and instead made a tirade against the performance of the company:

I have endeavoured, to the best of my ability, for more than twenty years to co-operate with your organisation, along the same lines that I have operated in other countries in which we do business; but, from our viewpoint, our endeavours have not been welcomed by your organisation.

We feel that the situation to-day is more serious and far-reaching than the matter of income tax, to which you refer. Mr. Braitmayer informs me that your competitor has more machines in use than your company. When we compare your business and the potentialities of your territory with the business done in other countries, it prompts me to respectfully suggest that you and Mr. Phillpotts, who, I understand, are the largest stockholders, come to the United States, and we will go into the matter . . .[45]

Watson's letter ended with a cheery comment 'Mrs. Watson and I were glad to know that your son is in New York, and we are going to invite him to our home this week. Mrs. Watson joins me in kindest regards and best wishes to Lady Chadwyck-Healey and yourself.' Several comment-ators have noted Watson's extraordinary ability to combine an aggressive business manner and charming social relations on two quite different planes. None the less, Chadwyck-Healey and Phillpotts had not the slightest intention of visiting the lion in his den. Chadwyck-Healey carefully composed a reply, which was discussed and amended by the full board. The reply did not mince words either:

. . . if you don't mind my writing with rather brutal frankness, I and my colleagues have been engaged in this business for over twenty years; my brother, myself and Phillpotts have made visits to all parts of the world in which we are doing business, and generally we and our organization are sparing no effort to get contracts. Under these circumstances, it would be difficult for me or any of my colleagues to listen with patience to anyone outside our organisation who said we were not making enough effort, and offered to show us how to do so. . . .

I have to repeat that we cannot afford to continue to pay you Royalties and, in addition, income tax on their amount. As I have said to you before, English law makes any agreement to do so null and void, and there is, indeed, a penalty enforceable here on any person who refuses to allow the deduction to be made.[46]

There is no more correspondence on file. On 26 June 1936 the IBM Executive Finance Committee in New York came to a decision that magnificently combined high-mindedness with commercial self-interest. The board 'passed a resolution that, since there would be no advantage of changing from a royalty basis to a service basis, no arrangement should be made which would evade payment of taxes to the British Government'.[47] At its meeting on 27 July 1936 the BTM board resolved, in future, to pay royalties with income tax deducted.

And there the matter lay. The boom of 1936-39 supervened, and after that the Second World War, so it was not until the early 1950s that a settlement was finally reached.

The boom period, 1936–1939

British Powers emerged from the 1929-32 economic crisis very rapidly.* At the end of 1933 it was able to award a bonus to its factory personnel, the first for several years. From that point on factory output increased steadily throughout the 1930s. A major factory extension was completed in 1934, and in 1935 total personnel passed the 1000 mark. Presiding over the British Powers operation since 1919 had been its chairman Sir Joseph Burn, who was simultaneously general manager of the Prudential (1920-1941); the general manager, F.P. Symmons, was also actuary of the Prudential. It is clear from the board minutes that although both Burn and Symmons were heavily involved in the strategic direction of the company, their full-time responsibilities as principal officers of Prudential precluded their heavy involvement in day-to-day operations. The executive officers who reported directly to the board (none of them were directors) were S.C. Downes, L.E. Brougham, C.E. Hunter, and W. Desborough.

The year 1936 can only be described as British Powers' *annus mirabilis*: in production, sales, and machine development every previous achievement was surpassed. One single statistic sums up the extraordinary growth in production during the years 1935-36: in May 1935 the company employed something over 1000 people; in October 1936 this

* In 1936 the manufacturing company changed its name to Powers Accounting Machines Limited, in preference to the archaic Accounting and Tabulating Corporation of Great Britain Limited. Internally the company tended to call itself British Powers when referring to the operations of the combined manufacturing and selling operations.

had risen to nearly 2000, of whom about 1700 were employed in the manufacturing company. The expansion of the manufacturing operation was mirrored by the growth of the selling company. In 1936 Powers-Samas took over a 10,000 square foot four-storey building, Powers-Samas House, from the Prudential in Holborn Bars, which was to remain the head office until the company merged with BTM in 1959. The sales personnel had risen from about 60 in 1929 to something in the region of 300. But perhaps more important than the sales organization itself, was Desborough's influence behind the scenes on the Development Committee which guided British Powers' expansion. There are several extant technical reports from the 1930s written by Desborough that vividly convey his firm grasp of product strategy.

By 1936, the Powers development department, headed by A. Thomas and his assistant F.G. English, had grown astonishingly in confidence and scale. In autumn 1936, coinciding with the opening of Powers-Samas House, three complete new ranges of machines were unveiled, one range for each of three new punched cards. Altogether there were some forty machines. The large-card machines had had their capacity increased from 45 to 65 columns (Fig. 4.1c, p. 83); technical development had enabled smaller holes to be used, although the capacity still fell short of BTM's 80-column slotted-hole card. The second range of machines applied the same improvements to the Powers Four range, 36 columns now being provided instead of 26 (Fig. 4.2b, p. 85); the Powers Four range now had very close to the capacity of the old 45-column machines, which were no longer sold other than to top-up existing installations. The 65- and 36-column ranges represented not so much a new direction as consolidation and technological refinement. The third range of machines, however, was an entirely new development.

Marketed as Powers One, the new range used tiny 21-column cards 'little larger than a tram ticket' (Fig. 4.2c, p. 85). The machines were simple in the extreme, their complexity and size being reduced to a minimum; they were non-alphabetic, and had modest operational speeds. The machines were aimed particularly at retail-stores accounting, where the low transaction value made large-card machines uneconomic. Needless to say, the whole scheme was master-minded by Desborough. The machines were originally developed for the Cooperative Wholesale Societies 'Climax Checks', with the expectation that they would quickly spread to other organizations that could not justify the cost of the medium- or large-card equipment.

In 1937 the development department formally became known as the Research and Development Department, and moved into its own building on the Croydon site. One of its first tasks was to improve on the standardization and interchangeability of parts in order to reduce stocks and production costs. (This was of course very much in line with the rest of the engineering industry, whose productivity generally increased by about 20 per cent during the 1930s.) During 1937 and 1938 there began several costly developments for ancillary machines, not all of which reached the market-place before the outbreak of war. Once again, the ancillary machines were produced in response to new machines developed by IBM and sold by BTM in the UK. The new machines included a multiplying punch, a cross-adding punch, an alphanumeric interpreter, and an interpolator.* The multiplying punch, announced in 1938, was the most spectacular: it was the only machine of its kind in the world capable of multiplying sterling quantities (that is, pounds, shillings, and pence). It was entirely mechanical, and of breath-taking internal complexity.

From about the mid-1930s British Powers began to be a much more active exporter, and in the period 1936-41 some 23 per cent of its total production went overseas. In 1936 an agreement with Remington Rand was made by which they would exchange technical information and market one another's machines in their territories. Either the American company, or the American user, would not take the British small-card machines seriously, and sales in Remington Rand's territories were no more than a few sets of machines a year—a great lost opportunity.

When the Remington Rand agreement was made in 1936 the territories of the two companies were rationalized: British Powers took the British Empire, Scandinavia, and the Middle East; France and the French colonies were shared; and Remington Rand had the remaining territories. The best overseas outlet continued to be the French SAMAS company, although it was by no means an easy territory, owing to fluctuations in the exchange rate. In order to obtain French Government orders it also became necessary for SAMAS to be 'Francizized', which meant having French ownership of a majority of the stock, and a majority of French nationals on the board. This was achieved, but Remington Rand found the arrangement unacceptable, and agreed to sell their French interests to British Powers in 1939 for £50 000. The next biggest overseas markets for British Powers machines were Australia and New Zealand, and Scandinavia. These were to be very important markets during the post-war recovery period.

---

* The *multiplying punch* multiplied two fields on a card, and punched the product on the same card; a tabulator could only add and subtract, so the multiplying punch was an important new machine for users such as the gas and electric companies, who charged customers on a unit-price-times-units-used basis. The *cross-adding punch* was another multiplying punch with characteristics tailored to certain accounting operations. The *interpreter* printed the information punched in a card so that it could be read by humans. The *interpolator* (or *collator* in the US) merged two sorted packs of cards into a single sorted pack.

The Croydon plant was consistently working flat-out during the second half of the 1930s, with factory output generally in the region of £400 000–£500 000 in world selling prices. This would have represented perhaps 150 sets of small-card machines, and half as many sets of large-card machines a year. The entire Powers production since 1928 had been the responsibility of the works manager C.E. Hunter, of whom very little is known.[48] Hunter died in 1937, and his place was taken by L.E. Brougham. In the summer of 1937, a backlog of 22 weeks' orders had accumulated, in spite of overtime working, a night shift, and expansion into a second factory; the selling company actually had to be prevailed upon to decline taking new orders. In 1938 money was poured into new plant and factory extensions, and the capital of the selling company was doubled. In that year the company, with 2500 staff, claimed to be operating the 'largest factory in Europe exclusively engaged in the manufacture of office machines'.[49] So far as can be determined no new stock was issued during this period, all growth being funded by retained profits. Nonetheless in 1938 the company was able to declare a dividend of 32.5 per cent to its sole investor, the Prudential Assurance Company.

Turning to BTM, its recovery in many ways paralleled that of Powers. Recovery began during 1933, and was complete by the end of the year. A harbinger of better times was the securing of the company's largest ever order from the Milk Marketing Board by Cecil Mead (later a managing director of the company). The importance of this order—apart from its value—was that it indicated that BTM had at last completed the transition from importer to full-scale manufacturer, and was accepted as 'British' by a quasi-government user. During 1933 to 1936 BTM's tabulating machinery on hire more than doubled, from £72 000 to £145 000, and revenues increased proportionally. In spring 1935 a second factory was acquired in Letchworth, to which the card-making plant was transferred, leaving more room in the main factory. As with Powers, 1936 was the beginning of a period of great expansion and prosperity: bonuses were given to the sales force, holiday pay was introduced for hourly-paid workers, and an apprenticeship scheme was introduced. (The apprenticeship scheme was particularly important for what Phillpotts liked to call his 'happy family'. One of the great strengths of the company was the affection in which it was held by families, two and sometimes three generations of whom had worked for 'the Tab'; this atmosphere persisted until the early 1960s, after which the switch to electronics led to a declining workforce and many redundancies.)

It was with this incoming tide of prosperity that Everard Greene judged had come the right moment to step down as general manager. Not quite sixty, he became a member of the board with special responsibility for service bureaux; this was a light enough load to leave him free to enjoy a long retirement (he died in 1963 aged 85), and a prosperous one—for many years his salary and commission had been in the region of £3000 a year.

To strengthen the board following Everard Greene's retirement, Victor Stammers and Cyril G. Holland-Martin were appointed 'deputy directors', with responsibility for sales and technical development respectively.[50] Stammers proved to be a splendid appointment, and he eventually became a managing director and deputy chairman of the company; Phillpotts and Stammers developed a particularly close, almost father-and-son, relationship that lasted until Phillpotts' death in 1950. Of Holland-Martin's appointment there are mixed views. He was a son-in-law of Sir G.E. Chadwyck-Healey, and a son of Robert Holland-Martin (who was a director of Martin's Bank, a shareholder in BTM, and a founder of the Office Machinery Users Association). Cyril Holland-Martin joined BTM in 1933, when he was in his late twenties, and was appointed deputy director three years later. A man of considerable technical gifts, and with a delightful personality, he was only partially successful in his post-war task of reviving BTM's products. He was the last of the 'gentleman' executive directors to be appointed.

From the time of Everard Greene's retirement, Phillpotts took a much more active interest in the company, and formally became chairman and managing director in 1938 at a salary of £2500. Phillpotts saw himself as a financial strategist (regrettably often a conservative one) with Stammers, Holland-Martin, and Max Browne in charge of sales, technical development, and production respectively.

Under Stammers, the sales operation expanded vigorously, the sales force approximately doubling during the period 1936–39. Although there was ample business for both Powers and BTM, the competition was nevertheless seen as being 'acute'. A publicity department was formed in 1936 (and not before time), and a proper sales-training program was set up. In 1936 new service bureaux were opened in Sheffield, Newcastle, and Bristol, in addition to the existing bureaux in Dublin and London, which had been operating since 1933. The bureaux took in tabulating jobs for customers who could not justify their own installations, and provided additional peak-demand capacity for other users. Although the service bureaux tended to operate at a loss, they were seen as an important aid to sales, bureau users often graduating to rent their own installations. The London bureau, incidentally, was one of the main providers of scientific computing in Britain before the war. L.J. Comrie, the leading authority on scientific calculation in Britain, was retained as a consultant by BTM throughout the 1930s.

As an exporter, BTM was fully as active as Powers. Overseas business consistently accounted for between a quarter and a third of total revenues.[51] In 1937 an Overseas Committee was formed to co-ordinate the export business, and directors and senior staff made regular tours of the overseas branch offices in Africa, India, Australia, and Egypt. The Australian branch, which had never been properly exploited (as IBM had pointed out to BTM on a number of occasions) was at last taken in hand by Max Browne, who returned permanently to his native Australia to take charge of the operation.

In order to meet the competition of the Powers small-card machines, BTM introduced machinery using a half-sized 38-column card (Fig. 4.3).

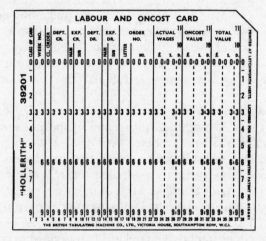

[Shown 70 per cent of actual size, $3^{11}/16 \times 3\frac{1}{4}$ inches]

Fig. 4.3 BTM 38-column half-card, 1936

This was a very simple development indeed: by using the short card, approximately half of the internals of the machines were eliminated, while using the standard 80-column card-feed mechanisms and bases. In May 1936 a production run of 20 sets of machines was authorized. Subsequently 24-column and 60-column cards were also introduced, but none of the short-card formats ever really caught on. On the other hand BTM's supremacy in the large-card machines could not be rivalled by Powers. In effect, during the 1930s, the two companies were beginning to split the market, sharing it largely on the basis of machines of high and low specification, and high and low cost. In fact BTM was renting all the 80-column equipment it could command, and Powers was selling all the small-card machines it could make. Attempting to enter the other's domain was less profitable for both companies. But it would not be until the 1959 merger that this situation reached its rational outcome.

BTM's financial statistics for the 1930s (Table 4.1, p. 78) show that from 1936 to 1939 the company expanded massively: tabulating machinery on hire more than doubled, from £145 000 in 1936 to £320 000 in 1939. During the same time the company headcount nearly doubled to 1225, but the expansion was largely in the sales force; factory personnel at Letchworth probably only increased by about 50, to 425 in 1939. On the whole Phillpotts' financial conservatism seems to have won the day; although the board occasionally overcame his circumspection, the increase in manufacturing capacity during 1936-39 was far less than it could have been. Studying Table 4.1 we see that during the mid-1930s BTM's plant enabled it to add to the value of its tabulating machinery on hire at the rate of £30 000 to £40 000 a year (including depreciation).* During 1937-39, however, the tabulating machinery on hire was increasing at a rate of over £80 000 a year. Even allowing for overtime working and some increase in manufacturing capacity, the conclusion is inescapable: BTM was obtaining a full half of its machines from the United States.

BTM's capacity was falling short in two respects: first in the development of new types of machine, and second in sheer volume. When the new generation of ancillary machines were developed by IBM in the first half of the 1930s, BTM was developing the Rolling Total Tabulator, and would have been in no position to undertake a development on the scale of a multiplying punch, for example. Most of the machines added to BTM's 80-column range during the late 1930s were developed by IBM. Table 4.4 shows BTM's 80-column range for the late 1930s, of which several machines were either imported complete or assembled from parts. Board of Trade statistics for 1937/38 show that in that one year Britain imported 182 complete punched-card machines—every one of which must have found its way to a BTM customer.[52] In a year in which BTM added to its machine population of tabulators and sorters by less than 60 each, this was importation on a grand scale. There is an anecdote that for BTM's overseas customers, some machines were sent directly from IBM, BTM name-plates being affixed in New York; to add to the illusion local Letchworth newspapers were shipped to the United States for use in the packing cases![53]

In order to increase BTM's manufacturing volume it seems likely that large quantities of parts were also imported from IBM for assembly in Letchworth. Board of Trade statistics show that Britain imported

---

* BTM's output of £30 000-£40 000 a year, and Powers' output of £400 000-£500 000 a year are not comparable, owing to differing accounting practices. Powers output was measured in 'world sales prices', whereas the BTM valuation reflected the cost of production, the machines subsequently being rented. The BTM valuation would have to be multiplied by a factor of 4 or 5 to get a proper comparison with Powers.

Table 4.4 Principal BTM 80-column punched-card machines, late 1930s

Machine	Price (£)	Speed (cpm)	Manufacturer
Card punches			
Hand punch	23[a]		BTM
Hand verifier	25[a]		BTM
Automatic key punch	110[a]		IBM
Duplicating key punch	130[a]		IBM
Alphabetic key punch	450[a]		IBM
Sorters			
Horizontal sorter	9	400	BTM
Tabulators			
Balancing tabulator	9	150	BTM
Auto-control tabulator	45[b]	175/120	BTM
Senior RTT (numeric)	57[b]	150/100	BTM
Senior RTT (alphabetic)	64[b]	150/80	BTM
Ancillary machines			
Reproducing punch	525[a]	100	IBM
Summary punch	575[a]		IBM
Multiplying punch	29[b]	10	IBM/BTM
Interpreter	16	75	IBM
Collator	19	250/500	IBM

Notes
[a] Outright selling price; all other prices are monthly rentals. Note that the IBM-BTM agreement allowed punches to be sold not rented; this was originally intended to apply to the hand punch (which sold for £15 in 1908) but BTM made use of the loophole to sell rather than rent any machine called a punch.
[b] Rental for a minimum specification machine.

Sources
'Machine Records' and 'Hollerith Electrical Tabulating Equipment', both n.d., late 1930s (ICL Historical Collection).

£750 000 of calculating-machine parts in 1937/38, although only a fraction of these could be accounted for by BTM. Powers was by no means oblivious to these massive imports from the United States (after all, Sir Gerald May was chairman of the Import Duties Advisory Committee). It was particularly aggrieved that:

... under the present laws it is possible to import a machine in a few sections, assemble the three or four sections, and label the completed machine as "British Built." ... It is perhaps unnecessary for us to add that Powers Machines as sold in Great Britain and throughout the British Empire are manufactured in their entirety at the extensive factory of Powers Accounting Machines Ltd., Croydon, England. Thus, there is no question that 'Powers' are both "British Made" and "British Built."[54]

In late 1937 the negotiations between the British and American Governments leading up to the Anglo-American Trade Agreement were taking place. Office machinery was one of many protected industries that were being examined, and at the time it was proposed that the import tariff on adding and calculating machines should be reduced from 20 per cent to 15 per cent. Powers made a formal representation to the committee that no reduction in the tariff should be made.[55] So far as adding and calculating machines in general were concerned, Powers lost the argument: in spite of years of protection there was still no indigenous calculating-machine industry to speak of, protection having served not so much to nurture a fledging industry as to increase industry costs generally. Powers did, however, win a major concession with regard to punched-card machinery. Britain now had a world-class manufacturer in Powers, which fully deserved protection: the duty on imported punched-card machinery thus remained at 20 per cent, while all other calculating-machine duties were reduced to 15 per cent.

Powers was understandably delighted by this result. Not content with winning, the company related the whole episode in a provocative article in *Powers-Samas Magazine* in March 1939.[56] The following month, however, it was obliged by BTM lawyers to print a retraction of some of its more contentious statements. This was the first and only time that the rivalry between the companies, which was always intense, spilled over into a public squabble. It was, however, spring 1939; war clouds were gathering, and in a matter of months the time for squabbling, public or private, would be past.

5

An interlude: the Second World War
1939–1945

Project Cantab
Keen . . . , together with a few of his principal assistants in the
development laboratory and the man in charge of the new factory,
were told the whole story of Hut 6. The workers on the assembly
line and in the factory, however, never knew what the machines
were intended to do. I hope this book will tell these people, and
their children and grandchildren, that what they did was enormously worthwhile.

—Gordon Welchman, *The Hut Six Story*, 1982.[1]

On 3 September 1939 Britain declared war on Germany, and in
December 1941 war was declared upon Japan. Victory in Europe came
on 8 May 1945, and Victory over Japan the following August. The
six years of war were a hiatus in the economic development of Britain, for
in that period everything was sacrificed to the national war effort:
'Foreign investments were sold, women conscripted, capital was run
down and not replaced, civilian consumption was drastically reduced,
exports were cut back.[2]' British industry was in the van of the contribution to the national war effort, and its control over its own destiny was
almost completely curtailed.[3]

There are really two separate aspects to describing how the war affected
the British punched-card machine manufacturers. The first is, so to speak,
the war story—the contribution of the companies to the war effort, the
impact of air-raid precautions (evacuation and so forth), and the secret
projects. The war story is interesting for its own sake, and for the contribution it made to the morale of the companies and their post-war culture.
But beyond that it is little more than a collection of good stories. The
second, and much more important, aspect of the war was the effect it had
on the long-term development of the companies. The most notable of
these effects were the wartime stagnation of R&D, and the creation of a
home and export market starved of office machinery. These conditions
were created in the period 1939–1943; the rundown from war during
1944–45, and the immediate post-war period, transformed the situation
only slowly. It was not until about 1950 that the effect of the war had
completely worked itself out of the system.

The coming of war

From about 1937 a European war had seemed inevitable to many contemporary observers. In September 1938 Chamberlain brought back the
famous 'peace in our time' message from Munich, but it was no more
than a respite. By early 1939 the drift into war was inexorable.

In January 1939, in its first recorded response to the coming war, the
BTM board approved a decision to build up machine stocks—presumably
in the expectation that imports from IBM could only become more difficult
in the event of a 'special emergency'.[4] During March and April a whole
series of measures were taken: an air-raid shelter for the Letchworth
factory was approved, an underground store for punched-card printing
dies was built, BTM staff became involved in the local anti-aircraft detach-
ment, and volunteers were granted leave to attend training courses for the
fighting forces. In May 1939 the company was placed on the list of
reserved businesses of national importance, which exempted its factory
staff from call-up. In the tense summer of 1939 detailed plans were made
for the evacuation of the London head office to Letchworth, and the para-
phernalia of air-raid precautions were put into place—blackouts, underground tools stores, and so on.

When war was declared, at the beginning of September 1939, many of
the company's staff enlisted in the armed services (eventually a total of
477 people served). At the board level these included H.V. Stammers,
who rejoined the RAF (he had served in the Royal Flying Corps during
the First World War), and C.G. Holland-Martin (an amateur pilot) who
joined the RAF in Canada to train British pilots. Leo Amery, who had
attended but one board meeting since the outbreak of war, officially
resigned in June 1940 to become the Secretary of State for India. The
executive direction of BTM now fell heavily on the shoulders of its ageing
directors Phillpotts and Baillie, both approaching seventy, who took up
residence in Letchworth to serve as managing director and assistant
managing director respectively.

At the same time that BTM (and indeed the whole of British industry)
was making its plans for wartime working, so too was British Powers.
Thus during the first half of 1939 plans for air-raid precautions at the
Croydon factory were implemented by Brougham, and efforts were made
to transfer the card plant to a safe area. On the outbreak of war, as with
BTM, there was a drift of staff into the fighting services. In many cases
these people became involved in operational punched-card units, their
technical work continuing in many ways unchanged, but under the very
different conditions of military uniform and discipline.

America did not come into the war until December 1941, although it
helped enormously with the war effort before that, particularly through

the lend-lease act. In 1939 war seemed a much less likely prospect in the United States than it did in Britain. Early in 1939, British Powers had agreed to pay Remington Rand £50 000 for its interest in SAMAS in five annual instalments of £10 000. As war became inevitable, it was realized by the Powers board that it would become very difficult to pay the instalments, owing to currency restrictions. Brougham and Downes therefore visited the American company, in what was to be their last trip to the United States for six years, to negotiate a settlement:

We had an awful time with Jimmy Rand. He was very truculent about the whole thing. . . . He said 'If you think we're coming to save you crowd again like we did in the First World War, you're wrong . . . what is more you're not likely to fight a war anyway'. In answer to these comments I said 'Well Mr Rand . . . all we're saying is, if we're at war, we just delay paying you. But you say that we won't go into war. Well then why don't you sign the agreement we want you to sign'. He said 'If you put it like that I'll sign right away'.[5]

In fact, after the outbreak of war the value of sterling fell so rapidly that Remington Rand agreed to settle outright for a sum of $130 000 in April 1940. This would have been an excellent outcome for British Powers had France not fallen two months later, making SAMAS more or less worthless. Relations with Remington Rand remained completely amicable throughout the war, but there was so little interaction between the companies that they were not a significant part of the war story.

The relations between BTM and IBM during the war changed completely from the abrasive character they had had before the war, and IBM became very supportive. It may have been that Watson's attitude was motivated not so much by affection for BTM itself as for Britain as a nation; but the most effective way of helping Britain was to help BTM. In view of the dollar shortage, on the outbreak of war Watson allowed BTM to bank royalty payments in sterling in London for the duration. Throughout the war the royalty account was used by IBM to make donations, typically of several thousand dollars a time, to such causes as YMCA huts for the forces and the American Ambulance in Britain. In December 1941 the Japanese attacked Pearl Harbour, and America finally joined the war. Watson sealed the alliance between the countries in a gesture that touched every member of BTM's personnel: each received a personally addressed food parcel, and a book of his own choosing, from 'friends across the sea'; and in Letchworth, London, and every district office, a Christmas lunch was held at IBM's expense.[6] Throughout the war, Watson kept up a barrage of recorded Christmas messages and morale-boosting food packages. He also opened up opportunities for BTM engineers to serve in Canada for the duration. Watson was extraordinarily patriotic, and he made similar gestures towards IBM's other outposts throughout the war, as well as putting IBM's manufacturing and research facilities at the disposal of the United States Government.[7]

Punched-card machine production

Like every engineering business during the war, the factory output of the punched-card machine manufacturers was dictated to a large extent by the Board of Trade. BTM was permitted to use 45 per cent of its capacity for punched-card machine production, the remainder being given over to production for the war ministries.[8] In the case of Powers, which had a larger volume of exports, 65 per cent was permitted.[9]

The punched-card machine industry, in fact, fared very much better than the rest of the light engineering sector, in being allowed to devote such a high proportion of its capacity to normal production. There were two reasons for this. First, office machinery had an important operational value in the war effort, and demand 'rose by leaps and bounds as administrative work and the collection of statistics expanded in the Services, in industry, and in Government departments'.[10] Second, the domestic office-machine manufacturers helped the balance of payments by reducing the need for office-machine imports, and in some cases were net exporters. The fact that the punched-card machine companies at no point had to suspend normal production was an important factor enabling their rapid post-war recovery. Other producers (such as the gramophone industry, domestic electrical appliances, and many others) experienced far more disruption.

On the outbreak of war, the immediate concern of the Board of Trade was the balance of trade. In order to conserve dollars for munitions purchase, an import-licensing system was immediately imposed for a whole range of goods, ranging from textiles to machinery. The range included office machinery, and BTM was refused a licence to import machines from IBM. This had the immediate effect of bringing BTM's rate of acquisition of punched-card machinery for rental, which had been heavily supported by imports from IBM, down to the levels of the mid-1930s. As Table 5.1 shows, the 'tabulating machinery on hire' did little more than keep pace with depreciation.

Alongside the restriction of office-machine imports, exports were strongly encouraged during 1939 and 1940: 'exports were the cheapest and most effective means of satisfying the war requirements of the country —that is, through import from abroad rather than by the diversion of home resources to war production'.[11] Thus manufacturers such as Powers were urged to export as much as possible to non-enemy countries; the foreign exchange earned could then be used for armaments purchased from the United States. Powers production for 1940 and 1941 was main-

Table 5.1 BTM financial statistics, 1940-45

	Assets (£000s)		Pre-tax profits (£000s)	Personnel
	Total	Tabulating machinery on hire		
1940	804	332	66	
1941	992	323	86	
1942	1126	320	83	2000
1943	1248	326	88	
1944	1597	371	100	2808
1945	1584	487	101	2009

Source
BTM Annual Reports, 1940-45.

tained at, and even exceeded, pre-war levels, one-third of output going overseas to its major markets of France, Australia, and Scandinavia (Table 5.2). But in spring 1940 Denmark and Norway were invaded by Germany, and France fell in June. At a stroke Powers lost its largest export market, in France, and its third largest market of Scandinavia. (The loss of neutral Sweden was, however, temporary; and it became the largest Powers export market, averaging sales of £60 000 a year during 1941-45.) BTM's exports were negligible during the early war years, almost all of its production going to the home market; but some overseas markets, such as Australia, were supplied directly by IBM on BTM's behalf.

Table 5.2 British Powers production, 1939-46

Year of production	1939	1940	1941	1942	1943	1944	1945	1946
Factory output (£000s)	482	546	577	366	414	738	483	1142

Source
Powers-Samas Deputy Chairman's Conference Papers, 24 October 1946.

After the fall of France, it became clear that Britain was committed to a long, hard war. A new sense of urgency gripped the nation, and government controls on industry became much tighter. Up to the summer of 1940, restrictions had mainly been aimed at improving the balance of trade; the emphasis now turned to the total control of the means of production towards the war effort. Although government departments generally took priority, it was recognized that it was essential to keep the capital equipment of the civilian sector intact, because the war effort was crucially dependent on the smooth running of the railways, the Post Office, the power companies, and so on. The Board of Trade controls were designed to ensure that just sufficient—'but only just sufficient'—machinery and supplies reached the essential civilian sector.[12] In June 1940 machinery licensing (including office machinery) was introduced (from which government departments were exempt) to prevent the unnecessary purchase of capital goods. Although a majority of civil applications for licences were accepted, the rejection rate was sufficient to prevent non-essential applications. A further measure to dampen the demand for machinery was the introduction of purchase tax. In October 1940 purchase tax on office machinery was set at $33\frac{1}{3}$ per cent. This seemed a harsh decision to the punched-card machine manufacturers, since unlike much of the office-machine industry they did not rely on imports; Ralegh Phillpotts and Sir Joseph Burn protested strongly, but without success.[13]

The effect of these controls was that during the first two or three years of war virtually all the punched-card machinery that was not exported was directly or indirectly taken by the government for the war effort. There is no detailed surviving data on the number or size of government installations, but an internal BTM history of 1957 listed some specific examples.[14] These included several small installations for the Royal Ordnance Factories and aircraft factories, for which many of the machines were probably requisitioned from non-essential users. Powers claimed that 'the greater part of the costing and accounting work of the Nation's armaments, aeroplane production and engineering in this country is being produced on Powers Machines'.[15] Most government departments used machines for statistical and planning purposes; these included the Treasury, the Ministry of Works, the Ministry of Agriculture, and the Ministry of Aircraft Production (MAP). Within the fighting forces there were some very large installations used for stores accounting and personnel records. BTM gained some publicity value from a mobile statistical unit that served in France, Belgium, and Germany at various stages of the war. In many respects the forces' units ran along similar lines to civilian installations, except for military uniform and discipline; and they were staffed where possible by enlisted men with tabulating-machine experience.*

* One example of such a unit was the RAOC No. 1 Statistics Unit attached to the Middle East Forces in Cairo, commanded by Lt. Col. C. Shread (a Powers salesman who was later to become Powers-Samas home sales manager). Shread's widow recently donated a very detailed record of the unit to the ICL Historical Collection.[16] The unit, which was of

In addition to the installations directly operated by government organizations and factories, all of BTM's service bureaux were dedicated to government work throughout the war. For example the London bureau was responsible for processing the raw materials requirements for the aircraft, tank, and wheeled-vehicle programmes. Because of their operational importance, all the bureaux were evacuated to safe areas (the London bureau was transferred to East Molesley, for example). The bureaux work made an important contribution to BTM's revenues during the war, when its scope for increasing revenues by renting more tabulating machinery was severely limited. From having been a loss-maker before the war, the bureaux became very profitable, and this continued after the war.

As so often in the past, the supply of cards gave altogether more problems than the machinery itself. The cards were the life-blood of the business, and both Powers and BTM duplicated their card plants in safe areas (Glossop and Alderley Edge respectively). The regular supplies of pulp from Scandinavia and Europe ceased early in the war, and the available raw material produced cards that were 'flabby and damp'.[17] The situation was further aggravated by shipping losses and air raids. The only solution was to import card stock from America, but it took time for the necessary paper licences to be granted. In the interim, it was seriously considered using the 'Valtat process' to manufacture cards: in this process two thin cards were glued together, so that the curling properties of the inferior card stock would cancel out, and metal impurities were isolated by the insulating layer of glue.[18] Fortunately this somewhat eccentric idea (though it was taken entirely seriously) never had to be adopted.

In spring 1941, when Britain's supply of dollars was near exhaustion, America introduced lend-lease, which enabled the lavish import of American armaments and goods without regard to the balance of payments. This enabled BTM to bring in a modest stream of IBM collators and model 405 tabulators for government installations. After lend-lease, the Board of Trade controls no longer acted to encourage exports, but rather to restrict them, since to export the same type of goods that America was supplying on lend-lease would have been contrary to the spirit of the act. This applied particularly to office machinery, for which

medium size, was staffed by 26 army personnel, and could call on up to 398 civilian personnel as required. The machine complement included 22 automatic key punches, 22 verifiers, 5 sorters, 3 standard tabulators, and a full range of ancillary machines. The routine tasks processed included stores accounting (for over 414 000 items), fighting troops personnel records (for 240 000 people), vehicle spares, and various statistical jobs. Shread's record is one of relatively few known examples of a really detailed record of a punched-card installation and its applications of any period.

imports actually exceeded pre-war levels.* Powers was permitted to continue exporting to allies such as Australia and India, where the machines were directly related to the war effort, but goods to non-allies (notably Sweden) were stopped altogether.

At this time the demand for office machinery generally so far exceeded supply that the Board of Trade took active steps to relieve the situation. To stimulate production, office-machine manufacturers were given Essential Works Orders which enhanced their status and prevented the conscription of skilled personnel to the fighting forces. Particular sectors of the industry were also carefully examined; for example typewriter manufacturers were encouraged to manufacture standard machines at the expense of portables.[20] In September 1941 the Directorate of Office Machinery was established, to directly co-ordinate production and distribution. This high degree of control reflected the great importance attached to office machinery by the government. Like many of the departments within the Board of Trade, specialist expertise was brought in from outside where civil servants fell short; in the case of the Directorate of Office Machinery, H.V. Stammers was temporarily seconded from the Air Force to act as an Assistant Director. The Office Appliance Trades Association, as the representative of the industry, acted as the main external advisor to the Directorate; the accounting machine section of this advisory body included A. Cranfield of BTM and S.D. Parker, representing Powers and Remington Rand.[21] In January 1942, the Directorate of Office Machinery brought in the Office Machinery (Restrictions) Order, which prohibited the breaking up or movement of any item of office machinery without a licence; this applied not only to manufacturers but also to users, and to second-hand machinery as well as new.[22] Under the Directorate's licencing system it was even possible to locate individual machines, so that firms and government departments could be informed of what machines could be made available to them. This was 'a closer control than any other exercised by the Board over acquisition and supply'; and the control was not relaxed until the autumn of 1943, and then only slightly.[23]

War production: sub-contracting

During the Second World War, industrial production was directed to the all-out war effort. Perhaps more than any other single statistic, aeroplane production sums up the scale of this effort: in the years 1938 and 1939 Britain built 2800 and 7900 planes respectively; in 1940, 15 000 planes

---

* Office machinery imports were: 1938, £847 000; 1943, £750 000; 1944, £1 500 000.[19]

were made; in 1941, 20 000; in 1942, 23 600; in 1943 and 1944 over
26 000 planes were built each year, an average of more than 2000 a
month.[24] BTM and Powers contributions to war production were of two
kinds: special projects and sub-contracting. The special projects were the
more interesting, and are described later; but sub-contracting, though less
glamorous, was also important.

To understand the structure of the wartime industrial effort, one has to
go back to the Weir Committee of 1933, which had been formed to advise
on rearmament if war should come.[25] The Weir Committee had recommended three means of increasing the nation's armoury. First, the
expansion of the two main armaments suppliers, the Royal Arsenal at
Woolwich and Vickers-Armstrongs. Second, the conversion of large-scale
engineering manufacturers to armaments manufacture in the event of
war; this was the so-called 'shadow industry', which included motor-
vehicle manufacturers, civil aircraft manufacturers, the heavy electrical
industry, and so on. Third, the utilization of the manufacturing capacity
of the entire engineering industry by sub-contracting. This arrangement
was rather like a shallow-sided pyramid: two firms at the top, a few tens in
the middle, and several thousands at the bottom. It was in this bottom
layer that BTM and Powers belonged; their contributions were therefore
somewhat anonymous—two cogs in the war machine.

The main contracting agencies were the Ministry of Supply, the
Admiralty, and the Ministry of Aircraft Production: these corresponded
roughly to the Army, Navy, and Air Force. Immediately on the outbreak
of war, Phillpotts took the view that it would be better to offer BTM's
capacity at the outset rather than to have machines commandeered. The
company thus immediately became a sub-contractor, manufacturing aeroplane parts for the Vickers agency factory at Chester, where Wellington
bombers were built, and for Handley Page, makers of the Halifax bomber.[26]
In general the administration of war production was superbly organized,
and advantage was taken of BTM's very high quality engineering resources
to make bomb-sights and other high-precision aircraft instruments. Early
in 1940 BTM also began to make watchmaker's lathes; here again,
advantage was taken of BTM's position as one of a comparatively small
number of firms with a well-developed machine-tool-making capability.

There is no data available either on the particular contracts fulfilled by
BTM, or on the revenue generated (in fact the company was not permitted
to disclose details at the time). Overall, however, the picture is fairly clear.
Between 1939 and 1943 turnover increased by a factor of three, the
labour force more than doubled, and three new factories in Letchworth
were taken over. Hollerith output probably increased only marginally
during this period, almost all the expansion being attributed to war work.
Phillpotts was prudent about taking on work that involved expenditure on

plant, and, as Table 5.1 (p. 107) shows, BTM assets increased at a much slower rate than output. Much of the additional plant was supplied by the government on short-term lease or on an agency basis.

For no very good reason (other than that the board minutes happen to be more detailed) the record of Powers' war work is better documented. Powers was one of thousands of firms engaged on the manufacture of ammunition components, almost all of which was sub-contracted to the light-engineering industry. Within the first two months of war, Brougham had secured contracts for bomb parts and fuses amounting to over £100 000. The ability to manufacture fuses and other ammunition components was very widely available in the light-engineering industry, since the main equipment needed was ordinary automatic screw-making machines and capstan lathes. Brougham found it difficult at first to get work that made full use of Powers' much higher capability in precision mechanical engineering; for example a visit to the Ministry of Aircraft Production in Harrogate resulted in nothing more than a listing for 'nuts, bolts and terminals'.[27] This was frustrating. First, because there was a wish to serve the war effort in the best possible way; and second, because there was a need to keep morale within the factory high, to prevent the drift of skilled workpeople into the fighting forces.

In fact Brougham's worries were short-lived, and the government's administrators of war production soon found contracts that matched the company's skills. By the summer of 1940 Powers was working on a Ministry of Supply contract for computing units and predictor gears for fire-control (that is, gun aiming) in the 40mm anti-aircraft gun, and a Ministry of Aircraft Production contract for stabilizing units. These were light engineering tasks of a real complexity, and called on skills comparable with punched-card machine construction:

Worst of all was the supply of fire control gear. Not only was the productive capacity barely sufficient to meet the total volume of requirements, but the requirements themselves were changing as a result of the rapid progress of design. Especially troublesome was the provision of fire control gear for light anti-aircraft guns.[28]

Powers' background of producing rapidly evolving punched-card machinery must have made it particularly suited to making fire-control apparatus.

In July 1940 £75 000 debentures were issued to fund further war contracts; these included a contract for 1200 stabilizer units, which must have represented a significant fraction of national production. The lower-grade work of fuse manufacture for the Admiralty continued to soak up any spare capacity, and hundreds of thousands were delivered. To achieve this output, while maintaining Powers production, weekend working was introduced in the summer of 1940, and all holidays were cancelled; this was of course the darkest period of the war 'when Britain stood alone', and there can be no doubt that the sacrifice was willingly made.

In 1942 additional factory accommodation was acquired to take on further war contracts. At one point the production of anti-aircraft gun predictors reached 300 per month. In addition to the predictors and stabilizers, in 1943 two large contracts were agreed for the supply of Typex (or Type 'X') coding machines, amounting to between 4000 and 5000 units. The production of Typex machines, predictors, and stabilizers—all machines of complexity comparable with that of an automatic key punch—must have bitten deeply into Powers total capacity, and no doubt accounts for the drop in punched-card machine production during 1942–43 (Table 5.2, p. 107).

Powers R&D: special projects

In the early 'phoney war' period, Powers R&D had continued on several punched-card machine projects started in 1938-39. In June 1940, however, following a visit by Arthur Thomas to the Royal Aircraft Establishment (RAE), the R&D facilities were put at the disposal of the Air Ministry 'for the manufacture of difficult and accurate components for one of their most urgent aircraft instruments'.[29] Powers would have been one of several firms involved in this work.* It is interesting to note here the blurring of research, development, and production common to many wartime projects. Although Powers' contribution was in the production of the instruments, rather than in their design, it was work that only an experienced experimental unit was capable of, and it had some parallels with the work of making special attachments for punched-card machines.

The Powers board was fully aware of the danger of sacrificing punched-card machine development to war work, in that it would weaken the post-war competitive position. In fact, Sir Frank Smith, Director of Scientific Research to the Admiralty, had advised the company not to devote more than 30 to 40 per cent of its R&D resources to the Air Ministry.[30] It is clear, however, that in 1941 and 1942 the proportion was far higher—this was patriotic, but a major strategic error, whose consequences would only become apparent in the late 1940s.

Throughout the war the development and use of aircraft instruments increased year upon year. These instruments, which ultimately amounted to a considerable fraction of the manufactured weight of an aircraft,

* The actual instrument is unknown. The RAE was, however, at that time involved in the design of an automatic sight for aircraft guns. Although tracer bullets and rudimentary gun-aimers existed at that period, the higher speeds and greater manoeuvrability of the new generation of German aircraft had made them ineffective. Summer 1940 was the height of the Battle of Britain, and an effective gun sight was a requirement of great urgency.

included devices for registering operational factors, bomb-aiming, automatic navigation, stabilization, and fire-control. The manufacture of these instruments was a very specialized business, which was limited to high-precision mechanical and electrical manufacturers, such as optical and scientific instrument makers, clock, watch, and camera manufacturers, and precision engineers such as BTM and Powers.[31] These were almost the only firms benefiting from government capital expenditure schemes.

The work was, naturally, secret; and in January 1941 the Powers factory was made a 'protected place', and personnel were issued with passes. In 1941, the company was asked to manufacture pre-production prototypes of 'a new and important Aircraft instrument'; and, more significantly, to make machine tools for mass production by other sub-contractors.[32] As the Air Ministry became more confident of the company's ability to deliver, it was asked to take on increasingly ambitious development projects. Outstanding amongst these was the Mark XIV automatic bombsight. This instrument enabled the accurate bombing of targets from very great altitudes, and was of enormous tactical significance in the bombing of Germany.[33] Powers' contribution to the project was to make 40 pre-production prototypes and machine tools for component production. This was only one of many government projects undertaken during 1941-1943. In his Annual Report for 1943, Thomas listed the government work undertaken during the year:

1. Urgent manufacturing work in cases where a small quantity of mechanisms were needed quickly, such as in the case of the Mark XIV computors and Torpedo Sights, for the Air Ministry.
2. Development work carried out in co-operation with the Government Research Departments, such as the Mark XV Computor and the Gun Angle Computor.
3. Development which we have been asked to take over completely, such as the Mark II Displacement Corrector and the Differential Unit for C.I.A. Instruments.
4. Work of a precision nature in which our accurate machining facilities have been in great demand such as Simplified Rifle and parts for various machine guns.
5. The production of special machines and fixtures which we had developed for the production of difficult components.
6. The production of sample instruments for which manufacturing contracts are in the factory.[34]

For his contribution to the Mark XIV bombsight programme, Thomas was awarded the MBE after the war.[35]

It is interesting to note, incidentally, the frequent appearance of the term 'computor' in Thomas's report. In the Second World War this invariably meant an analogue computer (although the term analogue was not then in use). Powers' experience of building mechanical analogue computers was alas of no value whatever in the construction of electronic digital computers in the post-war period.

BTM and the secret war

For a period of about thirty years the cryptography operation at Bletchley Park remained the best-kept secret of the Second World War, and nothing was publicly known until the publication of F.W. Winterbottam's book *The ULTRA Secret* in 1974. Since that date there has been an avalanche of books and articles about the Government Code and Cypher School (GC and CS) and its impact on the progress of the war.[36] The story has now been so well told, and in so many places, that the account below is confined to the more general background and to BTM's specific role.

In August 1939 the Government Code and Cypher School had been transferred to a Victorian mansion, Bletchley Park, in the town of Bletchley, some 25 miles to the west of Letchworth. During the war the organization was to grow from a few dozen people in 1939 to over 9000 by 1945. The enormous scale of the enterprise makes the long-sustained secrecy all the more remarkable.

The focus of the British code-breaking effort was centred on the German 'Enigma' coding machine. The Enigma was based on a commercial coding machine introduced in the 1920s; this was a simple machine no different in character to a number of machines developed around the same time, such as the Swedish Damm System and the British Powers-Samas Cryptograph.[37] The Enigma was adopted by the German forces for military communication during the second half of the 1920s. The Enigma consisted of a keyboard of 26 letters, and a lamp-board, also displaying the same 26 letters. In between the key board and the lamp-board was a diversifier or scrambling unit. To encrypt a message the cypher clerk would first initialize the diversifier of the Enigma, and then key in the plain text letter by letter. As each letter of the plain text was keyed in, some quite different letter would be illuminated on the lamp-board, which would be written down. What the cypher clerk had written down by the end of the process was the encrypted message; this would then be transmitted by Morse Code over the radio network. A particular property of the Enigma was that the encryption was reversible: to decode the message, the receiving station would set the Enigma to the same initial state, key in the encrypted text, and the original text would then appear letter by letter on the lamp-board. This only happened, of course, if the diversifier settings were the same on both machines; otherwise the result would be gibberish.

The British listening posts on the south coast of England and elsewhere would intercept Enigma messages transmitted on the radio networks, and

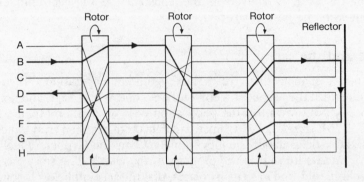

A simplified diagram of the Enigma for an 8-letter alphabet instead of the normal 26 letters.

(a) mechanism of the Enigma coding machine

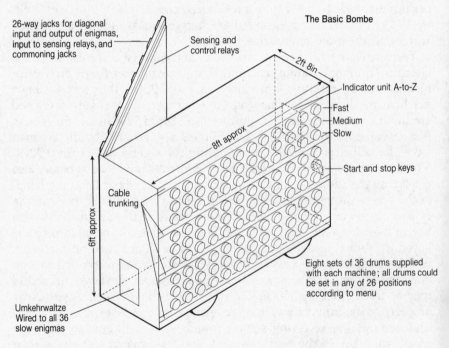

(b) a sketch of the BTM 'bombe'

[*Sources*: (a) A. Hodges, *Alan Turing: The Enigma*, Burnett Books, London, 1983, p. 166; (b) Redrawn from a sketch by N.F.N. Hedges.]

Fig. 5.1 Project Cantab

this was the raw material on which Bletchley Park worked. It must be understood that the security of the Enigma did not depend on the security of the coding machine itself (and indeed a machine had been captured by the allies). The security depended on the astronomical number of initial settings of the Enigma. To understand how the codes were broken, it helps to have some knowledge of how the Enigma operated. The Enigma scrambling unit (shown in Fig. 5.1a) included a set of three rotors, each of which had 26 input-output terminals on either side. The input-output terminals of the rotors were randomly connected, so that any letter entering a rotor emerged from it as some other letter. The three rotors in the machine were connected in the form of a counter (like the milometer of a motor car) so that as each letter was keyed in the left-hand rotor stepped on one position. When, after 26 letters had been keyed in, the left-hand rotor had made a complete revolution, the middle rotor would be stepped on one position; similarly when the middle rotor had completed a revolution, the right-hand rotor would step on one position. In this way, the rotors would only be restored to their original setting after 17 576 (that is, $26 \times 26 \times 26$) letters had been keyed in. This feature prevented an Enigma message of any reasonable length from being decoded by the traditional method of counting letter frequencies. Having passed through the three rotors, the current was returned back through them by the reflector or turn-around wheel (the *umkehrwaltze*—or Uncle Walter as it was happily known at Bletchley Park). It was the symmetry imposed by the turn-around wheel that gave the Enigma its reversible property of either encoding the text, or decoding it, depending on which was keyed in. Yet one final device, a plug-board (the 'steckerboard'), gave yet another letter-for-letter transposition. To set up the Enigma prior to encoding a message, the steckerboard would be plugged, three rotors from a set of five would be selected, and each of them would be given an initial setting. According to one source, this gave the Enigma 1 305 093 289 500 possible steckerboard arrangements for each of $6 \times 17\,576$ possible rotor settings.[38] The Enigma settings (or keys) were changed daily, and it was the enormous number of possible settings that gave the system its security: it was firmly believed by the enemy that it would take so long to break an Enigma key (if it was possible at all) as to make it completely secure. Because the Enigma was a machine, however, it was vulnerable to attack by machine. In fact, prior to Britain's entry into the war, Polish intelligence had already devised a machine known as a 'bombe' to assist in determining the Enigma key. Put at its simplest, the idea behind the bombe was to move a set of Enigma scrambler units in unison and at high-speed through all possible combinations until the key emerged. The machine was known as a 'bombe' on account of the electro-mechanical ticking it made.

On the outbreak of war the GC and CS enlisted a number of 'men of the professor type' whose task it was to solve the Enigma. These included the now famous Cambridge mathematician Alan Turing, and another mathematician, Gordon Welchman, who, along with Doc Keen of BTM, were the major players in building the early British code-breaking machines. Within BTM they were code-named 'the Cantab machines' on account of the academic origins of the inventors, but within Bletchley Park they were still known as 'bombes'. The original Polish bombes had by this time been rendered obsolete, by increasing the number of Enigma rotors from three to five; this had increased the number of possible Enigma keys sufficiently to make them impractically slow. Turing and Welchman's breakthrough was to discover, by the application of some sophisticated mathematical reasoning, a means by which the number of possible keys to be searched for could be reduced from astronomical trillions to millions; still a very large number, but within the realm of mechanization.

BTM was approached to construct a new form of bombe, and Doc Keen, and a small number of his immediate subordinates, were put in the picture about the Bletchley Park activities. The functional design was specified by Welchman, and Doc Keen and his team undertook the engineering work. Engineering development began early in 1941; and by the middle of the year two prototypes and between four and six production models had been delivered. Thereafter, they were delivered at the rate of about two or three a month. The development thus took well under six months, an astonishing achievement for such a complex machine. The functional design of the bombe has been described in detail by Welchman.[39] No photograph (if one was ever taken) has ever been released, but Fig. 5.1b is a sketch drawn from memory.

Output of bombes at the rate of two or three a month continued throughout 1941 and 1942. They were all assembled in a secure area in the Letchworth factory from sub-assemblies constructed in the main factory. By the summer of 1942, some thirty Cantab machines had been delivered, and they were operated by Wrens in machine rooms located at Bletchley Park, and in the nearby villages of Adstock and Wavendon. A maintenance team of eight men with telecommunications experience was conscripted by the RAF, and this reported to Doc Keen at Letchworth for training.[40] At this time, however, the tempo of the German offensive had begun to increase on all fronts, with the African campaigns and the great pincer movement to capture the oil fields of the Middle East. The increase in the offensive resulted in a greatly increased number of keys to be broken each day, and consequently a requirement for far more Cantab machines. Up to this point the machines had been built as a side-line in the main factory, but now a programme on a much larger scale was called for. This was the responsibility of G.H. Baillie, who as the assistant managing director of BTM, liaised with Bletchley Park. A government building (the Ascot Training Centre) was taken over in spring 1942:

As regards [this factory] it may be of interest to Shareholders to appreciate that it is possible for a British firm to hustle in a way which would command respect even among our American friends. The premises were turned over to us in the form of a large, quite bare empty building, of about 20,000 sq. ft. area, which had been used as a store, about 1st May. Aided by the Government in equipment and the provision of some hundred or more up-to-date Machine Tools, power, lighting, heating and ventilation were installed, and we were actually in production in the premises in less than sixty days, from the time they were handed to us, which reflects great credit on Mr Chalk, our Production Manager, and his Staff.[41]

A month or so later further space was taken over in another factory (the Spirella works—a manufacturer of corsets in peace time, but in wartime a maker of parachutes). There was apparently a hitch sometime during this period, when the formal contracts failed to arrive in time; on the personal assurance of the Bletchley Park liaison that funds would be forthcoming, the expansion of the Cantab programme went ahead without interruption. By September 1942 some 215 people were working on the day shift at the Spirella works alone, and 105 on the night shift; early in 1943 it was recorded that 'in view of the increased demand for Cantab machines a further 200 employees will be required'.[42] And this still was not enough: to overcome the shortage of female labour and the shortage of factory space, from September 1943 women were employed as outworkers to wire the Cantab machine drums. Altogether some 200 Cantab machines were constructed by BTM during the war. There are no financial or statistical records on the Cantab project in the ICL Archives, but the body of evidence suggests that at its peak perhaps a third of BTM's capacity was engaged in bombe production.

Operating the greatly increased number of bombes created logistical problems within the GC and CS. Both for reasons of lack of space at Bletchley Park, and for dispersal to reduce vulnerability to air raids, a large centre was set up at Stanmore on the outskirts of London, which also had residential accommodation for 500 Wrens to operate the machines.[43] Another centre was set up at Eastcote, to the west of London. The operations at Adstock and Wavendon were merged with the Stanmore centre, although other smaller machine-rooms were maintained at Bletchley Park and Gayhurst Manor nearby. In addition to BTM production, during 1943 the British bombes were supplemented by American machines made by NCR that worked on similar principles (though somewhat faster).[44] According to Welchman, some 2000 Wrens served to operate the machines.

It should not be supposed that the Cantab machines were all alike. In fact, as the Enigma machines and procedures were modified from time to time, so new bombes were devised. The machines went under names such as the 'basic' (the original model), the 'single-input' machine, and the 'double-input' machine; there were also a number of one-of-a-kind machines such as the 'eins' and the 'click' machines.[45] In February 1942, the German Navy replaced the *umkehrwaltze* with a fourth rotor, which increased the number of possible keys by a factor of 26; this created the need for a Cantab machine based on four drums instead of three, and operating at 26 times the speed to obtain the same results. To do this, a high-speed drum was introduced which rotated at 1000 rpm, the read-out being transferred via high-speed relays copied from a Siemens patent. Another machine for the four-rotor naval Enigma was built by linking together four bombes with three connecting shafts. Known as the 'Giant', the machine was too large to move, and was operated in the Letchworth factory; when the machine delivered a result, a special number at Bletchley Park was telephoned with the message 'the Giant has caught a whale', and the rotor settings would be given. The machine did not work well, however, as a result of slipping timing problems. The four-rotor bombes were working right up to the limits of electro-mechanical technology. In fact, electronic counters had been proposed, but Keen was scornful of this unreliable technology. In the event Post Office engineers went on to build the Colossus and other electronic machines, which were very close in spirit to the computers of the post-war period, and were to play the more important role in breaking the Naval Enigma. The bombes, however, continued to be the workhorses in breaking the Army and Air Force Enigma up to the end of the war.

After VE-day, on 8 May 1945, all use for the Cantab machines disappeared, and they were broken up with hammers and scrapped.[46] When peacetime conditions returned to something like normal, the end of the Cantab programme was celebrated with a dinner organized by BTM for all who had helped build the machines. But few knew the purpose to which they had been working. In the post-war honours, Ralegh Phillpotts was awarded a knighthood, Keen an OBE, and his principal assistant H.J. Morton an MBE. Phillpotts noted, with fitting modesty, that he who did the least, received the highest award.

The Cantab project is, justifiably, the best-known BTM contribution to the secret war. But there was another important activity that has received very little attention in the literature—this is the Hollerith installation within Bletchley Park itself. In the early days of the war, BTM gave the GC and CS some assistance with particular tasks, essentially on a bureau basis using machines in Letchworth. In May 1940 a job of some importance arose, and for reasons of secrecy a small installation was set up in a building on the outer perimeter of Bletchley Park. The Hollerith team consisted of F.V. Freeborn and two assistants. The initial programme of work was intended to last six weeks, and the job was completed on time; but in the interim the installation had proved of use in a number of other directions, and was asked to stay on. The work thereafter increased rapidly and the installation was transferred to within the secure area, where it was established in 'Hut 7'. The Hollerith installation was quickly set up on a 24-hour basis, using five shifts of operators (three on the day shift and two on the evening and night shifts). The most urgent work was undertaken for Hut 8 (which processed the Naval Enigma traffic). On heavy days this could involve the punching and verification of 3000 master cards, which when processed could generate up to 80 000 detail cards. Freeborn drove his staff (and himself) hard, working full-time seven days a week, and some evenings too. *

In time, a good many of the routine processing tasks were run on a daily, weekly, or monthly basis. The main effort then went into solving problems of a one-off nature. Often tasks would arise in the morning, a procedure would be devised in the afternoon, and the job would be processed on the evening and night shifts. As the same sub-problems began to recur, pre-wired plugboards were developed to handle them— these were given names such as 'multiple expansion', or given identifiers such as 'I.1.' (for 'indexing plugboard set-up number 1'). Freeborn strongly encouraged non-Hollerith people to become involved; this made for excellent relations between customer and supplier, and helped make the problem-solving easier, as the users got to know the limitations and capabilities of the machines.

The machines were generally grouped by type within the machine room, all the sorters together, then all the reproducers, then all the tabulators, and so on. In this way, dextrous operators could handle two or more machines of the same type. This was the arrangement at the time of Churchill's visit (probably in the summer of 1941):

Freeborn, who apart from his very high technical and administrative abilities, was always a showman, planned a memorable demonstration of the use of Hollerith equipment in B.P., for Churchill's visit to Hut 7.

On entering the Machine Room area, on his exit from the key punching room, the visitor was presented with a scene of intense activity. There would have been

---

* The exact nature of the work has never been disclosed. I am indebted to Ronald Whelan MBE, Freeborn's principal assistant, for the account given here. Whelan writes: 'Even were it permissible to describe the work carried out, the great range of tabulating procedures evolved to deal with these various tasks would present a daunting task to commit to paper, and unfortunately so many of the procedures are beyond the recall of memory. So it seems best to restrict my remarks to generalities.'[47]

about 45 machine operators in action and as many or more than this number of machines. Then all the machines were halted at the same instant, and in the complete silence which followed an introductory explanation was given to the visitor as the party stood upon the threshold of the area. As he was conducted towards the group of 12 or more Sorters all these machines were started into action at the same moment. They were run only for a short time and all came to a rest as one, so that their function and application could be explained without distraction.

Moving from the Sorters to the Reproducers the same arrangement held, i.e., all of these machines in action on approach, but at rest for explanation to be given; the same routine applying for each of the various types of equipment.

At the conclusion of the demonstration all the machines were brought into operation as the visitor was conducted to the exit, but all brought to rest as he paused on the threshold as he made his farewells.[48]

Shortly after Churchill's visit changes were made to the Enigma that put all the facilities of Bletchley Park under even greater strain. At this point a number of the senior Bletchley Park personnel (including Turing and Welchman) cut through the bureaucracy and wrote directly to Churchill on 21 October 1941 asking for more resources across the board, including the Hollerith section:

Owing to the shortage of staff and the overworking of his present team the Hollerith section here under Mr Freeborn has had to stop working night shifts. The effect of this is that the finding of the naval keys is being delayed at least twelve hours every day. In order to enable him to start night shifts again Freeborn needs immediately about twenty more untrained Grade III women clerks. To put himself in a really adequate position to deal with any likely demands he will want a good many more.

A further serious danger is that some of the skilled male staff, both with the British Tabulating Machine Company at Letchworth and in Freeborn's section here, who have so far been exempt from military service, are now liable to be called up.[49]

The effect was immediate. Churchill minuted his principal staff officer 'ACTION THIS DAY Make sure they have all they want on extreme priority and report to me that this has been done.'[50] Within a month the chief of the secret service reported back that every possible measure was being taken.

The Hollerith installation thereafter continued its expansion in terms of staff and machines. At its peak, the number of people employed was of the order of 300, including key punch and verifier operators, machine operators, punched-card filing clerks, and maintenance engineers, as well as the technical team developing procedures. With a card consumption of 2 millions per week, the Hollerith section was one of the largest, if not the largest, punched-card machine installation in Britain. On the cessation of hostilities Freeborn was honoured with an OBE, and stayed on with the Foreign Office for a period of three years, returning to BTM in 1949.[51]

The transition to peace

The national production of armaments peaked in 1943, continued at high level during 1944, and rapidly diminished in the early months of 1945 until VE-day in May. In 1943 victory, if not in sight, was assured; consequently industry began to plan for the transition from war to peace.

August 1943 saw a slight relaxation of wartime controls, in that it once again became possible to re-open order books (though not yet to deliver). The degree of pent-up demand for punched-card machinery was staggering: by spring 1944 Powers had a backlog of orders totalling £365 000, which represented about six months' production. For BTM the position was similar: it was impossible for the sales force to predict delivery dates for tabulators of any kind, nor for any machines imported from IBM. The companies were anxious to rebuild their export markets; but even had the government permitted exports, it is difficult to see how they could have satisfied the demand.

In the transition to peace the companies faced two problems. First, to convert from wartime production to peacetime manufacture with the minimum of disruption. Second, to develop new products. The first problem, though beset by innumerable tactical difficulties, was the more straightforward. It was clear from the sales interest of late-1943 and 1944, that the market would be able to absorb every machine that could be made. The companies therefore felt safe in retaining much, if not all, of their expanded capacity. In the case of BTM, its manufacturing capacity had more than doubled during the war, much of it at the government's expense. As Project Cantab wound down, the company was 'fortunately able to acquire on favourable terms an excellent lot of Machine Tools selected from those on loan from a Government Department for whom we were doing special work, and by this we have been able to replace worn Tools and add additional equipment to our Main Factory'.[52] BTM made a share issue in 1944 to fund expansion, which was very successful— £1 shares selling with a premium of over £2. The money was used to purchase an additional factory in Letchworth, and to buy 17 Park Lane, London, for an opulent head office befitting its post-war plans. In view of the immediate post-war building shortage these turned out to be wise acquisitions.

BTM was fortunate in that it proved possible to phase-in the increase of punched-card machine manufacture with the run-down of Cantab machine production and sub-contracting for aircraft firms. During 1943-45, the company's tabulating machinery on hire began to grow again at its pre-war rate, and soon exceeded it. Powers was less fortunate. In the year ending February 1944, punched-card machine production leapt to £738 000 (Table 5.2, p. 107), which was well in excess of its pre-war peak. During the following year, however, punched-card machine production had to be severely cut back to make way for war production of Typex machines and bombsights. This must have been a grave disappointment for the sales force, and the hardship was not helped by the refusal of the Directorate of Office Machinery to allow imports from Remington Rand to make up some of the shortfall. War production at Powers continued right up to the end of the war in Europe, and it was only a few days before VE-day that the Ministry of Aircraft Production cancelled its last order for 1000 Mark XIV bombsights, enabling normal production of punched-card machines to be resumed.

The second problem faced by the companies was to reconstruct their R&D activities. This problem was particularly acute for Powers, whose products were now beginning to show the result of several years lack of technical development. In 1943, as Powers' war-related research wound down, in the region of twenty projects clamoured for attention, ranging from a revised 65-column tabulator to a new hand punch. The resources were so inadequate that it was a question of pursuing the most promising handful of developments and suspending the rest. In October 1943, Sir Joseph Burn put all his weight behind a decision to concentrate a major part of the resources on the cross-adding punch, 'which afforded a golden opportunity for Powers to provide at the psychological moment the means to overcome customers' difficulties in dealing with "Pay as you earn".'[53] Unfortunately, in order to deliver the first few machines in time for the start of PAYE in April 1944, virtually all the development resources had to be given over to constructing pre-production models. The cross-adding punch was the only new product developed by Powers in wartime, and its cost in R&D terms made an already bad situation worse.

But beyond the obvious failure to develop new machines during the war period, there was a more subtle problem. This was the lack of product evolution over a five-year period. It was the cumulative improvements to the machines, especially the tabulator, that was the essence of the business. During the five-year period 1940–45 there had been only five minor improvements, compared with nineteen in the five-year period immediately preceding.[54] Moreover, five years was a long time in the office-machine industry, and product planning in Powers was seriously out of touch with the market place:

Owing to war, we have been more or less cut off from the rest of the world and we are therefore, unaware of the developments of other countries. As soon as possible after the cessation of hostilities it will be necessary for our representatives to visit the most important countries in order to find out exactly what others have been thinking and developing during the past four years. It would be unwise to go ahead now with a lot of research work entirely ignoring what may already be achievements elsewhere.[55]

In January 1944, the research committee structure within Powers was overhauled in response to the crisis: the new structure consisted of a strategic Research Board, to which a Technical Development Committee (the old Development Committee) now reported. Reorganization helped somewhat by bringing the R&D challenge into better focus, but it did not address the underlying lack of R&D resources. The main strategic decision the Research Committee made in 1944 was to develop a range of 80-column machines compatible with the BTM card:

It would be necessary to concentrate all available Research Dept. labour on this one project for approximately twelve months from the end of November 1944 to ensure the maturing of designs and models in time to make it possible for the Factory to have machines of the new capacity ready for sale by December 1946.[56]

This was a bold decision and, had the company stuck with it, it might even have worked. In fact, Powers was to vacillate between the 80-column development and the so-called 65/130 development, which enabled 130 columns to be punched on the standard 65-column card; and in the meantime the development of the small-card machines remained in limbo. With three ranges of machines already in need of revision, the introduction of a fourth entirely new range was unwise.

BTM, because it had never done a great deal of its own R&D, was far better placed than Powers. Its products, except for the Rolling Total Tabulator, were essentially the same as IBM's, which were the best on the market. During the war IBM had made promising developments in calculating punches and other machines, and BTM fully intended to profit from them: after all, that was why it paid royalties. Although BTM's Rolling Total Tabulator was a pre-war design, and there was little immediate prospect of improving it, it could certainly stand up to the Powers tabulator, the only competing machine in the markets in which it did business. BTM was not exactly complacent about its R&D, but it came well down the list of its priorities at the close of the war, and it would not rise to the top of the agenda until the 1950s.

6

Pent-up demand

1945–1949

In England . . . two firms of roughly comparable size competed
with one another in terms of the Hollerith and Powers systems,
and neither of them could be regarded as a giant comparable with
I.B.M. . . . The immediate post-war period found both companies
in the typical post-war situation of a booming demand for run-of-
the-mill products, a demand which had to be met despite all the
post-war insufficiencies of materials, tools and trained personnel.
Computers had in these circumstances to take second place to
more important considerations, and had to be developed at a
slower tempo than in the U.S.A.

—Lord Halsbury, 'Ten years of computer development', 1958.[1]

The post-war development of BTM and Powers, up to the merger in
1959, is encapsulated in the financial statistics of Tables 6.1 and 6.2.
These tables show that both companies expanded almost without interruption throughout the fifteen-year period; even allowing for inflation,
assets and production grew comfortably five-fold. The tables also show
that while the companies were finely balanced in terms of size, in terms of
profitability BTM was much the stronger.

The period 1945–1958 can be divided into three distinct phases, which
are the subjects of the remaining three chapters of Part I of this book. The
present chapter covers 1945–1949, the period of post-war reconstruction
and expansion, which ended with the termination of the agreements
between BTM and IBM, and Powers-Samas and Remington Rand.
Chapter 7 covers the period 1950–1954, when the companies were
coming to terms with being on their own, were entirely reliant on their
own R&D, and were first exposed to the competition of IBM. Chapter 8
describes the period 1955–1959, which covers the events leading up to
the merger between BTM and Powers-Samas. The merger was brought
about for several reasons, including the advent of electronic computers,
the escalation of R&D costs, and the decline in the profitability of Powers-
Samas because of the failure of its product strategy.

Table 6.1 BTM financial statistics 1946–1958

	Assets (£000s)	Pre-tax profits (£000s)	Personnel
1946	1926	116	c.2000
1947	2596	129	
1948	3397	145	
1949	4324	206	3000+
1950	4796	464	3900
1951	5764	490	
1952	7091	587	4475
1953	7765	631	
1954	8630	748	5414
1955	9261	891	6400
1956	11192	988	
1957	13198	1182	8100
1958	16019	1469	c.9000

Note
Pre-1949 figures exclude subsidiaries.

Source
BTM Annual Reports, 1946–58.

The post-war scene

Coming back to the immediate post-war period 1945–1949, these were years of 'repeated if not continual' economic crisis.[2] Although the most direct controls of wartime were swiftly dismantled, the punched-card machine companies, like other manufacturers, were far from free agents. The Labour Government elected in the autumn of 1945 continued controls in the form of building licences, raw materials restrictions, dollar restrictions, machinery licensing, and export quotas. These controls meant that the growth of firms was influenced as never before in peacetime by government economic policy. For the punched-card machine manufacturers, however, the effects were largely beneficial: the office-machine industry was at the very forefront of the export drive, and was more favourably treated than non-essential (that is, non-exporting) industries. These conditions enabled the companies to grow at a very rapid rate; for example BTM's factory output approximately trebled between 1945 and 1949. This was a faster rate of growth than even in the heady days of the boom period of the late 1930s.

Table 6.2   Powers-Samas financial statistics 1947-1958

	Assets (£000s)	Pre-tax profits (£000s)	Personnel
1947		359	c.3000
1948		562	
1949	4188	775	
1950	4445	701	
1951	5481	652	
1952	6431	673	
1953	7194	598	
1954	9037	600	5000 +
1955	12156	517	
1956	16025	397	7000 −
1957	18043	416	
1958	19448	557	c.8000

Source
Powers-Samas Annual Reports, 1950-58.

The period 1945-1946 for the British punched-card machine manu-facturers was one not so much of reconstruction as reorganization. Both companies emerged from the war in excellent financial and operational condition. Financially, the retained profits from the war years, notwith-standing excess-profits tax, had been highly beneficial, and both companies had all the cash that they needed from recent share issues or cash reserves. Operationally, war damage to the factories had been negligible; the manufacture of punched-card machines had continued throughout the war, and it remained only to turn plant devoted to war production back into punched-card machine manufacture.

Conditions in the United Kingdom have to be compared to the devasta-tion on the continent.[3] In Germany, the population was near starvation, industry was in ruins, and what industrial capital remained was prey to reparations. The German IBM subsidiary survived the immediate post-war period thanks to the American company's sending food parcels for its staff, and used machines for reconditioning and hire. German Powers had been dispersed to Paris and Prague during the war; the task of reconstruc-tion began in 1946, no doubt similarly assisted by its American parent Remington Rand. In France the post-war situation was worse than in Britain, though not nearly as bad as in Germany. SAMAS had been totally disrupted by the war.[4] Following the German occupation of northern France, it was obliged, as an English-owned company, to transfer to the unoccupied (Vichy) zone, where it led a precarious existence owing to the lack of new machines and spares. In the occupied zone, the assets of the company were effectively confiscated, and a new company CIMAC (Compagnie Industrielle des Machines de Comptabilité) was set up to exploit its St Denis, Paris, factory. On the cessation of hostilities, the problems of reconstruction were formidable from a physical point of view, the factory having been heavily bombed in 1944; but exchange controls and the Francisization of industry made matters worse. Powers-Samas retained a minority shareholding in SAMAS, but the company never regained its pre-war market position.

The emphasis for the British companies was thus not so much on reconstruction, as on modernizing their organizational structures and products. But these changes would not take place until the first generation of directors, now in advanced years, had faded away. In the case of BTM, reorganization on a large scale only began in 1951, after the break with IBM and the death of Ralegh Phillpotts. In 1945, Vic Stammers returned from war-service, in which he had attained the rank of Group Captain, and had served as Assistant Director of the Directorate of Office Machinery. Phillpotts returned to being chairman, and Stammers was appointed managing director. Further fresh blood was brought to the board in the form of a new works director, H.S. Briggs. But as for the rest of the board, the old guard remained on for a few years yet: W.G. Dunstall, G.H. Baillie, O.H. Stanley, Everard Greene, and the Chadwyck-Healey brothers. These men had all been associated with the company since its earliest days; the youngest of them was sixty-five, and the rest were in their seventies. The fact the company survived well enough was no doubt due to Stammers and his executive deputy directors: A. Cranfield (Secretary), C. Mead (Sales), C.G. Holland-Martin (Technical), and A.H. Haworth (Finance).

The Vickers' acquisition and the reorganization of Powers-Samas

Immediately after the war, the Vickers company took a shareholding in Powers-Samas and the most-aged members of the Powers board retired; and this opened the doors to a large-scale reorganization. The Prudential had decided to sell the Powers business towards the end of the war. The reason for the Prudential's selling the business is not on record, but the most plausible explanation is that Sir Joseph Burn, aged well over seventy, was ready to retire. The Powers business had always been Burn's special project, and it was not a logical part of the Prudential's business. It is also the case that 1945 was a particularly good time to sell. In September 1945 the merchant bank Morgan Grenfell arranged to sell 40 per cent of the business to Vickers, much smaller percentages to Remington Rand and the Impey group, and the remainder to the institutions, including the Prudential itself. The reason for Vickers acquiring a shareholding was very straightforward. According to Terence Maxwell, a director of Vickers at the time (and later chairman of Powers-Samas):

The problem which for a second time in this century had been placed before the Vickers Board, was to turn swords into ploughshares after the second world war. The large armament factories and plants had almost at once to stop production and we were faced with the major tasks of finding new products, techniques and new employment for the thousands of people who were then in the plants. One of those opportunities for going into refined engineering appeared to be the punched card systems . . . [5]

Vickers made a number of similar acquisitions at about the same time to transfer to the peace economy; but the Powers-Samas deal was the first to materialize.[6] So far as Vickers was concerned, the Powers acquisition solved the particular problem of its Crayford plant in Kent:

At Crayford the main post-war problem was to find suitable work for the fire control department with its highly skilled machine fitters and assemblers; it was the partial solution of this problem which the Board had been seeking in acquiring Powers-Samas, and the introduction of the Powers-Samas accounting machines, which began with orders for over £500,000 in 1946, thereafter averaged about £750,000 a year.[7]

Conversely, Powers-Samas (like BTM) urgently needed additional plants into which to expand. The fact that Vickers' Crayford plant and Powers' Croydon plant had been manufacturing identical fire-control equipment during the war gave considerable assurance that Crayford would be able to switch easily to the manufacture of punched-card machinery.

The board of Powers Accounting Machines was entirely reorganized at the time of the Prudential disposal in 1945. Sir Joseph Burn left the business altogether, although remaining life president of the Prudential until his death in 1950. The general manager, F.P. Symmonds, also left the company, although he continued to serve as the actuary of the Prudential. At the invitation of Morgan Grenfell, Sir Alexander Aikman was installed as chairman; Aikman was an accountant by training, who had served on the boards of numerous companies, including EMI and Guardian Assurance. Arthur Impey was appointed deputy chairman and managing director; although Impey had not previously served on the Powers Accounting Machines board, he had been a director of the selling company since its formation, and was the founder of SAMAS. Arthur Impey was unquestionably the best post-war chief executive that Powers-Samas was to have, and when he retired in 1950 the company ran steadily downhill. At the time of the reorganization the selling company was integrated into the company, so that Powers-Samas now effectively operated as two divisions: production and sales. The heads of production and sales were L.E. Brougham and W. Desborough, and the triumvirate of Impey, Brougham, and Desborough ran the operational side of the company.

A further major reorganization occurred in 1948. Up to this date, R&D had been run as a department of the Production Division. Although product planning and R&D was formally the responsibility of various planning and technical development committees, in practice it was run as part of L.E. Brougham's personal fiefdom. Impey realized that the future of the company depended largely on its product strategy, so that he removed all planning and R&D from the production division, making an autonomous Research Division under Arthur Thomas. This was unacceptable to Brougham, who promptly resigned and was replaced by a new production director, F.P. Laurens from Vickers. During this period of reorganization, finance was also centralized as a fourth major division.

Expansion

When, during 1944, the restrictions on office-machinery sales had been slightly relaxed, the extent of what was popularly known as 'pent-up demand' became apparent. This demand applied across the whole spectrum of manufacture, but the extent in office machinery was particularly acute; not only had the market been starved of office machinery throughout the war period, but the efficiency drives of war production and the shortage of clerical staff had greatly increased the demand:

The necessity for the efficient administration and control of the nation-wide war effort has been responsible for the intensive application of mechanised methods in the office . . . We learnt in the war how to tool-up our offices to match the prodigious tool-up of our factories.[8]

The pent-up demand for office machinery of all kinds was a great opportunity for the manufacturers. In the budget of spring 1946 purchase tax on office machinery was abolished, stimulating demand further, although supplies were strictly allocated to essential industries by a Ministry of Supply licensing system. In happier times the demand might have been satisfied by American imports, but following the abrupt ending of lease-lend in August 1945 the country had no dollars to spend. The British office-machine manufacturers thus found themselves, for a period of about two years, in a seller's market of an undreamed-of extent. Quite simply, the manufacturers could sell all that they could make: this was true even if the equipment was of an old-fashioned pre-war design, since although the latest American machines may have been superior, they were not to be had in Britain.

The office-machine manufacturers were actively encouraged by the government to increase their manufacturing capacity, since this helped the balance of payments, first by substituting for imports, and second by contributing to exports. The industry was generously treated in terms of building licences and transport, and priority was given in the allocation of raw materials. (Incidentally, office machinery was very attractive from a 'value added' point of view, because it consumed very little steel compared with the motor industry, for example.)

The apparent ease with which the industry expanded tends to under-emphasize what was in fact a most difficult period for manufacturing of every description. In the case of BTM it had been decided at the end of the war to double production with all speed (this was no doubt the reason that Phillpotts brought in Briggs as production director; he died in 1946, however, and was replaced by another external appointment, J.A. Davies).[9] The immediate priority for BTM, a fact realized even before the end of the war, was to manufacture at home those machines imported from IBM. Although there were long-term profit advantages to the company in local manufacture, it was the shortage of dollars that was the main spur. In September 1945, following the end of lease-lend, BTM technical personnel were sent to New York to bring back the plans for reproducing punches, collators, and interpreters which had formerly been imported.

There was only a modest scope for expansion at BTM's main (No. 1) Letchworth factory, and its second Letchworth factory was entirely given over to card production. To improve its position, the company took a majority shareholding in Challand Ltd, a local manufacturer of machine tools, in 1945, and it sought to sub-contract as much production as possible. Punched-card machines were essentially of two kinds: standard and non-standard machines. The standard machines, whose design never varied (sorters, collators, key punches, etc.), were increasingly sub-contracted to manufacturers with spare capacity following the lapsing of war contracts. The Letchworth factory continued to make non-standard machines, which included tabulators and all 'special' machines made to the requirements of customers. The tabulator was in fact a surprisingly non-standard machine, since the number of counters and printing arrange-ments (and therefore the rental) were tailored to the needs of the installa-tion. This meant that very close supervision was needed over manufacture and assembly, and this made it unsuitable for sub-contracting. Table 6.3 shows tabulator production at Letchworth over the period 1945 to 1950, and clearly indicates the rate of increase in BTM's total production. Powers

Table 6.3 BTM tabulator production, 1945-50

Year of production	1945	1946	1947	1948	1949	1950
Printing tabulators	98	138	168	212	244	244

Source
'Tabulating Machinery on Hire', 21 July 1955, BTM Board Papers.

adopted an essentially similar sub-contracting strategy. All tabulators and non-standard machines continued to be made at Croydon, while sorters and key punches were made at Vickers' Crayford plant. By 1947 the Crayford output contributed about one-third of Powers total production.

Towards the middle of 1946, following the abolition of purchase tax on office machinery in the spring, the volume of unfulfilled orders in the industry began to rise dramatically. The Powers-Samas order book at this time amounted to about two years of total output, a situation which Impey described as 'quite out of hand and most serious'.[10] There were two ways to deal with this situation. The first was to reduce the sales effort, to prevent the situation deteriorating further. The sales force was discouraged from taking on new prospects, and encouraged instead to concentrate on selling ancillary (that is, sub-contracted) machines to existing installations. Various kinds of rationing also had to be introduced, and advertising was stopped. The effect on the morale of the sales force was not good.

The second way of reducing unfulfilled orders was to increase production yet further. Both companies streamlined production methods within their own factories. There was ample scope for improvement, because the surviving pre-war practices and the 'cost-plus' mentality of servicing war contracts had made the factory administration somewhat casual over budgeting and stock levels. Neither Powers nor BTM had an efficient costing system. (Here was an example of cobblers' children being the worst shod: the office-machinery industry has not always been at the forefront in applying mechanization to its own industry.) In the case of BTM the engineering consultancy P.E. Ltd was brought in in 1947 to implement a production, planning, and control system. In Powers, F.R.M. de Paula, a director on the main board and one of the country's leading authorities on production control,[11] developed a comprehensive system for costing, forecasting, and budgeting with the Powers accountant S. Rae. Incentive and bonus schemes were also introduced, which increased output (and wages and prices).

Of course all these schemes foundered from time to time owing to the dislocation of industry during the difficult post-war years. There continued to be occasional shortages; for example BTM had difficulty in obtaining enamelled copper wire to make its relays, the order books of manufacturers being filled up to three years ahead. Machine tools, run down during the war, were replaced only gradually. The most notorious of the problems of the post-war period was the fuel crisis of the winter of 1947. Workers had to be laid off for a period of weeks, although card production was maintained as an 'essential service'. Powers estimated that the fuel crisis cost it £85 000 in lost production.[12] Since workers continued to be paid for a 34-hour week, this was a substantial loss; but the fair treatment was good for morale.

Research and Development

During the war, R&D had been held back, and the companies therefore inevitably began the post-war period marketing machines which had developed negligibly since the end of the 1930s. The immediate post-war years served only to aggravate this situation, for two reasons. First, the existence of the seller's market deflected the attention of both boards from the underlying weakness: to judge by the board minutes, the research issue scarcely surfaced until about 1948. Second, many of the development resources in the companies had to be diverted into satisfying the demand for non-standard machines or tooling-up for increased manufacture, rather than being devoted to their true purpose of prototyping new machines.

Of the two companies, BTM was in the less serious position, since it could ultimately derive its R&D from IBM. Such development as it did of its own merely contributed to its profitability, and where it fell short IBM could be relied upon to make up the difference. In a mid-1948 memo to the board, technical director C.G. Holland-Martin reported on progress of the two main new developments within the company: a new tabulator and an automatic key punch (these later emerged as the 900-series tabulator, and the Keystor punch).[13] The need for a new tabulator was the highest priority. In 1947 IBM had introduced its model 407 tabulator, which was superior in every way to BTM's ageing Rolling Total Tabulator. In a sense this did not matter, because BTM did not have to compete with IBM; but it was not a position that could be sustained indefinitely. In retrospect, perhaps a more worrying fact was that BTM chose to develop its own tabulator, rather than to take advantage of IBM's designs. Although BTM saved some royalty payments by making its own tabulator, it was more truthfully an example of the not-invented-here syndrome. By contrast, the automatic key punch was a relatively easy and unadventurous development, which was intended to substitute for the American model and hence avoid royalty payments. In retrospect, the most significant development, which came well down the list of priorities at the time, was an electronic multiplier. It was realized that electronics would be important, and the company had dipped a toe, though no more, into the water; but even this was opposed by Doc Keen, who continued to advocate electro-mechanical technology.

Within Powers, at about the same time, the main development was still the full range of 80-column equipment. The 80-column development had begun in the war years, but since the average time from inception to production was a leisurely eight years,[14] the machines would not be available until the early 1950s. Most of the remaining research effort was devoted to a new tabulator. A whole range of improvements to the tabulator were greatly needed, since the Powers tabulator was woefully inadequate even by the standards of the ageing BTM tabulator. Perhaps the most serious disadvantage was its mechanical connection box, which was far less flexible than the BTM automatic plug board; and one research programme aimed to replace this with an electrical system. It was also necessary to incorporate improvements in the printing, counter, and paper-feed mechanisms, all of which were showing signs of age. In short, the Powers tabulator was too slow, it was inflexible, and the print quality was poor; it was also only 65-column. The most interesting innovation in the tabulator was to separate the printing and arithmetic features into two separate mechanisms, to give 'two standard types of machine instead of the present day cumbersome tabulator'.[15] This may have been an interesting concept from the design and production point of view, but it did not address the short-term problems of the BTM competition.

During the first half of 1948, Arthur Impey became seriously worried about the inbred nature of the research of the company:

Powers only make one product, and their future success depends in very large measure upon their correct appreciation and anticipation of the needs of the market *many years ahead*. If they only follow competition or customers' demands, they will slowly but surely lose ground and prestige. Research is therefore *vital* and on the same level of importance as Sales and Production, and today it is behindhand.[16]

It was this anxiety that had precipitated Impey's reorganization of Powers-Samas, with a separate research division, described earlier.

The new research division enabled a much closer collaboration between production, sales, R&D, and product planning (or 'commercial research', as it was then still known). One of the first-fruits of the new structure was the decision to update the entire range of 36-column machines, the bread and butter of the Powers business. A new range using 40-column cards was announced as Powers Forty in 1950, after an elapsed time of about two years. Another development was the Powers Three tabulator, which filled a sales void identified by the commercial research department between the Powers One and Powers Four tabulators; this too was developed rapidly, and announced in 1949. There remained, however, one most serious weakness in Powers' research policy: this was the failure to introduce any serious electronics research. Here Powers was at a grave disadvantage compared with BTM. Although BTM's experience was remote from electronics, it was at least electrical, there was a willingness to become involved, and there was the example of IBM to follow. For Powers, steeped in decades of mechanical engineering tradition, electronics was wholly alien to its culture and experience. The company never really made the transition to the new technology.

The economic crisis and the export drive

Even before the war ended, the need for exports in the post-war period was in the air. In July 1944 a correspondent of the magazine *Office Equipment Industry* noted: 'Gone are the days when exports can be confined to the surplus over the needs of the Home market. We shall have to export to live!'[17] The post-war years were overshadowed by the persistent balance-of-payments crisis that began with the ending of lease-lend in August 1945. The government immediately began an export drive aimed at increasing export quotas to 150 per cent of the level of 1938 (later increased to 175 per cent). The exporting industries, given priority for materials, labour, and shipping, by and large performed extraordinarily well.

But no industry performed better than the office-machine industry, of which a Minister of Supply was subsequently able to say 'It would be hard to find an industry whose post-war expansion has been either more rapid or more successful than that of the office equipment manufacturers'.[18] Table 6.4 shows the export performance of the British office-machine

Table 6.4 UK office-machine exports, selected years, 1938–1949

	1938	1945	1948	1949
Total (£000s)	2100	4000	12199	15972
Export (£000s)	618	600	3637	3955

Source
Board of Trade, *Digest of Statistics*, as cited in *Office Equipment Industry*, *passim*.

industry. Within a year of the war's ending exports were running at nearly six times the 1938 figure: this was an extraordinary achievement, even allowing for the fact that the pre-war export performance had been poor. To some extent the situation was helped by the dollar shortage, which was almost universal. For example Denmark banned American imports altogether, so that Powers was able to take up the business that IBM could not satisfy.[19] Table 6.5 shows Powers-Samas' export statistics for the post-war period, with the pre-war figures for comparison. (The export performance of BTM was broadly comparable, but the fact that machines were rented rather than sold makes interpretation difficult.) The immediate post-war exports for 1946 were spectacularly good: by holding back home demand, nearly 50 per cent of output was exported. After 1947 exports stabilized at a more normal one-third of output, much the same as the pre-war proportion.

Table 6.5 Powers-Samas exports to principal markets, 1936–1949

	Average 1936-41	Average 1941-45	1946	1947	1948	1949
Total (£000s)	498	516	1142	1913	1988	n/a
Export (£000s)	115	136	518	677	819	739

Note
Powers-Samas' principal export markets, in order of size, were: Scandinavia, Australia, South Africa, Eire, Middle East, and India.

Sources
Powers-Samas Board Minutes and Deputy Chairman's Conference Papers, 1946-50, *passim*.

During 1947 Britain's balance-of-payments crisis worsened, in spite of the efforts of exporters. The situation was exacerbated by the fuel crisis of early 1947, which cost the country £200 million in lost exports. In summer 1947 the dollar shortage reached acute proportions, and inflation was becoming a concern. The government's response was to urge the exporting industries to greater efforts yet, to abandon sterling/dollar convertibility, and to give up its post-war cheap-money policy.[20] To stem the outflow of dollars, the government encouraged American industry to establish manufacture in Britain, offering ready-built factories in the 'distressed areas'. The first American office-machine company to arrive was NCR in 1947, with a plant in Dundee to manufacture accounting machines and cash registers; by 1950 it had been joined by several other American companies.

At this time the seller's market for BTM and Powers was still at its height, both at home and overseas. In 1947 BTM had increased its authorized capital and borrowing limits in readiness for expansion, and negotiated for a distressed area factory in Castlereagh, Belfast. The economic gloom made a share issue difficult, so that a £2.5 million loan was negotiated from the government-sponsored Finance Corporation for Industry, at favourable terms, and from Barclays Bank.* Negotiating loans of the order of £2.5 million was somewhat beyond the experience of BTM's board, but it was able to persuade Edward Holland-Martin (C.G.'s brother) to join the board and lead negotiations. Edward Holland-Martin, besides being a director of the family bank, had been a board member of the Bank of England prior to its nationalization in 1948; he remained a non-executive director of BTM and ICT until 1964.

As part of its expansion programme, in July 1948 Powers doubled its authorized capital to £520 000. At the same time the company was renamed Powers-Samas, and a quotation was obtained on the stock exchange; five-shilling shares opened at 42/6d, which spoke well for the favourable light in which the office-machine industry was regarded.[21] Powers-Samas did not require finance for factory expansion, since the Vickers plants were more than adequate. The cash was largely needed to finance the rental of machines, which was rapidly gaining favour over outright sales with customers. Rental not only saved the customer the immediate cash outlay, at a time when credit was expensive, but was also perhaps a reflection that the technology was changing at a rate that made the typical seven-year period to amortize an outright sale unattractive.

There had been a general inflation in Britain during the post-war years, and BTM and Powers were affected no less than the rest of industry. The companies had to increase prices from time to time, although with some caution, so as not to unbalance the competition between the companies: 'discussions now take place frequently between the two Companies to avoid uneconomic selling on the part of either for any reason whatever.'[22]† By and large the export performance of the companies was little affected by increased prices, since they rarely competed with the American punched-card machine manufacturers on their own territory. But in fact British punched-card machines were becoming increasingly disadvantaged wherever there was genuine competition. In France, the SAMAS position was deteriorating rapidly: from having been Powers' best overseas operation pre-war, taking 7 per cent of its output, it now took only about 2 per

* Although the chairmen of industry were swift to criticize the heavy taxation imposed by the post-war Labour administration, they were not so quick to praise an innovation such as the Finance Corporation for Industry (FCI). Established at the end of the war with resources of up to £125 million to finance large-scale industrial development for which funding was not readily available through ordinary market channels, the FCI was to be the main source of BTM's short-term borrowing for the next decade.

† The ethics of this collusion, which was not then illegal, never seem to have been questioned within the firms. After the Restrictive Trade Practices Act of 1956 such cartels had to be registered, and seen to be not contrary to the public interest.

cent. France of course had its own economic problems; and even had Powers-Samas machines been price-competitive, imports were unpatriotic. Although SAMAS was manufacturing key punches and other machines at its St Denis plant, the products of the wholly indigenous Machines Bull and IBM (which could afford not to repatriate its profits) were preferred. In Scandinavia, where Powers-Samas competed directly with IBM, the position declined alarmingly in 1948 as British products became less competitive and dollars became more freely available following the Marshall Plan. Powers' Swedish agents, Ericssons, complained in October 1948:

... our rental price for 65 col. on an average will still be 35 % above IBM and even 36 col. will be about 20 % above IBM. With the technical inferiority from which we suffer in so many cases the picture still looks pretty hopeless. We will however do the best we can in order to bridge over this difficult period until your new equipment is available. I must, however, repeat my warning that it may be found impossible.[23]

Powers did what it could to rescue the situation by discounting prices to the bone, but it could do no more than affect the position marginally. The uncompetitive prices were echoed by all the exporting industries, and by 1948 it was clear that sooner or later a devaluation of the pound would be necessary. Devaluation finally came in September 1949, when the pound was devalued from $4.00 to $2.80.

Termination of the Remington Rand and IBM agreements

On Sunday 18 September 1949 Sir Stafford Cripps, Chancellor of the Exchequer, broadcast to the nation on the devaluation:

I do appeal most earnestly and with all my strength to our manufacturers and exporters to redouble their efforts to sell their goods to the dollar markets . . . This is a step that we cannot and shall not repeat. It provides a great and immediate opportunity—let us seize it eagerly and with both hands.[24]

The effect of the devaluation of 30 per cent, generally agreed to be 10 per cent more than necessary, was to fully restore the competitiveness of British exports. For Powers-Samas in particular it meant that its small-card machines, whose competitiveness with IBM's 80-column machines had gradually been eroded, were now once more good value for money.

It was against the background of this 'great and immediate opportunity' that a month later, in October 1949, Desborough led a Powers-Samas mission to New York to renegotiate the Remington Rand agreement. The existing agreement provided three benefits for the two companies. First, there was the territorial agreement by which they avoided competition with one another. Second, they were empowered to act as agents for one another's products in their own territories. Third, the agreement provided for the exchange of technical information.

By autumn 1949 it was clear that the days of the first benefit, the territorial agreements, were numbered. The Remington Rand and Powers-Samas agreement was in fact at that time under review in the light of the Sherman Antitrust Act: 'Washington had told them that whilst the Agreement was not illegal such Agreements (including the similar Agreement of I.B.M. with B.T.M.) were "poisonous" to the United States Government'.[25] The second benefit, of acting as agents for one another's goods, had never operated satisfactorily for the simple reason that it was in neither company's interest to sell the other company's machines if its own could conceivably do the job. Over the years Remington Rand had sold only a negligible amount of Powers-Samas small-card equipment, and none of it in the United States, arguing that in its territories prices were not a primary consideration. It had never been clear to Desborough whether Remington Rand was being obstructive or whether it was an honest commercial judgement on the small-card equipment (however misconceived). Following devaluation government pressure to sell in the dollar areas was now greater than ever; and it was frustrating for Powers-Samas not to be able to take advantage. For example Canada, with its huge exports of wheat to the United Kingdom, was more than willing to trade with Britain. Again, in South America the Anglo-Argentine Trade Agreement provided for nearly £1 million a year of British office-machinery imports, of which Powers-Samas was precluded from taking a share. The third benefit of the agreement, technical collaboration, was again an arrangement that had never been fully exploited. For example both companies were simultaneously but independently developing a full range of 80-column machines, where collaboration was obvious and would have benefited both. Since the war Remington Rand had undertaken some electronic research, but it was equivocal about giving away this know-how, as it could not see that there would be any corresponding gain.

Under these circumstances Desborough's judgement was that Powers-Samas probably had more to gain by terminating its agreement with Remington Rand than by keeping it. This was a view confirmed by the very low morale of the entire Tabulating Machine Division of Remington Rand, which was far 'from being the apple of Mr Rand's eye', and was self-confessedly inferior to IBM. Desborough noted 'One wonders how long the unequal struggle can continue'.[26] The final impetus to terminate the agreement came on 25 October, when IBM announced the formation of its World Trade Corporation, and the ending of its agreement with BTM. It was time for Powers-Samas to do the same: three days later the company gave Remington Rand six months notice of its intention to terminate their main agreements. There was still time to withdraw the notice, if Remington Rand could be persuaded to make the agreement work, but this did not seem a likely eventuality.

The notice of termination of the Powers-Samas/Remington Rand agreement was not undertaken lightly, but compared with the break between BTM and IBM it was an event of minor significance. For BTM, the break with IBM was the single most momentous event in the history of the company (and indeed for the British computer industry). Unfortunately none of the BTM participants in the negotiations is known to be alive, and the surviving documentation is minimal. This is not to say that the event has ever been forgotten, and even today the topic is a lively one amongst the elders and retired of ICL; but on the whole the reminiscences probably contain more heat than light. Even IBM's account in its *History of Computing in Europe*, published in 1967, nearly twenty years after the event, is untypically intemperate: 'The past disagreements paled into insignificance with the new threat of a rupture of relations between the two allies'.[27]

The events leading up to the severance had begun as soon as war was over, with BTM's first post-war mission to New York in early 1946. The mission, led by Stammers, was largely a fact-finding exercise, but the royalty question would unquestionably have arisen in view of the dollar crisis, which put BTM in a vulnerable position. IBM's response, as it had been in the same circumstances pre-war, was to send in its accountants to inspect the royalty account before undertaking any negotiations. In spring 1947 Stammers made a second visit to New York, and was empowered by the BTM board to concede the Australian territory, and even the profitable Indian territory, for the right terms; these terms would have included, particularly, the abolition of royalties on expired patents. Again no progress was made, although the company received a by-no-means-hostile return visit from a team led by T.J. Watson Jr in 1947, when some concessions were made. BTM, for example, undertook to rent rather than sell its ancillary equipment (notably reproducing and summary punches), as was intended by the spirit of the agreement. On its part IBM actively considered the co-ordination of production between BTM's UK plant and the IBM plant in France, and even contemplated a jointly-owned factory in Britain. During the next year, while IBM ruminated on the royalty question, Stammers reported to the board: 'In the meantime, every effort is being made to maintain the friendliest relations and to encourage them to supply the maximum amount of auxiliary equipment for which dollars have been authorised, with the minimum delay'.[28]

When it came, in early 1949, IBM's considered response, from the office of T.J. Watson Sr, was a bomb-shell. The letter laid down three claims:

1. That your Company has not carried on its business in accordance with the wording of the Agreement of March 31st. 1908 . . . which agreement states that B.T.M. will proceed 'to introduce and develop the said business within the territory and will use its best efforts to make the business of renting the said tabulating and sorting machines and of selling the said cards and punches extensive and profitable.'
2. That B.T.M. has wrongfully deducted income tax to the extent of $1,465,087.65 before remitting royalties.
3. That B.T.M. has underpaid royalties on apparatus and cards to the extent of $353,333.[29]

In short, and in spite of the recent friendly relations, IBM's position had altered not one iota since the 1930s, except in so far as the amounts of the claims had grown larger. The response of the BTM board is not recorded, but it must have been incredulity. The board could have had little doubt of the strength of its position, but none the less took legal advice. On the allegation that BTM had failed to develop the business, the legal view was:

. . . on the facts as brought before us such as that in the last ten years (using round figures) B.T.M.'s turnover, approximately two-thirds of which is applicable to home trade and one-third to overseas trade, has increased from £477,000 to £1,761,000 its profits from £46,000 to £161,000 and the gross royalties paid in the same period from £66,000 in 1938 to £276,000 in 1948, we have no hesitation in saying that no special jury or judge in this country would hold that there was any foundation for the claim.[30]

That IBM could not claim for the deduction for income tax from royalties must have seemed equally beyond question. The legal advice was the same as it had been in 1926, when opinion was first sought: 'the Income Tax Act of 1918 not only entitle[s] B.T.M. to deduct income tax before paying royalties but make[s] any claim for payment in full void in English law'.[31] This opinion was subsequently confirmed by Sir Walter Monkton QC, and there can scarcely have been a higher authority. IBM's third claim, on the underpayment of royalties on BTM attachments, possibly had some substance; but the amount involved was much less than IBM claimed.*

The result of Watson's reply was that relations between the companies sank to their lowest ebb. In September 1949, 'Recognising that the Company may now have reached a turning-point in its affairs' Phillpotts and Stammers, accompanied by their legal advisor Sir Sam Brown, made

---

* The total IBM claim was eventually settled out of court in 1952 for a sum of £60 000.

one final mission to New York.[32] Phillpotts and Stammers went to New York, not to break the agreement, but to try to modify it. IBM, however, had already decided to disengage from the agreement if it was possible, and was willing to offer BTM terms that, on the surface, were not ungenerous. The terms were that in exchange for the cancellation of the agreement, BTM would be free to sell or rent its products, it would no longer have to pay royalties to IBM, and it could continue to use all its patents filed up to the date of the termination; moreover IBM would honour existing orders for machines and the transfer of technical information. These terms were probably ones that BTM would have been pleased to accept at any previous time in its history if it could have got them. On 14 October Thomas J. Watson Sr and Sir Ralegh Phillpotts signed the termination of the agreement. It was estimated that BTM would save some £300 000 a year in royalty payments. A few days later BTM issued a press release:

... The financial benefits immediately accruing to the Company in the new circumstances will be devoted to strengthening the business in every direction necessary to meet competition.

The Management not only have every confidence in the skill, determination and loyalty of their employees in every Division, Branch and Section of the Company to meet the problems that arise from the Company's independence, but believe that they, in company with the Management, will welcome this opportunity of proving that British effort and British skill can be matched successfully against any competitor in our business, whether national or international.[33]

What IBM gained from the termination of the agreement, of course, was a considerably increased sales territory, which now encompassed the whole world.[34] On 25 October 1949 it announced the formation of the IBM World Trade Corporation.

In retrospect, it can be seen that BTM's decision to break with IBM was the greatest mistake the company ever made. Because of IBM's anti-trust position, BTM had a far stronger hand than Phillpotts or Stammers ever realized, and they could have got much, much better terms than they did. As it was, for a sum that amounted to a mere £300 000 a year, it had cut itself off from IBM's R&D at the very moment that electronic accounting machines and computers would call for unprecedented financial and technical resources.

Electronic machines

1950–1954

'Electronic' is possibly a somewhat overworked designation for all developments involving electric currents, but, nevertheless, there are many interesting adaptations of war-time researches in this field. If it were possible to take a trip through the laboratories and experimental departments of the various equipment companies, no doubt many interesting possibilities would be revealed.

—W.B. Woods, a director of NCR UK, November 1949.[1]

Two themes dominate the history of the British punched-card machine industry during the early 1950s: independence from the American companies, and electronic developments.

The main consequences of independence were that the companies were exposed to competition from IBM, and that they were now entirely responsible for generating their own R&D. The companies had a breathing space of perhaps two or three years to come to terms with the new conditions, an adjustment which was made all the more painful by the fact that the post-war seller's market had come to an end. The early 1950s also saw the beginning of the transition from punched-card machines to electronic computers, a transition that was not completed until the middle of the 1960s. Although it was not fully realized at the time, R&D in electronics was the key to the future.

BTM's reorganization

The break with IBM was a turning point for BTM. Prior to 1950, the board had been somewhat amateurish and reactive, and it had rarely thought in terms of explicit product or marketing strategies, or organizational structures to implement them. As Arthur Humphreys (who joined the company in 1940, and rose to become managing director) has commented: 'the British Tabulating Machine Company was really run by English gentlemen, and I think the business came fourth after hunting, shooting and fishing'.[2] Phillpotts, for example, had long since retired to his Devonshire retreat, and the chairmanship of BTM was his single professional activity—and a fairly part-time one at that. G.H. Baillie had for several years been putting most of his energies into his passion as a connoisseur and collector of clocks and watches, and was preparing the latest edition of his famous book *Watch and Clockmakers of the World*.[3] And much the same for the other 'old gentlemen' directors.

To meet the competition which would soon be unleashed by IBM, the company needed to change rapidly, starting at the top. The change began on 1 October 1950, when Sir Ralegh Phillpotts, while still acting as BTM chairman, died at the age of 78. In a *Times* obituary, Leo Amery drew a characteristic portrait in words: 'friends will long remember with wistful affection the tall, loosely knit figure, the slow kindly smile, the wise judgement expressed so diffidently, the natural helpfulness of one who always seemed to be giving himself to others'.[4] Phillpotts was held in extraordinary affection by people at every level within the company, and his mild eccentricity was the source of many anecdotes. With the death of Phillpotts there was a sense of the passing of an era—a pre-war and a more leisurely era. During the following year, the remainder of the old guard—Everard Greene, Chadwyck-Healey, and Baillie—either retired or died.

A new chairman, Sir Cecil Weir, was appointed in July 1951. Weir was one of the leading industrialists of his generation, and one of the very few to rate an entry in the *Dictionary of National Biography*.[5] He was also a senior public servant, and during the war had served as Director General of the Ministry of Supply. After the war he was economic advisor to the Control Commission for Germany, and played a large part in its post-war reconstruction, described in his autobiography *Civil Assignment* (1953). As well as being chairman of BTM, he also served as a director of British Enka and Pyrene. Weir was a passionate advocate, somewhat ahead of his time, of the European Economic Community, and during 1952-55 he was head of the UK delegation to the European Coal and Steel Community. Weir was an outstanding public figure, and 'was one of those men who, reared in private business, found satisfaction in working incredibly long hours on the jobs that offered him the widest scope'.[6] Weir was an extraordinarily good catch for a company the size of BTM, and he stood head-and-shoulders above any of the existing board members in terms of business experience and influence in the corridors of power.

It was realized that the competition from IBM, when it came, would be in terms of the price, specification, and delivery times of its products, and in the professionalism of its sales and maintenance operations. Of all these factors, price-competitiveness was seen as being the most serious challenge. IBM, which in 1950 was over twenty times the size of BTM in terms of assets, had overwhelming economies of scale. The highest priority of Weir and his managing director, Vic Stammers, was therefore to increase the size of BTM as rapidly as possible, to achieve some of the same economies of scale.

To improve efficiency and maintain control during this period of rapid growth, BTM began to reorganize and evolve much more rapidly than at any previous period. Manufacturing and sales underwent large-scale reorganization under J.A. Davies and Cecil Mead respectively. Another change, under Arthur Haworth, who was made a board member in 1951, was to centralize accounting, to 'result in a tighter control and organisation'.[7] Research and development was also strengthened. When BTM had broken with IBM, it was always intended that the money saved by not paying royalties would be used to develop the next generation of products, which would no longer be obtained from IBM. The years 1951–52 thus saw the Technical Division move out of the factory environment and into two self-contained R&D units in Letchworth. In 1951, Cyril Holland-Martin was promoted to the main board with specific responsibility for R&D—the first time that a board member of either of the British punched-card machine companies had had formal responsibility for research.

Fig. 7.1 shows the organization of BTM in 1955, after the reorganization had been completed. With two principal divisions for production and sales, and smaller divisions for R&D, accounts, secretariat, etc., it was the typical functional structure of a one-product company.[8] It is interesting to note that while BTM was centralizing and becoming more bureaucratic, IBM was about to decentralize and become less bureaucratic, in order to respond more dynamically to the rapidly evolving office-machinery scene.[9] BTM's bureaucratic legacy is an important factor in understanding the progress of ICT and ICL in the 1960s and early 1970s.

While Weir was bringing about reorganization and making internal promotions to the BTM board, he also made some strong and influential appointments of external directors (Appendix 2a). These appointments included: Sir John H. Woods, former permanent secretary to the Board of Trade, and an executive director of English Electric and Marconi; W.E. Ogden, a senior partner of a City accountants', and chairman of the Delta Group; Sir Walter Puckey, a production engineer with a distinguished record of public service; and Sir John Whitworth-Jones, formerly Director General of Organization of the Air Ministry. Thus in the first four years of Weir's chairmanship, the BTM board had been greatly strengthened, and contained far better resources of talent in finance, production, and sales. If there was a weakness in the board, then it lay in the technical direction, where C.G. Holland-Martin was unsupported; although talent in this direction was thin on the ground, it was by no means impossible to find.

While Weir and Stammers were busily reorganizing BTM for the impending arrival of IBM, Powers-Samas was evidently not gripped with the same sense of urgency. Like BTM, it was planning for rapid growth, but

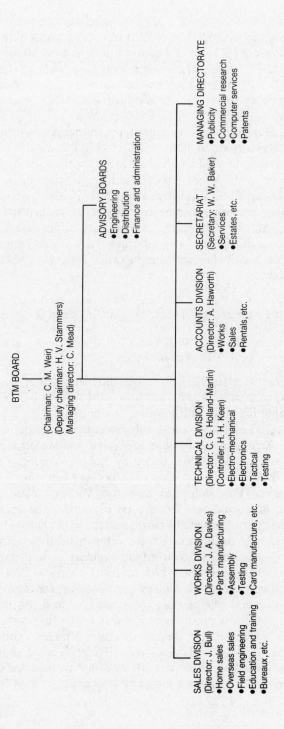

BTM BOARD

(Chairman: C. M. Weir)
(Deputy chairman: H. V. Stammers)
(Managing director: C. Mead)

ADVISORY BOARDS
●Engineering
●Distribution
●Finance and administration

SALES DIVISION
(Director: J. Bull)
●Home sales
●Overseas sales
●Field engineering
●Education and training
●Bureaux, etc.

WORKS DIVISION
(Director: J. A. Davies)
●Parts manufacturing
●Assembly
●Testing
●Card manufacture, etc.

TECHNICAL DIVISION
(Director: C. G. Holland-Martin)
(Controller: H. H. Keen)
●Electro-mechanical
●Electronics
●Tactical
●Testing

ACCOUNTS DIVISION
(Director: A. Haworth)
●Works
●Sales
●Rentals, etc.

SECRETARIAT
(Secretary: W. W. Baker)
●Services
●Estates, etc.

MANAGING DIRECTORATE
●Publicity
●Commercial research
●Computer services
●Patents

Fig. 7.1 BTM organization, c.1955

this it would do in the spirit of a Vickers mechanical-engineering subsidiary rather than as a competitor of IBM in the office-machine business. To fill its board vacancies, Powers-Samas was able to draw on the executive talent developed by its much larger parent company Vickers, which could claim to have 'all the talent they wanted in every expert side of their business'.[10] None of these sides of the business, unfortunately, was in office machinery.

Notable among the new Powers-Samas appointments was Colonel A.T. Maxwell, elected chairman in January 1952. Still a comparatively young man of 47, Terence Maxwell had had a meteoric career: he had been the youngest member of the Vickers board on his appointment in 1935, he was a director of the Bank of Australia and New Zealand, and served on the boards of several other companies. With his background in both finance and engineering, Maxwell's appointment augured well. If there was a shortcoming in Maxwell's appointment, it was that he was already heavily committed with directorships in other concerns. Maxwell subsequently remarked:

. . . when the Chairman of Vickers, Sir Ronald Weeks as he then was (subsequently Lord Weeks) sent for me and asked me to become Chairman of Powers-Samas, I raised that very point. I said, 'will I have time to do what is necessary there as well as my other jobs?' and he said, 'Well Terence, I should think you will find no difficulty—just look in every Tuesday afternoon'.[11]

This was of course a characteristic understatement, but it was symptomatic of the way in which Vickers did not see any real distinction between the office-machine business and its other businesses.

In 1950 and 1952 the two most able executive directors of Powers-Samas retired—Arthur Impey its chief executive, and Walter Desborough its sales manager. Impey was succeeded by Robert Wonfor, a man who had risen through the ranks of Vickers to become director of one of its minor subsidiaries. The ability to draw on Vickers talent had both advantages and disadvantages. On the positive side, the excellence of Vickers financial control was well known, and the importance of engineering came second only to finance. On the other hand the engineering in Vickers was very different in kind from the engineering in Powers-Samas, and this cannot have helped when the long-term direction of the punched-card machine industry was in a state of flux. Wonfor, for example, had a background in gun and rifle manufacture; however well this might have served him as a director of production, it was of little value in the strategic direction of the office-machine industry. Again, Vickers, with a virtual monopoly in the supply of armaments to the British Government, was not a sales-oriented company; there was a 'tendency to wait for orders, to assume that the company need not go and find work, at least in the way that other companies must'.[12] Consequently, Desborough's successor had to come from within Powers-Samas: he was Fred J. Nash, a protégé of the first sales director H.R. Russell in the early 1930s. Able as Wonfor and Nash were, Powers-Samas never made good the loss of Impey and Desborough. During 1950–1959, appointments to the Powers-Samas board tended to be of short duration (see Appendix 2b), most of them coming from Vickers, with a few promoted from within. As with BTM, the technical input to the board was not strong, and there was no technical director at all until W.E. Johnson was appointed in 1953. Johnson, with his twenty-year background of Powers-Samas mechanical engineering, faced formidable difficulties in responding to the challenge of electronics. A second weakness of the board was that it was composed almost exclusively of somewhat inbred executive directors, at a time when the right kind of non-executive direction could have helped steer the company through the uncertain future of punched-card machinery.

Competition and expansion

As things turned out, the arrival of IBM in the United Kingdom was something of an anti-climax. It was always realized that it would take IBM several years to establish selling and manufacturing operations in BTM territories, but even so the pace at which it did so was distinctly leisurely. Immediately after the break with BTM in 1949, IBM United Kingdom Ltd was formed with a capital of £2 million, of which 60 per cent was owned by IBM and 40 per cent by UK shareholders. Although IBM UK played host to the IBM European Convention in 1950, the first tabulating machine orders were not taken until 1953. By summer 1954, when IBM opened its first UK plant in Greenock, Scotland, it still had only 580 employees.[13] By contrast, BTM and Powers-Samas each had over 5000 employees. Even allowing for the fact that IBM UK was mainly a selling and maintenance organization, it was still on a very small scale compared with the British manufacturers. It was not until about 1960, following the formation of ICT, that IBM competition became genuinely aggressive.

There is no doubt that, had it chosen to, IBM could have entered BTM territories far more aggressively than it did. The understanding of Tom Hudson, who was managing director of IBM UK from 1951 to 1965, is that the reason for IBM's slow start was twofold.[14] First, IBM was not traditionally a large exporter of capital. Its policy had always been for its subsidiaries to grow organically—first by importing machines at cost, paying IBM a royalty of the order of 10 per cent, and using the retained profits to grow the business. Ordinarily, this process would be helped by a team of American IBM people who would develop the local marketing and maintenance operations. Only when the subsidiary had become self-sufficient would it venture into manufacturing. In the case of IBM UK, however, there was a second factor. According to Hudson, this was the result of some power politics between Tom Watson Jr, who headed IBM in America, and his brother, Dick Watson, who led IBM World Trade. As a result of a brotherly feud, World Trade was not viewed as a wise career-move for an up-and-coming IBM executive. Consequently, almost no American IBM personnel were seconded to help set up the British subsidiary. When Hudson arrived from IBM Canada to manage the UK operation in 1951, there were just six people. These six people recruited and trained the entire workforce of IBM UK during the 1950s. It is also possible that IBM's own policy towards BTM was uncertain in the early 1950s. Tom Watson Jr and Vic Stammers remained on good terms, and it is clear from the board papers of BTM that there were real hopes that the two companies might merge if amicable terms could be agreed. The main obstacles to such an agreement were Watson Sr, who would have opposed such a move, and IBM's anti-trust position.

The competition from Remington Rand proved to be even less of a problem than that from IBM. The Tabulating Machine Division had never been among the most profitable of Remington Rand's operations, and the company made little effort to enter Powers-Samas territory. Remington Rand was in fact expanding vigorously in Britain: it already had typewriter factories in Weybridge and Park Royal, London, and in autumn 1950 it opened its Hillingdon, Glasgow, factory, which made typewriters and calculating machines. But it neither made nor marketed punched-card machines in Britain.

In the early 1950s BTM and Powers-Samas set out on an uninterrupted programme of expansion. Both companies entered the 1950s in positions of great financial strength. BTM had always made a respectable profit and paid good dividends. In 1949 it had made a pre-tax profit of £206 000 (Table 6.1, p. 127), and it was estimated that the company would save £300 000 a year by no longer paying royalties to IBM. Even allowing for increased manufacturing and R&D costs, the result was that BTM's profitability effectively doubled. Even so, with taxation on undistributed profits of about fifty per cent, there was little scope for growth by the retention of profits. The company estimated that assets needed to grow at the rate of £750 000 a year. In the short term, loans were obtained from the FCI and the company's bankers, which were then repaid by rights issues made when stock market conditions were favourable. This strategy, of short-term loans repaid by rights issues, was sustained throughout the 1950s, enabling the assets of BTM to more than treble during the decade.

Although Powers-Samas did not receive the financial windfall that BTM inherited on breaking with its American parent, its position was very sound for two reasons. First, the company was very profitable: 'Our trading profit is far above the level needed to maintain the present dividend rate, and our manufacturing costs are tending to fall'.[15] Second, in 1951 Vickers acquired a majority share-holding in Powers-Samas; Vickers was a large and wealthy company that could meet all the capital requirements of its subsidiary so long as it was profitable to do so. Powers-Samas' assets expanded four-fold during the 1950s (Table 6.2, p. 128).

The steadily increasing assets of the two companies reflected growth from two factors: tabulating machinery on hire, and conventional fixed assets (factory buildings, plant, etc.). In the case of BTM, tabulating machines on hire accounted for the largest part of its assets.* In the long run, renting machines was far more profitable than selling them, and it was of course the reason for IBM's profitability and its immunity against recessions. For BTM, however, raising leasing capital had never been easy, and IBM's insistence on a leasing policy had certainly frustrated its growth. With the termination of the IBM–BTM agreement, BTM was now free to sell or rent machines as it saw fit. Unfortunately, the rental of machines had become the norm for Hollerith users, and the promotion of outright sales met with little enthusiasm from customers; this was not a point that BTM could insist on, since customers were now free to rent from IBM. An ingenious scheme was devised by BTM, known as 'Invest-ment Rental'. In this scheme the customer paid a high front-end cost, and thereafter a reduced rental; this would in effect reimburse BTM for the immediate manufacturing cost of the equipment; but the scheme was not very popular. In fact, it was not until the late 1950s that financial institu-tions began to come to grips with computer leasing, a development which followed in the wake of IBM's abandoning its rental-only policy in 1956.

Powers-Samas had always had a policy of either selling or renting equip-ment. Historically, the proportion of sales to rentals had been kept as high as possible to improve cashflow; and in 1950 the outright sales to rental ratio was 57:43. Since the average life of machines was well over ten years, this policy exchanged short-term solvency for long-term profit. Now, with the advantage of Vickers' cash, the policy was reversed, in order to bring the proportion of rentals up to about 65 per cent:

It is obvious, therefore, that the immediate effect of largely increased rentals would be a substantial drop in profits; on the other hand there is no doubt that a substantial rental income will always be a very steadying influence on the earning power of the Company, and the record of progress of I.B.M. is a striking proof of

---

* BTM Annual Reports for the 1950s show tabulating machinery accounted for 80–90 per cent of assets. This, however, included work-in-progress and stocks, so the proportion of machinery actually on hire to customers would be considerably less, perhaps 50 per cent of assets. No more precise data is available.

this, for they always weathered their financial storms in U.S.A. with less disturbance than almost any Company in that country.[16]

The capital outlay needed to achieve this objective over a period of years was estimated at £200 000 a year.

In terms of production, both BTM and Powers-Samas roughly trebled their output during the 1950s. Probably the best available indicators of growth are the number of personnel employed and the factory area. Between 1950 and 1959, the year of the merger, the number of BTM employees increased from 3900 to 9000, and the factory area rose from about 400 000 square feet to 900 000 square feet. Because of the economies of scale and improving efficiency, output grew proportionally faster.* The statistics for Powers-Samas are very similar.

Throughout the 1950s there was a steady programme of expansion. BTM expanded at both Castlereagh and Letchworth, and in 1951 acquired two subsidiaries, T.D. Tools Ltd (a manufacturer of light castings), and Collangular Ltd (a manufacturer of steel office furniture). In 1954 premises were acquired in Stevenage for electronic research and production, and a country mansion, Bradenham Manor, was taken over for a training school. Powers-Samas expanded in much the same way; in 1953 it took over Vickers' Dartford plant, and later its Chertsey plant. It also acquired a second building in High Holborn, London, for a sales and service centre.

Overseas operations and Powers-Samas' American venture

Immediately after its break with Remington Rand, Powers-Samas began an extraordinary expansion of its overseas activity. This expansion was set on course by Arthur Impey in late 1949; he was the most internationally-minded of Powers-Samas' chief executives, and it was his last act before retiring. In Europe, fairly close to home, branches or agencies were set up in Switzerland, Western Germany, Holland, Austria, Italy, and Spain.[17] These European countries were all existing Remington Rand territories, but they had never been fully exploited, and there was little chance that Remington Rand would defend them too vigorously. Further from home, particularly in South America, Powers-Samas was reluctant to challenge Remington Rand's much stronger markets, at least for the present. In

---

* The surviving records for machine production in the 1950s are very sparse, and in any case simple indicators such as the number of tabulators manufactured are misleading. For example within BTM the annual production of tabulators rose only slowly, from about 300 a year to 400, during this period; but the production of ancillary machines, notably electronic multipliers and calculators, began to account for a higher proportion of the business.

addition to these entirely new markets, existing territories were strengthened. For example a majority holding was taken in SAMAS, a share-holding was taken in the Danish agency, and a wholly-owned South African subsidiary was set up in place of the ailing agency with Mathieson and Ashley.

Early in 1950, Powers-Samas decided to set up an American branch. In 1950, as today, the United States was the most formidable overseas territory for any European company. The start-up costs of setting up an American subsidiary were very high, the road to profitability was a long one, and the possibility of failure on the way was considerable; this was true of any industry, but it was especially true for the office-machine industry, of which the United States was the acknowledged world leader.

The Powers-Samas board was not in the least naive about the problems of establishing an American venture; but all the difficulties were swept aside when reckoning the benefits of entry into the biggest office-machine market in the world. The first benefit, and perhaps the most important, would be the prestige and credibility that success in America would confer on Powers-Samas; it would establish the company as a world-class supplier of punched-card machines in a way that no amount of publicity could. Second, the American market had never been supplied with small-card machines: the bulk of Powers-Samas output was small-card equipment, it had been successful wherever the company had traded, and the board was convinced that the machines would do well in the United States; the launch of an American venture would also coincide with the replacement of the old Powers Four range by the newly developed Powers Forty, so that the time to introduce the machines could never be better. Third, Powers-Samas had to expand; if it could penetrate the American market then rapid expansion would be assured.

In early 1950 half-hearted discussions were held with Remington Rand to offer them the agency for America, but as they had already had the Powers Four rights for nearly twenty years, and not sold a single set in America, it was no surprise that the discussions quickly broke down. In June 1950 a fact-finding mission was sent to America, and a market-research survey commissioned. Every indication was favourable, and in autumn 1950 a small branch was established in Chicago. The American branch, initially with seven British sales and maintenance staff, traded under the name Samas (the company was prevented by Remington Rand from using the trade name Powers). The Samas-Forty and Samas-One small-card machines were exhibited at the Chicago Office Equipment Exhibition in February 1951, where the response was more than encouraging, and yielded several hundred inquiries. During the next few months American sales and maintenance staff were engaged and trained, and the sales force began to follow up some 1500 prospects.

The number of firm orders proved a major set-back. By the end of 1951, after nearly a year of full-scale operation, only eight orders had materialized, all of them in the Chicago area. It had originally been estimated in 1950 that Powers-Samas would have to spend £½ million over a three-year period before the American venture moved into profit. But these estimates were based on market research that now proved to be over-optimistic, and had assumed some outright sales, whereas not one installation so far had been other than rented. Clearly the venture would be far more expensive than originally projected; but the company had reached the point of no return. If it was now to withdraw:

We would . . . be placing in the hands of our competitors the most powerful argument to embarrass us in this country or in any other where we may operate. A Punched Card user rightly demands permanence in his source of supply and in maintenance; he insists on continuity of service, and that his supplier be as dependable as his Banker. If we withdraw from the United States, our eventual re-entry there or our entry into other territories such as Canada, Brazil or the Argentine, would be severely handicapped.[18]

During 1952 the situation steadily worsened, sales did not pick up, and with a payroll of thirty-five people the cost was alarming. The reasons for the failure of the American branch are subtle and complex, and even within Powers-Samas it was difficult to see where they had gone wrong, and how they could have managed things differently. Probably the dominant factor was the small scale of the operation and its lack of credibility: a single office in Chicago did not give the company the national presence needed to assure potential customers of the long-term viability of the machines, to which they were after all entrusting their businesses. (In fact—right up to the present day—no British office-machine or computer supplier has ever succeeded in penetrating the American market on a long-term basis, other than as an OEM supplier.)

In late 1952, Powers-Samas managed to make a graceful withdrawal by assigning the American agency to the Underwood Corporation based in New York. By a stroke of good fortune, H.R. Russell—the general manager of the British selling company in the early 1930s—was appointed to take over the Underwood-Samas division; although Russell may have lacked the drive of his youth, the business could scarcely have been in better hands. During 1953 sales offices were established in Boston, Hartford, Philadelphia, Detroit, and Chicago, and a full training pro-gramme was organized. The machines were exhibited at office-machinery fairs throughout the United States and Canada, and the small-card machines were taken seriously;[19] but, even so, sales were disappointing. In five years Underwood was unable to make the machines pay, and eventually terminated the agreement at the end of 1957.

BTM's overseas ventures during the 1950s were altogether more conservative (or perhaps more prudent) than those of Powers-Samas. During the early 1950s IBM opened up subsidiary companies in all the countries in which BTM operated, so that far from entering new territories BTM was in the position of defending those it already had. The most important of BTM's territories were South Africa, India, and Australia, which between them accounted for perhaps 80 per cent of overseas business, and a quarter of BTM's total revenues. Although BTM's home territory was safe for the time being, on account of its size, the overseas territories were far more vulnerable, since the overseas branches themselves were small, and IBM would very quickly be a serious threat. As things stood, BTM's only defence against the superior machines of IBM was the fact that the British machines could handle the eccentric currencies of the Commonwealth. The South African company, which was BTM's only wholly-owned subsidiary, was strengthened as rapidly as was practical: the authorized capital of the company was increased, the board of directors strengthened, a new card works was built, and the maintenance and spares operations were streamlined.[20] In India, in addition to IBM's entry, there were strong political pressures that resulted in the formation in 1952 of a wholly-owned subsidiary with a minority of national directors; and in Calcutta a card works was built and a small assembly operation set up. Very little was done for Australia. South Africa and India remained strongholds of BTM (and later ICT); but Australia was soon dominated by IBM.

Research and Development

The termination of the agreements with the American companies had more impact on R&D than any other aspect of the British punched-card machine companies. To ensure their survival in the second half of the 1950s the British companies had to produce equipment that was competitive with IBM in the shortest possible time.

Prior to 1950, research expenditure in both companies had been modest. In 1949, for example, the annual research expenditure in Powers-Samas was £50 000, a sum which represented less than two per cent of its revenues; and BTM's expenditure was probably less than this. As a percentage of sales, the R&D spending of the British companies was not out of line with British industry generally, but in absolute terms it was much too small compared with big American office-machine firms. For example, IBM at that time spent three per cent of its revenues on research, which would have amounted to not less than £2 million a year.*

---

* According to IBM annual reports, the company spent $2 million on R&D in 1944, and $7½ million in 1951.[21]

Table 7.1   R&D Expenditure 1950-1958

| | BTM | | Powers-Samas | |
	Expenditure (£000s)	As a percentage of revenues	Expenditure (£000s)	As a percentage of revenues
1950			139[a]	5
1951				
1952			200[a]	5
1953	80	2	268	6
1954	110	2	266	5
1955	270	5	309	5
1956	491	7	462	7
1957	649	9	512	7
1958	607[a]	7	564[a]	6

Note
[a] Estimate.

Sources
1950-52: Powers-Samas Research Committee Minutes, *passim*; 1953-58: 'Report Dated 21 April 1958 on Proposed Merger', Deloitte, Plender, Griffiths, and Company (ICL Archives).

Table 7.1 shows the research and development expenditure for BTM and Powers-Samas during the 1950s. Although the figures are incomplete, the trend is very clear. Immediately following the break with Remington Rand, Powers-Samas very nearly trebled its research expenditure, to £139 000 for 1950, and thereafter research spending was kept at between five and seven per cent of revenues. The surviving figures for BTM R&D expenditure are somewhat difficult to interpret. Immediately following the break with IBM it was planned to double the research activity as swiftly as possible; this was achieved by about 1954 or 1955, by which time staff strength was about 40 engineers and 120 supporting people. Although 'research' strictly interpreted still accounted for no more than two per cent of revenues, there was an enormous volume of development work, in bringing the remaining machines formerly imported from IBM into production; this probably accounted for in the region of four per cent of BTM's revenues during 1950 to 1953. From 1955, however, there was a leap in BTM's research expenditure through the funding of collaborative computer ventures, which are discussed in the next chapter.

Perhaps the most difficult problem, beyond the sheer scale of the research task, was to determine a policy on electronic research and development. The commercial advantages of electronic technology were, in 1950, unproven; but for non-technical management there was in electronics an unmistakable vision of the future, a sense that things were changing. In the post-war years, electronics captured the public imagination to an extent that was not to be seen again until the advent of 'microchips' in the late 1970s. The Second World War saw a rapid development in electronics, notably in radar and computing machines, and industry in general was under great pressure to exploit the new technology. Probably no industry was under more pressure to introduce electronics than the office-machine manufacturers. In the late 1940s and early 1950s 'electronic brains' received a good deal of press attention, much of it emanating from America. An article on 'office robots' in the respected business magazine *Fortune* was typical of the period:

The longest-haired computer theorists, impatient of half measures, will not be satisfied until a maximum of the human element and paper recording is eliminated. No intervening clerical operators. No bookkeepers. No punched cards. No paper files. In the utility billing problem, for instance, meter readings would come automatically by wire into the input organs of the central office's electronic accounting and information processing machine, which, when called on, would compare these readings with customers' accounts in its huge memory storage, make all computations, and return the new results to storage while printing out the monthly bills.[22]

It was of course easy to dismiss this kind of hyperbole, but at the same time it was clear that electronic calculators would play some future role in punched-card machinery. The qualities perhaps most needed at the highest levels of the research divisions at this time were an informed opinion and openness of mind, and a willingness to adapt and move forward with the new technology. These qualities unfortunately were conspicuously lacking.

In BTM the head of research Doc Keen was openly hostile towards the new technology, and in mid-1951 John Bull, one of BTM's outstanding managers, temporarily took charge of the situation.[23] Keen was gently but firmly moved to the sidelines as 'consulting engineer' to the company, in which position he remained the doyen of the old technology until his retirement in 1959; during 1952 a rising young engineer, John Drewe, was appointed head of research. A very similar sequence of events took place in Powers-Samas, although matters took rather longer to come to a head. In autumn 1952 the existing head of research, Arthur Thomas, was appointed a 'special director', and a younger, more adaptable engineer, W.E. Johnson, was appointed head of research in his place.

At the lower levels of the research divisions there was a problem for engineers in adapting to the new technology. This was a problem, commonplace today, that was almost unparalleled in 1950. There was really no prospect that engineers entrenched in pre-war mechanical and electro-mechanical technology could make the change, even had there been a willingness of spirit. The new expertise had to be imported from outside. In the case of Powers-Samas, an electronics group was established within Vickers' electronics research laboratory at Crayford, where it was kept well away from the mechanical research department at Croydon. Within BTM bright young electronic engineers were recruited, and eventually located at an electronics research laboratory at Stevenage. In fact, recruiting and keeping young electronic engineers—who were a rare breed—was not easy, especially with the housing shortages of the early 1950s, and it took three or four years to staff the electronics laboratories with people of real talent.

It would be wrong to suppose that traditional mechanical and electro-mechanical research suddenly gave way to electronics. Far from it; traditional products were to remain the main source of revenues for at least another decade, and the existing products were in urgent need of development.

Within Powers-Samas, there were three main research groups: mechanical, electro-mechanical, and electronic. These were also seen as being short-, medium-, and long-term research. The mechanical group was by far the largest, and its most urgent task was to develop the new range of 80-column machines. It is depressing to recall that the 80-column project was initiated in 1944, when it was decided 'to concentrate all available Research Dept. labour on this one project for approximately twelve months from the end of November 1944 to ensure the maturing of designs and models in time to make it possible for the Factory to have machines of the new capacity ready for sale by December 1946'.[24] It is very clear from the records of the research committees that one project after another had supervened over the 80-column range. In the years since the war much good work had been done, such as the Powers Forty range; but the effect was that the 80-column project had gradually lost all momentum.

The second Powers-Samas research group, electro-mechanical, was developing a 'new super-tabulator' in conditions of great secrecy. At that time the machine was known as the 'F-type' tabulator, and it was later marketed as the 'Samastronic'. The new tabulator had a remarkable specification, that promised to outclass every existing tabulator by a wide margin. Not least, the machine was intended to operate at 400 cards per minute, compared with the 150 cards per minute of IBM's fastest tabulator. The new tabulator was to be electro-mechanical rather than mechanical, and this would at last eliminate the old Powers connection box, which was a major competitive disadvantage against the Hollerith machines. The change to electro-mechanical technology was not without trauma:

Up to 1952 there had been virtually no electrical work associated with our organisation. Concentration on the Electro-mechanical type of Tabulator is therefore a major change in our outlook and in the type of personnel employed. We are also carefully investigating the change in production methods involved by the introduction of these new principles.[25]

It was unfortunate that Powers-Samas moved to the half-way house of electro-mechanical technology, instead of switching completely to electronics. Although the tabulator was later sold as the 'Samastronic', the name was no more than a cynical marketing device, for it contained no electronics whatsoever.

The BTM R&D effort of the early 1950s had a very similar pattern to that of Powers-Samas. There were three main activities, which were essentially short-, medium-, and long-term; these were developments for production, tabulator design, and electronics research. The principal aim of the short-term development activity was to bring the full range of IBM's pre-1949 electro-mechanical designs into production, now that they could no longer be imported. Not the least of these machines was the electro-mechanical multiplier; bringing this into production must have been a dispiriting task, for it was an horrendously complex machine, whose days were plainly numbered with the advent of electronic multipliers. The work of the tabulator group, established in 1948 to develop the model 901, took on a new urgency when the sales division reported on the competitive position with IBM in autumn 1950:

The situation is so serious that the Board are asked to give formal support to the project and to say that they attach the highest degree of priority to it, and to ask that all concerned shall work together with the object of producing these first machines at the earliest possible moment.[26]

The development of the 901 was crucial to BTM's survival in the buyers' market of the 1950s. One of John Bull's first tasks in his temporary role as head of the technical division was to give 'absolute priority' to the 901; but a production machine was still several years away.[27] During 1952 and 1953 the situation began to seriously affect sales, as customers deferred orders pending the announcement of the new tabulator, and production of Rolling Total Tabulators had to be cut back. This was the closest BTM came to laying-off workers in the whole of the 1950s; indeed, if the merger between Powers-Samas and BTM had taken place in 1953 or 1954, instead of 1959, there can be little doubt that BTM would have been the weaker partner.

The remainder of this chapter is concerned with electronic and computer research, which in the long run were of the greatest importance. Both BTM and Powers-Samas have been criticized for the timidity of their early computer developments. But this is a judgement made with hindsight and insufficient knowledge; the urgency of the 901 and Samastronic developments detailed above perhaps sheds some light on the conflicts of allocating resources to short-, medium-, and long-term research.

Early electronics policy: 'evolution not revolution'

Within the punched-card machine industry, electronics was initially seen as the latest phase of the piecemeal product improvement that had been taking place for more than forty years. This policy was admirably captured by the phrase 'evolution not revolution'. In a note to *Office Equipment Industry* in October 1949 Desborough gave the first public indication of the Powers-Samas view:

The new machines of the immediate future are unlikely to result in revolutionary *applications*, but unusual developments can be expected in a few directions in the principles upon which office machines operate. For example, just as the jet engine has not in any way changed the function of aircraft, but simply their motive power, so we may expect electronics to feature to an increasing extent in some office equipment of the future. The pattern of progress will remain evolutionary.[28]

Similarly, BTM's electronics policy was publicly stated to be 'A Balanced Policy: evolutionary rather than revolutionary'.[29]

This consensus view of electronics in punched-card machines was almost certainly unconsciously absorbed by IBM, which probably originated the phrase 'evolution not revolution'. IBM had in fact been involved in electronics research far earlier than is often supposed. In the early 1940s a project to improve the speed of certain electro-mechanical accounting machines had been started; these included 'the 601 multiplier, in which the operating speed was distressingly slow, being limited by the electro-mechanical devices then available'.[30] The 601 (which was imported by BTM as its model 501) operated at a speed of about ten cards per minute. In 1946 IBM announced the model 603 electronic multiplier, in which electronics enabled a speed of one hundred cards per minute to be achieved. One hundred 603s were sold before it was replaced by the model 604 calculating punch. The 604 was a much more powerful machine, which included the four rules of arithmetic, and could be programmed by means of a plug-board. The 604 was demonstrated in 1948, and some 5600 machines were sold over the next ten years.[31]

Taking their lead from IBM, both BTM and Powers-Samas cut their teeth on electronic multipliers (Table 7.2). Had the companies realized how swiftly IBM would replace its electronic multiplier with a full-scale calculating punch, however, it is doubtful whether they would have done so.

Table 7.2 Electronic multipliers and calculators

Model	Date delivered	Price	Description
BTM 541	1952		Electronic multiplier (sterling)
BTM 542	1954	£8100	Electronic multiplier (sterling)
BTM 550	1956	£13 200	Electronic calculator (36 program steps, 4 rules)
BTM 555	1957	£25 000	Electronic calculator (150 program steps, 4 rules; drum storage)
P-S EMP A	1953	£6550–£9000	Electronic multiplier (sterling)
P-S EMP B	1954	£6550–£9000	Electronic multiplier (sterling)
P-S EMP C1	1954	£6550–£9000	Electronic multiplier (decimal)

Note
All BTM machines were 80-column; Powers-Samas machines were 40- or 65-column.

Sources
Price data: R.H. Williams, 'Early Computers in Europe', *Proc. 1976 National Computer Conference*, AFIPS Press, Montvale NJ, 1976, pp. 21–29; D. Kilner, 'A Survey of Digital Computers Available in the United Kingdom', July 1959 (National Archive for the History of Computing).

BTM had an enormous advantage over Powers-Samas when embarking on electronic multiplier development, in that it actually possessed an IBM model 603 (which had been exhibited at the first post-war Business Efficiency Exhibition in 1947), and could make use of the IBM patents. Because it was a decimal machine, the 603 was unsuitable for British sterling currency, so a development team led by W. Woods-Hill developed entirely new electronics for the machine. Although there was a not-invented-here element in the wholesale redevelopment of the electronics, it was also an essential part of gaining experience and confidence in the new technology. First deliveries of this machine, known as the model 541, were made in late 1952. The 541 was quickly superseded by an improved multiplier, the 542, large-scale production of which began in 1954. Some one hundred orders were taken during 1954 for the 542 multiplier, making a significant contribution to BTM's revenues. The 542 was followed by two further developments, both full-scale calculating punches competitive with the IBM 604. The 550 calculating punch was introduced in 1955,[32] and the 555, which incorporated a drum store, in 1957.

In Powers-Samas' Crayford electronics laboratory, work started on an electronic multiplying punch (the EMP) in autumn 1950. The project, led by E.J. Gutteridge and R.P.B. Yandell, moved ahead with a confidence and speed that must have surprised outsiders. A prototype machine was completed in late 1952, and the first pre-production models of the EMP (the model A) were delivered on trial to customers in autumn 1953. A larger-capacity machine, the model B, was introduced shortly afterwards, followed by a non-sterling export model, the C1. All the Powers-Samas multipliers were technically and commercially successful, and hundreds were sold.

Origins of the British computer industry

The origins of the computer and the computer industry have now been well researched and much written about, although mainly from an American viewpoint. To understand the British perspective, and specifically the perspectives of BTM and Powers-Samas, it is necessary to review early American developments, and their take-up in Britain.

The first electronic calculator, the ENIAC, was developed in conditions of secrecy during the period 1943 to 1946 by a group led by J. Presper Eckert and John W. Mauchly at the Moore School of Electrical Engineering in the University of Pennsylvania.[33] Originally intended for ballistics calculations, the machine was completed too late for the war effort. When the machine was publicly inaugurated in February 1946 it received wide press coverage, and was largely responsible for the early public perception of 'electronic brains'. Although the ENIAC was a gargantuan machine of about 18 000 electronic tubes, its computing power was very limited, as a result of several design shortcomings that were appreciated long before it was completed. In late 1944, the American mathematician John von Neumann began to collaborate with the ENIAC group, and as a result he circulated a classic report, *First Draft of a Report on the EDVAC*, in June 1945. This highly technical report, which had a limited circulation, described what is now known as the 'stored-program computer'; and it established the functional structure of the modern computer. This functional structure is today frequently termed the 'von Neumann architecture', although this considerably slights the roles of Eckert, Mauchly, and others in the Moore School computer group.

Following the publicity surrounding the ENIAC, the Moore School received many requests for information on computers, and in the summer of 1946 a course of lectures was organized to promulgate the new ideas.[34] Some thirty people attended the course, including representatives from most of the academic and industrial computing laboratories in the United States, and two delegates from British universities (Cambridge and Manchester). Once the course was over, there was in every sense a race to build the first computer of the new type. During 1946 the Moore School team largely disbanded, one group under von Neumann joining the Institute for Advanced Study at Princeton, and Eckert and Mauchly forming their own company to develop a computer on a commercial basis. In 1946 Eckert and Mauchly were unique in seeing commercial possibilities for computers, every other group in the world being located in academic or industrial computing laboratories.

In Britain in 1946 there were three leading research centres where computers were under development: Cambridge University, Manchester University, and the National Physical Laboratory (NPL) at Teddington. The British groups rapidly came into the lead, and had two working machines before any were completed in America: a fact which is generally attributed to the modest scale of the projects in austerity Britain. At Manchester, a group led by F.C. Williams and T. Kilburn produced a 'baby machine', which first operated on 21 June 1948, and a full-scale machine came into operation the following year.[35] At Cambridge University the EDSAC, developed by a group led by M.V. Wilkes, first operated on 6 May 1949, and is generally agreed to have been the first practical stored-program computer to operate.[36] At the NPL, the head of the mathematics division, John Womersley, engaged the mathematician Alan Turing in 1945 to lead the computer group. Turing designed a machine known as the ACE; a scaled down version of this machine, the Pilot ACE, first operated in 1950.[37] These three groups were thus the focus of British computer activity; during the early 1950s several other research projects got under way (Table 7.3); but Cambridge, Manchester, and Teddington remained the three most influential centres.

In the late 1940s, computers were seen as being mathematical computing instruments for which there was no obvious commercial demand. For example Vivian (later Lord) Bowden, who was employed by Ferranti, sought the advice of Professor Douglas Hartree, outstandingly the best informed British expert, and the only one to have actually used the ENIAC:

He told me that, in his opinion, all the calculations that would ever be needed in this country could be done on the three digital computers which were then being built—one in Cambridge, one in Teddington and one in Manchester. No one else, he said, would ever need machines of their own, or would be able to afford to buy them. He added that the machines were exceedingly difficult to use, and could not

Table 7.3 Early British computer groups, 1945–55

Research group	Computer	Date	Notes
Cambridge University	EDSAC	1949	First 'practical' stored-program computer
Manchester University	Baby machine	1948	First operational stored-program computer
	Mark I	1949	Prototype of Ferranti Mark I
	Meg	1954	Prototype of Ferranti Mercury
National Physical Laboratory	Pilot ACE	1952	Prototype of English Electric DEUCE
Birkbeck College, University of London	ARC	1948	Based on IAS Princeton computer
	SEC	1952	Re-engineered ARC
	APE( )C	1953	Prototype of BTM HEC
Telecommunications Research Establishment	TREAC	1953	First 'parallel' British computer
Post Office Research Station, and Radar Research and Development Establishment	MOSAIC	1952	Based on NPL ACE computer
British Tabulating Machine Co.	HEC	1953	Prototype of 1200 series computers
Elliott Brothers	Nicholas	1952	Experimental nickel-delay-line computer
	401	1953	Prototype of 402 computer
English Electric	DEUCE	1954	Based on NPL Pilot ACE
Ferranti	Mark I	1951	Based on Manchester Mark I
	Mark I-Star	1953	Based on Manchester Mark I
J. Lyons and Co.	LEO	1951	Based on Cambridge EDSAC

Note Table excludes relay calculators.

be trusted to anyone who was not a professional mathematician, and he advised Ferranti to get out of the business and abandon the idea of selling any more.[38]

Clearly the market for computers would be a small one: optimistically machines would sell in tens, but certainly not hundreds; and they would be very expensive. This was, however, not an unnatural situation for the large electrical manufacturers, where the concept of selling very expensive equipment in very small numbers had some parallels with the selling of power-generation plant, for example. Furthermore, the electrical engineering industry had itself a need for large-scale scientific computation in product design. It was thus fairly natural that Ferranti should forge links with Manchester University, to which it was geographically close, and English Electric, whose chairman Lord Nelson was on the NPL executive committee, should forge links with that computer group. The results of these links were the Ferranti Mark I and Mark I-Star computers, and the English Electric DEUCE (Table 7.3). The first group in Britain to become interested in the application of computers to commerce was the bakery J. Lyons, which decided in 1947 to build an 'automatic office'.[39] The company was unable to interest a manufacturer, and so assembled its own team to build the LEO computer in collaboration with the Cambridge University Mathematical Laboratory. The project was so successful that a subsidiary company, Leo Computers Ltd, was formed in 1955. It cannot be said that Lyons' entry into computer manufacture fits any logical or rational pattern. As noted in Chapter 2, the closest parallel is with the Prudential's entry into the punched-card business; it was essentially the whim of a highly placed executive with a mission to improve business operations.

Apart from the LEO, all the other computers that were being developed in Britain were being constructed in computing laboratories as 'mathematical instruments'. BTM had good and regular contacts with British computing laboratories, since it supplied Hollerith punched-card equipment to most of them, including Cambridge University, the NPL, the RAE, and others.[40] Maurice Wilkes, director of the Cambridge University Mathematical Laboratory, recalls in his *Memoirs*:

A fairly frequent visitor was C.G. Holland-Martin, of the British Tabulating Machine Company, who kept a close eye on what was going on in the Laboratory, and we were always glad to see him. I have a very clear recollection of a visit he paid in the latter part of 1948 or the early part of 1949 when the EDSAC was in an advanced stage of construction. At that time the mercury batteries were accommodated in wooden boxes—known colloquially as coffins—placed behind the racks containing the corresponding electronic equipment. We were sitting on one of these coffins and I had been going into various technical details. We fell silent, and I realized that he was trying to make up his mind whether this enterprise was a mad university escapade or whether it heralded the world to come; in more immediate terms what, if anything, his company should do about it.[41]

At this time BTM's policy was to do not very much at all: it would continue to watch developments with interest, but it did not see any place for itself manufacturing mathematical computing machines. This was also the policy of Powers-Samas, although it must be said that it was a less well-informed decision. *

Probably the main catalyst for the punched-card machine companies' entry into computer manufacture was the formation of the National Research Development Corporation (NRDC). The NRDC was announced by Harold Wilson, President of the Board of Trade, in May 1949, with the stated aim that it would foster the patenting and the commercial exploitation of British inventions.[42] The first managing director of the NRDC was Lord Halsbury, a research administrator of great experience. On its formation, the NRDC acquired the Manchester University patents for the 'Williams Tube' memory, and one of Halsbury's first tasks was to negotiate a licence for IBM in New York. IBM needed the Williams Tube memory for the 'defence calculator' it was developing under contract for the United States Government (later sold as the model 701). Although the defence calculator was a scientific computer, Halsbury came away convinced that it was only a matter of time before IBM produced a commercial data-processing computer. It was vital that Britain should not be left behind, and he therefore tried to bring together a consortium of the British punched-card machine and electronics manufacturers with the aim of developing a commercial computer as a joint venture. It took six months to bring the manufacturers round the table, and the so-called Advisory Panel on Electronic Computers held but one meeting, in December 1949:

The outcome of the Advisory Panel Meeting was that both the electronic manufacturers and the punched-card machine manufacturers respectively represented that they were individually in positions to tackle the problems of an electronic computer development project as well as, for example, the International Business Machines Corporation in the United States. It was pointed out to the punched-card machine manufacturers that, in the opinion of the Corporation, they had inadequate electronic staff and resources. It was apparent also that the manufacturers were not willing that the Corporation should take the initiative in

---

* Unlike BTM, Powers-Samas had no machines installed in mathematical laboratories. The reason for this was that the automatic plug-board of the Hollerith tabulator enabled it to be programmed very rapidly for exploratory calculations. Because the Powers connection box had to be made in the factory, at considerable expense, the tabulator was not suitable for mathematical work.

launching a development project but agreed that the Corporation could usefully co-ordinate activities.[43]

Finding the proposal that the firms should collaborate on an NRDC contract to construct a computer had fallen on stony ground, in January 1950 the NRDC invited BTM and Powers-Samas to assist it in satisfying itself that a market for electronic computers 'did, in fact, exist'.[44] As a result of these discussions Halsbury formed the view that Powers-Samas was 'an almost completely fossilised organisation',[45] whereas BTM was far more go-ahead. He therefore informally offered the prospect of a development contract to BTM's C.G. Holland-Martin. Halsbury marshalled his best arguments in a letter of March 1950 to try to coax Holland-Martin away from BTM's evolutionary policy towards electronics:

I believe it would be fatal to confuse the two separate issues of
    a. developing a reliable computer functioning electronically,
    b. introducing electronics into your standard equipment.
The first project must stand on its own two feet. Out of the experience gained, valuable contributions will be made to the second project. The second project, however, will always be subordinate . . . nothing will come of it except itself.[46]

Encouraged by the NRDC offer, BTM determined to enter the computer field. Less encouraged, Powers-Samas continued to stand at the sidelines.

In April 1950 the BTM board had at last begun to evolve a computer policy:

The BTM view may be summarised as follows:

(a) That as a commercial proposition the manufacture of the small number of machines required for semi-scientific computation work is not financially attractive, but

(b) it is important that we should, if possible, avail ourselves of the research work required for the development of the semi-scientific Computer, as this may well give a lead to the design of the commercial Computer.

(c) Were we to neglect the opportunity now offered us, we might well be leaving the field open to IBM to import their 604's and thus establish a firm footing in this country.[47]

During 1950 negotiations with the NRDC continued, and a possible link with Ferranti was explored; but both sets of negotiations faded away. The proposed NRDC contract had begun to take shape at the end of 1950, when, following a visit to America, Halsbury suggested that BTM 'manufacture a small computer, to a relaxed specification, for sale in the U.S. market'.[48] BTM, who perhaps understood the American market better than Halsbury, declined the offer. The negotiations between BTM and Ferranti continued somewhat longer, and there were meetings at the highest levels between the companies. It had originally been intended to develop a machine for the Festival of Britain; but this fell behind schedule, and once that early impetus was lost the negotiations eventually broke down over the commercial exploitation of any machine developed. BTM, whose selling organization was far more sophisticated than that of Ferranti, felt unable to proceed unless it had unfettered control of marketing.[49]

Early computer developments at BTM and Powers-Samas

While BTM's negotiations with the NRDC and Ferranti were under way, the company's own expertise and confidence in electronics were increasing rapidly, the prototype 541 multiplier having come into operation in autumn 1950. At about this time J.R. Womersley joined the company to lead computer research, resigning his post as superintendent of the NPL Mathematics Division in order to do so. This proved to be an excellent appointment, since Womersley combined a considerable scientific standing and knowledge of the computer field with an entrepreneurial flair and a reputation for opportunism.

By this time, late 1950, BTM's computer policy had firmly fixed itself upon constructing a small low-cost 'semi-scientific' computer, and it proposed to do this independently of the NRDC and Ferranti, and entirely from its own resources, in order to retain all the rights to its own inventions.[50] Soon after his appointment Womersley offered a consultancy to specify such a machine to Dr Andrew D. Booth, who was building a small computer at Birkbeck College in the University of London. Booth was in fact somewhat on the fringe of British computer developments, and his team, consisting of himself and a single research assistant (later his wife), must have been the smallest in the country. Booth was, however, a protégé of the famous British scientist J.D. Bernal FRS, who had opened doors for Booth, as a result of which he had spent several months in 1947 working with von Neumann's group in Princeton.[51] Booth thus had an exceptionally clear insight into the functional structure of the stored-program computer, and his limited resources had caused him to evolve a conservative design based round a low-cost drum store. Booth's project was thus much closer to BTM's aim of producing a low-cost machine than any of the large-scale projects which involved high-speed electrostatic or mercury delay-line memories, and high-speed arithmetic units.

The BTM computer development group, under the technical leadership of a young electronics engineer, Raymond Bird, immediately began work on constructing a machine known as HEC (Hollerith Electronic Computer) to Booth's specification.[52] By mid-1951 the plans had been approved by Booth, prototype chassis were under test, and the specification for a drum store handed over to the Letchworth workshops. In early

1953 an HEC prototype* was demonstrated to the public at the Business
Efficiency Exhibition in Olympia, for which purpose a program to play
the game of bridge had been developed by R.L. Michaelson (then BTM's
only computer salesman, and later a President of the British Computer
Society).[53] During 1954 two pre-production prototypes known as the
HEC 2M (M for marketable) were developed, the first of which was
delivered in early 1955. In the event only six HEC 2M computers were
sold, but the development had succeeded admirably in its original objective
of equipping the company with know-how on computers and a feel for
their commercial potential. On the basis of the HEC 2M development, a
commercial version known as the HEC 4 began in 1954; during the
second half of the 1950s this was to outsell every other British computer.

Powers-Samas made a far less successful entry into computers than did
BTM. Perhaps the outstanding reason for this was that Powers-Samas
failed to become involved in a collaborative venture at an early enough
stage or, as BTM had done, to import computer expertise. In parallel
with the development of electronic multipliers, in the autumn of 1951
planning began at the Crayford electronics laboratory on what was initially
called a Punched Card Calculator (PCC). This machine, originally envisaged as containing 100–200 valves, was intended to occupy much the
same sales niche as the IBM 604 calculator or the BTM 550, and would
cost £5000–£6000. By early 1954, however, the design was 'developing
as a computer rather than as a calculator but work was proceeding with
[the] definite object of keeping the machine within the specified cost'.[54]
The machine was announced in August 1954 as the 'Programme
Controlled Computer', and orders were taken for delivery in the second
half of 1955. By this time the machine was to use two thousand valves
and its projected price was £13 000.

Although styled a 'computer', the PCC was not a computer in either
the strict sense of the term, or in terms of performance. Table 7.4 lists the
characteristics of the PCC and the machines offered by BTM. This table
shows very clearly that in the spectrum of these machines the PCC was
without any question a calculator. Because the PCC was called a computer, however, in the computer surveys of the period the PCC was
generally classed as a computer, whereas the BTM 555 was not. This no
doubt gave the PCC a cachet and attention it would not otherwise have
had; but the fact remained that Powers-Samas was not yet in the computer
business. In fact, while the PCC was under development, the Powers-
Samas chairman Maxwell, whose technical knowledge was slight but
whose intuition was sound, came to the view that all was not well, and
that the company's computer group needed an injection from outside.[55]

---

* The HEC prototype is preserved in the Birmingham Museum of the History of
Science and Technology.

Table 7.4   The PCC in context

	BTM 550	P-S PCC	BTM 555	HEC 2M
Speed				
cards per minute	100	120	100	—
operations per second	—	—	—	400
Storage				
plugboard (instructions)	36	160	150	—
registers	3	6	3	2
drum (words)	—	160	105	1024
Price	£13 200	£19 500	£25 000	£25 000

In March 1954 he sought the advice of the scientist Thomas Merton FRS, a fellow-director on the Vickers board and a former scientific adviser to the government. Merton's opinion was that it was imperative that Powers-Samas should collaborate with an electronics manufacturer, and in his opinion the field was led by Ferranti. The company also commissioned an independent report from the scientist Dr Denis Gabor of the University of London, whose ear was closer to the ground.[56] Gabor's view was that collaboration with Ferranti would buy the company two years of development.

As it happened, a semi-formal collaboration had been in existence between the two companies since mid-1952, when Powers-Samas had begun to develop punched-card input-output equipment for Ferranti computers. Powers-Samas' role up to that point had been a subordinate one, as a peripheral equipment supplier rather than as a full partner; but the sales and technical staff of both companies were convinced that they could jointly develop and market a commercial data-processing computer. Top-level discussions were held between Maxwell and Sir Vincent Ferranti, and in September 1954 a full-scale collaboration was formally agreed.[57]

8

Computers and the merger
1955-1958

Competition by the entry of new Suppliers into our field is becoming
more fierce and our ability to meet it depends largely on our rate of
development keeping pace with that of our main competitors.

—C. Mead, November 1955.[1]

By about 1955 BTM and Powers-Samas began to feel for the first time the
full force of the competition from IBM, and for both of them it, rather
than the other British company, was now the most serious competitor.
To become international business-machine companies capable of
competing with IBM, the British punched-card machine companies had
three strategic objectives: first, to expand in order to sustain their market
share; second, to improve their traditional punched-card products; and
third, to make an effective entry into the computer market. The manner
in which the companies tried to achieve these three objectives is the
substance of this chapter. In short, however, we may say that while BTM
fell somewhat short of meeting all its objectives, Powers-Samas failed to
meet any of them. In fact, the most obvious way for the companies to
meet the competition from IBM was for them to merge, but it was not
until 1958 that the need for concentration finally overcame the old
rivalries, and a merger was agreed. By the time the merger was agreed,
Powers-Samas had been weakened to a degree that would have been
inconceivable in 1955. BTM and Powers-Samas went into the merger
with net assets of £6.6 million and £9.3 million respectively, but in the
new company BTM received 62 per cent of the net equity and Powers-
Samas 38 per cent—yet even this, as events later showed, was over-
generous.

Expansion

In 1955 business investment in Britain, after remaining flat in the early
1950s, was rising at the phenomenally rapid rate of 15 per cent a year.[2] A
significant proportion of business investment was in office machinery, so
that the climate for expansion of the British punched-card machine
manufacturers was exceptionally favourable. The strength of the office-
machine market is well illustrated by the fact that delivery times for

British punched-card machines had lengthened to typically two years, and even longer for the newer and more attractive equipment. Indeed, one of the main competitive advantages enjoyed by IBM was that it was able to offer delivery times of six months, rather than the two years of the British manufacturers.

During 1955, in readiness for a major expansion of Powers-Samas, Vickers bought out the remaining minority shareholdings, and the company became a wholly-owned subsidiary, and was no longer publicly quoted. This arrangement, made at the recommendation of the chairman Terence Maxwell, enabled the company to borrow and expand at a greater rate than would otherwise have been possible. The company ceased paying dividends, and ploughed back all profits to fuel the expansion.

With the vast financial resources of Vickers, Powers-Samas expanded spectacularly during the period 1955-56. In January 1955 it assumed ownership of the Vickers Dartford plant and 800 employees, and in the following autumn it announced the acquisition of an engineering works with 900 employees as a going concern in Southport. The existing plants in Croydon and St Denis, Paris, were also expanded, and work was also begun on a self-contained research centre in Whyteleafe, Surrey. To finance this expansion Powers-Samas had to make very large borrowings from the parent company. As Table 8.1 shows, capital employed more than doubled, from £6.8 million at the end of 1954 to £13.8 million at the end of 1956: an increase of 30 per cent in 1955, and an astonishing 56 per cent in 1956. Some £5 million of the new capital was taken up in expenditure on plant, stocks, and work-in-progress. To bring all this new

Table 8.1 BTM and Powers-Samas (P-S) revenues and capital employed, 1953-1957

| | Revenues | | Funds employed | | Net equity | | Borrowings | |
	BTM	P-S	BTM	P-S	BTM	P-S	BTM	P-S
1953	4440	4383	6306	5333	3451	4538	2856	794
1954	4922	4995	7179	6784	3870	4711	3309	2073
1955	5419	5853	7742	8844	4626	6966	3116	1878
1956	6551	6204	9245	13849	5077	8084	4168	5765
1957	7540	7283	10728	16665	6592	9320	4136	7346

Note
All figures in £000s.

Source
'Report Dated 21st April 1958 on Proposed Merger', Deloitte, Plender, Griffiths, and Company (ICL Archives).

plant rapidly into production to meet interest charges was a considerable operational challenge.[3] In fact, as the revenue figures of Table 8.1 show, expansion of output during 1955–56 fell considerably short of target, and the impact on profits was dramatic. Adjusted profits fell from £599 000 in 1954 to £396 000 in 1955, and fell again to £276 000 in 1956 (Table 8.2).

Table 8.2 BTM and Powers-Samas (P-S) profits, 1953–1957

	Adjusted profits (£000s)		As a percentage of revenues		As a percentage of funds employed		As a percentage of net equity	
	BTM	P-S	BTM	P-S	BTM	P-S	BTM	P-S
1953	632	597	17	14	12	11	18	13
1954	841	599	20	13	14	10	22	13
1955	883	396	18	9	13	6	19	6
1956	975	276	18	8	13	4	19	3
1957	1169	382	18	11	13	5	18	4

Source
'Report Dated 21st April 1958 on Proposed Merger', Deloitte, Plender, Griffiths, and Company (ICL Archives).

Although BTM expanded its revenues to much the same degree as Powers-Samas during 1955–58, it did so at a much lower cost, with an annual growth rate of capital employed of a fairly steady 15 per cent, year upon year. One very good reason for this conservative expansion was that BTM had to go to the city for its short-term finance; its borrowings were thus kept to a level that its past profits record could justify.[4] BTM's expansion, however, was not held back only by the limits of its borrowing. In fact in the summer of 1955, while Powers-Samas was expanding at an unprecedented rate, the BTM board made a policy decision to 'damp down' its expansion.[5] There were a number of reasons for this policy. First, expansion was proving difficult operationally. In Britain as a whole, the economy was seriously over-heated, and demand was very intense.[6] The boom conditions that created the strong demand for office machinery also caused a labour and housing shortage that made expansion almost impossible in Letchworth, and in Castlereagh steel shortages were holding up expansion of the factory. Second, there was a degree of labour unrest and inflation with which BTM's management was unfamiliar: a strike was brewing at Castlereagh, and engineering workers were pressing for double-digit wage increases. Rising prices had to be passed on in increased rentals, and there was concern that BTM's rentals seemed to be ever-increasing, while those of IBM remained static. But perhaps the main reason for the conservative expansion was that for Cecil Mead, who had replaced Victor Stammers as managing director in December 1955, the very future of punched-card machines was in doubt. Thus while production of electronic calculators and computers was increased at a new plant in Stevenage, the expansion of traditional machinery was held in check:

It might be unwise in view of the possible effects of competition from electronic machines not necessarily using Punched Card apparatus, to increase this side of our business too largely on a rental basis, as we might find we might have to face a large replacement programme before machines in service had "earned their keep".[7]

This policy has to be compared with that of Powers-Samas, for whom the possibility that the market for punched-card machinery might one day evaporate seems scarcely to have been considered. While Powers-Samas went into a headlong expansion in 1955, BTM took active steps to reduce the selling effort on traditional equipment.

Relieved of the pressure to sell, the opportunity was taken to step up the training of BTM's sales force in computer techniques. In October 1956 an autonomous Training Division was formed, which spearheaded this operation. If computers did replace tabulating machines, then BTM would have the best-trained sales force in the country; and if they did not, then not a great deal would have been lost.

Competition and traditional products

In the 1960s the main source of competition from IBM would be its computers, but in the 1950s the force of competition was in traditional punched-card machines, which still accounted for well over 90 per cent of revenues. To survive the competition in the next few years, both British companies were committed to introducing new tabulators: the BTM 901, and the Powers-Samas Samastronic.

The existing BTM Rolling Total Tabulator of pre-war design was completely outclassed by IBM's 400-series accounting machines, and there was anxiety both at home and overseas. During 1955, for example, BTM's overseas income fell from a quarter to a fifth of its revenues, reflecting IBM's superior tabulator and shorter delivery. In South Africa, BTM's largest overseas market, there was a strong vestigial loyalty to Britain, but this was not a situation that could be relied upon indefinitely: 'The need for *901*s is considerable and it is hoped that we will be able to speed up delivery of these. . . . The tabulator is *the thing* upon which the whole of our business depends'.[8] In Australia, where this loyalty did not exist, IBM had grown very rapidly from nothing in 1950 to a position where it now had half as many installations in place as BTM. To meet this situation an Australian subsidiary was formed in 1956; but the only long-term solution was to improve products and deliveries.

The 901 development had started in autumn 1950, and in 1954 the first few prototypes were installed in test sites. The prototypes proved unreliable in operation, and had many teething problems. None the less, in face of the competition from IBM, it was decided in January 1955 to open the order books for the 901, and to switch tabulator production to the new model. The early 901s required a great deal of maintenance, and needed regular modifications in the field. Besides not being very reliable in service, the 901 tabulator was not a particularly advanced machine of its kind. With a limited character set and a printing speed of only 100 lines per minute (lpm), it was still a functionally inferior machine to the standard IBM accounting machines, and it was much slower than IBM's fastest 200 lpm model. At the end of 1956, when the production problems of the 901s had settled down, the decision was taken to develop a number of variants of the basic machine: a 200 lpm model (the 906), a low-cost version (the 902), and various others. These were, however, some years away; and BTM's tabulator position remained fundamentally weak.

Powers-Samas' position *vis-à-vis* IBM was, if anything, worse than that of BTM. In 1955 its Powers Forty small-card machines (which represented 50 per cent of factory output) were becoming uncompetitive, and its large-card (65-column) machines were virtually unsaleable. To answer the competition in the medium term the Samastronic tabulator was being developed; but this remained at least two years away. In 1955, therefore, the company rushed into production its so-called 'restyled' range, in both 65- and 80-column versions. The restyled equipment, particularly the 80-column range, which had taken a decade to develop, was introduced with little fanfare, in order not to detract from the sales of the existing ('classical') ranges during the change-over period. This was perhaps fortuitous, since the early restyled machines had to be withdrawn from the market owing to teething problems, and were not reintroduced until mid-1956.

In ordinary circumstances the lack of competitive tabulators would have been a serious problem for the British companies; but, with order books filled two years ahead, in 1955 the dominant short-term problem remained quantity rather than quality. In fact, because Powers-Samas had the Samastronic under development, which had a better specification than any machine on the market, it saw its position as being potentially very strong.

The Samastronic has an interesting history.[9] The principal selling-point of any tabulator was its printing speed, which in 1949, when the Samastronic was conceived, was a maximum of 150 lpm in any machine on the market. In that year W.E. Johnson of Powers-Samas visited a number of American research laboratories, where *inter alia* he saw wire-matrix printing methods under development; although very fast, these devices were expensive and bulky, and not readily adaptable to tabulators, which continued to use print-bars or print-wheels. On his return to England, Johnson devised a modification to the wire-matrix printing technique. Instead of a matrix of wires, he envisaged a single stylus, which would oscillate in a horizontal direction against the constant motion of the paper in a vertical direction (Fig. 8.1). Thus the character would be drawn in a way analogous to a television raster. This comparatively inexpensive mechanism was to be the basis of the Samastronic print unit. In 1950 a project group was established under C.A. Jones, which eventually built up to some fifty research and ancillary staff. By a happy accident, a market for computer printers had developed during the first half of the 1950s, so that in addition to a tabulator Powers-Samas now also found itself with a printer suitable for computer output. In spring 1955 the Powers-Samas board decided to expedite the Samastronic development to ultimately replace all large-card tabulators, and it authorized the manufacture of 300 machines for delivery in 1957–58.

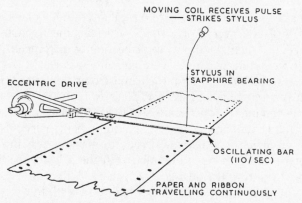

Fig. 8.1   The Samastronic printing mechanism

This was a high-risk strategy, for even at the time success for the Samastronic was by no means assured. First, no working prototype tabulator had actually been constructed, and all past experience should have indicated that target dates for development usually proved over-optimistic. Second, the finance division noted that 'estimates of cost and selling price have revealed a completely inadequate margin';[10] to produce the Samastronic at a reasonable price would entail an unreasonably optimistic reduction in manufacturing costs. Third, if the Samastronic proved a great success it would possibly provoke a flood of returns of rented classical equipment, seriously depreciating the company's investment in machines on rental. All these problems, however, were wished away, and Powers-Samas would survive or perish with the Samastronic.

Ad hoc R&D: Pluto and Apollo

The period 1955–56 was the most difficult yet in which to determine an R&D strategy; a fact which is confirmed by the number of disparate projects entered into by both BTM and Powers-Samas. During this two-year period both companies spent roughly the same amount (£¾ million) on R&D; this represented about 6 per cent of their revenues, and accounted for between 300 and 350 technical and ancillary staff in each company. The companies perceived three areas in which they needed to have an R&D position: traditional punched-card machines, automation, and data-processing computers.

The development of traditional punched-card machines, to defend their current market position, was unquestionably the highest priority of both companies, and consumed the highest proportion of the research budgets:

Whilst it is certain that new fields of business will be opened to us by [electronic] equipment, much remains to be discovered regarding the extent to which it may be employed in partial substitution in some of our existing installations. We think it most important in present circumstances to continue to maintain our electro-mechancial research effort at full scale in parallel with our electronic research effort.[11]

In both companies, the biggest single research and development projects were to produce the new tabulators, the Samastronic and the 900 series. Powers-Samas also had substantial programmes to develop new ancillary machines, including a mark-sense card reader, a Kimball Tag reader, and a paper-tape-to-card converter; these projects were in addition to the normal volume of piecemeal improvement on its range of approximately 80 different punched-card machines. BTM maintained a much lower spend on ancillary machine development, preferring instead to devote a higher proportion of its expenditure to electronics research. To maintain its competitive position in electro-mechanical equipment, however, it struck up a deal with Machines Bull of France, by which it imported multiplying punches and interpreters.

The second area in which the companies sought to move was 'automation'. This was an umbrella word that was just coming into vogue, and included such areas as materials handling, factory automation, and control systems. This was a realm of activity that, in retrospect, belonged more naturally to the electronics manufacturers, such as Elliott Brothers and Plessey; but things were not so clear-cut in 1955. In BTM a 'special projects department' was set up to handle automation projects that were potentially lucrative but did not fit comfortably into either punched-card or computer developments. Typical of these special projects was the 'Plastab' materials handling system developed in collaboration with ICI, but eventually dropped for the lack of enough other customers. Both BTM and Powers had several similar, now little known, projects.

A particularly important automation area was the mechanization of the clearing banks: Powers-Samas already supplied the bulk of accounting machinery to the British banks, and Maxwell intended that Powers should remain a major force in this sector. The major requirement to enter bank mechanization was a cheque-reading machine. Developing devices to handle punched cards was an area in which Powers-Samas had a great deal of experience, quite sufficient to know that developing a reliable cheque-reader was entirely beyond its resources. It was this fact that caused Maxwell to arrange an historic and secret meeting with BTM in September 1956. The meeting was attended by Maxwell, his managing director F.P. Laurens, his sales director F.J. Nash, and their opposite numbers in BTM: Weir, Stammers, and Mead. In the course of this meeting:

Col. Maxwell went on to say that, as the result of his talks, he and his executives had come to the conclusion that, if the Banks business was to be secured by the British punched-card companies, success would be more likely to be achieved by collaboration than by competition between the two Companies.[12]

As a result of this meeting a joint working party was set up to determine a strategy for a joint venture in bank mechanization. This was the first step towards a merger.[13]

The third area in which the companies were active was the development of data-processing computers. There is no doubt that BTM saw far more clearly than Powers-Samas at this time that its business in the 1960s might well depend on the ability to market a large-scale computer. In retrospect, however, it is clear that neither company saw at all clearly the potential of the market for computer peripherals: this was a great lost opportunity.

Powers-Samas' short-term computer development was based on its PCC. The PCC had been exhibited at the Business Efficiency Exhibition in June 1955, where some 70 orders were taken. The immediate priority was therefore to bring the PCC into production with all speed, and all other electronics research was 'savagely cut' to this end.[14] The first two prototypes were delivered in autumn 1956, but because of mechanical and electronic problems they took many months to settle down. Regular deliveries began in mid-1957.

For the rest of its computer research, Powers-Samas relied entirely on its collaboration with Ferranti. After the signing of the agreement between the companies in September 1954 there had been high hopes of the collaboration. By July 1955 a joint working party had arrived at a detailed research programme:

From the 14 "building block" specifications the first four data-processing machine specifications have been composed and it is hoped that these four specifications will be finalised and ready for development action during next month. It is further hoped that prototypes of these machines will be completed during the second half of 1956.[15]

The target date of the second half of 1956 for working prototypes was of course optimistic to say the least. As events turned out, it is clear that the July 1955 joint policy bore little relation to reality, and Ferranti's collaboration with Powers was less than whole-hearted. At that time Ferranti had three main computer developments: a large scientific computer (the Mercury), a large data-processing computer (the Perseus), and a small general-purpose computer (the Pegasus). From Ferranti's viewpoint the collaboration with Powers was focused on the Perseus computer, but this had the lowest priority of Ferranti's three developments, and was the last to materialize. On the other hand the immediate objective that Powers-Samas sought from the collaboration was not a large-scale machine, but a small tape-processing computer, as a successor to the PCC. There was thus an almost complete mismatch between the objectives of the two companies.

During 1955–56 almost nothing emerged from the collaboration of value to either company: neither a small tape-processing computer nor a large data-processing computer. The Pegasus had, however, emerged as one of the more successful small general-purpose computers of its generation. It was decided by Powers to attach its punch-card input-output equipment (and hopefully eventually magnetic tape) to a Pegasus, and sell it as the Powers-Samas Pluto computer. Ferranti found this a curious arrangement, since it already sold the Pegasus with BTM input-output equipment, and the Pluto was no more than a Pegasus with Powers-Samas input-output. For Powers-Samas to suppose that it had in Pluto a serious entrant into the data-processing market bordered on self-deception.

BTM had, in 1955, already made a successful entry into the computer market with its HEC 2 computer, and had a lead of at least two years over Powers-Samas. The HEC 2 was a semi-scientific computer, so during 1954–56 in-house development focused on a data-processing version, the HEC 4. The first HEC 4 (the type 1201) was delivered in November

1956, and a version with a larger drumstore (the type 1202) was delivered from late 1957. Over a hundred 1200s were sold, making it commercially the most successful of the first generation of British computers.[16]

As early as 1954 BTM had decided that in addition to the small HEC computer it would need a large-scale data-processing computer, although at the time no one in the company could have drawn up a detailed specification for such a machine. It was also clear that the company would need to collaborate with an electronics manufacturer, and intuition suggested that an American company would be the better bet. It happened that BTM had already established a connection with a small American computer concern, the Laboratory for Electronics (LFE) in Boston, which was building a large-scale computer known as Apollo. In order to avoid buying peripherals from IBM, LFE had approached BTM to supply card-readers in 1954. By another piece of good fortune, the BTM's Holland-Martin family was well-connected with American banking circles, and learned that David Rockefeller of the Chase Manhattan Bank had invested venture capital in LFE.

Holland-Martin and Mead visited Boston in August 1954. LFE was a thriving company with 700 personnel, including 150 electronic engineers, and had a turnover of $3 million, mainly from radar contracts with the United States defence agencies. LFE had established a computer-development activity centred on a small group of about thirty-five engineers and technicians; the group included some outstanding computer engineers, and had a number of on-going projects. These projects included a CRT display terminal, magnetic core logic, character recognition, and a high-capacity storage drum of 2 million characters (2 Mchar). All these projects were well developed, and compared favourably with any work of a similar kind that Holland-Martin had seen in Britain. The LFE's weaknesses, in terms of entering the computer business, were its lack of marketing expertise and input-output equipment. These were of course BTM's strengths, and an agreement to develop a computer jointly was drawn up. While negotiations between the companies were under way, the Chase Manhattan Bank placed an order with LFE for a large-scale random-access computer, for delivery during 1956. The specification of this machine,[17] which was expected to cost about £50 000–£60 000, matched BTM's requirements (in so far as they were able to state them); and it was decided to build two copies of the machine: Diana for the Chase Manhattan, and Apollo for BTM.*

An important aspect of the collaboration for BTM was to be able to transfer back to the UK not just the Apollo machine, but also the know-how to its electronics personnel. To this end BTM seconded a team of

---

* The name Diana—Goddess of the Chase—was suggested by Kenneth Elbourne, head of BTM's Commercial Research Department, and a classical scholar.

Robert P. Porter (1852–1917)

Sir Ralegh Phillpotts (1871–1950)

C.A. Everard-Greene (*c*.1878–1963)

BTM founders
In 1904 The Tabulator Limited was founded by Robert P. Porter and R.B. Phillpotts, with C.A. Everard-Greene; the company was re-incorporated as the British Tabulating Machine Company (BTM) in 1907. Porter, who was chairman of the company until his death in 1917, was formerly director of the US Census (1890) and an influential industrial journalist. Phillpotts, a lawyer by training, was general manager and later chairman of BTM until his death in 1950. He was knighted in 1945 for his services in the Cantab code-breaking-machine project. Everard-Greene, an engineering graduate of Cambridge University, was general manager of the company from 1904 until his retirement in 1936.

Sir Joseph Burn (1871–1950)

Sir Joseph Burn, a director and sometime president of the Prudential Assurance Company, was responsible for the Prudential's decision to acquire the British rights to the Powers punched-card machines. Burn was chairman of the British Powers operation from 1919, until it was acquired by Vickers in 1945. He is seen here (*right*) escorting the Duke of York on a visit to the Prudential tabulating-machine section about 1930.

W. Desborough (*c.*1890–1956)

Walter Desborough was managing director of the British Powers selling company from 1931 until his retirement in 1952. A prolific writer and lecturer on office mechanization, Desborough was one of Britain's foremost authorities on business machinery. He was particularly associated with the decision to market the highly successful Powers Four small-card machines in 1932.

BTM executives, the 1950s

The 1950s saw the complete separation of ownership and management within BTM, as the old-style manager-owners were replaced by professional executives. The photograph of Sir Ralegh Phillpotts and G.E. Baillie (*left*), taken at the BTM sports day in 1946, evokes the latter-days of the 'gentleman' directors. Following the death of Phillpotts in 1950, the industrialist Sir Cecil Weir (*overleaf*) was appointed chairman. During the 1950s the executive management of BTM (*below*) was dominated by managing director Victor Stammers and his two assistant managing directors Cecil Mead (sales) and J.A. Davies (production).

Sir Ralegh Phillpotts (*right*) and G.H. Baillie, 1946

Left to right: Cecil Mead (1900–79), H.V. Stammers (1894–1971) and J.A. Davies (1901–87)

BTM-Powers-Samas merger signing ceremony, 1959: seated *right*, Sir Cecil Weir (1890–1960) and *left*, Col. A. T. Maxwell (1905–)

ICT chairmen and managing directors, 1959–68

In 1959 Sir Cecil Weir and A.T. Maxwell (*above*) agreed to merge BTM and Powers-Samas to form International Computers and Tabulators (ICT). Following the death of Weir in 1960, Sir Edward Playfair (*facing page, top*) was appointed chairman. Basil de Ferranti joined the ICT board following the acquisition of the Ferranti computer department in 1963. The photograph (*facing page, bottom*) shows de Ferranti demonstrating the ICT Standard Interface at the 1900-series launch in September 1964; in December 1964 he was appointed managing director to lead the 1900-series programme. Following a financial crisis in 1965, Terence Maxwell and Cecil Mead respectively replaced Playfair and de Ferranti as chairman and managing director.

Sir Edward Playfair (1909–),
ICT chairman 1961–65

Basil de Ferranti (1930–88), ICT managing director, 1964–65

Foreground, left to right: Sir John Wall (1913–80), Prime Minister Harold Wilson, and Arthur Humphreys CBE (1917–)

ICL chairmen and managing directors, 1968–80

ICL was formed in 1968 as the result of a government-inspired merger between ICT and English Electric Computers. The first chairman was Sir John Wall, formerly a managing director of EMI and head of the Post Office. The first managing director was Arthur Humphreys, who had played a major part in reorienting ICT from punched-card machines to computers during the 1960s. In the photograph (*above*) Wall and Humphreys are seen showing a computer circuit board to Prime Minister Harold Wilson. Humphreys recalls that whenever he met Wilson he would ask 'How is my company doing?'

Facing page: In 1972, following the computer recession of 1970–71, Tom Hudson, who had been managing director of IBM (UK) 1951–65, was appointed chairman of ICL. At the same time, an American-trained managing director Geoff Cross was brought in from Univac to lead the recovery. When Cross returned to the United States in 1977, an internal appointment was made for his successor— Dr Chris Wilson, formerly head of international sales.

Tom Hudson CBE (1915–), ICL
chairman 1972–80

Chris Wilson (1928–), ICL managing
director 1977–81

Geoff Cross (1925–), ICL managing
director 1972–77

Left to right: P.L. Bonfield CBE (1944-), Sir Christophor Laidlaw (1922-), David Marwood, and Robb Wilmot CBE (1945-)

Peter L. Bonfield, chairman and chief executive of ICL, 1986-present

ICL executives, 1981-

In 1981 a new management team was introduced into ICL in response to a financial crisis brought about by competition from US and Japanese computer suppliers, and the economic recession in the UK. The new management team included: chairman Christophor Laidlaw, formerly deputy chairman of BP; managing director Robb Wilmot, formerly managing director of Texas Instruments in Britain; and direct of operations Peter Bonfield, formerly with Texas Instruments, United States. the photograph (*above*) the managemen team is assembled at a retirement ceremony for David Marwood, compan secretary 1962-84. Since 1986, Bonfield—himself the son of a former BTM manager—has been chairman an chief executive of ICL.

six engineers to Boston; the BTM team was led by Ralph Townsend, who had taken a leading role in BTM's successful electronic calculator development.[18]

BTM: evolution of computer strategy

In 1955, deliveries of computers in Britain in any volume were only just beginning, and, excluding one-of-a-kind research machines, there were fewer than twelve installed computers, almost all of which were scientific machines.

The data-processing computer was, however, becoming the concern of forward-thinking management: 'Electronic Computers in the Office' was the subject of the national conference of the Office Management Association in May 1955,[19] and was also the theme of the conferences of the Institute of Production Engineers and the British Institute of Management the same year. Table 8.3 shows the computers that were available or projected at the time of the Office Management Association's Conference, and represents probably the best available 'snapshot' of the British data-processing computer market at that time. That the market was in a considerable state of flux is evidenced by the number of machines which were not subsequently developed, and the number of new machines that were to appear in the following year or two from other British manufacturers such as EMI, STC, and AEI. It is also noteworthy that two manufacturers (English Electric and Ferranti) could only offer scientific machines that were not true data-processing computers at all.*

It was the function of BTM's Commercial Research Department, led by Kenneth B. Elbourne, to advise the board on computer policy. The Commercial Research Department, an elaborate and well-staffed organization costing £30 000 a year to run, could predict the sales of punched-card machines with considerable accuracy; but the prediction of computer sales was an entirely different matter. The Commercial Research Department had two main sources of information: market-research surveys of users, and the developments of its competitors. So far as computers were concerned, the normal techniques of market research generated as much noise as information: in 1955 it was really the case that users would know what they wanted when they saw it.

---

* The distinction between 'scientific' and 'data-processing' computers was an important one. A scientific application tended to involve a large amount of arithmetic processing, but relatively little input-output; whereas a commercial application was just the other way about. Consequently scientific computers generally had powerful arithmetic-processing facilities, but poor input-output, and often no magnetic-tape storage. For a data-processing computer, card-based peripherals and magnetic tape were essential, while the processor was of secondary importance.

Elbourne's group kept itself well informed on the developments of its competitors; this was the function of its 'intelligence department', which was run by an ex-navy intelligence officer. The computer developments of BTM's competitors were essentially those listed in Table 8.3; although BTM knew as much as anyone about unannounced developments, the information at its disposal was not qualitatively different. As the table shows, there was very little in the small-machine market that was superior

Table 8.3　Firms offering 'office' computers in Britain, spring 1955

Manufacturer	Model	Class
BTM	1201	Small data-processing
Burroughs	E-101	Small scientific
	UDEC*	Medium data-processing
Elliott Bros	402	Medium scientific
	405	Large data-processing
English Electric	DEUCE	Medium scientific
Ferranti	Mark I-Star	Medium scientific
	Pegasus	Medium general-purpose
IBM (UK)	650	Medium data-processing
	704	Large scientific
	705	Large data-processing
Leo Computers	LEO II	Large data-processing
NCR	NATRON*	Medium data-processing
Plessey	PEP*	Small data-processing
Powers-Samas	PCC	Small data-processing
Remington Rand	UNIVAC I	Large data-processing
	File Computer	Medium data-processing

Note
Computers marked with an asterisk were not delivered.

Source
The Scope for Electronic Computers in the Office, Office Management Association, London, May 1955.

to the HEC, and there were no large-machine developments to which BTM urgently needed to respond. In mid-1955 it was learned that IBM was developing a random-access computer, the 305 RAMAC, based on a disc store, and that Remington Rand was developing the Univac File Computer, based on a drum. This market intelligence arrived when BTM had already agreed to develop the Apollo random-access computer in collaboration with LFE; the news confirmed the soundness of the technical specification of Apollo; and by early 1956 it had become the cornerstone of BTM's large-machine strategy.

BTM now committed itself to spending a very large sum on Apollo, estimated at some £300 000 over a two- or three-year period, representing more than a quarter of its total R&D expenditure. It was well known to BTM that LFE, like many high technology start-ups, tended to live on a knife-edge of under-pricing and over-running on government defence contracts, and had periodically come close to financial collapse. In order to protect its investment in Apollo, on which a great deal now depended, BTM decided to form a joint subsidiary with LFE. The International Computer Corporation (ICC) was formed in May 1956, with Denys Nelson, one of BTM's senior managers, installed as president.

Another piece of market intelligence that BTM learned in late 1955 was that several of its British competitors were developing small data-processing computers. BTM had in the HEC model 1201 the most successful small data-processing machine in Britain. To maintain its leading position, the question of finding a successor to the HEC now became a very high priority. In the short term the Stevenage computer-development group was working on the model 1202, with a larger drum memory: this would maintain the HEC's leading position for a year or two; but in the longer term a completely new machine was needed, provisionally known as the HEC V.

To design and manufacture the HEC's successor, BTM decided that it needed to collaborate with an electronics manufacturer: the main reason for such a collaboration was that BTM's electronics expertise was already fully committed, with a team of six in Boston working on the Apollo, and the remainder working on the HEC 1202 and the model 555 calculator at Stevenage. Furthermore, during 1955 BTM's head of computer research, J.R. Womersley, resigned, and the computer group was currently without a head of high calibre. Approaches to several academic and industrial computer researchers had failed to bring forward a person in whom the board had full confidence.

In 1956, Britain had several manufacturers with electronics and computer expertise, whereas experience in the office-machine industry was far more rare, and to BTM's view of far more value. (This was also understood to be the view of American office-machine manufacturers such as Burroughs, Underwood, and NCR, which were also establishing links with electronics firms.) BTM saw itself as a bride with many potential suitors, and it chose with care. Top-level negotiations were conducted by Stammers and Mead with English Electric, Elliott Brothers, and GEC, and somewhat less serious discussions were held with Decca, EMI, and AEI. After a great deal of deliberation, an agreement was finally made with GEC, mainly on the grounds that it had no declared intention of

marketing computers (it was the conflict over marketing that had led to
the breakdown of the BTM and Ferranti joint computer venture in 1951).
Another advantage of GEC was that its mainstream electronics business
insured it should be well placed to survive any rapid changes in memory
or processor technology: 'They are committed to the development of such
elements of computer construction design as transistors, which are
thought likely to play an increasingly important role in future electronic
techniques.'[20] In July 1956 an announcement was made of the formation
of a subsidiary company, Computer Developments Ltd (CDL), jointly
owned by BTM and GEC.[21] The company began operations in November
1956, initially with three projects: an inventory computer (P1), a small
scientific computer (P2), and a small commercial computer (P3).[22]

Events were now moving very rapidly in the data-processing computer
market. By late 1956 several more machines had been announced, particularly in America, so that there were now very much clearer percep-
tions both by BTM and its customers of the kind of data-processing
options that were available. Thus, while in 1955 customers had wanted a
computer *tout simple*, they were now able to specify much more detailed
information on the price-range, the peripherals needed, whether magnetic-
tape storage was wanted, and so forth.

Coinciding with these stronger market signals, more realistic manufacturing costs of the Apollo computer were becoming available, which
suggested that it would now cost £150 000–£200 000, rather than the
£50 000–£60 000 originally projected. Elbourne's group saw no significant market for a machine in this price-class in Britain. It was therefore
decided that BTM would have to develop another machine, code-named
Atlanta, in the £50 000–£70 000 price-bracket. It was, however, decided to maintain the momentum of the Apollo project, since, even if
only two or three machines were sold, they would have a high prestige
value; the file-drum under development at ICC was also of considerable
potential value, and it was also hoped to use the processor technology in
Atlanta.

In late 1956, BTM's computer policy would have seemed confused to
an outsider, and probably to an insider. In a masterly stroke, however,
Elbourne, in collaboration with the various engineering and research
groups, pulled all the threads together, and emerged in January 1957
with a blueprint for a computer strategy to take BTM into the 1960s (see
Fig. 8.2).[23] BTM was to produce a range of machines covering the price
spectrum £40 000–£90 000. In the short term the HEC 1202 would
bridge the gap between the low-specification 1201 and the arrival of its
successor. The HEC's successor, to be known as the 1300 series, would
be based on the P3 project under development at CDL. The 1300 would
exist as a basic version (the 1301), a version with magnetic-tape storage

(the 1302), and a model with a random-access drum (the 1350). The medium-price computer market would be supplied with the Atlanta, to be known as the 1400 series. The 1400 series would be offered in a basic version with magnetic tape (the 1400), and a model with a random-access drum (the 1450). Finally, the Apollo computer—to be known as the 1550—would be offered to the handful of organizations requiring a very large machine.

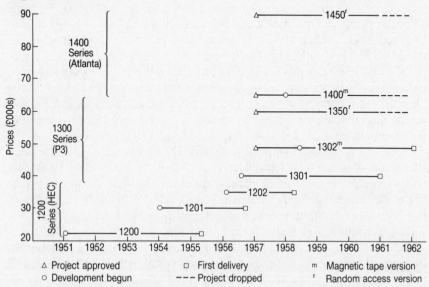

Fig. 8.2 BTM computer strategy, 1957

BTM's very clear computer strategy in 1957 has to be compared with that of other contemporary British manufacturers. BTM's main competitors, Ferranti and Elliott for example, were attempting to produce both scientific and commercial machines: in the former they were well qualified to proceed, but in the latter they had nothing like the commercial knowledge or marketing expertise of BTM. In the event, Ferranti's commercial computers (based on Pegasus and Perseus) were not a success, and Elliott linked up with NCR to market its commercial machine (the 405). Most of the other manufacturers in Britain had much narrower objectives, often based on a single machine (such as Leo Computers with its LEO II). There can be very little argument that of all the computer manufacturers in Britain, BTM had outstandingly the clearest and broadest vision of the computer market of the 1950s. As it happened, not all the plans came to fruition in the 1960s; but this was due to problems of changing technology and American competition, rather than to an ill-conceived strategy.

During 1957-59, BTM's computer R&D was therefore strongly focused on fulfilling its computer plans. At CDL all development resources were devoted to designing the 1300 processor, and this proceeded successfully, though rather slowly. BTM's other joint venture, ICC, suffered a serious setback when the Chase Manhattan Bank decided to cancel its contract for the Diana computer, because of late delivery and cost overruns. This event completely undermined LFE's confidence in the project; it withdrew from data-processing computers, and ICC was wound up in early 1958. A prototype machine was completed, however, and shipped back to England in December 1957. Attempts were made to sell the machine to the Milk Marketing Board; but it was not interested in what was essentially a one-of-a-kind prototype, and one that did not have magnetic tape either. BTM cut its losses, and scrapped the machine. The demise of the Diana/Apollo computer, which was to have been sold as the 1550, was not damaging from a commercial viewpoint, since only two or three sales had been anticipated. More serious was the fact that development of the 1400-series processor had been held back throughout 1957, in the hope that much of it could be derived from the Apollo project; now that Apollo had arrived, however, this appeared impractical, because the specifications of the machines were very different. From early 1958 all the resources of the Stevenage computer development group were concentrated on the 1400; but much precious time had been lost.

To accompany the processors, BTM needed a full range of peripherals. In terms of punched-card peripherals, it was completely self-sufficient, and in fact was developing a market selling punched-card input-output equipment to other computer manufacturers. BTM experienced greater difficulty in making a satisfactory high-speed printer, and, apart from casting envious eyes over the Powers-Samas Samastronic printer, sought to make a licensing agreement with one of the American manufacturers Anelex or Shepard.

A fact often overlooked in the history of the computer, is that good peripherals were more difficult to manufacture than central processors. The most notoriously difficult peripheral was a magnetic-tape storage unit. Britain was very late to develop magnetic-tape systems, largely because it was a development that looked easy, but was in fact costly and difficult, and never got the priority it deserved. Halsbury summed up the situation admirably in 1958:

In fact, the construction of a good tape transport mechanism is a difficult and tricky piece of not only mechanical but aerodynamic engineering, and the main reason for their failure to produce a viable solution of the problems involved is that electrical engineers have refused to recognize that fact and tackled their problems in a spirit of facile optimism. As a result we have not a single tape-deck in the U.K. able to compete with U.S. equipment, and, when I enquire the price of the best competitor to it, I am shocked to be quoted for the equivalent of one and a half *Continental* Rolls-Bentleys with Hooper coachwork and purchase tax![24]

In July 1957, recognizing the difficulty of the problem, BTM acquired a 51 per cent holding in a small British company, Data Recording Instruments, to develop a magnetic-tape unit, which would ensure its self-sufficiency in the long term; for the medium term negotiations were started with American manufacturers. In terms of magnetic storage, BTM did, however, have one very strong card in its hand: the random-access file drum developed by ICC. This was a working entity, with a capacity of 2 Mchar, that, apart from the IBM RAMAC disc unit, was ahead of anything offered by any other manufacturer in America or Britain.[25]

The merger

During 1956 and 1957 Powers-Samas experienced a financial collapse which culminated in the merger with BTM. Tables 8.1 and 8.2 (pp. 172 and 173), the only directly comparable financial statistics of the companies for any period, show very clearly the extent of the financial decline of Powers-Samas.* In 1953 and 1954 the revenues and capital employed of BTM and Powers-Samas had been within a few percentage points of one another; and although Powers-Samas profits were somewhat lower, this could be accounted for by its higher R&D expenditure. But, during 1955 and 1956, when Powers-Samas expanded very rapidly, revenues failed to increase sufficiently to meet interest charges, with a consequent drop in profits. In 1956, only a 3 per cent return was achieved on shareholders' funds, compared with BTM's very respectable 19 per cent. The crisis for Powers-Samas came in the autumn of 1957: the principal causes of the collapse were rising production costs, and the failure to produce the Samastronic tabulator.

The main cause of rising costs was UK inflation, which was entirely outside the control of the company. Between 1949 and 1957 UK prices rose 30 per cent: this increase entirely wiped out the competitive advantage that Stafford Cripps' 30 per cent devaluation of 1949 had given exporters. Powers-Samas' main export, the Powers Forty range, was once again no longer competitive: the American operation petered out during 1956, and in the same year business in Scandinavia, its largest overseas market, declined 80 per cent. With the strength of competition at home and abroad from IBM, and to a lesser extent from BTM, it was impossible to pass on increased costs in higher prices and rentals.

* Tables 8.1 and 8.2 are based on the financial report produced by Deloitte, Plender, Griffiths, and Company on the merger between the companies. Some figures differ from the published annual reports, in an effort to derive a common basis for comparison.

Powers-Samas might well have survived the financial crisis, had it not made a fatal tactical blunder. In June 1957 it prematurely announced the Samastronic tabulator at the Business Efficiency Exhibition: the new tabulator promised to be a remarkable machine—it had a printing speed of 300 lpm, and a flexibility that unquestionably put it ahead of any other machine in the world. Two hundred orders for the Samastronic were taken at the exhibition; and during the following few weeks the order book for Powers' out-moded classical and restyled equipment collapsed. Only at this point did it become clear to the board, apparently for the first time, that the Samastronic was months if not years away from production. Managing director F.P. Laurens called for a full report from his technical director. Johnson's report revealed an awesome list of shortcomings:

It would not be equipped with any adding. . . . It would be capable of feeding stationery only at a constant speed, i.e., no line spacing or long feeding. . . . Its printing coils would have a limited life to the extent that it would be necessary when running the machine to replace or repair coils at the rate of approximately one every four hours. . . . It would need to be operated without the print head cover and possibly without other covers in order to minimise trouble due to overheating. . . . It would not be equipped with a Summary Punch.[26]

Taking the chair of his executive committee, Laurens' reactions bordered on panic:

The Chairman said that the information in the report was catastrophic, only just coming to light at this late stage, and asked when clear information would be given to Production. It was evident that this year we are not going to get any tabulators and doubtful about printers and this was a very serious situation indeed as it was only four-months to the year end. . . . The general outlook position of the Company was now entirely controlled by this situation. . . . The Chairman said that the whole position must be set down in writing. It was a very serious blow, in fact, a catastrophe.[27]

The final blow to Powers-Samas came in September 1957, when Mr Thorneycroft, Chancellor of the Exchequer, began a deflationary credit squeeze. The bank rate rose to 7 per cent, with a consequent further falling-off in orders, particularly for non-rented equipment. To stimulate sales, it was proposed halving the selling prices of Powers Forty machines. Prices were cut, though only by 20 per cent, and other incentives were introduced. These measures were not enough to keep the factories occupied, however; a pay-freeze for the entire work-force of Powers-Samas was introduced, and the decision was taken to close the Southport factory.

As the financial crisis within Powers-Samas deepened, a merger with BTM was agreed between the companies. According to Maxwell the decision was taken during an informal lunch with Sir Cecil Weir on 22 August 1957.[28] Which of Maxwell and Weir proposed the merger has never been revealed to this day, but the evidence no doubt speaks for itself. It must also remain a matter of conjecture as to how, or whether, Powers-Samas could have survived the 1960s had a merger not taken place: although Vickers had the financial resources to keep Powers-Samas afloat, it was not a company given to sentiment.

In retrospect it is clear that BTM was, particularly in view of its position in computers, in a far stronger position to survive the 1960s than Powers-Samas, and the question remains as to why it should have potentially weakened itself by taking on such a wounded partner. The principal reason was that Weir, like Maxwell, judged that a concentration of the British punched-card machine industry was essential for its survival: there would be economies of scale, and more importantly their R&D resources would be united against IBM, rather than in competition with one another. Philosophically, Weir was strongly in favour of large industrial units to meet American competition; and his aims for the British punched-card machine companies paralleled his lofty aims for the integration of the European Coal and Steel Community.[29] Maxwell's view, perhaps less grand than Weir's, but born of his particular experience of bank mechanization, was that it was essential for the companies to combine their research efforts.

Apart from the long-term benefits of concentration, BTM saw two short-term gains: the Samastronic, and production capacity. The BTM board saw in the Samastronic a solution to its own weak position in tabulator development: 'the Samastronic at 300 lines a minute is on the market now, and the earliest that we can contemplate for a machine of our own at similar or higher speeds is 1960'.[30] Had the company realized how far the Samastronic was from being on the market, it is doubtful if the merger would have proceeded at all. The second attraction of the merger was that it would enable a rapid increase in production capacity; BTM's order books for traditional equipment were very swollen, and its plant capacity was inadequate. If the terms were right, then a merger with Powers-Samas, whose plants were under-utilized, offered a perfect opportunity to expand at the fastest possible speed at the lowest possible cost.[31]

In conditions of the greatest secrecy, a merger was agreed in principle; and it only remained to determine the appropriate financial basis. As it happened the accountants Deloitte, Plender, Griffiths, and Company served as auditors for both companies, so that they were able to produce a financial assessment without a whiff of suspicion being aroused either in the companies or in the City. The accountants' report concluded:

. . . we are of the opinion that, taking all known factors into account, the interests in the combined profits of the new organisation should be apportioned within a bracket 70% and 65% to B.T.M. and 30% to 35% to Powers.[32]

This valuation was based primarily on the proportion of future revenues that were secured by rented equipment, and the historic and future profit trends of the two companies. The report took no account of the research positions of either company, and had it done so it would no doubt have found still further in favour of BTM.

In the event, Weir and Maxwell struck up a gentlemanly deal that BTM shareholders would hold 62 per cent, and Vickers 38 per cent of the equity in the new company. The low valuation of Powers-Samas was a profound shock to its management, but there was no real alternative to a merger. In July 1958 the companies issued a joint statement of their intention to merge their interests in a new company, International Computers and Tabulators Limited.

Part II
Computers

9

The decline of the tabulator

1959–1961

They [IBM] believe, as I.C.T. do, that the discontinuance of
orthodox punched card equipment is not yet in sight, and I gather
that they are experiencing some feeling of relief and added security
now that they have introduced the 1401 [computer] in its
defensive role.

—H.V. Stammers, February 1960.[1]

As a company, ICT existed for about eight years, before finally merging
with English Electric Computers Limited to form ICL in 1968. Although
ICT's revenues grew at an overall rate of 15 per cent a year during this
period (Table 9.1), this fell far short of the 30 per cent annual growth rate
hoped for when ICT began operations. There was also considerable
volatility from year to year, and profits generally failed to keep pace with
revenue growth—both in absolute terms and as a return on funds employed. The company's head count also tended to rise and fall with these
financial vicissitudes.

ICT's uneven performance is accounted for by the rapidly changing
nature of its business, as punched-card machinery gave way to the
computer during the period 1962-65: while ICT managed to increase its
gross revenues, the computers it sold were either imported direct from the
United States or contained a much higher proportion of bought-in components than its traditional electro-mechanical products. The effect was
that margins were eroded and labour had to be shed. The tide only began
to turn in 1966 when, after a low point in 1965, the ICT 1900 series
computers began to sell in treble figures.

ICT: initial structure and strategy

The first two or three years following the 1959 merger saw the top management of ICT tackling the operational and cultural problems of merging
two companies that were once competitors and were now partners. Two
sales forces had to be combined, one previously paid on a commission
basis and one not, and each with distinct traditions and sales experiences.
The entire product range, now with very large areas of overlap, had to be

Table 9.1 ICT financial statistics, 1960–67

	Revenues (£000s)	Pre-tax profits (£000s)	Personnel
1960	24504	2452	19616
1961	28116	2518	21823
1962	31071	2115	24285
1963	40156	1437	21129
1964	59495	2593	20359
1965	55250	− 509	22883
1966	63353	2331	23708
1967	66821	3029	24765

Note
No comparable figures are available for 1959.

Source
ICT Annual Reports, 1960–67.

rationalized; and this rationalization eventually percolated down to plant level, where the problems of sustaining morale were severe, particularly for the personnel of Powers-Samas—seen as the weaker partner. The R&D operations also had to be merged: Powers-Samas' prestigious Whyteleafe research laboratories were eventually sold off, and their personnel transferred to Letchworth and Stevenage. The ICT chairman Sir Cecil Weir, and his managing director Cecil Mead (who were both very good at the job) made a constant round of morale-boosting visits to the UK plants and laboratories, and to the overseas branches. The morale problems were not confined to the factories and sales offices, however, for at every level of management there were now effectively two occupants of every post; it took several years for a genuine rationalization to be achieved. The unwieldy eighteen-man ICT board (Appendix 2c) carica- tured the merger problems: there were two deputy chairmen (Victor Stammers and Terence Maxwell), one vice-chairman (A. Hird), two directors of production and engineering (J.A. Davies and F.P. Laurens), two sales directors (John Bull and F.J. Nash), two research directors (C.G. Holland-Martin and W.E. Johnson), and so on. It took a number of years to lose some directors with appropriate dignity, and to find distinct roles for others.

Both BTM and Powers-Samas had been heavily centralized companies, and there was now a strong desire to take on the more fashionable decen- tralized structure adopted by the likes of IBM and RCA in the United States,[2] and which was beginning to be adopted by other firms in the

UK.[3] This was not, however, a nettle the board felt equal to grasping until the merger pains were over; but by 1965—following the acquisition of the Ferranti computer department—the company had become decentralized, and a much more modern and reactive organization.

Once the merger had been agreed in 1958, joint director-level and executive-level planning groups were established to smooth the operational problems of integration, and to formulate a long-term strategy.[4] The latter was the responsibility of a group led by Arthur Humphreys from BTM and Lyon Lightstone from Powers-Samas—both high fliers in their respective companies, and later directors. Thus ICT began operations—probably for the first time in the history of either company—with a clear, explicitly-stated strategy. The ICT strategy had several dimensions, but the key objectives were:

1. To become a large-scale vertically-integrated data-processing equipment manufacturer.
2. To supply products for the traditional punched-card machine market, and to diversify into small and medium EDP computers.
3. To become a peripheral manufacturer and OEM supplier.[5]*

The first objective, of becoming a large-scale vertically-integrated manufacturer, very much matched Sir Cecil Weir's vision of the company as the dominant British supplier of data-processing equipment, and eventually the leading European company, second only to IBM. This was not so much growth for growth's sake as the need for economies of scale to compete with IBM: achieving scale had been the principal reason for the merger, and indeed had been BTM's and Powers-Samas's principal strategic objective throughout the post-war period. To achieve this growth, the ICT Planning Division was set to work to devise a business plan incorporating a long-term 30 per cent annual growth rate. An important prerequisite to sustaining a high growth rate was to find some means of financing rentals. Inadequate leasing finance had frequently restricted growth in the past; and although the punched-card machine companies generally muddled through, a permanent solution to the problem had yet to be found. This was to be the specific responsibility of Deputy Chairman Terence Maxwell, who was a trained banker, and a former managing director of the bankers Glyn, Mills, and Company.

In hindsight, ICT's second strategic objective, of basing future growth on punched-card machinery, and merely diversifying into computers, was almost fatally wrong. When it became obvious that computers were in the ascendant, ICT had neither the technical capability nor the organizational structure to react. IBM faced just the same uncertainties as ICT in

---

* EDP: Electronic Data Processing. OEM: Original Equipment Manufacturer.

responding to the computer, but its defensive strategy was much more effective. By the mid-1950s IBM had recognized that the industry might undergo a revolutionary technical change; and it set about developing expertise and an organization able to react if such a change should come. Thomas Watson Jr subsequently stated:

During these really earth-shaking developments in the accounting machine industry, IBM slept soundly. . . . Finally we awoke and began to act. We took one of our most competent operating executives with a reputation for fearlessness and competence [T.V. Learson] and put him in charge of all phases of the development of an IBM large-scale electronic computer. He and we were successful. . . .

By 1956 it became clear that to respond rapidly to challenge, we needed a new organisation concept. . . . In late 1956, after months of planning, we called the top one hundred or so people in the business to a three-day meeting in Williamsburg, Virginia. We came away from that meeting decentralised.[6]

Although ICT had developed a tolerable defensive position so far as computer R&D was concerned, when the collapse of the punched-card machine business arrived it was quite unable to switch its electro-mechanical production to electronic equipment and computer peripherals with anything like the necessary speed.

ICT's third strategic objective, of becoming a peripheral supplier to other computer manufacturers on an OEM basis, was well-conceived; but it was not vigorously pursued until it was almost too late. The manufacture of electro-mechanical peripherals should have been the perfect exit strategy from ICT's declining punched-card machine business, but in fact the company ended up importing peripherals from American suppliers— even printers, an item which above all it should have been able to make for itself. Through its holding in the Data Recording Instrument Company (DRI), ICT was only partially successful as a magnetic-tape-drive supplier—however, it is fair to say that ICT was by no means alone in discovering that the technology of magnetic storage devices was formidably difficult.

Product rationalization and the Samastronic débâcle

At the time of the merger, ICT had a good deal more scale than economy. With nearly twenty thousand employees, it had no less than 21 factories sprawled across England, and a major plant in Castlereagh, Northern Ireland. Its punched-card machine products encompassed four distinct ranges (Table 9.2), each with a different card format and size, and the Hollerith 80-column range itself had two size-variants. In addition there was a hotchpotch of punched-card machine and computer research projects in various states of completion. There was very little contention that in the future there would have to be a single large-card range based on the

Table 9.2 ICT punched-card machine ranges

Before merger		After merger	
Range	Columns	Range	Columns
Hollerith	80/38	ICT 80	80
Powers-Samas	65/130	dropped	
Powers Forty	40	ICT 40	40
Powers One	21	ICT 21	21

Hollerith 80-column card, and one small-card range based on the Powers-Samas 40-column card. In future, Powers large-card equipment would only be sold to existing installations, and most of that would be supplied by refurbishing machines returned from the field. (The tiny 21-column machines continued to be made and sold, but their sales accounted for very little revenue.) This rationalization meshed in very well with ICT's expanding business, so that during 1959–61 output was increased by 50 per cent, with only a 20 per cent increase in the direct workforce, and no additional factory space.

So far as punched-card machine R&D was concerned, there were two key projects within ICT (Table 9.3). First, a high-speed printing tabulator, and second, a second-generation transistorized calculating tabulator to replace the PCC and the model 555.[7] In addition, there were a number of smaller development projects for new machines, such as a 2000-card-per-minute sorter, and a transistorized calculating punch for the ICT 40 range; these projects were all aimed at maintaining competitive parity with IBM, which was now a strong competitor in the UK as well as overseas.

For some years both BTM and Powers-Samas had been in fear that IBM would introduce a high-speed tabulator, printing at perhaps two or three times the speed of its existing 150-lines-per-minute accounting machines. In the event, IBM never did market such a machine; but the anxiety in the British companies was none the less real. BTM had seen great promise in the Powers-Samas Samastronic, and, following the merger, BTM's own high-speed tabulator project was dropped. It did not take long for experienced former-BTM engineers to discover that the electro-mechanical design of the Samastronic arithmetic units was an amateurish mess, and that there was no real prospect that the machine could ever be made to work with acceptable reliability.[8] Many machines prematurely released into the field in the last months of Powers-Samas's existence had to be either withdrawn or maintained at enormous cost. Even the print unit was unable to deliver reasonable print quality, or to print multi-part forms, and

Table 9.3   ICT R&D budget, 1960/61

Project	£000s	Percentage
Punched-card equipment		
Tabulators and calculating punches	169	13.0
975 calculating tabulator	246	18.9
Other	233	17.9
Total	648	49.7
Computer equipment		
Processors	417	32.0
Peripherals	156	12.0
Magnetic tape (DRI)	82	6.3
Total	655	50.3
Total	1303	100

Source
'Design Programme: 1960/61, 1961/62, 1962/63', 17 February 1961, ICT Board Papers.

so ICT's hopes for developing a computer printer from the Samastronic had to be abandoned, leaving it without an acceptable product for several years.

In November 1960 the board took the decision to put an end to the Samastronic once and for all. So far as the balance-sheet was concerned, the total cost of the débâcle was put at about £1½ million—a figure that exceeded ICT's entire annual research budget.[9] In fact the position was to prove even worse in the long term, because in order to fulfil the cancelled Samastronic orders—there were well over 200—output of Hollerith equipment had to be increased at great cost, or the business would have been lost to IBM. The failure of the Samastronic also cost ICT dearly in goodwill, and a product that might well have secured some competitive advantage against IBM, albeit temporary.

ICT's second major punched-card development was the model 975 calculating tabulator. The 975 calculating tabulator consisted of a transistorized calculating punch and a tabulator, integrated in a single unit. IBM had no comparable product; and ICT hoped the 975 would prove highly competitive against IBM's more orthodox transistorized accounting machines. (Sperry Rand was also developing a calculating tabulator with a very similar specification—the Univac 1004—of which more later.) The calculating tabulators and punches were an important bridge between the traditional electro-mechanical accounting machine and the new stored-program computer. But because they occupied 'that ill-defined boundary which divides computers from calculators',[10] they were generally ignored by analysts of the 1960s computer scene. This tends to indicate a much sharper divide between computer and non-computer EDP equipment than was truly the case, and ICT classed these machines as 'small computers', which from a marketing point of view they were. Indeed, ICT derived more revenue from this class of machine than from all its computers put together during the first half of the 1960s.

Computer developments

During the lead-up to the merger, the joint planning staff took stock of the computer development plans of the two companies. Powers-Samas' Pluto project was seen as hopelessly uncompetitive, and was cancelled straight away, leaving ICT's future prospects dependent entirely on BTM's computer projects.[11] This was one of the main reasons that Maxwell had accepted the 62:38 valuation of the merging companies.[12]

These computer plans were based on two machines, the 1300 series and the 1400 series, and a random-access file drum (Table 9.4). The

Table 9.4 ICT computer developments, *c*.1960

Range	Model	Price (£000s)	Announced	Description
1300	1300	45 +	Jan 1963	Small, card-based
	1301	65 +	May 1960	Small/medium, card or magnetic tape
	1302	175 +	Mar 1964	Medium, magnetic tape
	1350		Cancelled	Medium, random access
1400	1400		Cancelled	Medium, magnetic tape
	1450		Cancelled	Medium, random access

Sources
'Computer Development Plans', 21 January 1957, BTM Board Papers. 'ICT Product Plans', 8 May 1964, ICT Board Papers.

1300 series was to be offered initially in two models: the 1301, a small/medium system, and the 1350, a random-access version; smaller and larger versions, the 1300 and 1302, were to be introduced subsequently. The 1400 series was to be offered in two models: the 1400, a medium-sized magnetic-tape-based system; and the 1450, a random-access version. Had these plans matured, ICT would have had an excellent range of equipment; but during 1960 much of the commercial potential evaporated, because of technical obsolescence and development delays.

The 1400-series 'balanced data-processing computer' was ICT's prestige computer project. It had been heavily publicized since 1958; but during 1959 not a single sale had materialized. The 1400 was a first-generation computer based on thermionic valves, and this technology was being rapidly overtaken by the new transistor electronics. The 1400 could not compete against second-generation machines, such as the IBM 7090 or the EMI 2400. The planning staff, concerned at this obsolescence risk, had commissioned a report from the Stanford Research Institute (SRI) in America.[13] The consultants reported in autumn 1959 that there was no prospect of selling the machine in the 1960s. As a result of this advice, the entire project was scrapped, and the prototype sold off to Dr Andrew Booth at Birkbeck College for a token £5000.

Another major disappointment occurred with the random-access file drum derived from BTM's collaboration with the Laboratory for Electronics in Boston. Up to 1960 this had seemed competitive against the IBM RAMAC disc store used in the IBM 305 computer. But in that year IBM announced the model 1301 disc drive, with an average access time of 165 milliseconds, and a capacity of 56 million characters;[14] against this specification, BTM's file drum with a similar average access time (200 milliseconds), but a capacity of only 2 million characters, had no real commercial potential, and the plans for random-access machines had to be put into abeyance. ICT was, in fact, one of a number of casualties of IBM's pre-eminence in disc-drive technology: RCA was developing a magnetic-card-based random-access store (the RACE), and Univac a drum-based system (the FASTRAND drum), neither of which were successful.[15]

The ICT 1301 computer, although developing slowly, was in considerably better shape than the 1400, in that it was a second-generation machine based on transistors. The computer had been designed by the ICT and GEC joint subsidiary Computer Developments Limited (CDL), and was being developed and manufactured in GEC's Coventry telecommunications factory. The relative success of the 1301 served to underline the value of collaboration with an electronics manufacturer with an awareness of the component business. The 1400 had been developed entirely in ICT's own Stevenage electronics laboratory. In addition to the 1301 computer project, in 1959 ICT had a string of peripheral developments in progress: card-readers and punches, paper-tape devices, printers and console typewriters. And with its major stake in DRI, its position in magnetic-tape storage looked secure. So, despite the disappointments of the 1400 series and the file drum, in terms of the traditional time-scales of the British punched-card machine industry, ICT's position did not seem unduly alarming. Although the short-term position in computers was weak, since the first-generation 1200 series was rapidly approaching obsolescence, computers accounted for such a small fraction of the business that it appeared of little immediate consequence. The fact was that in 1959 and 1960 the punched-card machine business was extra-ordinarily buoyant. For example, two-year delivery times for ICT 80-column equipment were being quoted, and the main anxiety within ICT was to increase production to avoid sales losses to IBM, who were able to quote six-month deliveries.

It would be a harsh judgement to accuse ICT of complacency in computer development during 1959. Although computers accounted for only 10 per cent of ICT's output, it was devoting a full 50 per cent of its R&D budget to them.

The event which completely transformed the outlook for computers, and precipitated the collapse of the punched-card machine market, was the announcement of the IBM 1401 computer in October 1959. The 1401 was originally intended by IBM to be a second-generation successor to its first-generation model 650, in much the way ICT's 1300 series was intended as a successor to its 1200 series. But the 1401 captured the American EDP computer market to an extent that took IBM by surprise, and exceeded all forecasts: a thousand orders were taken in the first few weeks following the announcement, and the machine went on to sell a total far in excess of ten thousand installations, outselling the 650 by a factor of ten.[16] The success of the 1401 has often been attributed to the model 1403 chain printer that accompanied it; printing at 600 lines per minute, it enabled a single 1401 to replace four conventional tabulators. (Ironically, the chain printer was first conceived by IBM France in the late 1940s, and the idea was offered to BTM; a team visited Vincennes in 1949, but they turned it down.[17] IBM in America adopted the idea when it had failed to develop wire matrix printers.[18])

The IBM 1401 was an instant success in the UK too, and in May 1960 ICT was forced to make a premature announcement of the 1301; this was partly for prestige reasons and partly to ensure that at least some sales of this class of computer accrued to ICT. The credibility of the 1301 announcement was tempered more than a little by the two- to three-year delivery times, and the modest specification: the basic 1301 was promised for mid-1962; the magnetic-tape version would not be available until 1963; and there were no plans to announce a random-access version at all. By contrast, delivery for the IBM 1401 was 6–12 months, and magnetic-tape and random-access storage were immediately available.

If one had to chose a point in time when the true scale of ICT's deficiency in computers dawned on the board, it would be November 1960, when the American business magazine *Fortune* carried an article with the faintly alarming title:

Q. What Grows Faster Than I.B.M.?
A. I.B.M. Abroad.[19]

The article included a good deal of detail on IBM's competitive strategy that was evidently new to the board, and provided the agenda 'for an informal and down-to-earth discussion between the resident Directors concerning the possible implications of this information on I.C.T.'s present and future policies.'[20] The single most revealing item in the article was the extent to which the computer had penetrated the American data-processing market, and would soon, according to Dick Watson, President of the IBM World Trade Corporation, take over the European market:

By 1964, according to Dick Watson's estimate, some 40 per cent of World Trade's revenues will be from electronic data-processing equipment (EDPM), compared with perhaps the 10 per cent it represents today. In the U.S., an estimated 35 per cent of I.B.M.'s business is in EDPM.[21]

If the European EDP market in three years' time was to be 40 per cent electronic computers, then ICT would need to develop products to fill the vacuum.

As a first step, in March 1961, ICT took over the GEC staff who were developing the 1300 series at the GEC Coventry telecommunications works. The 1300 team was merged with ICT's own R&D staff as a subsidiary company, ICT (Engineering) Ltd, in which GEC took a 10 per cent shareholding.[22] The managing director of the new development company was E.C.H. (Echo) Organ, who had been manager of the 1300-series computer development in GEC. At the same time, CDL, which had now served its purpose in specifying the 1300, was taken over, and became the nucleus of a new product-planning group.

The 1300 series itself was to be built in the GEC works, since ICT lacked the manufacturing capability; over 200 machines were eventually delivered. Even so, the 1301 remained unavailable for delivery until mid-1962, while other manufacturers, both British and American, were offering delivery of comparable or better second-generation machines in 1960 and 1961 (Table 9.5). The most obvious competitors to the 1301, apart from the IBM 1401, were the EMI 1100 and the Univac SS-80 File Computer, both of which were in the same price-class as the 1301, and were being actively marketed. In the medium/large class, ICT had no machine at all to offer against the IBM 7090, the EMI 2400, the English Electric KDP10, the Honeywell 800, or LEO III. ICT's immediate need, then, was for a small/medium computer to sell against the IBM 1401 in

Table 9.5 Second-generation EDP computers on the UK market, *c*.1960

Manufacturer	Model	Price	First UK delivery
EMI	1100	180	1960
	2400	500	1961
English Electric	KDP10	400	1961
Honeywell	800	400	1962
IBM	305	70	1960
	1401	120	1960
	1410	200	1960
	7090	1000	1960
ICT	1301	120	1961
Leo	LEO III	200	1962
Univac	SS-80	100	1960

Notes
Price is for a typical system, in £000s.

Sources
Delivery data: *Computer Survey*. Price data: J. Hendry, *Business History*, 29, 1987, pp. 73–102.

the short term, and the design and manufacturing capability for a medium/large computer in the medium term.

In the meantime, the extraordinary paradox was that, in spite of all the signals about the booming computer market, in 1960 computers still accounted for less than 15 per cent of ICT's business, and the sales of punched-card machines appeared to be rising inexorably.

The switch to computers

To outsiders and pundits, the decline of the punched-card machine was seen as inevitable from the early 1950s; but in fact the decline took much longer than is commonly supposed—indeed, throughout the 1950s sales of punched-card machinery actually increased without a single reversal.

ICT was by no means alone in supposing that the traditional punched-card machine was not yet on the point of expiry. In 1960, IBM World Trade launched an entirely new line of punched-card machines, the 3000 series, of which it was reported:

The commercial success of the 3000 has been extraordinary. Though aimed at the small businessman, it has also unexpectedly appealed to large firms such as Volkswagen, which bought thirty of them for its agencies, and to chainstores and branch banking houses. Since it was introduced in the spring of 1960, nearly 800 sales have been recorded, and in five years World Trade expects to install over 6,000 of the systems in Europe alone.[23]

The 3000 series, designed by IBM Germany, used a small-card format not unlike that of the ICT 40-column machines.

As late as October 1960, the ICT board accepted the view of the Planning Division that: 'There was and is no evidence of a slackening demand for conventional equipment, and unless we increased our output to take care of the growing demand and to improve our lead times, more of this business would go to I.B.M.'[24] Supported by this evidence, ICT continued to increase its production of traditional machinery, and set in motion a programme of expansion to boost output by over 50 per cent over the next four years. During 1961–62 in the region of three and a half thousand additional work-people were taken on, new plants acquired, and a good deal of expensive tooling-up undertaken. This was of course the very antithesis of a conventional exit strategy for what was shortly to prove a declining business.

The collapse of the punched-card machine business started between autumn 1961 and spring 1962, and it came on with a devastating sudden-ness, even as ICT was stepping up its production. At the time, there was some mystification as to the cause, and indeed whether it was just some temporary downturn in the business cycle. In fact, the cause was the IBM 1401: during 1961–62, IBM installed nearly one hundred systems in the UK, accounting for a third of all computer sales. The great majority of these replaced one of ICT's existing—and usually multi-tabulator—installations. The impact on ICT's operations was made particularly acute by a nasty gearing effect: as newish machines were returned from the field, they could be refurbished at minimal cost and shipped straight back out again, thus reducing further the need for the production of new machines. During the 1961/62 financial year, orders for punched-card machines fell short of the target of £25 million by one-third.[25] A decline in profits, and a reduction in the work-force, followed in 1962/63, as surely as night followed day.

As the punched-card machine market began to collapse, the need for computer products became urgent, and above all there was a need for a coherent computer strategy. The overall responsibility for devising this strategy was given to Arthur Humphreys, head of product planning. Humphreys' strategy, in short, was for ICT to make an orderly transfer from being primarily a punched-card machine manufacturer to being a large-scale EDP-computer manufacturer, with computer sales amounting to 50 per cent of revenues by the mid-1960s. In the short term ICT would have to import and resell machines from a United States manufacturer. In the medium term it would obtain its own EDP manufacturing capability by acquiring the computer division of another British concern, such as English Electric, EMI, or Ferranti. Finally, ICT would re-orient its electro-mechanical R&D towards computer products, such as printers and punched-card peripherals, for sale to other American and British manu-facturers.[26]

This formation of a coherent computer strategy took place against a number of changes in the ICT board and senior management. In October 1960 Sir Cecil Weir died in office, and a successor had to be found. To maintain the balance between the BTM and Powers-Samas factions on the board, an outside appointment was sought. As it happened, Sir Walter Puckey, an ICT non-executive director, was a founder of Management Selection Limited (MSL), who recommended two candidates to the board.[27]

The candidate selected by the ICT board was Sir Edward W. Playfair, who took up office in August 1961. Playfair was not an industrialist, but a career civil servant, and at the time of his appointment was Permanent Secretary in the Ministry of Defence. His appointment was perhaps a tacit recognition that government was likely to play an increasing role in the high-technology industries; and Playfair's move was one of three similar appointments made at around the same time in different industries.* Victor Stammers retired at the time of Playfair's appointment, Cecil Mead and Terence Maxwell became deputy chairmen, and John Bull became managing director. While John Bull took on the unenviable, if not impossible, task of holding together ICT's operations during the transition from punched-card machines to computers at home, Playfair, Mead, and Maxwell—plus Arthur Humphreys—were to be the key actors in the period of negotiations that lay ahead.

* This migration of senior civil servants into industry is described by Anthony Sampson's *The New Anatomy of Britain* (1971) in less than glowing terms: '. . . it cannot be said that permanent secretaries have had a dynamic effect on industry through their closeness to it, and their network has not been notable for bringing in bright young men or ideas: Vickers, Albright and Wilson and International Computers have all been in the doldrums'.[28] The candidate ICT turned down, incidentally, was Sir Arnold Hall FRS, one of Britain's outstanding industrialists. The ability of the boards of ICT and ICL, when faced with a choice of chairmen, to pick the less suitable has been almost unerring.

10

Negotiations and mergers

1961–1963

> ICT, then, emerged when its industry was in a critical condition.
> Second generation machines were on the way, but no more;
> British industry was still unused to computer applications, beyond
> the most elementary digital programs for payroll and stock control;
> and high capital costs combined with slow payback were squeezing
> the marginal firms out of the business and into mergers.
>
> —*The Manager*, March 1965.[1]

During 1961–63, ICT was involved in an almost constant round of
negotiations with virtually every major computer company in America
and Britain, as well as Machines Bull in France. The threads of this
tapestry of negotiation are very difficult to untangle. For example, ICT
and Machines Bull were both independently talking to RCA and General
Electric in the United States, at the same time as they were talking to each
other; and simultaneously ICT, English Electric, and RCA were considering some tripartite agreement. There were thus at least six separate, but
interlocking, sets of negotiations involving just these companies. The
course of these negotiations becomes much clearer when viewed in the
context of ICT's objective in seeking liaisons with other companies. ICT's
objective was to strengthen its position in computers in two ways. First, it
needed to close the technology gap between its own computers and those
available in the United States—this implied a close relationship with an
American company. Second, it needed to increase its electronic production facilities—this implied either merging with, or acquiring, another
British computer company.

The technology gap

In 1961, when it became a matter of urgency for ICT to obtain second-
generation computers, the only place to look was the United States,
because it was so far ahead of the UK and Europe. An examination of the
causes of this technology gap throws some light on the problems of the
UK computer industry in general, and ICT in particular.

Superficially, the structures of the US and UK non-military computer
industries were similar. They had both developed during the 1950s, and

there were three main types of entrant (Table 10.1). First, there were the business-machine manufacturers seeking to diversify into computers; these companies were the most like ICT in spirit, and included IBM, Sperry Rand, Burroughs, and NCR. Second, there were the electronics and control manufacturers establishing computer divisions: RCA, General Electric, and Honeywell; their British counterparts were Ferranti, English Electric, Elliott-Automation, and EMI. Third, there were the newly established computer companies: the Control Data Corporation (CDC) was the most significant American start-up in the early 1960s; probably Leo Computers Limited was the closest that Britain had to a start-up.

Table 10.1 Principal US and UK mainframe computer companies, 1960

Entrant type	USA	UK
Business-machine manufacturers	IBM Burroughs Sperry Rand NCR	ICT
Electronics and control manufacturers	RCA General Electric Honeywell	English Electric Ferranti Elliott-Automation EMI
Newly established manufacturers	CDC	Leo Computers

Table 10.1, incidentally, lists only the eight dominant American computer manufacturers of the early 1960s, often known as 'IBM and the seven dwarfs'—a journalistic epithet that captured exactly the extent to which IBM dominated the industry. There were, in reality, some thirty American manufacturers in total, including such well-known names as Bendix, Clary, Digital Equipment Corporation (DEC), Friden, Monroe, Packard Bell, Philco, Royal McBee, Sylvania, Underwood, and so on.[2] Most of these firms eventually withdrew from the business, or were bought out by the larger companies. Likewise in Britain, in addition to the firms listed in Table 10.1, AEI, Decca, GEC, Marconi, Plessey, and STC all developed computers, and some of them were marketed; but none of them stayed in the computer business long enough to become significant members of the UK industry.

Beyond this superficial structural similarity, however, the viability and maturity of the US and UK computer industries were very different. In the mid-1950s it was probably true to say that the two countries were very much on a par, certainly in technological capability, if not in scale. But by the early 1960s the situation had been completely transformed, and the UK industry had fallen at least two or three years behind the United States. This was the technology gap.

American computers were considerably in advance of those available from European manufacturers in terms of the three components of a computer installation: processors, software, and peripherals. By 1960, virtually all computers on the American market had second-generation transistorized processors. Software was also considerably in advance of that available in the UK: the programming languages FORTRAN and COBOL were widely available, and operating systems and real-time applications were far in advance of any software products routinely offered by UK vendors. (The term software, incidentally, which was coming into use in America in 1959 or 1960, did not become widely used in Britain until about 1962—this was itself perhaps indicative of the technology lag.) In terms of peripherals, the most significant difference was in magnetic-tape and disc-storage technology. The former was very well established in the US, with several suppliers, and the latter was maturing rapidly. By contrast, in Europe there was little capability in magnetic-tape-drive manufacture, and none whatever in disc-drive technology.

The existence of the technology gap between the United States and Europe—which spread far beyond computers—was recognized at the time, and was extensively researched, particularly in the second half of the 1960s, and particularly by such quasi-governmental organizations as the Organization for Economic Co-operation and Development (OECD), the UK National Economic Development Office (NEDO), and the science policy research units of universities. There was a consensus that there were three main causes of the technology gap: managerial and cultural differences, the question of scale, and the extent of government support.[3]

In managerial and cultural terms, ICT was a distinctly centralized and bureaucratic organization compared with American computer companies, although in British terms it was not out of the ordinary; indeed, Cecil Mead was considered an innovative manager—he was chairman of the British Institute of Management 1963-64, and was knighted for his services to industry in 1967. In the second half of the 1950s three of the major US computer companies—IBM, RCA, and Burroughs—had adopted decentralized organizational structures; and ICT saw IBM in particular as being a role-model. IBM had split its business into autonomous divisions (Data Processing, Data Systems, Federal Systems, General Products, etc.); and this is the structure to which ICT moved during the next few years. Visitors to the United States were constantly impressed by the cultural differences between the countries:

The American is perhaps less set in his ideas than the Englishman; he is more prepared to change his job and tackle something new—even if only within his own organisation. This is only a personal opinion but it is mentioned as it may well be a factor in enabling I.B.M. to produce their type of flexible decentralised organisation.[4]

There was not a great deal that ICT could do at that time to import the enterprise culture; but it is notable that ICL was later (1972 and 1981) to accept American-nurtured managing directors to pull the company through difficult times.

The question of scale was largely to do with the size of the American computer market. Just as in an earlier generation the United States manufacturers had dominated the world supply of office machinery on the strength of their domestic market, so the same was now happening with the computer industry. The American market was at least two or three years ahead of Europe in its per capita consumption of computers. Thus, while in 1959 there were 3810 computers in the United States, there were just 550 in the whole of Europe.[5]

At the level of the firm, however, the contrast in scale between American companies (excluding IBM) and ICT was less than is sometimes supposed. In both the United States and in continental Europe IBM completely dominated the computer scene. In 1960 it had about three-quarters of the American data-processing market, and probably about two-thirds of the European market. Only in Britain, where it came comfortably second to ICT, was IBM not the dominant data-processing equipment supplier. (Their UK and Commonwealth revenues were about £25 million and £12.5 million respectively in 1959.)[6] Thus, while ICT was certainly disadvantaged in terms of scale compared with IBM, its relative position was not qualitatively different from the other main American computer manufacturers. For all these companies the need for scale was at least as acute as for ICT, and when the British company held negotiations with them, they were always conducted as between equals, for ICT remained the dominant non-American data-processing company.

An important difference between Britain and the United States was the nature and extent of government support. The need for spending on R&D in computers was very high. One estimate put the cost of developing a range of EDP computers as between £8 million and £16 million:[7] this was almost certainly a considerable underestimate, but in relation to ICT's total annual R&D budget of perhaps £2 million it was still astronomical.

Although there was no direct subsidy of R&D in computers by the American Government, there was a heavy investment in military R&D contracts, which had considerable derivative value in civil products. The scale of spending was massive in British terms—for example, in the period 1950–59 IBM was awarded contracts totalling $396 million, accounting for 60 per cent of its total R&D spending.[8] One of the most important IBM contracts was for a large number of computers for the SAGE defence system in the early 1950s. This programme had several spin-offs: for example, the core-memory technology developed for the SAGE FSQ-7 computer was later incorporated in the 700 series, and IBM developed invaluable experience in developing large-scale real-time software.[9] By contrast, in the UK during the 1950s the sole form of government support for the industry had been Halsbury's National Research Development Corporation, which had funds of a mere £5 million, and had moreover to be self-financing.

In 1956 both IBM and Sperry Rand embarked on projects to develop very high-speed computers that would advance the state of the art by a factor of one hundred. IBM developed the Stretch computer (later sold as the 7030) for the Los Alamos Laboratory of the Atomic Energy Commission, and Sperry Rand developed LARC for the Lawrence Livermore Laboratory.[10] Again, the American Government did not directly underwrite the development costs of these computers, but it guaranteed to buy the computers at a fixed (and generous) price when completed. As it happened, neither IBM nor Sperry Rand made money directly out of these high-speed computers, but IBM in particular derived considerable spin-off in its 7000 and 360 series of computers.

The American high-speed computer projects became something of a *cause célèbre* in the UK, as the most conspicuous manifestation of the computer technology gap.[11] Eventually this concern led to the NRDC funding the Atlas and the EMI 3400 computer projects; there is little doubt, however, that these efforts were misplaced, and sponsorship of the EDP computer industry and the peripheral industry would have been far more effective in closing the technology gap.

American negotiations: the Univac and RCA agreements

While ICT was negotiating with American companies it was constantly aware of IBM's pre-eminence in the field. Unfortunately, while IBM was obliged to disclose its old punched-card machine technology, there was no prospect of ICT obtaining access to IBM's computer technology. ICT visitors were received with courtesy by IBM on many occasions; but the possibility of commercial collaboration had been signed away in 1949.

America's number-two computer company was Sperry Rand, which had been formed in 1956 by a merger between Remington Rand and Sperry Gyroscope.[12] The Univac Division of Sperry Rand had started out as an operation with immense technical promise, but it was rapidly eclipsed by the superior marketing of IBM; in the memorable phrase of a contemporary observer Univac 'snatched defeat from the jaws of victory'.[13] The most notable Univac fiasco was the second generation SS-80 File Computer, which was marketed in Europe from 1957, but was not sold in the United States until 1959, in order to protect the old Remington Rand 90-column punched-card business (the SS-80 used 80-column cards). In 1957, the SS-80 would have been very competitive against the IBM 650; but soon after it was launched in the United States in 1959 the IBM 1401 was announced; and the 1401 was a far superior machine.

In 1959, Sperry Rand had approached ICT with a view to acquiring the manufacturing and selling rights of its 80-column tabulators. As part of the deal Univac offered ICT the SS-80 computer. In fact, nothing came of these negotiations, largely because neither company would relinquish the European market, and also because the SS-80 was approaching obsolescence.[14] In 1960–61 Univac announced a number of new products, including a large EDP computer, the 1107, the 490 real-time system, and a small calculating punch, the 1004. All of these were offered to ICT. Peter Ellis, Arthur Humphreys' chief assistant, could see a market for about two 1107s in ICT territories—this was a figure that amazed Univac, since the machine was selling in dozens in the United States. In the event, ICT took on neither the 1107 nor the 490. The 1004, however, was a different matter, since it had a very similar specification to the ICT 975 calculating tabulator, which was still a long way from production. In autumn 1962, Humphreys agreed to take an initial batch of one hundred machines, and between 1963 and 1966 nearly five hundred were sold. The 1004 was the single most important factor that enabled ICT to survive its financial crisis of 1965, and it was probably the best deal that Arthur Humphreys ever made for the company. The 1004 also enabled the 975 development to be cancelled, allowing the R&D resources to be diverted to computer and peripheral development.

ICT had excellent relations with Burroughs that went back to the early 1950s; and of all the American companies Burroughs' current business problems were most like those of ICT. As the premier manufacturer of mechanical desk-top accounting machines, and the leading supplier to banks, Burroughs faced identical problems of switching production to electronic-based technology, and diversifying into computers to secure its future business. Indeed, in the mid-1950s a jointly-owned development company had been negotiated (and a name had even been dreamt up— 'HoBo'—for Hollerith-Burroughs); but the talks faded away, largely because Burroughs' computer research at the time was considerably behind even ICT's. During the intervening period, Burroughs had re-structured and developed a first-generation computer, the 220, which it supplied mainly to its banking customers. ICT supplied punched-card peripherals to Burroughs on an OEM basis, but at the critical time, in 1961, Burroughs had no major computer technology that ICT could take up on a reciprocal basis. This was bad luck, because Burroughs was about to embark on the development of its model 5000 computer; this was a machine that was technically one of the most adventurous of its day (and which was later one of the design inputs to ICL's new range in 1969).[15]

None of the major electronics and control-based computer companies (Honeywell, General Electric, and RCA) nor CDC had significant EDP marketing operations outside the United States in 1961, so that all of them were interested in some form of arrangement with a European company. There were early talks with Honeywell, and with CDC, which offered ICT its large 3600 computer. Neither of these negotiations came to anything, mainly because the products offered did not fit in with ICT marketing plans. Both Honeywell and CDC eventually set up their own European marketing organizations. Many discussions took place with General Electric (GE), starting in 1961 and going on through to the mid-1960s. As it happened, ICT's Terence Maxwell had a family connection with a director of GE, which made for easy relations between the companies.[16] Even though GE's computer division was small, GE itself was a vast enterprise, with revenues nearly twice those of IBM. GE's policy was to achieve a merger with a European business-machine company, to give it a European sales force and manufacturing capability; and it held negotiations with both ICT and Machines Bull in France. ICT's negotiations with GE probably went further than with any other American company, and there was a period of a few months in the middle of 1961 when it seemed likely that GE would take a stake in ICT, perhaps in the region of 25 per cent, and discussions were held with one of the British Government departments as to whether this would be compatible with the public interest. While these talks were under way, however, for a variety of reasons—including the question as to the desirability of American ownership, and the fact that GE had become involved in an anti-trust suit—ICT broke off the talks. GE did, eventually, join up with a European company, by acquiring Machines Bull in 1964; but the link-up was not a commercial success.[17]

Unlike GE, RCA had a policy of restricting its marketing operations to the United States. As a new entrant to the business-machine industry it had had to develop its domestic sales force from scratch (largely by poaching from IBM and others),[18] and it had no desire to take on an international selling operation. In 1960 RCA was marketing an excellent range of second-generation EDP computers in the United States, the models 301, 501, and 601 (Table 10.2). It also had a major development programme under way for smaller and intermediate-sized machines (the

Table 10.2 RCA EDP computers, 1961

Model	Price (£000s)	Announced	Licencees
301	60-150	Apr 1960	ICT (model 1500) Machines Bull (Gamma 30) Hitachi Siemens
501	200-350	Dec 1958	English Electric (KDP10)
601[a]	450-600	Apr 1960	[ICT]

Note
[a] The 601 was cancelled in 1962; RCA delivered only four machines, none of them to ICT.

Sources
Prices: 'Report by Messrs. Lightstone and Humphreys on . . . RCA and EE', 26 January 1961, (ICL Archives). Announcement dates: F.M. Fisher *et al.*, *IBM and the U.S. Data Processing Industry*, Preager, New York, 1983, pp. 73-4.

201 and 401); and it was developing high-speed magnetic-tape drives, the RACE random-access store, and high-speed logic and memory elements. Perhaps the biggest area of development was in software—RCA employed 650 programmers in its EDP division, probably more than were employed in the entire UK computer industry. British visitors found this activity quite staggering in its scale. In order to recoup its development expenditure, RCA was actively seeking licensing agreements with companies outside the United States, and was already talking to English Electric, Machines Bull, Siemens in Germany, and Hitachi in Japan. English Electric, in fact, had a long standing cross-licensing agreement with RCA, through its Marconi subsidiary;[19] and in 1960 it began to manufacture the RCA 501 under licence, as the KDP10.

ICT's first involvement with RCA occurred as the result of a suggestion from Charles Odorizzi, head of the RCA computer division, that the two companies, together with English Electric, should consider the formation of a tripartite computer company to exploit the computer market outside the United States.[20] A joint study team from the three companies, which included Arthur Humphreys and Lyon Lightstone from ICT, and W.E. Scott, managing director of the English Electric computer division, met at RCA's headquarters in early 1961. The ICT group was enthusiastic about the formation of a joint company, focusing initially on the European market.[21] Individually, each company was too weak to make a successful assault on IBM—RCA lacked the marketing capability, although its electronics R&D and production were good; English Electric lacked a sales force and its R&D was weak, but its electronics manufacturing capability was strong; ICT was weak in electronics, but it had marketing strength and a promising peripherals business. Combined, the companies would have all that was needed to make a successful entrée into the European EDP market. Unfortunately, like so many of these early negotiations, the talks came to nothing. RCA did not, in the cold light of day, see the arrangement working out from a financial viewpoint; and Lord Nelson, chairman of English Electric, preferred to carry on independently, apparently oblivious that computers were becoming a high-stake, high-risk business. (Playfair reflected that Lord Nelson going into computers was reminiscent of a gentleman going into farming!)[22]

Although the possibility of a joint computer company fell through, in September 1961 Mead and Humphreys negotiated several important deals with RCA. First, they arranged for ICT to import over a hundred model 301 computers during 1962–65; sold as the ICT 1500, this machine occupied the product gap in between the 1004 and the 1301, and also filled the sales vacuum until the 1301 came into full production. Second, they arranged to buy the model 601 when it became available, which would become ICT's medium/large machine. (In fact, the 601 was cancelled 'almost as soon as the ink was dry' on the agreement, in favour of the model 3301.)[23] Third, to restore the balance of trade between the companies, ICT arranged to supply RCA with punched-card peripherals on an OEM basis. Finally, and most important, they negotiated a long-term non-exclusive licence to use RCA computer technology; the overall cost of this agreement, which was related to ICT's turnover, was to be approximately £10 million over the fifteen-year term of the licence.

Negotiations with British companies

What ICT had achieved from its American agreements were products to sell in the short term, and a licensing arrangement that would enable it to manufacture and sell RCA's state-of-the-art computers in the longer term. What it now needed was a large-scale electronics manufacturing capability in the UK. This capability could only be achieved by taking control of the computer division of another manufacturer. Obtaining control, rather than merging, was a cornerstone of ICT's policy: it was convinced that no other British company had the planning and selling capability to compete with IBM or the other American companies. But this was not necessarily the view of the other British companies. Table 10.3, which shows the UK market shares during 1950–59, illustrates ICT's very poor showing during the formative years of the industry, during which it had secured only a measly 7 per cent of the market. This poor performance was probably one of the reasons why negotiations were so difficult: if ICT had little confidence in the marketing capability of its competitors, those competitors in turn had little reason to have much faith in ICT.

Table 10.3   UK market shares, 1950-59

	Value (£000s)	Percentage market share	Number of computers sold
Elliott-Automation/NCR	3930	32.4	25
Ferranti	3190	26.4	36
Leo Computers	2000	16.5	10
English Electric	1875	15.5	25
ICT	870	7.1	29
IBM	240	2.0	2

Source
Derived from Table 12 in C. Freeman *et al.*, 'Research and Development in Electronic Capital Goods', *National Institute Economic Review*, 34, 1965, pp. 40-91.

None the less, the scene was ripe for merger activity. Table 10.4 shows the extraordinary array of computers that had been put on the market by British computer manufacturers in the period 1950-63. Although the UK market was expanding, only £15 million worth of computers were sold during 1960-61, so that it is unlikely that anyone was making money. Eventually, all the British companies would merge to form ICL, but this would involve several steps of rationalization (Fig. 10.1). The first merger wave occurred during 1962-63, and this resulted in three British firms: ICT (which absorbed the computer interests of EMI and Ferranti), English Electric-Leo-Marconi, and Elliott-Automation.

Of the British computer manufacturers, Elliott-Automation had been the most successful during the 1950s, having taken a 32 per cent share of the market. Elliott Brothers had been a company rather in the doldrums following the Second World War; but, under its maverick managing director Sir Leon Bagritt, it became the *enfant terrible* of the electronics and control business. It was renamed Elliott-Automation in 1957, and at that time was probably Britain's fastest-growing company; it grew largely by acquisition, and by 1960 it had several dozen subsidiary companies.[24] Although discussions were held between Bagritt and ICT's Cecil Mead on several occasions, a merger was never a strong possibility for a number of reasons. Probably foremost, was the fact that Elliott-Automation, with a price/earnings ratio in the fifties or sixties, would have been a very expensive acquisition. Also, Elliott-Automation's main computer business was in process-control and automation, rather than EDP, so its

Table 10.4 UK-manufactured computers, 1951–63

Manufacturer	First delivery	Model	Average price (£000s)	Generation	Type (C/S/P)	Number sold
AEI	1960	1010	250	2	C	B
Elliott-	1955	402	25	1	S	B
Automation	1956	405	125	1	C	C
	1958	802	17	2	P	B
	1959	803	35	2	P/S	E
	1961	503	80	2	C	C
EMI	1959	1100	180	2	C	C
	1961	2400	600	2	C	A
English	1955	DEUCE	50	1	S	C
Electric	1961	KDP10	400	2	C	B
	1962	KDN2	20	2	P	B
	1963	KDF6	60	2	S	B
	1963	KDF9	120	2	S	C
Ferranti	1951	Mark I/I-Star	45	1	S	B
	1956	Pegasus	50	1	S	C
	1957	Mercury	120	1	S	C
	1959	Pegasus II	120	1	C	B
	1959	Perseus	150	1	C	A
	1961	Sirius	17	1	S	B
	1961	Atlas	2000	2	S	A
	1963	Orion	300	2	C	A
Leo	1957	LEO II	95	1	C	B
	1962	LEO III	200	2	C	C
ICT	1955	HEC 2M	25	1	S	B
	1956	1201	33	1	C	D
	1959	1202	45	1	C	B
	1961	1301	100	2	C	E
STC	1958	Zebra	28	1	S	C

Notes
The table excludes one-of-a-kind machines and prototypes, and imported machines.

Type: C = commercial   Sales: A = 5 or less
     S = scientific   B = 6–15
     P = process-control.   C = 16–50
                                      D = 51–100
                                      E = over 100.

Sources
Delivery dates and volumes of sales: *Computer Survey*. Price data: R.H. Williams, 'Early Computers in Europe', *Proc. 1976 National Computer Conference*, AFIPS Press, Montvale NJ, 1976, pp. 21–29; with corrections from other sources.

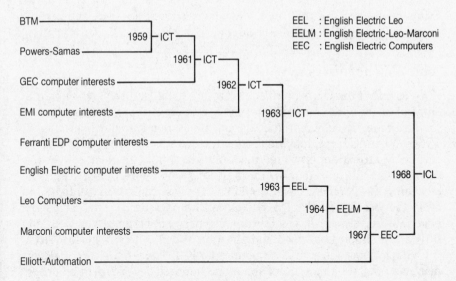

Fig. 10.1 Evolution of ICL, 1959–68

expertise did not blend well with ICT's objectives; and in so far as Elliott-Automation had any aspirations for the EDP computer business, these were already being met by a marketing arrangement with NCR's English subsidiary.

A much better business case could have been made for a merger between ICT and English Electric, since their EDP marketing and technical strengths were complementary. English Electric had begun making computers in 1947, and during the 1950s and early 1960s it had developed an excellent range of scientific machines, the most recent of which was the KDF9, which had an elegant 'stack-based' architecture. There had been talk at one point of ICT marketing the KDF9 for English Electric. Unfortunately, once the joint talks between RCA, ICT, and English Electric broke down in 1961, the impetus for a closer relationship was lost, and was not regained until 1967. In the event, English Electric did manage to acquire the EDP and marketing expertise it was seeking by gaining control of Leo Computers in April 1963. The Leo Computers management had become increasingly aware of the escalating costs of the computer industry during 1962, and a sell-out to English Electric was achieved very discreetly and quickly through the merchant bankers Lazards.[25] ICT at no time held merger talks with Leo Computers, for the reason that Mead was simply too busy to pursue them.[26] The formation of English Electric Leo Computers Limited constituted a real second force in the British computer industry. In 1964 the company absorbed the computer interests of the English Electric Marconi division, and became known as English Electric-Leo-Marconi (EELM).

The EMI acquisition

EMI, as one of the UK's premier electronics manufacturers, was a natural entrant to the UK computer industry, although it was slightly late on to the scene, its first commercial machines not being delivered until 1960. When ICT was looking around for partners in 1961, EMI had the particular attraction of being the only electronics company that was actively seeking to exit from the business, since it recognized that the escalating development costs would call for vast capital investment, and even then commercial success was far from assured. This made the negotiations between ICT's Edward Playfair and Terence Maxwell, and EMI's Sir Joseph Lockwood and Sir John Wall, fairly straightforward.

EMI had some substantial attractions for ICT. It was a highly competent manufacturer; it had a team of about one hundred development engineers in Feltham and Hayes, Middlesex, which would practically double ICT's capability; it had a small, well-trained sales-staff, and some prestige customers, including the banks; and finally it had no less than three second-generation computers, at a time when ICT had none. EMI's smallest machine, the model 1100, was broadly in the price/performance class of ICT's 1300 series; but it had the advantage of being available, with magnetic tape, at a time when the ICT machine was still in the proto-type stage. Although ICT had arranged to buy in the RCA 301, the 1100 was slightly more powerful; and in any case a home-built product was always to be preferred to an import. EMI's second machine was the 2400. This was a highly competitive large-scale EDP machine that was a useful addition to ICT's product range. The EMI 2400 had been developed under the auspices of Lord Halsbury and the NRDC, and was intended to be Britain's answer to the IBM 7090 large-scale EDP computer. This it would have been, had it not had profound reliability and software problems. This, of course, was unknown to either EMI or ICT at the time of the negotiations. In the event only three 2400s were ever sold.[27] EMI's third machine was the 3400 prototype. This machine had been developed with the aid of a £250 000 development contract from the NRDC, and, along with the Ferranti Atlas, was intended to be Britain's answer to the IBM Stretch and the Univac LARC. The giant-machine market was one that it was ICT's policy to eschew, so the 3400 had very little attraction, and was never developed beyond the prototype that ICT inherited.[28]

On 9 July 1962 ICT acquired EMI's computer interests, for which it paid 275 000 ICT ordinary shares—which valued the business at £1¼ million. Although only the model 1100 computer lived up to expectations, ICT considered it did well out of the deal; and it was, after all, 'one move towards consolidation of the industry, by the friendly removal of one competitor who has a good name in the world of electronics.'[29]

The Ferranti talks

The EMI acquisition remained little more than a step in the right direction. A merger with Ferranti offered something much more sub-stantial. Talks were held on several occasions, dating from the mid-1950s. There had been serious talks at the time of the BTM/Powers-Samas merger in 1959, with ICT seeking to market the Pegasus; but Ferranti was unwilling. If ICT and Ferranti had joined forces in 1959, the history of the British computer industry would no doubt have been very different. By 1963, however, Sir Vincent de Ferranti, chairman of Ferranti, had decided to make an exit from the computer business, for much the same reasons of escalating development costs that had caused EMI to withdraw the previous year.[30] ICT's reactions to Ferranti's overtures were initially lukewarm, for two reasons. First, ICT was in the throes of shedding labour, because of the decline in punched-card machine sales, and its share price was so low that, whatever it paid for Ferranti, it would have been a high price in relation to the assets acquired. Second, although Ferranti's computer R&D and production were outstanding—unquestion-ably the best in Europe—its current range of products was not at all attractive to ICT.

Ferranti's first-generation machines were no longer being actively sold, and it had only two second-generation machines, Orion and Atlas, neither of which was attractive. The Orion, although it was a large-scale EDP machine, was too close in performance to the EMI 2400 which ICT was already intending to sell. Moreover, Orion had major reliability problems, owing to a novel electronic technology known as the 'neuron'. The neuron eventually had to be abandoned, and a successor machine, Orion II, had to be developed.[31] The Atlas was even less of an attraction than the Orion. The Atlas, like the EMI 3400, was a very-high-speed scientific computer, intended to compete with the American Stretch and LARC; and it had been partially underwritten by £300 000 funding from the NRDC. Developed in collaboration with Manchester University, the Atlas was a major technical triumph, doing much to recapture Britain's lost prestige in advanced computer design. It had pioneered techniques in virtual storage and operating systems that were perhaps two years ahead of American manufacturers. But although the Atlas was strong on prestige, it was an asset that ICT did not want, any more than it had wanted the EMI 3400. At the time of the merger talks, only two Atlases had been sold.

What the Ferranti acquisition therefore offered ICT was not a range of machines, but R&D potential and a manufacturing capability. The R&D potential was certainly very high, particularly in software. The Ferranti programming division, managed by Peter Hunt, had developed the Atlas operating system, which was well in advance of anything offered by American manufacturers, and it had produced a commercial programming language, Nebula, for the Orion that was at least equal to those offered by American manufacturers. As a computer manufacturer, Ferranti's computer plant in West Gorton, Manchester, was the largest in Europe.

Computer Leasings Limited and the FP6000

Two events helped transform the attractiveness of Ferranti to ICT in spring 1963. The first was the formation of Computer Leasings Limited; and the second was the FP6000 computer, developed by Ferranti's Canadian subsidiary.

The leasing problem had always been endemic to the punched-card machine industry; but the problems in the computer industry were much more severe. Because of the high obsolescence risk of computers—nobody knew if an individual model would last three, five, or ten years—customers almost invariably leased computers rather than buying them outright. IBM was happy to offer leasing arrangements to UK customers, as were wealthy companies like English Electric; and so ICT was forced to do the same. However, if ICT acquired Ferranti, then, as its computer output rose to perhaps fifty per cent of production, it would no longer be able to supply adequate leasing funds. Ordinary bank-borrowing would produce much too high a degree of financial gearing; and the possibilities of issuing debentures or ploughing-back profits were very limited.

The solution lay in a leasing company, of the kind that existed in America. In America, with the arrival of second-generation computers, especially the IBM 1401, the anticipated life of computers became considerably longer than the five years that IBM traditionally used as its depreciation basis. The first of the American leasing companies was the Greyhound Company, which began operations in 1961. Greyhound, in effect, bought machines from IBM and leased them out to users, typically under-cutting IBM rates by twenty per cent. By working on a depreciation basis of eight to ten years, the leasing companies became a highly profitable branch of the United States computer industry.[32]

The concept of a computer-leasing company drifted across the Atlantic to Europe during 1962 and 1963, at a time when ICT in Britain and Machines Bull in France were both wrestling with the problem of financing the growing volume of rentals. It seems curious, in retrospect, that European leasing companies were so slow to emerge; but it was probably due to the much stronger traditions of leasing capital goods in the United

States. The idea was first brought to the attention of ICT's Terence Maxwell in September 1962 by Bernard Clarke, joint general manager of Midland Bank, one of ICT's main bankers.[33] After an intense round of negotiations in spring 1963, Maxwell brought together a consortium of lending institutions to invest up to £24 million in an ICT subsidiary, Computer Leasings Limited (CLL). The financial details were highly technical, but in essence the arrangement was that ICT would sell its computers for cash to CLL, which would then lease out the machines and distribute the revenues to the investing participants at a rate of one or two per cent above the bank rate; the bulk of any additional profits went back to ICT, which continued to bear the obsolescence risk. The initial £24 million of leasing funds in CLL would enable ICT to expand as rapidly as it could, at least until 1966, when more funds would be needed. (Around the same time that ICT formed CLL, Machines Bull also formed a leasing subsidiary, Locabull. It is perhaps a reflection on the different economic climates in the United States and Europe, that in the former leasing companies were quite distinct from, and regarded as parasitic by, the computer manufacturers; whereas in Europe they could only prosper as subsidiaries of the computer companies.)

The second event that changed the balance of value to ICT of Ferranti's computer division was the discovery of a medium-sized computer known as the FP6000, developed by Ferranti's Canadian subsidiary, Ferranti-Packard. The FP6000 had originally been specified in England as an overtly 'commercial' computer by one of Ferranti's salesmen, Harry Johnson; and the design had much common ancestry with the Ferranti Pegasus. But because Ferranti had most of its resources committed to the Orion and Atlas, it was not developed in England. The design was picked up by the Canadian subsidiary, however, where it was developed into a product during 1962, and by spring 1963 four systems were on order. The FP6000 was first described publicly at the American Spring Joint Computer Conference in April 1963.[34] The FP6000 was a very advanced machine, incorporating a multi-programming system, derived from Orion, of unusual sophistication in a machine of its size. Implicit in the design of the FP6000 was that it could support a spectrum of machine sizes, priced from as little as £50 000 up to perhaps £500 000. The performance could be extended in a fairly continuous manner by having core-store sizes from 4 Kword* up to 32 Kword, with speeds from 6 microseconds to 2 microseconds, and various processor options. The software for the system would be invariant with system size; and this would enable users to upgrade their systems without the reprogramming costs of changing to an entirely different architecture.

* Kword: 1024 (or occasionally 1000) words. An FP6000 word contained 24 bits, the equivalent of four 6-bit characters or three 8-bit bytes.

In March 1963, a Ferranti team visited Canada to make a detailed technical evaluation of the FP6000, and concluded:

There are certain facets of the system we do not like. However, were we to begin designing now a machine in the same price/performance range as the FP6000, we would have in some 18 months' time a system that would not be significantly better—if indeed it were any better—than the FP6000.[35]

A follow-up visit was made by ICT's Arthur Humphreys and Echo Organ the following month. Although ICT had its own computer projects under way, it was clear that the FP6000 was far more developed than any of them. Moreover, the circuit technology of the FP6000 had already been proven in the field, as it was identical to that used in a machine known as the Gemini, which had been installed with Canadian Airways and was working well. The first FP6000 had been delivered to the Federal Reserve Bank, New York, and was in the process of being commissioned. Although no application software had been developed, the multi-programming operating system and much of the basic software had been completed.

Immediately after Humphreys and Organ returned to England, Humphreys went to see Cecil Mead at his office in Park Lane, London, on Easter Monday, April 1963. Humphreys recommended to Mead that ICT should adopt the FP6000 specification for the small/medium computers it then had under development at Stevenage—PF 182 and PF 183.[36] Mead gave Humphreys authority to go ahead, and the following day the two projects were re-oriented to the FP6000 design. The reasons for this decision were essentially to reduce the lead-time and development costs, but implicit in the decision was the concept of a compatible range of computers. This was not the only development project at Stevenage, as there was another joint development project, 'Poplar', with RCA, to develop a computer to be known as the 2201; and another processor, the X4, had been inherited from EMI.[37]

The decision to adopt the FP6000 long predated the formal acquisition of Ferranti, of which the terms had yet to be negotiated. There was also an unwritten understanding that Basil de Ferranti, the second son of Sir Vincent, should be managing director designate. Interestingly, Sir Vincent Ferranti had a succession problem with his two sons, Sebastian and Basil, not unlike the succession problem that Thomas Watson Sr had with his two sons, Tom and Dick, in IBM. Sebastian stayed with the Ferranti firm, and Basil joined ICT. Aged thirty-four, 'Boz' de Ferranti was not an easy person to assimilate into ICT. During 1957–64 he had been a Conservative M.P., and briefly Parliamentary Secretary to the Minister of Aviation. Prior to that he had been managing director of the Ferranti Domestic Appliance Department. He had a well-deserved reputation as a play-boy and a scientific gadfly. Although he radiated charm, and had an infectious enthusiasm for computers, he had very little operational business experience. As a chairman of ICT he would have been excellent; but he lacked the flair for finance and administration needed in a managing director, and he was to prove a disappointment.[38]

Agreement in principle for ICT to acquire Ferranti's computer division was reached in June 1963, and the formal agreement was signed by Playfair and Sebastian de Ferranti on 26 September 1963, the first day of ICT's financial year. Ferranti received cash and ICT shares, valuing the business at about £5.3 million. The deal included about 1900 personnel, and the development and manufacturing facilities at West Gorton, Manchester, and Bracknell, Berkshire. The Ferranti Digital Systems Department, which manufactured process-control computers, was not included in the deal. Following the Ferranti acquisition, there were major board changes in ICT. Most notably, Basil de Ferranti was appointed deputy managing director for R&D; and, while he was being groomed to be managing director (which he became in December 1964), Cecil Mead took over as managing director from John Bull. Eric Grundy, a founder of the Ferranti computer department in 1947, joined the ICT board as a non-executive director representing Ferranti; and Peter Hall—manager of the Ferranti computer department—was appointed a deputy director. Within ICT, Humphreys and Organ were appointed directors, and some of the old-guard directors retired to make way (Appendix 2c).

It should perhaps be mentioned that while ICT was negotiating with Ferranti, it was also talking simultaneously to Machines Bull, and certainly in early 1963 the French connection had seemed the more likely. The basis for collaboration was very good, in 'that they both had licensing agreements with RCA and were selling the model 301 (as the ICT 1500 and the Gamma 30, respectively); they had been exchanging punched-card machine know-how for years; and they were both strong in their own countries, but weak elsewhere in Europe. The negotiations continued long after the Ferranti acquisition had been agreed; but in October 1963 Machines Bull had a major financial crisis, and negotiations came to a halt. In December 1963 the American company General Electric put in a rescue bid; and, although there was initially some reluctance on the part of the French Government (as there would have been under similar circumstances in Britain), in April 1964 GE was allowed to take Machines Bull over.

Rationalizing the product line

Following the Ferranti acquisition, ICT had an impressive array of incompatible computers (Table 10.5). In the short term (1963-66), there was little that could be done but accept the position as it was. There were too

Table 10.5 ICT Product Plans, October 1963

Date	small <£50K	small/medium £50–150K	medium/large £150–400K	large £250–750K	giant £1M+
1963-66	1004	1101 1300 1301 1500 (RCA 301)	1302	Orion	Atlas
1965-68	1004—enhanced	PF 182 2201	1900 (FP6000) 1600 (RCA 3301)	Orion II	Atlas II
1968-72	900 (PF 183)	← —— PROJECT SET —— →			no plans

Source
'Computer Product Plan', 7 October 1963, ICT Board Papers.

many competing machines in the small/medium range; the medium-priced machines were not particularly competitive; of the large machines, the EMI 2400 had been abandoned, and the Orion was unreliable; and such enthusiasm as existed for the Atlas came only from Ferranti. For its medium-term plans (1965-68), ICT would be selling an enhanced version of the 1004 as its smallest machine. In the small/medium class it had the PF182 project under way for a successor to the 1100 and 1300 ranges, and the joint development with RCA for the 2201. In the medium/large class it had the FP6000, to be sold as the ICT 1900, and a somewhat larger machine, the RCA 3301, to be marketed as the ICT 1600. Finally, for the large and giant machines it had the successors to the Ferranti Orion and Atlas. Thus, for its medium-term plans, ICT had a full spectrum of machines, although the software and hardware compatibility between them was negligible. For the longer term, it was intended that all of ICT's medium-to-large EDP computers would be made from a single 'project set', which would have compatible software and peripherals throughout the range. It was planned that such a range of computers should be available by 1968, and that the range would either be developed in collaboration with RCA, or by development of the FP6000.

Which way to go—the RCA route, or via the FP6000—was still under active investigation when, on 7 April 1964, IBM astounded the computer industry by announcing its System/360 compatible range of computers.

11

The response to the IBM System/360
1964-1965

I.B.M.'s $5,000,000,000 Gamble
The new System/360 was intended to obsolete virtually all other
existing computers . . . It was roughly as though General Motors
had decided to scrap its existing makes and models and offer in
their place one new line of cars, covering the entire spectrum of
demand, with a radically redesigned engine and an exotic fuel.

—Tom Wise, *Fortune*, September 1966.[1]

On 7 April 1964, IBM announced System/360, a compatible family of
third-generation computers. System/360 consisted of six distinct
processors and forty peripherals, which were intended to replace all IBM's
current computers, except the smallest and largest. The scale of the
announcement was entirely unprecedented, and all the evidence is that it
took the rest of the industry largely by surprise. Although ICT's product
planners had received intelligence in late 1963 that IBM was working on
a compatible range of computers, they knew nothing of the range architecture, or when it would be launched.[2]

The SPREAD report and System/360

IBM's decision to launch System/360 is generally regarded as one of the
great business success stories of the second half of the twentieth century.
Certainly, within the IBM culture it has taken on a symbolic significance,
as the true beginning of the computer age.[3]

For many years, the only authoritative account of the rationale behind
System/360 was two articles 'I.B.M.'s $5,000,000,000 gamble' and
'The rocky road to the market place', written by Tom Wise of *Fortune*
magazine.[4] Although factually accurate, the hyperbole of Wise's articles
—the quotation at the head of this chapter is a typical example—gave
IBM an aura as a technological pioneer which was scarcely justified. The
fact is that the concept of a compatible family was well understood within
the computer industry; IBM's achievement was to be the first in the
market-place with such a range. In recent years, much more information
about the origin of System/360 has become available, including the

SPREAD Report of 1961, which originally proposed the introduction of a compatible family of computers.[5]

In 1961 IBM had no less than seven incompatible computer architectures. This proliferation of computer models was causing major problems in marketing, manufacturing, and software development.[6] In terms of marketing, the large number of architectures necessitated multiple selling forces, each expert in a particular machine. The market-place was fragmented: small commercial users were supplied with the 1401, medium-sized users with the 7070, and large-scale users with the 7080. The scientific market was similarly fragmented. Users also had problems upgrading their installations by more than a factor of about two without changing to an entirely different machine, with all the attendant problems of reprogramming. Manufacturing problems were acute, and were threatening to undermine IBM's traditional economies of scale. For example, some 2500 different circuit modules were used in the different processors. Apart from the large amount of capital this caused to be tied up in stocks, it was also very difficult to implement improvements in electronic technology in any systematic way. Peripherals also represented a problem, since it was necessary to develop a special-purpose controller to interface each peripheral with each processor: given m processors, and n peripherals, this represented a possible $m \times n$ controllers; the only way to contain the problem was to limit artificially the number of peripherals offered with each processor. The same combinatorial explosion was occurring in software, where each processor required a full portfolio of systems programs and applications. In practice, the programming effort was kept within bounds; but software was beginning to dominate development costs, and it was realized that the problem would have to be tackled sooner rather than later.

It should be emphasized that these problems were common to the industry. ICT, for example, had almost as many incompatible architectures as IBM, and was responding to the problem in its own way. By 1962, for example, it had already developed a 'standard interface' for the 1302 computer, under the technical leadership of Ronald Feather.[7] Once the standard interface had been developed, it was possible to attach any peripheral to any processor, provided they both conformed to the standard interface specification. ICT was also labouring under no less than 18 different magnetic-tape formats on its various computers, so that it was acutely aware of the need for the standardization of file and data formats.[8]

The concept of a compatible family of computers was widely discussed in IBM during 1961, but was far from universally accepted.[9] Sales of the 1401, for example, had not yet begun to peak, and there were plans for smaller and larger models that would keep it marketable for several years. There was also an 8000 series under development, which would replace the 7000 series, and IBM's UK laboratories at Hursley had also developed a small scientific computer. In total, however, these developments threatened to do little or nothing to improve IBM's development, manufacturing, and sales problems. It was against this background that in November 1961 IBM's top management set up the SPREAD Task Group (SPREAD: Systems Programming Research And Development) 'to establish overall plans for data processing products'.[10] The SPREAD Task Group included several of IBM's most senior managers and technical staff, from various divisions, both domestic and world-trade. The group worked quickly, and its recommendations were made in a final report dated 28 December 1961.

The SPREAD Report concluded that a compatible family of computers was both commercially desirable and technically feasible. Most importantly, the report specified in considerable detail the marketing implications and the technical problems involved. For example, one major marketing strength was that a user, once committed to the compatible range, would become 'locked in' to the series. (One marketing problem not so clearly foreseen, however, was the emergence of 'plug-compatible manufacturers' who, by conforming to IBM standards, would be able to sell peripherals for attachment to IBM processors.) The SPREAD Report recommended the development of five distinct processors, to serve a spectrum of users from small to large, both scientific and commercial. The different processors would have identical instruction codes, but they would be constructed using different technologies, and with core memories ranging from slow to the fastest available. By means of a standard interface, most processors would support most peripherals. It was recognized, however, that it would not be possible to accommodate very small and very large machines within the technological framework of the computer range, and this was to prove a serious competitive disadvantage. The great technical challenges in implementing the new range were fully recognized by the SPREAD Report. The several processors and many peripherals would have to be developed simultaneously in IBM's several geographically dispersed development laboratories. This would entail a rigorous regimen of standards-enforcement and meticulous management.

The family concept was clearly a high-risk, high-reward strategy; Wise reported one IBMer as saying 'We called this project "You bet your company".'[11] However, in early January 1962 the IBM board accepted the recommendations of the SPREAD Report, and the R&D and manufacturing programs within IBM were reoriented to what was to be called System/360. It was estimated that the R&D budget for System/360 was about $500 million, and that the total cost of development and manufacturing was $5 billion.*

* The R&D cost of $500 million has since been confirmed as 'not terribly far off— probably not a factor of two off, one way or the other'.[12]

The System/360 announcement and competitive responses

The announcement strategy of System/360 was debated at length in IBM during 1962-63. There were two conflicting requirements. On the one hand, there was the need to derive maximum sales potential from the compatible-range concept, which suggested the simultaneous announcement of all the computers in the range. On the other hand, it was necessary to protect IBM's existing product lines, and to switch gracefully production from the old lines to the new; which implied a phased announcement over at least a two-year period. The SPREAD Report had envisaged a 'scatter' announcement of two processors in the first quarter of 1964, two more in 1965, and the last in 1966; during the announcement period, the old-line products would be systematically enhanced to maintain their short-term competitiveness and to avoid revenue fall-off. However:

In December 1963 all the debates on announcement alternatives were terminated after Honeywell's announcement of the H200—the first competitive announcement of a system that was architecturally almost identical to a leading IBM system. Honeywell's new system was touted to be four or more times faster than IBM's 1401.[13]

The concept of a 1401-compatible computer is attributed to J. Chuan Chu, Honeywell's EDP engineering chief, who argued that, by reason of its anti-trust position, IBM 'was too smart not to let us take 10 percent or so of the market'.[14] Following the H200 launch, Honeywell ran a provocative series of advertisements that featured the 'Liberator', a software aid to automatically convert IBM 1401 programs to the H200. The H200 was also plug-compatible and file-compatible with the 1401, enabling users to upgrade their installations using the H200 in a very straightforward way.

The success of the H200 was spectacular, taking more orders in the first week following the announcement than Honeywell had made in its eight previous years of operation.[15] This produced a dramatic fall-off in 1401 orders, and a flood of returns from the field. IBM briefly considered releasing an enhanced 1401—the 1401S—but decided instead to announce the entire System/360 range, as being the most effective response. On 7 April 1964 six processors in the 360 range were simultaneously announced (Table 11.1). The smallest model, the 360/30 was intended to replace the 1401 (and presumably the H200), over which it had a greatly improved price/performance. The largest machine, the 360/70, had a performance of about five times the IBM 7090, making it a very large EDP machine indeed, especially in European terms.

System/360 produced two major competitive challenges to other manufacturers: first, the concept of a compatible range, and second, a several-

Table 11.1 IBM System/360 announcements, 1964

Model	Price (£000s)	Announced	Delivered (USA)	Delivered (UK)
20	36	Nov 1964	Dec 1965	Apr 1966
30	152	Apr 1964	Jun 1965	Mar 1966
40	257	Apr 1964	Apr 1965	Apr 1966
50	538	Apr 1964	Aug 1965	Mar 1967
60/62	857	Apr 1964	Nov 1965	May 1967
67		Aug 1964	May 1966	Dec 1967
70	1,500	Apr 1964	Jan 1966	May 1967
91		Nov 1964	Oct 1967	

Notes
Price is for a typical or average system.
Models 60/62 and 70 were redesignated 65 and 75, and delivered on the dates shown.

Sources
Delivery data: US: A. Padegs 'System/360 and Beyond', *IBM Journal of Research and Development*, 25, 1981, pp. 377-90; UK: *Computer Survey*. Price data: 'Computer Characteristics', *Datamation, passim* and M. Phister, *Data Processing: Technology and Economics*, 2nd edition, Digital Press, Bedford MA. Prices originally stated as monthly rentals in dollars, converted to selling prices on the basis of 60 times monthly rental, and £1 = $2.80.

fold increase in price/performance over existing computers. In the hiatus of ordering that followed the April 1964 announcement, while the market digested the implications of System/360, all of IBM's competitors formulated their responses. There were three broad strategic responses available:

1. To develop a range of computers fully hardware-compatible with System/360, but with a comparable or better price/performance.

2. To develop a range of computers, not compatible with System/360, but with a comparable or better price/performance.

3. To focus on 'niche' areas not well-served by System/360.

Given sufficient resources, it was possible to pursue more than one of these options. Within the three broad responses, it was also necessary to take tactical advantage of the few competitive weaknesses of System/360:

1. The quoted delivery times of System/360 were 16-24 months, which was long by industry standards, and unprecedented for IBM.

2. The range lacked both very small and very large machines.

3. System/360 used a conservative electronic technology, known as SLT, which fell short of true third-generation integrated circuits.

4. The architecture did not adequately support real-time or time-sharing applications.

Most of these shortcomings arose from the technological uncertainties of the period 1961–63, when System/360 was under development, and from its accelerated introduction following the H200 launch.

The best-known examples of the first strategy, developing a 360-compatible range, were the RCA Spectra 70 and the English Electric System 4 (see below). Univac also introduced a somewhat lower-key 360-compatible range, the 9000, in spring 1966. The issue of IBM compatibility was a high-running controversy at the time. The strategy had been first introduced by Honeywell, and it was not clear in 1964 whether the 360 announcement would completely undermine the H200, or whether Honeywell would reap the 1401 customer base, whose machines had been rendered obsolete by the 360.

Several manufacturers adopted the second strategy, that of launching a non-compatible computer range.[16] In June 1964 Honeywell announced the model 2200, compatible with the H200; in February 1965 it introduced further models, the 120, 1200, and 4200. These turned the H200 into a compatible family of computers with a comparable price/performance to System/360; and the short lead-times of the 200 series secured a significant tactical advantage. Burroughs also took an existing model, the B5000, and turned it into the 500 series, initially with the model 5500; a larger machine (the 6500) and smaller machines (the 2500 and 3500) were introduced subsequently.

The most successful exponent of the third competitive response, aiming for a niche market, was CDC. By 'hitting IBM where they are weakest',[17] CDC rapidly came to dominate the large-machine market. CDC had already moved towards a niche strategy by announcing its 6600 super-computer in July 1962; but following the 360 launch it announced the 6000 series in December 1964—a range of three processors, the 6400, 6600, and 6800. Univac and Burroughs also developed niche strategies as part of their response to IBM. Univac specialized, through its model 1108, in real-time transaction processing systems, and secured many prestige orders, particularly with the airlines. Burroughs, taking advantage of its origins as a supplier of accounting machines to banks, became a major supplier of real-time financial systems. General Electric capitalized on the 360's weakness in 'multi-access' computing, a technique that allowed many programmers and users to share the computer simultaneously using typewriter terminals. * During the period 1964–66, GE dominated the American and European market for multi-access computers. IBM

---

* The terms 'real-time', 'multi-access', and 'time-sharing' were used somewhat interchangeably during the mid-1960s. The terms have generally been used here in their modern sense.

responded by announcing a time-sharing computer, the 360/67, in August 1965.

This, then, was the competitive environment created by the System/360 announcement. As a computer manufacturer in the international market place, ICT was forced into adopting one or more of these competitive responses.

The RCA and ICT responses: Spectra 70 and the 1900 series

From about 1963, well before the 360 announcement, both RCA and ICT had been independently evolving plans for compatible ranges of computers. These were, however, long-term plans; in the case of ICT there was certainly no intention of delivering its compatible 'project set' much before 1968.[18] The effect of the 360 announcement in April 1964 was therefore to compress into months development programmes that had been intended to take years.

Although RCA and ICT had been jointly developing the 2201 computer as a medium-term successor to the RCA 301/ICT 1500, their long-term plans were not at all integrated. While ICT had been contemplating a range based on the FP6000, RCA had quite separate plans, which would include some form of IBM compatibility. In autumn 1963, RCA decided to cancel the 2201 in order to devote all its technical resources to a new range of machines; this it did with the certainty of losing its short-term market share. The 3301, which had been announced the previous August, had passed the point of no return, however, and continued to be marketed both by RCA in the United States and by ICT in the UK (as the ICT 1600). By early 1964, RCA's new product plans were sufficiently advanced to be presented to ICT's top management. In March 1964, Cecil Mead and Terence Maxwell visited RCA's American headquarters, where General Sarnoff and Elmer Engstrom, the RCA chairman and president, reaffirmed their policy of remaining a significant force in the computer industry.[19] Mead and Maxwell were given a formal presentation of RCA's future range, on which it was proposed to spend $50 million in R&D. The range was to consist of a family of five compatible computers: deliveries of small machines, using conventional discrete electronics, were to begin in 1965, and large machines, which would use integrated circuits, were scheduled for 1966. The plans were sufficiently flexible that RCA would be able to emulate or adopt the instruction code for IBM's future range—then thought to be the 8000 series—which 'they believe will become a standard code for America and probably for the rest of the world' as soon as it was announced.[20]

The hardening of RCA's plans now forced ICT to confront the dilemma of whether to follow the RCA line, which was clearly technically very advanced, or to become fully committed to an FP6000-based compatible family. At the beginning of April 1964, an ICT planning and technical team, which included Basil de Ferranti, Arthur Humphreys, Peter Ellis, Peter Hall, Derek Eldridge, and Raymond Bird, visited RCA's Cherry Hill laboratories to make an appraisal of the RCA range.[21] As luck would have it, the System/360 announcement of 7 April 1964 occurred at the very moment of the ICT visit. There was no industrial espionage, and RCA obtained details of the 360 from the publicly available manuals.[22] While the ICT team toured the United States on other business, RCA immediately investigated the implications of System/360 for the RCA range. When the ICT team returned a week later, RCA had decided to make the new line fully 360-compatible. The new RCA range was subsequently announced as Spectra 70.

ICT was entitled to manufacture the RCA series under licence, but declined to do so on three main grounds. First, on the policy of IBM-compatibility; second, on the question of lead-times; and third, because of its growing commitment to the FP6000-based range. IBM-compatibility was seen to be a poor competitive strategy for ICT.[23] The only logical argument for a user buying an IBM-compatible computer in preference to a machine manufactured by IBM, it was argued, was because it had a better price/performance, or technical superiority. Given IBM's relative economies of scale, a price advantage could only be achieved at the cost of very low profits, if it could be achieved at all. And given IBM's R&D resources, and the fact that an IBM-compatible manufacturer would have to follow IBM developments, since it could scarcely anticipate them, technical superiority would also be extremely difficult to achieve. There was also the question of the damage that copying IBM would do to its image as an innovator. The question of lead-times was at least as decisive. Although the RCA planners believed they could bring machines on to the market in 18-24 months, the ICT team was highly sceptical. And in any case, they would be left without any product at all during the development period. RCA was a rich company, and willing to withstand a short-term loss for the eventual high rewards; but ICT did not have this luxury. Finally, although the FP6000-based range had not yet passed the point of no return, sufficient development work had been done to make it ICT's only real option in the short to medium term.

The FP6000 was architecturally less advanced than System/360 , but it had the great advantage of being available, working, and already in the field. The ICT team was convinced that an FP6000-based compatible family could be delivered well ahead of System/360. Probably the main perceived disadvantage of the FP6000—and this was to be brought up time and again over the next decade—was that it used a 6-bit character, where System/360 used an 8-bit byte. But even this, in 1963, was seen as far from being a disadvantage, since it meant that the core-storage requirement—which accounted for 25 per cent of processor costs—would be six-eighths that of a byte-organized machine. The ICT range needed to have a 10 to 15 per cent price/performance advantage over System/360, if it was to sell at all; and this went no small way to achieving it.[24] Similarly, although the FP6000 was in electronic terms a second-generation discrete-component machine, the technology was very well established, and therefore cheap. Although integrated circuits were faster, they were much more expensive; and, in cheaper models especially, processor speed was of less consequence to throughput than peripheral speeds.

Before flying back to England, the ICT team had decided to recommend that the FP6000 be developed into what was to become the 1900 series. There and then, Peter Ellis worked out the model numbers of the new series, and the logistics of implementation. The original FP6000—already announced as the ICT 1900—would be renamed the 1904, putting it firmly in the middle of the range. Below the 1904 there would be three smaller models, the 1901, 1902, and 1903, and above it there would be a large version, the 1906.[25] The two main Stevenage processor developments, PF182 and PF183, became respectively the 1902/03 (there were two models but only one processor) and the 1901, the smallest member of the 1900 series. At West Gorton, projects were established for the large 1906 processor, and for scientific variants of the 1904 and the 1906 (known as the 1905 and 1907). During the following months, private presentations of the 1900 series were made to potential customers, and the decision was made for a public announcement in the autumn.

The press launch for the 1900 series took place on 29 September 1964. It had been realized that something special would be called for in order to match the very high-profile launch of System/360. A bright new PR firm, which had spun-off from the 'Tonight' television team, was brought in to make a filmed presentation, with a script by Anthony Jay (later of 'Yes, Minister' fame). The film, which included presentations by Playfair, Mead, de Ferranti, and Humphreys, was shown simultaneously around the world.[26] Seven models of the 1900 series were announced at the press launch, priced from £40 000 up to £750 000 (Table 11.2). The small 1901 was not announced, in order to protect the 1004 and to keep R&D costs under control; but the numbering of the range was designed to imply that such a low-cost model would become available. In addition to the processors, twenty-seven different peripherals were announced. All the basic punched-card peripherals and printers were ICT's own make, including a very competitive 1350-lines-per-minute printer—'the apple of

Table 11.2 ICL 1900-series announcements, 1964-65

Model	Price (£000s)	Announced	Delivered
1901	65	Sep 1965	Oct 1966
1902	105	Sep 1964	Sep 1965
1903	175	Sep 1964	Aug 1965
1904	260	Sep 1964	May 1965
1905		Sep 1964	Jan 1965
1906	700	Sep 1964	mid-1967
1907		Sep 1964	mid-1967
1909		Sep 1964	Oct 1965

Notes
Price is for a typical or average system.
Models 1905, 1907, and 1909 were scientific versions of the 1904, 1906, and 1903, respectively, equipped with a floating-point processor.

Sources
Delivery data: *Computer Survey*. Price data: 'Development Plans', 28 April 1967, ICT Board Papers.

ICT's eye'—that went on to sell on an OEM basis.[27] All the fast magnetic tapes and discs, however, were to be imported—a fact which was not advertised at the launch. A full range of software was announced, including a multi-programming executive, programming languages, and application packages. The keynote of the press launch, however, was to emphasize the availability of the 1900 series—that 'it's here, you can see it'; and deliveries of under one year were promised.[28] At the Business Equipment Exhibition the following week, at Olympia, two prototype models—the 1902 and the 1904—were demonstrated;[29] this was unusual for any product announcement, but unique in the history of ICT. The timely delivery of computers had never been one of ICT's strong points, so the demonstrations went a long way to re-establishing its credibility.

The impact of the 1900-series launch exceeded all expectations, and orders poured in, both from Britain and around the world. Morale in ICT soared. The 1900 series, once thought of as a stop-gap, now looked to be a major success. Basil de Ferranti reported to the board:

. . . the thoughts of all concerned with I.C.T. were leading to the view that the right course for I.C.T to follow on future computer development was to continue on the 1900 Series order code, or an improved order code developed by I.C.T., and not to copy the IBM order code. The final decision on this matter would be a very major one for I.C.T.'s future.[30]

Reorganization for the ICT 1900 series

The development of the 1900 series 'made a company out of a consortium', and helped the rapid integration of Ferranti into ICT.[31] On 1 December 1964, Basil de Ferranti succeeded Cecil Mead as managing director, with the primary objective of bringing the 1900 series into production as rapidly as possible. Recognizing de Ferranti's limited experience in running a big company, an executive committee, which included Mead, who was now deputy chairman, was interposed between the main board and de Ferranti to oversee financial control and strategy implementation. At the same time, the entire company was restructured and decentralized (Fig. 11.1).[32] The new structure, which had some similarities with IBM's organization, consisted of three functional groups: computer equipment, data-processing equipment, and marketing. Within the groups, profit-centre concepts were introduced, and each group had profit and loss accountability for its own operations: 'the concept of operating in groups with profit and loss responsibility at all levels is an imaginative one for a functional company like ours which does not have a number of discrete ranges of product'.[33]

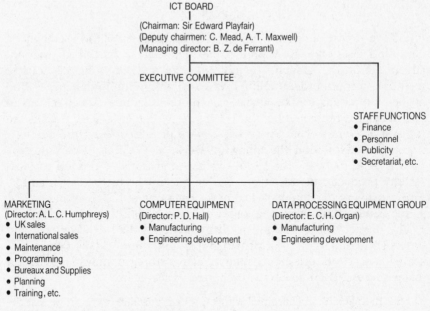

ICT BOARD

(Chairman: Sir Edward Playfair)
(Deputy chairmen: C. Mead, A. T. Maxwell)
(Managing director: B. Z. de Ferranti)

EXECUTIVE COMMITTEE

STAFF FUNCTIONS
• Finance
• Personnel
• Publicity
• Secretariat, etc.

MARKETING
(Director: A. L. C. Humphreys)
• UK sales
• International sales
• Maintenance
• Programming
• Bureaux and Supplies
• Planning
• Training, etc.

COMPUTER EQUIPMENT
(Director: P. D. Hall)
• Manufacturing
• Engineering development

DATA PROCESSING EQUIPMENT GROUP
(Director: E. C. H. Organ)
• Manufacturing
• Engineering development

Fig. 11.1   ICT organization, 1965

The Computer Equipment Group at West Gorton, effectively the former Ferranti computer department, was headed by Peter Hall, and was responsible for designing and manufacturing the larger processors. The Data Processing Equipment Group, headed by Echo Organ, was responsible for the design and manufacture of the smaller processors and all ICT peripherals. It also continued to be responsible for the design and manufacture of traditional punched-card equipment, although this was now rapidly declining. The Computer Equipment Group and the Data Processing Equipment Group were conventionally organized production units, but the Marketing Group was new in concept. Arthur Humphreys was appointed to head the group, and was made deputy managing director at the same time. The Marketing Group had the general role of tightly co-ordinating planning, production, and sales, and the specific role of managing the 1900-series introduction. The Marketing Group also included the Programming Division, since software was still seen largely as an aid to sales, rather than as a marketable product in its own right. Although de Ferranti recognized that 'The battle ahead lies in software, not hardware',[34] ICT, like the rest of the industry, had not yet thought in terms of selling software to generate revenues directly.

The 1900-series processors proved to be the least troublesome aspect of design and production. Although several processors were being developed simultaneously on two sites, design co-ordination was not a major problem. This was largely because rigorous and implicit specifications had already been imposed and frozen by the physical existence of the FP6000 hardware and software, and the ICT standard interface. (The development of the 2900 series was later to prove a much bigger co-ordination problem.) The mid-range machines were quickly derived from the FP6000, and rushed into production. The first production 1905 was delivered to Northampton College, London, in January 1965—only four months after the 1900-series announcement—and was officially inaugurated by Lord Bowden on 15 March 1965. The short lead-time of the 1900 series proved to be a major competitive advantage over System/360. Although the first machines from the IBM range were delivered in the United States in spring 1965, there were production problems that held back deliveries in the UK until spring 1966.

Since one of the main competitive advantages of the 1900 series over System/360 was its lower price, de Ferranti placed a major emphasis on investment in automated manufacturing and the use of standard modules to reduce manufacturing costs, rather than on technical innovation in circuitry. Several Milwaukee-matic numerically controlled milling machines were bought from America at enormous expense, and 'fine-blanking' metal-shaping machines installed. The ICT plants became something of a show-piece of industrial automation, attracting ministerial attention,[35] although the cost-effectiveness of some of the investment was debatable. Capacity of the West Gorton computer plant was increased to about 300 processors per year, and investment in automation reduced manufacturing costs to about one-fifth of those of the Orion.[36]

Major problems were encountered with peripherals, but mainly those imported from the United States. ICT's punched-card peripherals and printers were already well developed before the 1900-series programme was begun, and were selling well on an OEM basis to other manufacturers. Because no random-access memory devices were available from the UK or European manufacturers, ICT had arranged to import discs from Anelex in the United States, and to use the RCA RACE magnetic-card file, both of which were still under development at the time of the 1900 series announcement. The Anelex disc in the event never materialized, and discs were eventually bought from CDC—but not until mid-1966. This lost ICT a lot of ground in the growing transaction-processing market, in which IBM and Univac had been strong since 1960; ICT had yet to put a computer with a disc store on to the market. The RCA RACE also had problems—it was very late arriving and never really worked well, and was not particularly competitive with the IBM Datacell.

The biggest development problems, however, were encountered with software. A new programming division under Peter Hunt was established in January 1965; but ICT, like every manufacturer, was unprepared for the escalation in user demand for software on third-generation computer systems, and the lack of reliable tools for estimating costs and production time-scales. Another major problem was the shortage of programmers in Britain. An urgent advertising campaign was begun in early 1965 to roughly double the ICT programming establishment by attracting one hundred additional programmers; but it took the full year to get that number of recruits; in the meantime several of the applications packages promised for the 1900 series were shelved, or deliveries lengthened up to two years. The ICT Programming Division built up to about 600 people by 1966,[37] built largely on the expertise of Ferranti, which had world-class skills in compiler-writing and operating systems that ICT had lacked before the merger.

By January 1965, ICT had taken 124 orders for the 1900 series: a small figure in world terms, but unprecedented for a British computer. This success, inevitably, caused the order book for the older models to collapse. Moreover, de Ferranti's attention on the 1900 series had allowed electro-mechanical production—on which ICT was still highly dependent—to languish. ICT was soon caught up in a major financial crisis (see Chapter 12) that threatened the 1900-series R&D. ICT's financial crisis occurred at a time when it was becoming clear that the £4 million annual R&D budget was insufficient to maintain the momentum of the 1900 series, especially to keep it competitive with System/360.

During 1965, IBM had announced major operating systems for System/ 360 to which ICT had to respond for the 1900 series. This spawned projects for the GEORGE 1 and 2 operating systems in 1965, and for GEORGE 3 in 1966.* Software costs escalated to £1.7 million during 1965, which was about 50 per cent more than budgeted. In November 1964, IBM responded to the competitive pressures on the 1401 by announcing a low-cost addition to the 360 range, the model 20. To respond to this announcement ICT was forced to bring forward the 1901 development, which was announced in September 1965. The projected R&D costs for the next two or three years were now about £5.5 million a year. This still represented a little under 10 per cent of revenues; but ICT's profits were so low that the additional expenditure would have meant ICT's operating at a loss. Harold Wilson's Labour Government was, however, well disposed towards ICT, and Basil de Ferranti was able to secure a development loan of up to £5 million from the NRDC in May 1965. The NRDC loan was paid in four instalments during 1965-68, and was repayable during 1970-76 on a profit-related basis.[38] It is doubtful whether the 1900-series development could have continued without the NRDC loan.

It is interesting to compare the R&D cost of the 1900 series of about £20 million over four years (approximately $56 million) with the $500 million IBM expended on System/360 R&D over a comparable period. It has often been observed that IBM's R&D expenditure is greater than ICL's total turnover, and this has led at least one observer to note that 'the efficiency of their R&D process is therefore of commendable quality'.[39] This is certainly true; but it is not the ten times greater efficiency that the R&D spending ratios might imply. One major difference, for example, was that IBM was a far more integrated manufacturer, and made all its own peripherals and most of its electronic components. By contrast, ICT bought in virtually all its magnetic-storage peripherals, semiconductors, and core memories, so that their development costs did not form a component of ICT's overall R&D budget. Again, IBM put far more resources into applications development than did ICT, which simply did not compete with IBM in the more esoteric applications. On the other hand, there is plenty of evidence that ICT was more cost-conscious and design-minded. Probably the most well known example of IBM's profligacy was its operating system, OS/360, which was said to have taken 5000 programmer-years of effort, and to have had over 1000 programmers working on it at its peak.[40] The ICT GEORGE 3 operating system involved no more than about 75 programmer-years of effort, and was generally considered to be a much better system.[41] There is no doubt that ICT's

---

* Although GEORGE was an acronym, it was really a tribute to George Felton, the doyen of ICT's programmers.

shortage of development funds worked to its advantage in this instance. IBM's problems had been due to an understandable, but mistaken, belief that by throwing human resources at the task it could shorten the development time—in fact this just made it harder to manage.[42]

The English Electric System 4

Soon after the merger between the English Electric Computer Division and Leo Computers had taken place in April 1963, planning activity began on a range of third-generation machines. There were essentially three options available: to base the new range on the KDF9, to base it on LEO III, or to develop a completely new architecture.[43] Very early in 1964, a technical working party was established by W.E. Scott, managing director of English Electric Leo, to select one of these alternatives. Because the KDF9 and LEO III both had technical limitations that prevented their easy enhancement, it was decided to develop an entirely new range, which was known internally as Project KLX. During 1964, the KLX architecture was developed in detail, software was specified, and some engineering prototyping done. An important aspect of the latter was the decision to make use of Marconi integrated circuits rather than discrete transistors. Marconi, a division of English Electric, had made a strategic move into integrated circuits in 1962, and during 1963 had produced the Myriad process-control computer; the Myriad was probably the first computer in the world to use integrated circuits.

With the announcement of System/360 and the 1900 series during the course of 1964, the pace of innovation quickened, and it was clear within English Electric that if KLX was developed entirely from its own resources it would lose competitiveness because of its late introduction. Also, because English Electric had only about 15 per cent of the UK market, there was a need to contain development costs, especially for software, within realistic bounds. Scott decided, therefore, to investigate whether it might not be possible to make use of English Electric's technology agreement with RCA to integrate KLX with the Spectra 70.

A three-man study team, consisting of David Caminer (sales), Denis Blackwell (product planning), and Colin Haley (engineering development) visited RCA for a three-week period during November/December 1964.[44] RCA, in fact, made the Spectra 70 announcement during their visit, on 8 December 1964.[45] The Spectra 70 range, as then announced, consisted of four machines, the models 15, 25, 45, and 55 (Table 11.3). These model numbers were chosen to suggest their relative performance against System/360. The two smaller models (15 and 25) were to use conventional discrete components, and were offered with a twelve-month delivery, and the larger models, which were to use integrated circuits, were offered with an eighteen-month delivery. Although RCA adopted the System/360 instruction code so far as users were concerned, the 'hidden' operations for multi-programming and time-sharing were considerably more elegant and advanced.

Table 11.3   RCA Spectra 70 announcements, 1964-65

Model	Price (£000s)	Announced	Delivered
15	41	Dec 1964	late 1965
25	101	Dec 1964	late 1965
35	156	Sep 1965	
45	189	Dec 1964	mid-1966
55	370	Dec 1964	mid-1966

Notes
Price is for a typical or average system.

Sources
Delivery data: F.M. Fisher *et al.*, *IBM and the U.S. Data Processing Industry*, Praeger, New York, 1983, pp. 208ff. Price data: D.T. Caminer *et al.*, 'Report and Recommendations Following Visit to RCA . . . 1964' and 'Computer Characteristics', *Datamation*, *passim*.

RCA was at this time very keen to make a licensing arrangement with English Electric. Although it had secured licensing agreements with Hitachi and Siemens, it had recently severed its connection with Machines Bull following its acquisition by General Electric, and ICT had decided against adopting Spectra 70. English Electric was therefore offered the rights to Spectra 70 on very favourable terms.

It was clear to English Electric that by adopting Spectra 70 it would greatly accelerate the introduction of its new range, and would greatly reduce the development costs, especially of software. There were, however, two considerations that made the decision not entirely straightforward: the first was the question of IBM compatibility, and the second was the apparent loss of technical leadership. English Electric did not regard the matter of IBM compatibility as being a particular advantage in the UK market, since, unlike America and elsewhere, it was not dominated by IBM's *de facto* standards. Indeed, IBM compatibility was seen as a slightly negative marketing point:

A prospective customer might well ask why, if there is no essential difference between our model and IBM's, they should not go to the originator. The simple answer is that so far as we are concerned these are industry standards with which we have no quarrel, but in the positive sense we should be able to say that . . .

throughout the range we give better cost/performance curves than IBM and that we will back our equipment with better service in the field.[46]

On the question of technical leadership, both English Electric and Leo Computers had enjoyed a strong reputation in the British computer industry. The KDF9 was regarded as a highly innovative computer, and sold well in universities; and the LEO III also had great prestige. In order to secure government orders, English Electric had to be seen as something more than a manufacturer of computers under licence, and there was also the worry that 'the sales force may initially recoil at the idea of selling products that are "Not Invented Here".'[47] In reality, however, the Spectra 70 range offered ample scope for Anglicization: first, English Electric would be able to develop a big machine, which the RCA range lacked, and which could be sold to large university and commercial customers; second, by using integrated circuits for the small machines, where RCA had used discrete components, English Electric would be perceived as highly innovative by offering a 'true' third-generation range in hardware terms, unlike System/360 or the 1900 series—only the middle-range machine would be directly derived from RCA.

The decision was therefore taken to adopt the RCA Spectra 70 architecture for the English Electric range, which was to be marketed as System 4. The development of a full computer range, given English Electric's small market presence, was a major investment. English Electric was, however, Britain's third largest electrical engineering company, with an annual turnover of £200 million, and Lord Nelson had decided that it would make a strategic entry into both integrated circuits and electronic computers.[48] It was fully understood that the order books would not hold out on the basis of the existing second-generation products, and it was anticipated that there would be heavy trading losses during 1966. This was, however, a loss that English Electric could easily stand as 'a calculated risk'.[49]

The full range of four machines was announced in September 1965 (Table 11.4), with deliveries promised for early 1967. The model 4-50 was derived directly from the Spectra 70/45; it was therefore the first to be delivered, although deliveries in quantity were much later than had originally been planned. The two small machines, the 4-10 and 4-30, were developed by the Marconi division of English Electric. Although the functional specifications from RCA were used for these machines, almost everything else was 'invented here'. The use of integrated circuits, unfortunately, meant that the machines were not particularly economic. The 4-10, in particular, was not price-competitive against the IBM 360/20 or the ICT 1901, and was eventually cancelled before any were delivered.[50] The large 4-70, however, was a considerable technical triumph. Unlike

Table 11.4 English Electric System 4 announcements, 1965

Model	Price (£000s)	Announced	Delivered
10	100	Sep 1965	Cancelled
30	172	Sep 1965	Jun 1967
50	271	Sep 1965	May 1967
70	600	Sep 1965	mid-1968

Notes
Price is for a typical or average system.
Models 40, 45, 60, 65, 72, and 85 were added to the range during 1966-70. '[T]he first
4-50 . . . was delivered months before production 4-50's were ready' (EEC Board
Minutes, 29 March 1968).

Sources
Delivery data: *Computer Survey* and ICL sources. Price data: 'ICL Corporate 5-Year
Business Plan, 1968/69-1972/73', 5 October 1968, ICL Board Papers; and
'Rationalisation of Certain Companies in the British Computer Industry', 27 September
1966 (ICL Archives).

System/360, it had been designed in the expectation that the future
growth in large-scale computing would be in real-time and multi-access
systems. During 1966-67 many of the prestige orders for large systems
from the British Government and nationalized industries went to the
4-70: these included several machines for the Post Office, the National
GIRO Bank, the electricity boards, the UK Atomic Energy Authority,
and universities. The 4-70 completely outclassed the ICT 1906, which
had to be withdrawn from the market until a faster model (the 1906A)
could be announced in 1967.

The reaction within ICT to System 4 was initially fairly sceptical. The
idea of a British company, with no real export market, competing with
IBM head-on was considered ill-advised, to put it at its best. English
Electric's delivery schedules were also considered over-optimistic, since it
was well known in the industry that System/360 deliveries were running
three or four months late, owing to manufacturing problems with its SLT
circuits; in the event volume deliveries of System 4 did not begin until
well into 1968. Although integrated circuits were attractive from a
marketing viewpoint, ICT took the view, like IBM, that technology was
secondary to reliability and prompt delivery. This was evidently also the
view of the market: in the year following the September 1965 System 4
announcement, just £3 million worth of orders were taken; this was
equalled by the orders for the ICT 1901 alone, which was announced
the same month. None the less, a major effect of System 4 was to force

244 ICL: A business and technical history

ICT into introducing integrated circuits into the 1900 series as rapidly as possible, particularly to restore the competitiveness of the 1906. One interpretation of this situation was that ICT and English Electric were not so much competing against the Americans, as nibbling at each other's share of the British computer market.

12

Government relations and the formation of ICL

1964–1968

The American Challenge
The war is industrial, and its major battle is over computers. This battle is very much in doubt, but it has not yet been lost.

—J.-J. Servan-Schreiber, 1968.[1]

Servan-Schreiber's famous book *Le Défi Americain* (*The American Challenge*), which appeared in 1967, marked a turning point in the passive European acceptance of American domination of the market for high-technology goods. The book was a best-seller in France and in England, and it articulated the fears of politicians and industrialists, which had been growing for more than a decade. During the 1950s and early 1960s American manufacturers had increasingly come to dominate the advanced-technology industries. These industries included aerospace, nuclear power and weapons, radar and defence electronics, and computers. All of these were regarded as strategic industries, in the sense that it was considered that long-term prosperity, not to mention national prestige, depended upon them. The strategic importance of computers was highlighted in France in 1965, when the United States Government placed an embargo on a CDC 6600 ordered by the French atomic research authorities. During the mid-1960s, European governments poured money into the high-technology industries, sometimes independently, sometimes as international consortia. A sprinkling of the names of cherished, but often ultimately abandoned, projects is enough to evoke the spirit of the times: TSR-2, Concorde, ELDO and Euroatom, and many more.

In both France and Britain, anxiety over the computer industry came to a head in about 1963. In France, de Gaulle's Government created a five-year 'Plan Calcul' (the national computer plan), the official justification being that 'Government has a *de facto* predominance as the only entity capable of promoting a coherent policy on the national level, both by means of various influences at its disposal and through the size of its orders'.[2] The Plan Calcul ultimately led to the formation of the *Délégation à l'Informatique* in 1966, and a high-profile national computer company, Compagnie Internationale pour l'Informatique (CII), in 1967.

The beginning of Britain's direct government sponsorship of the high-technology industries, in a spiritual sense at least, dates from Harold Wilson's famous speech to the Labour Party Conference at Scarborough in October 1963, when he evoked the image of 'the Britain that is going to be forged in the white heat of the scientific revolution'.[3]

Mintech and the computer industry

When, in October 1964, Harold Wilson's Labour Government came into power, one of its first acts was to establish a Ministry of Technology, envisaged in *The New Britain*, an organization to 'guide and stimulate a major national effort to bring advanced technology and new processes into British industry'.[4] Mintech was to be in part the 'NRDC writ large'; but also it had a much wider mission to strengthen Britain's technological industries, and to diffuse advanced technologies throughout the rest of the industry.[5]

Of all the industries which Mintech was set up to help support and rationalize, Wilson viewed the computer industry as being that most urgently in need of assistance:

My frequent meetings with leading scientists, technologists and industrialists in the last two or three years of Opposition had convinced me that, if action was not taken quickly, the British computer industry would rapidly cease to exist, facing, as was the case in other European countries, the most formidable competition from the American giants. When, on the evening we took office, I asked Frank Cousins to become the first Minister of Technology, I told him that he had, in my view, about a month to save the British computer industry and that this must be his first priority.[6]

Accordingly, in November 1964, the newly appointed Minister of Technology held talks with both ICT and English Electric, in what was to be the first of many attempts to persuade them to bring together their computer interests. The major reason that a merger did not take place at this time is that it would not have been commercially advantageous for either company, especially in the short term. For both ICT and English Electric, the introduction of their new ranges of computers had passed the point of no return, and there could be very few advantages of integration until the time came to produce a new range of machines, in the early 1970s. A second issue was the question of control: neither ICT nor English Electric was at this time willing to yield control to the other.

During early 1965, Mintech therefore put the rationalization of the computer industry to one side in favour of the more tractable business of stimulating and diffusing computer technology in Britain, which was after all a prerequisite of a thriving computer industry. On 1 March 1965, Cousins made a statement on the computer industry to the House of

Commons that 'The Government consider that it is essential that there should be a rapid increase in the use of computers and computer techniques in industry and commerce and that there should be a flourishing British computer industry'; and he announced four initiatives to that end.[7]

First, a Computer Advisory Unit was to be established to encourage and advise on the use of computers in the public sector. From the computer industry's viewpoint, this initiative addressed one of its strongest grievances against the British Government, that it had been extremely tardy in adopting computers: in 1964 only 150 computers were in use in the public sector, compared with the 1700 in the United States.[8] The Computer Advisory Unit also initiated an informal beginning to the government's procurement policy: 'this advice is unbiased, but draws attention to the merits of British computers where these may be being overlooked or discounted'.[9] An important fiscal stimulus to the adoption of computers by industry was their special treatment under the investment allowances scheme, which subsidized their cost by a minimum of 20 per cent, and sometimes by as much as 45 per cent.

The second Mintech initiative was a full-scale review of the computer requirements of higher education and the research councils, with the aim of establishing a major procurement programme during the remainder of the 1960s, initially at the rate of £2 million a year. The review body, known as the Flowers Committee after its chairman Professor Brian Flowers (now Lord Flowers), issued its report *Computers for Research* in 1966.[10] An important and highly political conclusion of the Flowers report was that large American computers (for example, CDC 6600s) should be purchased for regional computer centres in London and Manchester. The Flowers report had a major effect in highlighting the strengths and weaknesses of the British computer industry, particularly its weakness in large computers.

The third Mintech initiative was to stimulate technological innovation in computers by sponsorship of R&D. The NRDC was considerably expanded, one of its first actions being to grant the loan of up to £5 million for ICT's 1900 series in May 1965. Basic and pre-competitive research were stimulated by the Advanced Computer Technology Project (ACTP) which funded advanced computer research on a cost-shared basis with industry. ICT had a number of programmes under this initiative, the most important of which was J.K. Iliffe's 'Basic Language Machine' (BLM) project for an advanced computer architecture, which was later to be a major input to the ICL 2900 series.[11]

Fourth, Cousins proposed a National Computer Centre (NCC), to improve the diffusion of computing by training in computer techniques and software development. The NCC was established as an independent company with headquarters in Manchester in July 1966; for over twenty years the NCC has been one of the more successful and durable of the Wilson Government's high-technology initiatives.

The large-computer project and Project 51

A fifth initiative, not announced by Cousins in his March 1965 statement to the House of Commons, was to invite ICT to lead a European consortium in making a proposal for a very large computer. During 1963-1964 the Atlas, then Europe's largest computer, had been eclipsed by three American high-speed computer projects: in August 1963 the CDC 6600 had been announced, with an estimated power of three to four times that of the Atlas; a more powerful machine, the IBM 360/91, had been announced in August 1964; and finally in December 1964 the CDC 6800 had been announced, with a power some four to five times greater than the 6600. As it happened, the 360/91 was ultimately late in delivery and a commercial failure, and the 6800 was not proceeded with. But the American announcements none the less set the agenda.

ICT's Edward Playfair—who spoke fluent French—took the lead in negotiating with English Electric and CITEC, the French computer company.* In July 1965, a formal proposal for a 'Large Computer Project' was submitted to the British and French Governments.[12] This proposal recommended the construction of a machine five to ten times the power of the CDC 6800—or a staggering 100-Atlas power—and the development cost was put at about £10 million. The proposal 'made it very clear that this whole project must be at Government expense',[13] since all experience had convinced the consortium that it was impossible to make money from giant computers, especially ones that stretched the technology to the extent proposed. The benefit of a large-computer project, it was argued, was not so much a commercial one for the developers, but rather a benefit to the collaborating nations in terms of prestige and technological spin-off. Indeed, there was mounting evidence that the spin-off from the Atlas project in terms of hardware and software innovation had been of considerable value in enabling Britain to develop its third-generation computer ranges. A second advantage of the project would be that the two nations working on a common project—small in scale compared with the Concorde, but similar in principle—would pave the way for the eventual integration of the European computer industry against the forces of IBM and the big American companies.

---

* CITEC was a consortium of the computer interests of CSF and CGE. France's other computer company, Machines Bull, having merged with the American company General Electric, was no longer considered French.

In September 1965, ICT and English Electric made a joint presentation on the Anglo-French Computer Project, as it had then become known, to Mintech.[14] The Ministry did less than jump at the offer, £10 million no doubt seeming a great deal of money, so the response was the conventional one in such circumstances—a committee was set up to deliberate on the matter. The committee, chaired by Ieuen Maddock of Mintech, included representatives from both ICT and English Electric, as well as Mintech's computer consultant Professor Stanley Gill, and several other technical luminaries. The committee met six times during November and December, and issued its report on 29 December 1965.[15]

The Maddock Committee took the view that the large computer problem was inseparable from the general problems of the computer industry, and widened its brief accordingly. It recommended, in particular, that the British Government should increase substantially its procurement of computers, and implement without delay the proposals of the Flowers Report. So far as the Anglo-French Computer Project was concerned, however, the Maddock Committee brought matters firmly down to earth, in the light of recent American developments, where the problems with the IBM 360/91 and the CDC 6800 were the talk of the industry. The committee also recognized that there was not room for more than one large-computer project in Britain, and recommended that only one of ICT or English Electric should be funded to develop a machine of roughly 10-Atlas power at the top end of its current range. ICT, which was so much further ahead with its 1900 series than was English Electric with its System 4, was subsequently promised limited Mintech support for such a large computer. This computer—to be known as the 1908, but known internally as Project 51—in fact never materialized, but perhaps succeeded in generating more column-inches of press speculation than any other British computer project of the 1960s. In reality, ICT attached relatively little importance to the large-computer project, for it actually needed financial help of a much more solid kind to resolve the financial crisis that had begun to overtake it during the early months of 1965.

ICT's crisis of 1965

Harold Wilson's estimate on coming to office that he had 'about a month' to save the British computer industry proved not very far short of the mark. In early 1965, ICT faced its most serious financial crisis to date. A budgeted cash inflow of £2 million had turned into a projected cash outflow of £4½ million, and profit projections had withered away altogether. The primary cause of ICT's financial problems was not, however, the American competition that Wilson feared, so much as the internal strains of introducing the 1900 series, compounded by industrial relations problems and the continuing decline of the punched-card machine business.*

The launch of the 1900 series had been a major success, with over 200 machines on order by spring 1965, which ensured ICT's medium-term survival. In the short term, however, the very success of the 1900 series had caused heavy cancellation of all of ICT's current computers. The downward spiral of sales of traditional punched-card equipment had also taken another twist, with sales 50 per cent below target. The deteriorating order book was exacerbated by an even worse delivery position. The

Table 12.1   UK market shares, 1964-1969

	1964	1965	1966	1967	1968	1969
UK-owned						
ICL	41.4	32.0	34.4	32.4	41.0	49.4
Other—UK	1.1	2.5	1.1	0.6	0.9	1.9
TOTAL—UK	42.5	34.5	35.5	33.0	41.9	51.3
US-owned						
IBM	40.0	35.1	43.2	42.5	23.4	27.7
NCR	7.6	9.6	6.1	9.5	10.7	7.9
Univac	2.5	3.3	3.0	3.3	8.8	3.1
Burroughs	0.9	1.5	3.9	1.3	6.4	3.0
Honeywell	5.2	10.9	5.8	6.9	5.4	7.9
CDC	—	0.6	1.1	—	1.1	1.5
DEC	<0.1	0.2	0.6	0.8	0.4	0.5
Other—US	0.1	1.6	0.2	0.5	0.7	0.6
TOTAL—US	56.3	62.8	63.9	64.8	56.9	47.2
Other—non-US	1.2	2.7	0.6	2.1	1.1	0.4
TOTAL	100	100	100	100	100	100

Note
The table is based on selling prices by 'notional value', roughly equivalent to the average selling price.

Sources
[HC272], p. 4 and [HC621-II], pp. 25-9.

  * Although the American share of the UK market did increase during 1965-67, this was due to production shortfalls among the British manufacturers who were introducing their new ranges; the market share of the indigenous manufacturers recovered in 1968. See Table 12.1.

industrial relations problems that dogged the British economy throughout the 1960s were as acute within ICT as anywhere. The English plants, following the lay-offs of 1962-63, had become increasingly unionized, and an overtime ban was in operation in support of a 20 per cent wage-claim. In Castlereagh the position was still worse, and output had dropped to a level where the ICT board seriously considered pulling out of Northern Ireland altogether. In the light of these financial problems, the May 1965 NRDC loan of up to £5 million over four years proved absolutely crucial to the short-term survival of 1900-series R&D within ICT. Had the loan not been available, R&D would have been drastically pruned to stem the cash outflow.

In his interim report, published in June 1965, Playfair prepared share-holders for the worst: 'the Board expects the results for the second half of the current year to compare much less favourably with the figures for the corresponding period last year'.[16] The City's reaction could scarcely have been worse, and the price of ICT shares fell nearly £1 to thirty shillings. As the end of the financial year approached, in August 1965, Playfair put the position fair and square to the board. ICT faced a major liquidity crisis. For the first time in its history, the company would announce a fall in revenues and a trading loss; and once the Annual Report was published it was feared that the banks would withdraw their credit. So far as Playfair could see, the only long-term options open to ICT, other than bankruptcy, were a merger with an American partner or to go 'cap in hand' to the government for support.[17] But neither of these could be moved upon until the immediate financial crisis had been put right.

Sir Anthony Burney, a non-executive director of ICT and a partner of the accountants Binder Hamlyn, was invited by the board to bring in his firm to make an independent report with all speed. The Burney Report[18] reached some unattractive conclusions: that in order to survive ICT should sell some of its assets and subsidiary companies, that it should reduce overheads (including R&D), and that it should abandon unprofit-able overseas activities (which was most of them). The main conclusion that Burney reached, however, was that the principal officers of ICT—Playfair and de Ferranti—had allowed decentralization to go so far that they had effectively lost financial control over the company. By the time that ICT's financial crisis had become apparent the situation was almost beyond remedy. Under the circumstances, conventional refinancing of ICT would be impossible: a rights issue with the current share price was unthinkable; the permissible number of debentures had already been issued; and approaching the banks might well precipitate their withdraw-ing credit altogether. The only real solution was to approach the govern-ment; but that could not be done until ICT had at least shown signs of putting its house in order.

Playfair had no option but to resign, and at the board meeting of 22 September 1965 he stepped down from the office of chairman. Cecil Mead was appointed chairman and chief executive in his place, with the mission of restructuring the company and restoring its profitability. To support Mead, Arthur Humphreys was given responsibility for all operations, and Basil de Ferranti made a lateral shift away from operational matters to become managing director of strategy.

A strategy for survival

When Cecil Mead became chairman and chief executive in September 1965, he and Arthur Humphreys faced a monumental task in restoring profitability and morale, and in determining some plausible future for the company. First, there was the immediate problem of improving cash-flow. Some assets were sold off, and machine rentals were raised—so far as the market would bear, and only just ahead of the prices and incomes freeze of July 1966. R&D expenditure was reduced, first, by negotiating a suspension of the RCA agreement, which saved nearly £½ million a year, and second, by cutting back on long-term research—short-term software and applications development were left intact. Organizationally, the manufacturing groups were re-integrated under the sole direction of Echo Organ, and the worst of the industrial relations problems were sorted out. The UK and overseas sales operations were rationalized, and loss-making operations cut back—for example in Germany, where the battle against IBM was inexorably being lost, several of the branch offices were closed down.

The three main strategic issues facing the company in its straitened circumstances were product strategy, marketing strategy, and the integration of the industry. These issues were especially the province of Basil de Ferranti.

Basil de Ferranti's appointment as managing director for strategy, in September 1965, came at the very moment that English Electric announced its System 4 range computers. ICT's product strategy, therefore, had to respond not merely to the company's impoverished circumstances, but also to the competitive threat from System 4. System 4 had three main competitive advantages over the 1900 series: first, it was a truly third-generation machine using integrated circuits throughout; second, it was System/360 compatible, including an 8-bit byte, which gave it an air of authority and modernity in the market-place; third, System 4 had excellent real-time capabilities, considerably better than either the 1900 series or System/360. In spite of the 1900 series' disadvantages, however, the fact remained that its popularity had exceeded all expectations—probably because machines were in the field and running even before System/360, and System 4 machines could not be delivered until 1967 at the earliest. Under all these circumstances the optimum strategy—and certainly the cheapest—appeared to be to extend the life of the 1900-series architecture into the early 1970s, while gradually introducing integrated circuits, a real-time capability, and other enhancements to maintain its competitive position. During 1966, therefore, a large proportion of R&D resources went into the enhancement of the 1900-series processors. The small/medium machines (1901-4) were re-engineered with integrated circuits, and became known as the A series, and the larger processors were enhanced with both integrated circuits and the fastest available discrete components (the E and F series). So far as enhancing the real-time capability of the 1900 series was concerned, there was very little that could be accomplished within the basic architecture; and this remained a severe technical weakness, and made a new range necessary in the long run.

De Ferranti's second task was to review ICT's marketing strategy. The trend at this time was increasingly for all computer manufacturers—other than IBM—to specialize in vertical markets or particular niches where IBM's competitive position was relatively weak. With the former strategy, Burroughs was to prove highly successful by capturing virtually all of the British banking market during the 1960s; and Univac, by specializing in real-time applications, was to take the lion's share of the British airline-reservations market. Some degree of market specialization had already been implicit within ICT, of course; but by commissioning a number of market surveys and economic intelligence reports, the formal policy was adopted of specializing in the six basic industries that accounted for 60 per cent of sales, as well as the public sector, where ICT enjoyed a preference on political grounds.

So far as the integration of the industry was concerned, the major challenge of 1965-66 was to resist an enforced take-over by English Electric, which had been proposed by Mintech. There was a conviction within ICT that English Electric had overreached itself, and that it would only be a matter of time before ICT emerged as the slower but steadier runner. In fact Basil de Ferranti—who was very European-minded—was thinking much more in terms of integration within Europe than within Britain. The detailed picture of the European computer market was rather unclear at the time, a fact remarked upon by the OECD report *Gaps in Technology: Electronic Computers*, which noted 'the existence of a major statistical gap, not only between the various producing countries, but also between the computer industry and all other industries'.[19] Table 12.2, abstracted from the OECD report, illustrates the trends. First, the European market was growing very rapidly, even faster than the American market. In the five-year period between 1962 and 1967, the population of computers in the three main European markets, Britain, France, and

Table 12.2 European computer populations, 1962 and 1967

	UK		France		Germany	
	1962	1967	1962	1967	1962	1967
IBM	56	649	139	855	341	1641
Other—US	5	249	0	160	44	496
UK-owned	248	1303	6	204	21	61
French-owned	3	51	141	748	16	279
German-owned	0	0	0	2	107	364
Other	0	0	0	0	10	22
TOTAL	312	2252	285	2008	548	2963
Percentage of US-manufacture	20.5	55.4	50.9	65.5	75.5	78.3

Notes
Percentage of installations of US-manufacture includes computers made under licence.

Source
OECD, *Gaps in Technology: Electronic Computers*, Paris, 1969, p. 41 and Tables 2, 4, and 6 in statistical appendix.

Germany, had grown more than six-fold, from a total of 1145 computers in 1962 to 7223 in 1967. Second, IBM had achieved a dominant position in all three countries, with a larger market-share than any single manufacturer. IBM's share of the market, in 1967, was about 40 per cent by value in Britain, 63 per cent in France, and 68 per cent in Germany.[20] And the market-share of American-designed computers—either made in America or made under licence—was well over 50 per cent of installations everywhere. Third, Britain and France, and to a lesser extent Germany, had indigenous computer companies with a large fraction of their domestic market, but a negligible proportion of each other's markets.

The obvious conclusion was that the best way for European computer manufacturers to compete with IBM and the other American companies was to combine their interests and open up their markets to each other. The times, however, did not yet favour significant co-operation on a European scale. In France, for example, attention was focused on the Plan Calcul, by which it was hoped to first establish a thriving national industry, so that it could later join any European consortium from a position of strength. In Germany, Siemens, the largest company, was selling RCA Spectra 70s under licence, and could therefore contribute little to any European consortium. The other German computing companies, notably Zuse and Telefunken, were thriving well enough, but mainly in the process-control area rather than in EDP, which was the larger market, and where the American threat was greatest.

Although the long-term aim for an integrated European computer industry remained on the agenda, negotiations drifted into a lower key, and did not liven up again until 1972-73.

The merger: part 1[21]

In his first six months as chairman and chief executive, Cecil Mead and his management team had achieved a remarkable recovery in ICT. By spring 1966, the company was operationally in better shape than it had been for a long time, and strategically it had a much clearer, if more limited, sense of long-term direction. The strain on Cecil Mead had taken its toll, however, and he had to retire through ill health in late 1966.* His role as chairman was taken over by Terence Maxwell, and it was Maxwell who was to be chief negotiator in the two years of talks that led up to the formation of ICL in March 1968.

On 31 March 1966, Wilson's Labour Government was re-elected with a safe 97-seat majority, ever more determined *inter alia* to revitalize Britain's industrial base. The two most important instruments for this revitalization were Mintech and the Industrial Reorganization Corporation (IRC). During 1966, the role of Mintech was expanded to include responsibility for the government's relationships with the engineering, vehicles, and shipbuilding industries; it took over responsibility for government research laboratories and the industrial research associations; and in June 1966, by merging with the Ministry of Aviation, it assumed responsibility for the aerospace industries and the development of defence and civil aircraft, including Concorde. The Industrial Reorganization Corporation (IRC) had been established during the last months of the old government, charged with 'promoting industrial efficiency and profitability and assisting the economy of the UK'.[22] Under its chairman Sir Frank Kearton, and its managing director R.H. Grierson, its efforts were initially focused on the electrical and electronics industries. During 1966-68, it encouraged the acquisition of AEI by GEC and the merger between English Electric and Elliott-Automation; it played an early part in the formation of ICL by the merger of ICT and English Electric Computers; and finally it brought about the merger between GEC and English Electric. The IRC also fostered concentration in the mechanical engineer-

---

* Sir Cecil Mead formally retired from the ICT board on 2 February 1967. From 1970 until his death in 1979 he was a director and sometime chairman of Software Sciences International Ltd, a firm headed by his son-in-law, Colin Southgate.

ing and vehicles industries, the best-known merger being that between British Motor Holdings and Leyland Motors in 1968.

During 1965, when ICT had been at the height of its financial crisis, Mintech had prepared a merger scheme for English Electric to take control of ICT. The scheme had been rejected by English Electric, not least on account of the incompatibility between System 4 and the 1900 series. ICT was, naturally, unwilling to be the junior partner in any merger scheme, and was moreover philosophically opposed to the IBM-compatibility of System 4, which it considered to be commercially unsound, not to say defeatist. Another major objection was that ICT considered it essential to be free to buy components from any supplier in the world; as a subsidiary of English Electric it might well be forced to buy its components from other English Electric subsidiaries—especially integrated circuits, in which English Electric had made such a massive investment—so that gradually its competitive edge would be eroded.

By spring 1966, the conditions of the three main British computer companies—ICT, English Electric-Leo-Marconi, and Elliott-Automation—had changed considerably. ICT's position, following the success of the 1900 series and Cecil Mead's new management, had markedly improved, to the point where it was making profits and was easily the strongest of the three companies. The position of English Electric-Leo-Marconi, following the launch of System 4, had worsened considerably: the development costs of the new range had produced the anticipated heavy losses during 1966, and the delivery of the new range in early 1967, on which success depended, was uncertain. The third company, Elliott-Automation, was in still deeper trouble. A sizeable proportion of Elliott-Automation's business had been defence contracts associated with the TSR-2 aircraft programme, which had been cancelled in April 1965; Sir Leon Bagritt, Elliott-Automation's managing director, was therefore now actively seeking some form of merger.

With the changing fortunes of ICT and English Electric-Leo-Marconi, the possibility of a merger surfaced again within Mintech, but this time with the likelihood that ICT would be the senior partner. In order to gain a clearer view of the dynamically changing position, Sir Maurice Dean, permanent secretary of Mintech, instructed the accountants Cooper Brothers to review the affairs of the two companies and to make proposals on how progress could be made. The Cooper Brothers inquiry was led by S. John Pears, a senior partner of the firm, and his report, 'Rationalisation of Certain Companies in the British Computer Industry', appeared in September 1966.[23] The Pears Report came down firmly against the idea of a merger between ICT and English Electric-Leo-Marconi. The main reason for this conclusion was the incompatibility of the 1900 series and System 4:

As a result of our discussions and enquiries, we consider that it would not be appropriate at the present time for H.M.G. to sponsor a merger to take place between I.C.T. and E.E.L.M., nor for either party to take over the other. The main factors which have led us to this conclusion are as follows:-

(a) The 1900 series and system 4 are incompatible and each company is convinced of the technical superiority of its product over that of its competitor. It would also be impossible at this juncture for one system to be evolved from a joint operation except perhaps on a long term basis.

(b) Both systems are too far advanced in development and marketing for it to be rational to call a halt to one or other system. If such a decision were to be taken, it would be more than likely that the prospective customers would turn to I.B.M. or to some other overseas or overseas controlled manufacturers.[24]

What the Pears Report did, however, recommend was some form of co-operation in the joint development of compatible peripherals, software, and applications, and 'In the long run it would be hoped that joint efforts would produce one successor to the 1900 series and system 4'.[25] The Pears Report also recommended the formation of a joint leasing company.

It was in fact on the question of leasing finance that ICT was convinced its survival depended. Computer Leasings Limited (CLL), which had been set up in 1963 to finance domestic leasings, was running close to its ceiling of a total of £24 million, and this threatened to frustrate the growth of ICT from the beginning of 1967 onwards. With CLL, ICT carried all the obsolescence risk, so that should machines be returned in bulk from the field, then ICT would bear all the cost; this was an obvious and necessary guarantee for the lending institutions to provide low-cost, low-risk finance. However, as the volume of leasing finance increased, ICT's tangible assets would no longer be sufficient to guarantee the loan. During 1966, therefore, ICT made proposals that the government should underwrite a guarantee which would give ICT 'a gilt-edged status' which would enable the continued provision of low-cost funds from the institutions.[26]

The provision of leasing finance, and support for the large-computer project, were in fact all that ICT ever asked of the government. The view of Mintech, however, was hardening towards a much more radical restructuring of the industry. On 3 July 1966 Frank Cousins had resigned from the Cabinet as a protest against the government's economic policy, and he was replaced as Minister of Technology by Anthony Wedgwood Benn. Wedgwood Benn was determined to see a large-scale rationalization of the British computer industry, rather than the piecemeal initiatives and R&D subventions wanted by ICT:

... it became quite clear, of course, when one thought about it, that the scientific emphasis was an illusion. [The Ministry] was about industry, and when one looked at industry it was about the difference between big industry and small industry.[27]

Wedgwood Benn referred ICT's request for leasing guarantees to the IRC, which not only had the power to make *ad hoc* arrangements of the kind wanted by ICT, but also to make them conditional upon reorganization.

The IRC accepted the recommendation of the Pears Report that a merger between ICT and English Electric Computers was not feasible, and it took the view that ICT should instead consider joining forces with the troubled Elliott-Automation. ICT was against such a merger largely because Elliott-Automation derived most of its revenues from process-control computers and automation. ICT had a strategy of several years' standing to concentrate its limited resources and managerial talent on the EDP sector, in which it had expertise, rather than the industrial auto-mation field, in which it had none; this was, incidentally, the policy also adopted by IBM. Furthermore, even had ICT been interested, Elliott-Automation, notwithstanding its recent problems over the TSR-2 cancel-lation, remained a glamour stock, and the price of its shares was still at a 'ridiculous level'.[28] ICT fared rather badly from this encounter with the IRC, since having failed as a marriage broker between ICT and Elliott-Automation, the corporation washed its hands of the leasing problem too, and handed the whole problem back to Mintech in December 1966.

In fact, the recognition that there were two distinct parts to the computer business, EDP and process-control, proved to be the key to the rationaliza-tion of the British computer industry, but one that had taken a surprising amount of time to be identified. The rationalization of the process-control sector, considered as a separate exercise, was comparatively straight-forward, since it was much the smaller sector (less than 10 per cent of the world market by value), and it did not have the same problems that the EDP sector faced in terms of competition from IBM and the other multi-nationals. Rather than joining with ICT, a merger between Elliott-Automation and one of the electrical giants, GEC or English Electric, made a much better strategic fit. The early months of 1967 saw intense negotiations between GEC and Elliott-Automation, and subsequently, when these talks foundered, between English Electric and Elliott-Auto-mation. On 24 June 1967 English Electric announced a bid valued at £41 million for Elliott-Automation, the acquisition being supported by a £15 million loan from the IRC, interest-free for eight years. The new English Electric subsidiary was to be known as English Electric Computers Limited.[29]

The feasibility of a new range

By April 1967, Mintech had formed the view (precisely contrary to its view of two years earlier) that ICT, with its stronger management and marketing expertise, should form the nucleus of the British EDP computer industry, a view which was increasingly being accepted by English Electric in the light of its problems with System 4.

On 26 April 1967, Wedgwood-Benn and his technical advisers called a meeting with Maxwell and Humphreys of ICT, and Lord Nelson and Sir Gordon Radley, the chairman and the managing director of English Electric.[30] At this meeting Mintech offered a three-item package of financial support to bring about a merger between the companies' EDP interests. First and foremost, Mintech accepted the conclusion of the Pears Report that the main impediment to a merger was the incompatibility of the current ranges. The Ministry therefore offered a non-repayable grant in the region of £25 million towards the development of a new range of computers for delivery in the early 1970s. Second, it offered, separately, to fund the development of ICT's large computer, the 1908. Third, it offered to underwrite an obsolescence guarantee for ICT, to enable it to extend its low-cost leasing finance with the institutions. Wedgwood Benn made it clear, however, that this financial aid depended on the ultimate merging of ICT and English Electric Computers. Moreover, if the companies did not merge, Mintech would abandon the British computer industry altogether, and simply implement its policy of promoting the use of computers in industry, whether purchased from Britain, America, or Europe.

In fact, the threat was scarcely necessary. ICT had appreciated for some months that it could not proceed to develop a new range of computers without government finance. Also, ICT had become increasingly aware of its weakness in developing real-time systems. System 4 and its real-time operating system would not only fill the void in ICT's short-term product range, but would strengthen its R&D capability immeasurably in this area. So far as English Electric was concerned, following the Elliott-Automation acquisition it had decided to focus on process control and automation, so that the opportunity of divesting its loss-making EDP business to the much more commercially-minded ICT was becoming attractive. Everything depended, however, on the feasibility of designing a new range of computers for the early 1970s. The range not only had to be competitive with IBM, but also had to be compatible with the 1900 series and System 4, in order to lock in existing customers. The argument ran that if compatibility with the existing ranges was not achieved, then customers replacing their machines would inevitably look at all available machines on the market, and would become prey to the American manufacturers. It was not at all obvious, in 1967, that compatibility with the two very disparate architectures could be achieved without affecting technical performance, so that a joint ICT–English Electric working party was established for a feasibility study.

The working party met in secret for an intense three-day session in the

Hotel Cavendish, London, 3–5 July 1967.[31] The group consisted of three of ICT's senior planners and technical people (D. Eldridge, P.V. Ellis, and G.E. Felton), and three from English Electric (D.J. Blackwell, A.C.D. Haley, and J.M.M. Pinkerton). Both teams were motivated towards finding a positive solution. The English Electric team, especially, was under the pressure of their mounting losses, said to be running at the rate of £½ million a month. The working party was not, in fact, able to give a categorical assurance on the compatibility criterion for the new range, but was guardedly optimistic:

We are agreed that there is no prima facie reason why it should not be possible to plan a range of systems meeting the basic requirements of competitiveness and of acceptable compatibility with the current ranges of both companies.

The overall success of such a planning operation cannot be predicted, in that sacrifices in competitiveness directly attributable to securing satisfactory transfer from both current ranges cannot yet be estimated. However, there are good reasons (e.g. the general rapid advance of technology, the successful current activities in emulation, the increasing use of high level languages) to believe that the chances of an acceptable outcome are good.[32]

The working party had in fact gone as far as it could in determining the feasibility of a new range. To proceed further it would be necessary to involve many more people from the technical and the planning sides of each company, and they would need access to confidential trading information that had been withheld from the working party. Since secrecy would then be impossible, future progress implied some form of announcement of the new-range studies, with the obvious implication of an eventual merger. This was a step that neither company was yet quite ready to take, and the top-level negotiations continued their leisurely pace.

The merger: part 2

On 24 August 1967, however, the calm of ICT and English Electric's deliberations was shattered when Terence Maxwell received an informal bid for ICT from John Clark, deputy chairman of the Plessey Company.[33] Plessey, along with Elliott-Automation, had been one of the *enfants terribles* of the electronics industry; its aggressive take-over activity had been much admired in the City, it was cash-rich, and there was no question that it could have solved ICT's cash problems.

In early 1967 Plessey had taken on Tom Hudson, formerly managing director of IBM (UK), as director of finance and corporate planning, and he had initiated a technical strategy based on the convergence of computers and communications. Taking the advice of American consultants, Hudson had become convinced that the future lay in computer networks linking real-time mainframe computers, and he urged Clark to put in a bid for ICT.[34] Through its XL12 communications processor, then under development, Plessey hoped to become a major force in computer networks, and a link-up with ICT's mainframe business seemed a natural move. The view within ICT was quite different: first, unless it merged with English Electric Computers, then it would have very little real-time expertise to offer Plessey; and second, it saw Plessey's strengths as being very much in the process-control area rather than EDP.

Although the Plessey bid had been made in secret, the City was rife with rumour, and ICT's share-price leapt by a quarter in the next few days. On 7 September 1967, two weeks after the Plessey offer, Maxwell received a second take-over bid—this time from Sir John Wall, managing director of EMI. This bid made far less strategic sense than the Plessey offer, and it never assumed a like importance.

Apprised of the situation by Maxwell, Mintech reached the view that the greater national interest would be served by a merger between ICT and English Electric Computers, rather than either of the other two companies, notwithstanding the fact that substantial government funds would be needed to achieve the merger. The Ministry persuaded Plessey and EMI to stay their hands for one month, in order to give ICT and English Electric the opportunity of achieving the basis for a merger. At the same time, the government finally gave ICT the financial guarantee it needed to secure its future leasing funds. From this point on, Maxwell was under strong moral pressure to consummate the merger.

In fact, it took about three months to achieve a consensus on terms between ICT, English Electric, and the government. The principal cause of the delay was ICT's valuation of English Electric's assets in the light of its persistent problems with System 4, now many months behind schedule and with no machines yet delivered. Indeed, ICT's view was that the System 4 programme was becoming less credible by the day, and English Electric was nervous that ICT would simply drop the series after a merger, throwing away all that it had achieved. In the event, a formula was agreed whereby, with a grant of about £30 million from the government, the two firms would amalgamate their EDP interests. In the mean time, City rumours over an outright bid by English Electric or Plessey reached fever pitch. To dampen down speculation, on 12 December 1967 a joint ICT-English Electric press conference was arranged, where it was stated that merger talks were in progress and a new computer range was being evaluated.[35]

If ICT and English Electric had moved decisively, a merger on the agreed terms would no doubt have been achieved, but the delay—each hoping for marginally better terms—was to prove disastrous. First, the economic climate had worsened dramatically during the autumn, culminating in the devaluation of the pound from $2.80 to $2.40 on 18

November 1967. Second, impatient at the slow progress towards the merger, on 9 January 1968 Plessey's chairman, Lord Harding, renewed his company's bid, and ICT's shares soared to a new high of sixty shillings. The Plessey bid was most unwelcome, but it could not be made to go away, and Maxwell faced a real dilemma. On the one hand, if he rejected Harding's overture, then it would probably provoke a formal, aggressive bid. On the other hand, if ICT pacified Plessey with a significant share-holding, then the scenario was even worse: English Electric would almost certainly withdraw altogether; government funding would fall through; the ICT share-price would collapse; and Plessey would get 100 per cent of ICT at a bargain price anyway. Wedgwood Benn personally expressed his grave displeasure to Lord Harding over the possibility of his wrecking the rationalization plans for the British computer industry; but Harding was adamant that Plessey must have equal participation with English Electric in the computer company, or else he would make an outright bid.

These events did not, however, displease the Treasury, which was trying to cope with the after-effects of the November devaluation and the January 1968 public expenditure cuts. Now that cash-rich Plessey had joined the merger talks, a government subvention of the order of £25–30 million was seen as politically unacceptable, and the Treasury was now thinking in terms of about half that amount.[36] Suddenly, the whole deal was looking less and less attractive from ICT's viewpoint. The level of government funding was now uncertain, but would almost certainly prove inadequate. System 4 looked ever worse: a prestigious order to the Midland Bank had been cancelled because of delivery delays, and English Electric was unwilling to underwrite any losses subsequent to the merger. And now, with a combination of Plessey and English Electric as potential partners, ICT's freedom of action in purchasing components could be a problem in the future. But, in effect, Plessey 'had blown up the bridge', and there was no going back. If ICT were now to withdraw, the government's preferential buying policy would be withdrawn, and with it the last vestiges of faith in the British computer industry would be destroyed, giving 'a heaven sent opportunity to IBM'.[37]

In what were to be the busiest few weeks of Maxwell's life, a compromise deal was finally hammered out between ICT, English Electric, Plessey, and Mintech. They would each take a share of the equity of a new company, International Computers (Holdings) Limited (Table 12.3). ICT's existing shareholders—who included Vickers and Ferranti, with large blocks of shares and board representation—received 53.5 per cent of the equity in the new company. Plessey and English Electric each received equal shares of 18 per cent of the equity: Plessey, in exchange for £18 million cash, and English Electric in respect of EDP assets and plants valued at £17 million. Finally, the government put £17 million into the

Table 12.3 Principal shareholders of ICL

	Number of ordinary shares (millions)	Percentage of ordinary shares
Existing ICT shareholders (including Vickers and Ferranti)	17.8	53.5
English Electric	6.0	18.0
Plessey	6.0	18.0
Ministry of Technology	3.5	10.5
TOTAL	33.5	100.0

Source
ICL Annual Report, 1968.

company: £13.5 million as a non-repayable grant to develop the new range and the large-computer project, and £3.5 million in respect of three million shares issued at par. Mintech's equity participation in ICL was in fact the first use of the Industrial Expansion Act of January 1968.[38] On 21 March 1968, the Minister of Technology presented a white paper to the House, *Industrial Investment: The Computer Merger Project*,[39] and a press conference was held announcing the proposed formation of ICL. The Industrial Expansion Act received Royal Assent on 12/13 June 1968, and ICL was vested on 9 July 1968.

The merger: an assessment

It must be said that only a minority in ICT wanted a merger with English Electric Computers, especially on the terms that were eventually obtained. Maxwell, to be sure, always saw a merger as an inevitability; but even he was disappointed by the financial outcome. Of the major shareholders, Sebastian de Ferranti also thought the deal was not a good one. Within ICT, Arthur Humphreys never really wanted the merger, but would have 'cracked on and driven the company forward'.[40] Echo Organ was troubled all along by English Electric's lack of openness; it was only when the merger terms had been agreed that he had the opportunity to examine the manufacturing costs of System 4, and he found them to be even worse than he had suspected.[41] Of all the parties in the merger, English Electric probably did the best, since it received a handsome compensation for its troubled System 4, which was to cause major problems for ICL, much as the Samastronic had blighted the early years of ICT. Plessey did less well from the deal, having paid a good deal more for its stake in ICL than it was later worth; and it would not be until 1979 that it could finally sell its stake for a modest profit. But the real damage that Plessey did to ICL was that its injection of cash 'was a different kind of money'[42] to the direct subvention that ICT had originally wanted from the government. Plessey expected a commercial return on its investment, and did not intend to allow it to be appropriated for long-term R&D.

Perhaps the most striking feature of the computer merger, was the very small amount of money the government put in, in relation to the rationalization it achieved. In fact, although the Treasury may have rubbed its hands over its financial prudence, its mean-mindedness meant that ICL was financially hobbled from the day it began operations. As Professor Stanley Gill put it, much later, in 1973:

Benn held power during the one brief period within the last years when there seemed real hope that the Whitehall establishment might be persuaded to undo the damage that it had been doing to our computer industry since the latter began. He did not rise to the opportunity. In comparison with what it could and should have been, the British computer industry is very little better today than it would have been if he had left it alone.[43]

13

ICL and the New Range

1968-1972

I.C.L. has to succeed because the government says it must. If we
fail as managers, we can be replaced. But I.C.L. will go on.

—Sir John Wall, August 1969.[1]
[Sir John Wall resigned as Chairman of ICL in February 1972.]

The financial statistics of ICL (Table 13.1) have an uncomfortable similarity to those of ICT during the 1960s. Although revenues increased at
an average annual rate of about 15 per cent, taking inflation into account
this was no better than 10 per cent; this gentle growth was punctuated by
two financial crises, in 1971-72 and 1980-81, with attendant reductions
in profits and in the head count.

ICL always faced the choice of being a world-class EDP supplier, or a
relatively small niche computer company. Except for occasional moments
of crisis, the former was always the key strategy:

ICL has no wish to [be] a specialist supplier to a limited market with the inherent
low return on funds and low growth rate. The fundamental goal will therefore be
to attain the position of being the third largest D.P. supplier in the world market
by 1980.[2]

The implication of this policy was that ICL had not merely to keep up
with, but to outperform, its American competitors such as Honeywell,
Univac, and Burroughs. This ICL never managed to do; and consequently
its history has not been uniformly happy.

ICL: initial structure and strategy

In February 1968, Terence Maxwell met with the two principal representative shareholders of ICL, Lord Nelson of English Electric and Lord
Harding of Plessey, to agree on a board structure for the new company.
One of the chief problems that Maxwell foresaw in a conventional single-
tier board structure would be the inevitable conflict of interest between
the executive directors of ICL and the representative directors of the
major shareholders. In particular, Maxwell foresaw problems in terms of
the freedom of ICL to buy components on the open market, independently
of English Electric's and Plessey's vested interests as suppliers. Maxwell

Table 13.1 ICL financial statistics, 1968–85

	Revenues (£millions)	Pre-tax profits (£millions)	Personnel
1968	92.2	3.8	34058
1969	115.4	5.5	34001
1970	130.9	7.7	36329
1971	150.9	8.6	32669
1972	154.3	3.3	27701
1973	168.6	10.9	28798
1974	200.5	13.4	29718
1975	239.8	16.2	28069
1976	288.3	23.1	27317
1977	418.7	30.3	32156
1978	509.4	37.5	33978
1979	624.1	46.5	34401
1980	715.8	25.1	33087
1981	711.1	−49.8	25564
1982	720.9	23.7	23581
1983	846.7	46.1	22573
1984[a]	1124.4	32.1	21275
1985	1037.8	53.8	19962

Note
[a] Results for 1984 are for 15 months, owing to a change of accounting year.

Source
ICL Annual Reports.

decided, in consultation with his advisors at Morgan Grenfell, to have a two-tier board.[3] The senior board, International Computers (Holdings) Limited, would consist largely of non-executive directors, and would be responsible for broad policy and co-ordination. The junior board, International Computers Limited, would consist of executive directors, and would be responsible for operational matters.* The two-tier structure— described by one commentator as 'a classic one-over-one situation'[4]— turned out badly, and was one of the contributing factors to ICL's financial crisis in 1971–72.

So far as a managing director of ICL was concerned, the natural choice

---

* Where the distinction between the International Computers (Holdings) board and the International Computers Limited board is unimportant, 'ICL' will be used hereafter.

was Arthur Humphreys, who with Cecil Mead had turned around the fortunes of ICT during 1965-67. Humphreys' achievements with the 1900 series had been recognized by the 'Marketing Man of the Year' award in 1967,[5] and he was an immensely popular figure within the company. The search for a chairman of ICL took some time. It proved difficult to attract any of the really major industrial figures of the day. Eventually Lord Beeching came forward, and he was Humphreys' preferred choice, but for one reason or another the appointment fell through. Failing that, a top person from the electrical sector was to be preferred, but not anyone directly associated with the major shareholders (English Electric, Plessey, or Ferranti), or associated with a major competitor, such as GEC. The position was eventually offered to Sir John Wall. At the time of his appointment, the fifty-six-year-old Wall was deputy chairman of the Post Office, having been previously with Unilever and EMI; and he came with the blessing of the government.

Wall and Humphreys were the only executive directors on the senior Holdings board. The other members of the Holdings board (Appendix 2d) were three non-representative non-executive members from ICT (Terence Maxwell—deputy chairman; Sir Alan Wilson—chairman of Glaxo; and Sir Anthony Burney—chairman of Debenhams), and seven representative directors: Sir John Clark and Tom Hudson of Plessey; Lord Nelson and G.A. Ridell of English Electric; Basil de Ferranti of Ferranti; F.T. Davies of Vickers; and John Duckworth, managing director of the NRDC, the Mintech representative. English Electric was acquired by GEC in 1969; and although Lord Nelson continued to serve on the board, the formidable managing director of General Electric, Arnold Weinstock, played a hidden role behind the scenes; he had a hand in forcing through management changes in 1972.

The most notable feature of the ICL operational board was the almost complete lack of representation of English Electric. Although the technical people from English Electric were regarded as excellent, they were generally considered to be lacking in 'management depth'; the only important exception to this was William Barlow, managing director of English Electric Computers, who was considered outstanding; but he was not offered the top ICL job, and resigned after the merger. Out of nine directors, only one, Cliff Robinson, was from English Electric; and he would eventually be dropped. Apart from the newly appointed John Wall, all of the remaining directors were from the ranks of ICT: Humphreys as managing director, Echo Organ and Peter Ellis as assistant managing directors, Basil de Ferranti (technical strategy), Peter Hall (computer group), Lyon Lightstone (sales) and Alan Scott (finance).

With 34 000 employees and a turnover approaching £100 million, ICL was now a relatively large company, and by a considerable margin the largest non-American EDP-equipment manufacturer. Humphreys had the immediate task of achieving a measure of rationalization and integration. Some plants were closed down and some duplication in peripheral manufacture was eliminated; but the big savings would not emerge until ICL had a single range of computers in the mid-1970s.

To accelerate integration and to improve control of the business, as well as exploiting new business opportunities in the service sector, two of ICL's activities were hived off as independent subsidiaries. The most important of these was the software house Dataskil. This was in part a response to IBM's 'unbundling' decision of May 1968 in the United States (June 1969 in the UK) by which hardware and software were to be priced separately, instead of charging for hardware only and supplying software 'free'. The unbundling decision gave a major impetus to the software industry, in which ICL had had a rather low profile, in spite of having the largest programming organization in Europe, with two thousand staff. Dataskil was formed from the corpus of ICL's applications and contract programming teams, and was formally incorporated in May 1970. The second growth and rationalization opportunity was seen in computer services. The service business was growing at 30 per cent a year, which was considerably faster than the industry as a whole; but it had become increasingly dominated by American manufacturers and time-sharing companies. The former ICT and English Electric bureaux activities in the UK and overseas were incorporated as International Computing Services Limited (ICSL) in 1968; and in 1970 ICSL merged with the computer services activities of Barclays Bank to form BARIC.

Once ICL had rationalized and integrated, its overall strategy would be very simply stated: it was to become an EDP manufacturer in the same league as the more successful American companies. In September 1968, the first five-year business plan for ICL aimed for a modest revenue growth at an annual rate of 15 per cent. Given that the demand for computers was predicted to grow at an annual rate of about 18 per cent in the UK and ICL territories (slightly less in the US), this was an unambitious target; but to assume that ICL could do better than merely maintain its market share with its current ranges would have been unrealistic.[6] Once ICL had new products, however, more rapid growth would be possible. Humphreys was quoted as saying, in a moment of characteristic ebullience: 'In ten years' time, the market will be worth £10 000m., and if we only have ten per cent of that, we'll be bigger than ICI is now'.[7] To secure a ten per cent share of the world market ICL needed a sustained growth rate of perhaps 20 per cent a year, and to become the world's third largest EDP supplier. But none of this could happen until ICL had made the transition from its current ranges to the new range.

The two-range dilemma

When ICL was formed, it took on what Arthur Humphreys described as 'the largest range of incompatible computers in the world'.[8] That ICL should simply drop all but one of its current ranges was politically un-acceptable, at least in terms of the White Paper of March 1968:

The group will continue to develop, manufacture, market and service the ICT 1900 Series and English Electric System 4 ranges of computers, with enhancements; it will also continue to manufacture, market and service the Elliott 4100 range of computers as well as ICT's other existing ranges of equipment. In addition, it is intended to develop for the 1970's a new range of computer systems to be competitive, both technically and commercially, on an international basis . . .[9]

It was intended that the new range would be launched in autumn 1972, so that the existing ranges would have to continue to be sold exclusively for the next four years, and for another two years beyond that during the change-over period.

Of ICL's three ranges of computers, the Elliott 4100 series was the most easily dealt with, since it had relatively little political support in the new ICL, dominated as it was by ICT and English Electric people. The 4100 was, in any case, a rather narrow range of machines, and not particularly advanced architecturally; it had, however, sold quite well to scientific users, especially the universities; so it would continue to be sold in ones or twos, but no more money would be spent on development other than for minor and largely cosmetic enhancements. Manufacture was discontinued altogether in 1970, and the factories closed down.

System 4 was an altogether different matter. There is no question that the dominant ICT faction of ICL was predisposed to its own 1900 series. First, there was the much larger installed base of the 1900 series, with several hundred machines in the field at the time of the merger, compared with the handful of System 4 computers actually installed. Second, ICT had always been philosophically opposed to IBM-compatibility, and the success of the 1900 series had only served to reinforce that view. But third, and most important, System 4 was at the time of the merger a far from proven range, having experienced many teething problems and delivery delays. None the less, ICL was politically committed by the terms of the merger agreement to sell and enhance System 4, whether it wanted to or not. And, in fact, System 4 did have two strengths: first, it had an excellent real-time capability, which the 1900 series did not; and second, it appealed to certain users, including some in the Eastern Bloc, who wanted IBM-compatibility but were unable or unwilling to buy from IBM. It was therefore decided at the time of the merger that the 1900 series would be marketed to the bulk of users with ordinary needs, and System 4 would be sold to users with advanced real-time applications. On that assumption, it was expected that ICL's projected computer sales of £100 million in 1968/69 would be roughly three-quarters 1900 series to one-quarter System 4.

As Table 13.2 shows, in terms of price and power there was a large overlap between the two series, so that the ICL planners were faced with formidable problems in achieving rationalization and yet maintaining the credibility of both ranges. Humphreys had initially hoped that it would be possible to make a 'bridge' between the 1904A and the large members of

Table 13.2   ICL 1900 and System 4, 1968

1900 series			System 4		
Model	Price	Power	Model	Price	Power
1901A	85	20	4-30	100	40
1902A	200	75	4-40	172	90
1903A	200	170	4-50	271	140
1904A	400	300			
1906A	900	1200	4-70	600	500
1908A	1600	5000			

Notes
Price is for a typical or average system in £000s.
Power measured in Post Office Work Units.

Source
'ICL Corporate 5-Year Business Plan, 1968/69–1972/73', 5 October 1968, ICL Board Papers.

System 4, so that small/medium users would continue with the 1900 series, and large users would migrate to System 4. This solution proved to be not technically feasible, however, so more drastic pruning was called for.[10] To some extent the fate of the small System 4s was sealed by the launch of the IBM 360/25 in January 1968. The IBM 360/20, the smallest member of the 360 family, had not been a true compatible, but the 360/25 now filled this compatibility gap, and offered much stronger competition to the small System 4s. It was therefore decided to axe both the 4-30 and 4-40 in favour of the small 1900s. A particular attraction of this decision was that the 4-30 was subcontracted to English Electric's Marconi division, so that it was English Electric that faced the redundancy burden rather than ICL, which would have been the case had the 1901A been cancelled. To make the most of the transaction-processing market, it was decided to enhance the upper range of System 4 by introducing several new models—the 60, 65, 72, and 85—which would sell to big real-time users.

It has been argued that ICL would have done better to phase out the admittedly ageing 1900 series in favour of System 4. Apart from the IBM-compatibility issue, this was never a practical possibility. One problem had been that many of the orders for System 4 proved to be non-existent once the merger had taken place. But even had the order book proved solid, it would not have been possible to deliver System 4s in sufficient quantity and with acceptable reliability. Not the least of the System 4's reliability problems was 'The Crinkle Pin Affair', by which deteriorating soldered connections in all System 4 processors in the field had to be replaced by flexible 'crinkle pins' at a cost estimated at £200 000. By the end of 1968 there was a 30 per cent shortfall in System 4 deliveries, amounting to over £6 million. The shortfall was sufficiently bad for Wall to consider taking legal action against English Electric for misrepresentation during the merger negotiations. This was a matter of some delicacy, given the presence of Lord Nelson and Sandy Riddell on the Holdings board. Wall commissioned a detailed investigation by Cooper Brothers in December 1968, but its conclusions, in short, were that it was a case of *caveat emptor*, and that ICL had no strong case for legal redress.[11]

New-range planning: the strategic options

In autumn 1968, only a month or two after ICL had formally begun operations, Humphreys and his head of product planning Mike Forrest began to think about the new range. Up to this point, nothing of significance had been done since the joint ICT–English Electric study team had met in July 1967. It was always realized that funding a new range would be difficult, and initially attempts were made to share the cost with another mainframe manufacturer. In November 1968, Humphreys and Forrest made a number of trips to the United States, where they had discussions with several firms, including RCA, CDC, and Burroughs, to see if it would be possible to find a 'ready-made' solution for the new range, or if a joint development would be possible.[12] None of these discussions produced any worthwhile result; and so it was decided that ICL would have to develop the new range entirely from its own resources. The specification of a completely new range of computers was a once-in-a-lifetime opportunity, and inevitably the protagonists of the various architectural solutions within ICL, and without, were anxious to see their particular vision implemented. In particular, Basil de Ferranti and Gordon Scarrott (head of advanced research) were proposing the Basic Language Machine architecture, while others—notably Professor Tom Kilburn at Manchester University—were proposing the MU5 computer architecture.

These were powerful intellectual and emotional positions. In order to defuse the situation, and to avoid emotional commitment from determining the new-range architecture, it was decided to create a formal planning structure to try to arrive at a rational solution.

The New Range Planning Organization (NRPO) was formed in January 1969, under the general management of Mike Forrest.[13] The specification of the new range occupied most of 1969. During the first phase (January to April) the possible options for a new-range architecture were evaluated in the context of an assumed marketing environment; this was done in a leisurely and systematic fashion, because 'The main risk to be guarded against was that of being emotionally committed to the form of a solution rather than to spend time studying the options.'[14] In the second phase, which occupied the remainder of 1969, detailed specifications for the selected architectural option were elaborated, and implementation and introduction strategies explored.

The nucleus of the NRPO consisted of ICL planning staff (from both ICT and English Electric), who had expertise in corporate planning, market research, and technical product planning. To this nucleus, staff with appropriate expertise were added—manufacturing personnel, hardware and software designers, sales staff, and so on. Altogether, some sixty people, and fifteen staff-years of effort, went into the first phase of new-range planning during the first quarter of 1969. In addition, about a dozen senior academics were retained as part-time consultants. The NRPO was divided into a dozen or so small teams, none of them more than six people in size. These study groups were broadly classified as 'aims', 'options', and 'assessment' teams. The function of the 'aims' teams was to determine the market environment from the mid-1970s up to the mid-1980s. This called for detailed market research surveys, at home and abroad, and forecasts for world computer demand and usage in the 1980s. The job of each of the 'options' teams was to investigate in detail one of several possible architectural options for the new range. Finally, the task of the assessment teams was to determine criteria by which to measure the options, and to independently identify and specify key criteria to be met by the new range—for example the need for 'bridging' techniques to ease transition from the current ranges, the need for resilience and security, and the need for advanced database and compiler techniques.

The first major assumption about the marketing environment in which the new range would exist, was that IBM would dominate it, just as it had in the 1960s, with well over 50 per cent of the world market. On the other hand, no assumptions could be made about IBM's product strategy: its 'future series', expected in the early 1970s, might be an enhancement of the 360 architecture, or it might be an entirely new architecture with emulation and other aids to assist the migration of users. It was this uncertainty over IBM's future series that made ICL view an IBM-compatible architecture as being too high-risk as a long-term strategy. A second major assumption as to the future computer market was that there would be a transition from primarily batch-processing computers to primarily real-time transaction-processing systems. This in turn would imply a shift from a market dominated by first-time users, which had characterized the 1960s, to one of mature users replacing batch computers with more powerful real-time models. In evaluating the success of the new range (subsequently announced as the 2900 series) it is important to understand the uncertainties of the market environment for which it was designed. As it happened, IBM did not change its machine architecture (and at the time of writing still has not). Also, although large real-time computers were a major growth area in the 1970s, a much bigger growth occurred in small decentralized computers, for which the 2900 series was not well adapted (nor was System/360).

Altogether, seven 'option' teams were established to evaluate different architectural options for the new range, the only constraint being the assumed marketing environment. Although there were seven options, they in fact amounted to three basic choices: first, to enhance one of the current ranges; second, to use an existing advanced architecture; third, to develop a new architecture. In the event, the third choice was taken; the arguments for this choice, detailed below, are unavoidably technical, but non-technical readers need not dwell on the detail to follow the general flow.

1. Options 1 and 2: enhancement of current ranges

The most conservative and cheapest choice was to enhance one of the current ranges, the 1900 series or System 4. The '8-bit 1900', as it was called, was under active study in ICT long before the merger, both by an internal team and externally by the Auerbach consultancy.[15] The three main problems with the 1900 series were its 6-bit character and 24-bit word, its lack of a real-time capability, and the fact that it was perceived as old-fashioned. The first was easily put right, and both study teams recommended a 32-bit-word architecture downwards compatible with the 24-bit 1900. Enhancing the real-time capability was also possible, although this was less straightforward. But the 1900 series was an ageing architecture, and it was judged that there was no real prospect of sustaining it beyond the mid-1970s.[16] Consequently there was little support for 1900 series enhancement, other than for short-term tactical purposes while some longer-term range was under development.

System 4 had real merit, even without enhancement, as ICL's new range. It already used an 8-bit IBM-compatible byte, and it had real-time facilities that were much better than those of System/360. Moreover, a good deal of work had been done on future development within English Electric, and ICL had access to RCA's new product-line, then under development to replace Spectra 70. The System 4 option consequently had strong support, especially from the English Electric faction within ICL, and the technical arguments were very strong. The principal argument against a 360-based architecture was whether ICL should go IBM-compatible. The arguments against IBM-compatibility had been iterated so many times in the past at ICT, that there was really nothing else to be said on the subject that had not been said many times before. It is doubtful, even had the technical arguments for enhancing System 4 been overwhelming, that the ICT faction could have been persuaded by them.

2. Options 3-6: existing advanced architectures

If ICL was to adopt a new architecture, then there was some merit in using an existing one, which would be less of a leap into the dark than developing its own *ab initio*. In fact, there was no architecture to which ICL had access that met all its requirements, so that the four architectures examined served largely as inputs to the 'synthetic option' (see below). The four architectures studied were the 'New Series Branch' option, the High-Level Language option, the Manchester University option, and the Basic Language Machine (BLM) option.

The New Series Branch option began, in effect, as a shopping list from ICT software writers of desirable features in a new range. It was a minor input to the synthetic option, but was otherwise something of a 'paper tiger'.[17]

The High-Level Language option was to adopt the Burroughs design philosophy of a machine oriented to a particular high-level programming language. On its own, this design philosophy was insufficient for the market of the 1970s, but as with the MU5 architecture (below) the need to execute high-level languages efficiently was subsumed in the synthetic option.

Manchester University had had very close links with ICL (via ICT and Ferranti) going back many years, so it was natural that ICL would seriously consider their latest machine, the MU5, then coming into service as a successor to the Atlas. Designed for a 'number-crunching' environment, the architecture was insufficient as the sole basis of a new range, but it contained many useful innovations, and was one of the two major inputs to the synthetic option. Five of the Manchester University faculty held consultancies on the design of the new range.

ICL's own BLM project was the second major inspiration for the new range, for it resolved in a very generalized but efficient manner problems of data management, language processor technology, and process management for real-time working, that had been tackled in an *ad hoc* manner in existing architectures.

3. Option 7: the synthetic option

The synthetic option, which was to be the basis of the new range, was generated by a small team given the brief of bringing together the best of current thinking on computer design to synthesize an architecture whose only constraint was that of the assumed market environment (that is, one dominated by real-time transaction-processing systems, using high-level languages, and large-scale databases).

From BLM and MU5 came advanced process-management concepts that would dramatically improve the efficiency and robustness of operating systems. (GEORGE 3 and OS/360 had both been notoriously resource-consuming and unreliable.) From sources such as Burroughs and MU5 came concepts of efficient high-level-language execution. And from BLM and MU5 came ideas on data management that would enhance the construction and efficiency of database systems.

Without any question, the new-range architecture was masterly. It was elegant, efficient, not in the least baroque, and in advance of anything offered by any other manufacturer (and this arguably remains true in the late 1980s).

New Range: implementation and introduction plans

The output of Phase I of the new-range planning, which ended in April 1969, was a large body of reports produced by the individual study teams.* These reports were examined by, and presentations were made to, ICL's middle and senior management drawn from across the company. In May 1969 the ICL board officially endorsed the decision to base the new range on the synthetic option. The following month, ICL gave its first public indication of its commitment to a new range by cancelling the 1908A in favour of a new machine, to be known as Project 52, which would be available in 1973.[19]

From mid-1969, the detailed specification of the new range began to take shape. What had actually been produced by the synthetic option team up to this point was a rather slim document describing the broad architectural concepts. To develop a complete specification the original option team of six was expanded to a full-time team of twelve, led by Alan Bagshaw. The team included about three on the marketing side, and the

---

* Arthur Humphreys has a favourite anecdote about the large volume of new-range documentation. As the number of reports lying in his office grew and grew, one day he asked Colin Haley, one of his senior planners, what he was supposed to do with them. 'Well,' said Haley, 'if you stand on them, you can see further into the future'.[18]

remainder were involved in the technical specification; of the latter, Virgilio Pasquali and Brian Warboys took leading roles in the hardware and software specifications respectively.[20] Team members worked closely with Manchester University and the BLM group to distil their ideas into the new-range architecture. The real problem with the MU5 and BLM options had been that they were too 'pure'. Neither option, in the view of the ICL planners, on its own addressed all of the needs of the commercial-EDP user. Neither Manchester nor the BLM people were happy with having their visions diluted, and this was the source of quite a lot of friction.[21]

In early 1970, work was started on a marketing plan for the new range under the general direction of Chris Wilson, head of marketing and product strategy. It was intended to support a range of six processors (P0 to P5) within the new-range architecture, ranging from a low-power machine (P0) up to a machine several times the power of the 1908A (P5). In fact, the low-power P0 processor was seen as an entry-level machine of limited appeal; and the P5 processor (Project 52) was seen as being too expensive to develop without a guaranteed government purchase of at least ten machines, and it was never much more than a paper exercise.[22] Attention was therefore focused on processors P1 to P4, which were viewed largely in terms of a replacement range for ICL's current computers. For example, P4, the most powerful processor (about 10-Atlas power) would be targeted at existing 1906A users and potential 1908A customers. P3—with about the power of a 1906A—would be the natural upgrade for current 1904A and System 4-70 users. And so on down the range.

The announcement strategy for the 2900 series received a great deal of attention, since there was much accumulated experience in ICL's planning division—dating from the Samastronic onwards—of the problem of a collapsing order book following the introduction of a new range.[23] The essential problem was that if all the processors in the new range were announced simultaneously, then 'the effect on 1900 sales would be catastrophic'.[24] Users of the 1900 and System 4 would naturally cancel their orders until the new range was available, and ICL would have nothing to sell during the two years it might take to switch production from the old range to the new. The ingenious strategy was therefore adopted of a 'top-down' introduction. The largest processors (P3 and P4) would be announced first, thereby securing the all-important 1904A and System 4-70 replacement market. By demonstrating (hopefully) the ease with which users migrated to the 2900 series, and by differential pricing, it was hoped to continue selling the 1901A to 1904A segment of the 1900 range until the P1 and P2 processors became available.

Even though the new-range development was now committed only to

HEC 4 data-processing computer, *c.*1957

HEC 4 chassis

The HEC 4 computer

BTM's first data-processing computer was the HEC 4, also known as the model 1201. The HEC was a first-generation machine, based on thermionic-valve electronics; a typical chassis from the central processing unit is shown *left*. The HEC series was the best-selling early British computer, over 100 being delivered between 1957 and 1964, at a typical system price of around £40 000.

Diana prototype, Stevenage, 1958

Random-access
drum store

The Diana computer

Diana was a very large random-access computer developed in Boston MA, in a
collaboration between BTM and the Laboratory for Electronics, during 1955–58.
By the time the prototype (*top*) had been installed at Stevenage in December
1957, it was already approaching obsolescence because it was based on first-
generation technology and had no magnetic-tape storage. The machine was never
marketed and the prototype was scrapped. A major part of the development was
the 2 Mchar random-access drum (*above*). But this, too, was overtaken by a
superior technology (magnetic-disc storage) before it could be developed into
a product.

ICT 1301 computer, 1962

1301 circuit card

The ICT 1301
The 1301 was designed by Computer Developments Limited, a development
company jointly-owned by BTM (later ICT) and GEC. Built at GEC's Coventry
works, the 1301 was a second-generation transistorized machine; a circuit card
from the processor is shown *above*. The first deliveries were made in mid-1962,
and over 200 systems were sold at an average system price of £100 000.

Ferranti Orion *c*.1963

Orion commissioning area, West Gorton, *c*.1963

Artist's sketch of the Ferranti Atlas, *c*.1961

The Ferranti acquisition

In September 1963, ICT acquired the Ferranti computer department. The deal included all of Ferranti's mainframe computers, including the Orion and Atlas, and the West Gorton, Manchester, manufacturing plant. The Orion (*facing page, top*) was a large-scale data-processing computer with a typical system price of £400 000. The West Gorton plant (*facing page, bottom*) was said, at the time, to be the largest computer-production facility in Europe. The Atlas computer (*above*) was a very high-speed scientific machine developed in collaboration with Manchester University and costing about £2½ million. Although the Atlas was not a commercial success (only five systems were delivered) it pioneered techniques in virtual storage and operating systems well-ahead of its time.

1900 OPERATING SYSTEM

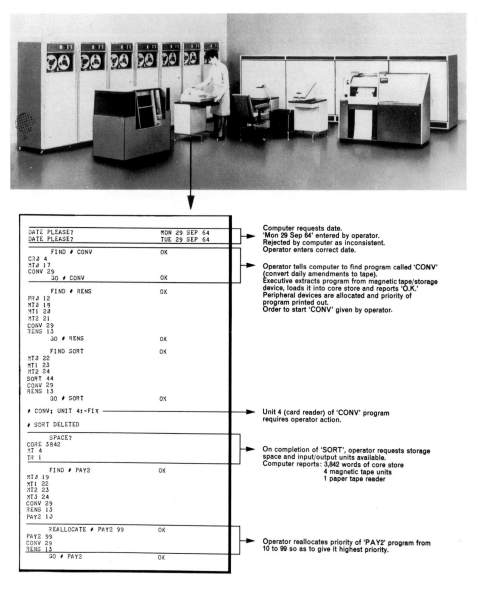

DATE PLEASE?	MON 29 SEP 64	
DATE PLEASE?	TUE 29 SEP 64	
FIND ⚡ CONV	OK	
CRⱭ 4		
MTⱭ 17		
CONV 29		
ⱭO ⚡ CONV	OK	
FIND ⚡ RENS	OK	
PRⱭ 12		
MTⱭ 18		
MT1 20		
MT2 21		
CONV 29		
RENS 13		
ⱭO ⚡ RENS	OK	
FIND SORT	OK	
MTⱭ 22		
MT1 23		
MT2 24		
SORT 44		
CONV 29		
RENS 13		
ⱭO ⚡ SORT	OK	
⚡ CONV: UNIT 4:-FIX		
⚡ SORT DELETED		
SPACE?		
CORE 3842		
MT 4		
TR 1		
FIND ⚡ PAY2	OK	
MTⱭ 19		
MT1 22		
MT2 23		
MTⱭ 24		
CONV 29		
RENS 13		
PAY2 1Ɑ		
REALLOCATE ⚡ PAY2 99	OK	
PAY2 99		
CONV 29		
RENS 13		
ⱭO ⚡ PAY2	OK	

Computer requests date.
'Mon 29 Sep 64' entered by operator.
Rejected by computer as inconsistent.
Operator enters correct date.

Operator tells computer to find program called 'CONV'
(convert daily amendments to tape).
Executive extracts program from magnetic tape/storage
device, loads it into core store and reports 'O.K.'
Peripheral devices are allocated and priority of
program printed out.
Order to start 'CONV' given by operator.

Unit 4 (card reader) of 'CONV' program
requires operator action.

On completion of 'SORT', operator requests storage
space and input/output units available.
Computer reports: 3,842 words of core store
4 magnetic tape units
1 paper tape reader

Operator reallocates priority of 'PAY2' program from
10 to 99 so as to give it highest priority.

Publicity slide illustrating the 1900-series multiprogramming executive,
September 1964

An ICT 1900 series advertisement, 1966. The advertisement won the first national prize in the Premio Europeo Rizzoli contest in Milan.

At I.C.T it's all go

I told the wife I delivered seven 'undred thousand quids worth of computers for ICT this week and she said pity you don't 'ave time to weed the garden.

I.C.T. now have over 500 orders for 1900 Series computers, announced only twenty one months ago. Of these 131 have been delivered, together with the necessary software. Delivery rate is building up to eight a week. What's more, these I.C.T. systems will be there for a long time. No matter how a business grows, the I.C.T. 1900 can grow with it. It was designed that way—to keep the buyer's original investment secure. That's why 500 systems — worth £61 million — have been ordered: a third of these for export.

Britain can be proud of **I.C.T.**

International Computers and Tabulators Limited

The ICT 1900 series

The ICT 1900 series was a compatible range of computers launched in September 1964, in response to the IBM System/360 announcement the previous April. The 1900-series processors were initially based on a conservative second-generation technology, but uprated A-series and S-series processors using third-generation integrated circuits were announced during 1967–70. A particular feature of the 1900 series was the multiprogramming 'executive', which reduced operator intervention and streamlined the flow of work through the computer. The illustration on the *facing page* shows a typical dialogue between the executive and an operator. ICT advertising (*above*) played on the fact that the 1900-series hardware and software were available in Europe well ahead of System/360, for which deliveries did not begin until 1967. By 1968 over 1000 ICT 1900-series systems had been ordered and 600 delivered. The 1900 series was a turning point for ICT that marked the end of its transition from being primarily a punched-card machine firm to being a full-scale computer supplier.

System 4 computer at the National GIRO Centre, 1968

English Electric System 4
When ICT merged with English Electric Computers to form ICL in 1968, it acquired the System 4 range of computers. Originally announced in September 1965, System 4 was an IBM-compatible computer range made under licence from RCA (although with a significant UK design and technology content). The large System 4 computers were particularly suited to real-time applications and several prestige orders were secured from government departments and nationalized industries.

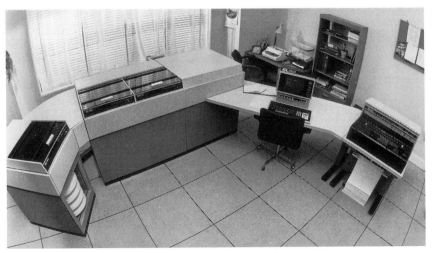

Fish-eye publicity shot of the ICL 2903, 1973.

ICL 2903
Launched at the Hanover computer fair in April 1973, the ICL 2903 computer was designed to capitalize on the booming market for small business systems in Europe. It was ICL's most successful product of the 1970s: at its peak it contributed 30 per cent of total revenues, and several thousand systems had been delivered by the time it was replaced with the ME29 in 1980.

ICL 2970, October 1974

2900 P-series circuit board, 1974

The ICL New Range
ICL was established in 1968 with the explicit mission to design a new range of computers for the 1970s, to which existing ICT 1900 series and English Electric System 4 users would eventually migrate. The new range was announced as the 2900 series in October 1974. The early P-series processors were based on medium-scale integrated circuits (*left*) and core memory, but the later S-series processors used large-scale integrated circuits and semiconductor memory. Software development for the new range accounted for 35 per cent of the total development expenditure—the photograph *overleaf* shows the Bracknell computer hall, which supplied prodigious computing power for the ICL Software Development Organization.

ICL Bracknell computer
hall, 1974

The Singer acquisition

In 1976 ICL acquired the international division of Singer Business Machines. The acquisition gave ICL a well-established European customer base in small business systems, and a portfolio of new products. These products included the System Ten computer, the model 1500 intelligent terminal system, and Point-Of-Sale terminals (*right*) that enhanced ICL's position in retail systems.

ICL/Singer POS terminal, *c*.1976

ICL DRS 20, 1981

ICL One-Per-Desk, 1984

The Networked Product Line

With the Networked Product Line, announced in October 1981, ICL made a major entry into the office-systems market. Several new products were announced —some based on existing ICL products, some developed in collaborative ventures, and others bought in from North American manufacturers. Typical products were the DRS 20 distributed-resource system (*above, left*), evolved from the Singer 1500; and the One-Per-Desk (*above, right*), a combined personal-computer-telephone which was developed in collaboration with the British micro-computer firms Sinclair and Psion.

ICL 2966 and Series 39 processors, 1985

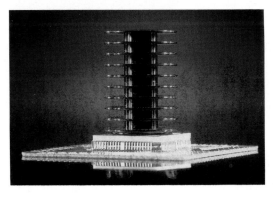

Fujitsu ECL chip

Series 39

In 1981 ICL's most urgent problem was the declining sales of its 2900 series computers, owing to competition from IBM and Japanese mainframe manufacturers. In October 1981, the company secured an agreement with Fujitsu to obtain access to its semiconductor technology for future ICL mainframes. Based on Fujitsu technology, the ICL mainframe range was relaunched as Series 39 in April 1985, with the initial announcement of the medium-sized level 30 and the large level 80. The new technology brought about a dramatic improvement in performance and reduction in size: the photograph (*top*) shows the relative sizes of the Series 39 processors compared with the powerful 2966 introduced in 1981: the level 80 with four times the processing power of the 2966 occupied only half the floor space, while the level 30 with a half of the power was only one-fifth the size. The model 30 used Fujitsu's relatively inexpensive VLSI CMOS technology, while the model 80 used expensive, but much faster, ECL chips—with their characteristic 'top hat' cooling fins (*above*).

the P1 to P4 processors, funding remained a problem. ICL's total R&D spend, which was projected at about £90 million for the five-year period 1968-73, had not only to support the new-range development, but also the continued enhancement of the current ranges.[25] The negotiations for joint ventures with other companies therefore continued. The most promising alliance at this time was with the French national computing company CII, since a European partnership would be good politically, and commercially might enable ICL to improve its dismal 2½ per cent share of the European market. ICL offered CII the full design of the new range, with the aim of joint manufacturing and development.[26] Unfortunately CII, like ICL, needed to have compatibility with its own current ranges, operating systems, and data formats. To achieve easy migration to the new range from a third architecture in addition to the 1900 and System 4 was not feasible, and, failing to reach a compromise, the CII negotiations petered out. Talks were also held with CDC. The hope initially had been that they could jointly develop the P5 as a super-computer; but eventually the talks focused on a more realistic European-standards company with CII. A joint company, Multinational Data S.A., was formed in 1971, with the equal equity participation of ICL, CDC, and CII.[27]

The effect of these negotiations, which entailed many revisions of the new-range specifications to accommodate different data standards and interfaces, was to hold back development of the new range almost completely during 1970.[28] And during that period the marketing environment itself had changed direction, and the industry was about to fall into recession.

The computer recession and the changing market environment

The two year period 1970-71 saw the first major recession in the computer industry. The recession was precipitated by the general economic downturn in the United States, which began in late-1969. The capital goods sector was the first to be hit by the recession, and during 1970 United States computer deliveries fell by about 20 per cent. As well as cancelling actual orders, users became more cost-conscious, and this further eroded margins. The first casualty of the computer recession in the United States was General Electric. General Electric's entire capital-goods business (nuclear reactors, jet engines, steam turbines, etc.) was hit by the recession, leaving it short of funds to develop its computer products, which were approaching obsolescence. In May 1970 it sold its computer interests (including the French Bull stake) to Honeywell. The fall in American home demand led to an increased competitiveness from United States manufacturers in Europe and in the UK. This exacerbated a trend that had begun in the late 1960s, owing to the differential growth rates of the computer market in the United States and Europe. (Because the United States was some two to three years ahead of Europe in computer diffusion, when the American market began to mature in 1968, with an annual growth rate of about 18 per cent in the United States, the growth rates in Britain and Europe remained a buoyant 21 per cent and 27 per cent respectively.)[29]

As a result of the recession, in 1970 IBM experienced a decline in rentals and sales, an event which was almost without precedent in its history. This led to unprecedented competitive responses from IBM, which drove the rest of the computer industry into deeper recession. As the press aptly put it, it was the case of IBM sneezing and the rest of the industry catching a cold. IBM essentially made three competitive reactions: first, it improved its position in small-business systems; second, it announced System/370; and third, it began price-cutting.

The drive to small third-generation business systems, which reached its peak in the mid-1970s, was not at first appreciated by the traditional EDP manufacturers. There was a widely held industry view that 'the major trend in both demand and technical development was towards very powerful machines, with remote access or time sharing facilities being used with a large number of remote terminals'.[30] This was the conviction that underlay much of ICL's new-range strategy, as articulated by Humphreys:

Concerning the future, I believe that larger systems will substantially take over from smaller systems, but that a smaller system will not be a small system, free-standing in its own right, but is likely to be a terminal . . .[31]

Two developments, however, began to undermine the trend towards larger systems. The first was the drop in the cost of integrated circuits and peripherals, which made it possible to have very low-priced installations, opening up a large market of new users who previously could not even have afforded a punched-card machine installation. Second, there was a general disenchantment among managements with large computer systems, which tended to be unreliable (particularly in terms of operating systems); and the economies of scale in large computers were proving to be more apparent than real. This led to an alternative EDP strategy of having several low-cost decentralized computers, instead of a single centralized machine.

Since the launch of System/360 in 1964, IBM had tended to ignore the small-machine market. The adherence (albeit partial) of the 360/20 and 360/25 to the System/360 architecture meant that they were relatively expensive; and this allowed lower-cost machines, such as the NCR Century 100 and the Honeywell 120, to take sizeable market shares, while in the UK the ICL 1901A sold very well. In July 1969, however, IBM launched the System/3 low-cost computer, which abandoned 360-compatibility altogether, and hence could be made to much lower costs. An entirely new set of punched-card peripherals using a small-sized card was introduced,* along with a fully third-generation processor and magnetic-tape and disc storage. System/3, like the small System/360 machines, was also equipped with the Report Program Generator (RPG) programming system, which was especially geared to the needs of first-time users and former punched-card machine installations.

System/3 not only opened up a new market for small-computer systems, but, because of technological leapfrogging, it also attacked the market for small mainframe computers such as the 1901A. System/3 was very successful, over 1600 systems being installed worldwide in the first year of delivery, and some 25 000 systems eventually being sold.[32] In October 1969, ICL's sales director, Lyon Lightstone, reported to the board 'with the introduction of System 3 on top of the NCR Century 100 and the smaller Honeywell systems, the 1901A is no longer competitive in this market'.[33] To meet the competition it was decided to develop the small (P0) new-range processor, which had been in abeyance; but this was a long-term project (1974 at the earliest), so in the short term an RPG translator was developed to attack the small IBM computers, and in the medium term a completely new small-computer development, code-named PF73, was begun (launched as the model 2903 in 1973).

IBM's second move in the computer recession was the launch of System/370, the successor to the 360, in June 1970. The new models, which used integrated circuits throughout, and had semiconductor memories, were true third-generation machines offering a price/performance of up to four times that of System/360. The 370 range was announced 'top-down' (as was planned for ICL's new range); but it seems likely that competitive pressure from RCA forced IBM to accelerate the announcement of successive models, which 'made the entire System/360 line obsolescent, and led to massive returns of leased System/360 equipment to IBM, which sharpened the effects of the recession on the firm'.[34] During 1970–72 all the other American manufacturers followed suit by enhancing their existing ranges with integrated circuits and semiconductor memories. These included the Burroughs 700 series in October 1970, the Univac 1110 in November 1970, and the Honeywell 6000 series in February 1971. It is, of course, arguable that these enhancements were motivated as much by general technological progress as by IBM's competitive pressure.

---

* The small-sized IBM card was developed from the 3000 series of punched-card machines introduced in 1960. The 3000 series had been abandoned in 1962, when it was eclipsed by the 1401 computer.

The effect of System/370 on RCA was much more dramatic. In response to the System/370 announcement in June 1970, RCA prematurely announced four small/medium models of its new product line the following September (the models 2, 4, 6, and 7). The intention had been to 'intercept' the System 370, but in fact: 'By introducing the RCA series, RCA "obsoleted," "intercepted," and "blew . . . out of the water" its own Spectra 70 series.'[35] By autumn 1971, RCA's crisis had so deepened that it decided to withdraw from the computer business altogether, and sold out to Sperry Rand. It was estimated that RCA lost $241 million on its computer operations during 1958-71.

The System/370 announcement provoked a number of reactions in ICL. First, in April 1971, ICL announced the 1900 S-series, in a press release designed to continue to show long-term commitment to the 1900 series, while at the same time not appearing to back-track on the new range:

The chain of logic which started in 1964 still runs strongly through the concept of the 1900 S series. It did not end with this series, and when some newer range of equipment is announced in some future year, ICL will have kept the significance of this continuing link in mind.[36]

Apart from bringing out the S-series, perhaps the main reaction within ICL was general relief that IBM had either abandoned or deferred its future series, which could have undermined its own new range. It also highlighted the risks of IBM-compatibility, and the demise of RCA gave every reason to be thankful that after the merger ICL had made the 1900 series the dominant range. System 4 sales, already producing a loss, were generally run down after 1971 except for large systems.

In May 1971 IBM cut the prices of most of its peripherals by 15 per cent. This competitive action was actually aimed at manufacturers of plug-compatible equipment, rather than the other EDP manufacturers; but all of them had to reduce their prices in line with IBM or lose market-share. In fact, IBM had never been particularly price-competitive in the past, and the removal of its 'price umbrella' was a rude shock to the industry. The development of the plug-compatible manufacturers had been one of the consequences of the decision to manufacture System/360 with a standard interface. By 1970, the plug-compatible manufacturers had grown to take 11 per cent of the IBM magnetic-tape drive market, and 4 per cent of the disc market.[37] The sole competitive advantage that the plug-compatible manufacturers had was in terms of prices, which were typically 20-30 per cent below IBM's. Consequently, IBM's main response had to be in terms of price-cutting. It was believed that IBM's manufacturing costs were less than 15 per cent of the price charged to users, so that price-cutting, while not an attractive option, was certainly sustainable. By contrast, ICL's manufacturing costs were in the region of 50 per cent of selling prices, so that price-cutting was never a viable option.[38]

The Select Committee on Science and Technology: an inquiry into ICL

The impact of the computer recession on ICL was to be a very public affair. In early 1970, the government established a sub-committee of the Select Committee of Science and Technology to examine 'The prospects for the UK computer industry in the 1970's, including the possibilities of international collaboration and the functions of Government in this field, both as policy maker and user'.[39] Sir John Wall noted, however, that the event 'turned out in practice to be an inquiry into ICL'.[40]

The Select Committee on Science and Technology had been established in the last year, 1969/70, of the Labour Government; and it was a major, and enduring, constitutional innovation. The aim of the Select Committee was to provide a forum for debate on science and industrial policy in a depth and length that was not feasible within the confines of a parliamentary debate. Three sub-committees of the Select Committee were set up to undertake exhaustive inquiries into three specific areas of science and technology: the nuclear industry, defence research, and the computer industry. Each of the sub-committees was composed of a group of well-informed MPs from all parties, and the open and fair-minded way in which they conducted their inquiries attracted worldwide commendation and interest from the financial and technical press.

The committee of inquiry into the computer industry, known as 'Sub-Committee D', took its evidence between February and May 1970. The committee was chaired by Airey Neave M.P., and it included several parliamentarians with significant knowledge of the computer industry. There were three particular areas concerning ICL to which the sub-committee addressed itself: the nature of the government's procurement policy; a quantitative as opposed to a qualitative assessment of ICL's R&D needs; and the competence of ICL's senior management. These were issues that had been widely aired prior to the hearings in the financial and computer press.

The government's procurement policy had never been formally documented, and its unofficial status was 'shrouded in mystery'.[41] The sub-committee succeeded in prizing out of the Civil Service Department its unpublished guidelines for computer purchase:

(1) To acquire large computers (those more powerful than Atlas) by single tender action from I.C.L., subject to satisfactory price, performance and delivery dates.

(2) To acquire smaller computers by single tender action (normally from I.C.L.) when they are intended to lead-in to the use of a large computer of the same family or where there are other reasons for seeking compatibility or flexibility by the use of machines of the same family, subject to the same proviso about price, performance and delivery.

(3) In all other cases, including large computers where I.C.L. are unable to meet all the conditions specified in (1) above, to seek competitive tenders from not less than 3 firms, . . . allowing preference in favour of any British machine provided that there is no undue price differential as compared with overseas supplies, that the British machine is technically suitable and that no undue delay is involved.[42]

This revelation confirmed what all of ICL's competitors had long suspected, and they now used the platform of the select committee to voice their strong objections. Between 1969 and 1971 ICL's share of government orders had risen from 69 per cent to 90 per cent; and although ICL was inclined, in public, to account for this fact as being merely a reflection of its competence in the marketplace, no one—least of all the members of the sub-committee—was convinced: 'We have had a certain amount of evidence which suggests that there is rather a special relationship between I.C.L. and the Government. While you discount it, I think yours is the only single voice. This is to be recognized.'[43]

Unsurprisingly, American manufacturers complained about the preference given to ICL. Honeywell, in particular, pointed out that its machines used more British components than ICL's, and that it had a factory in Scotland which it had set up in the expectation of receiving orders from the public sector, in accordance with Wedgwood Benn's stated policy that 'machines made in Britain by subsidiaries of foreign firms are regarded in this context as British'.[44] On the other hand, as further evidence to the sub-committee revealed, American manufacturers were well protected by the Buy American Act, and the French, German, and Japanese governments were each protecting their own computer industries. In fact, ICL's view was that the procurement policy, while the government accounted for a mere 15 per cent of national computer orders, was something of a distraction. In the United States, government orders accounted for perhaps one-third of the overall market. If the British Government merely increased its demand in proportion, it would be of more value to ICL than the procurement policy.

ICL made an ambivalent and ambiguous case for R&D support from the government. On the one hand, John Wall strongly criticized the level of government-funded research and development:

If you compare the development money being put by Government into this vital industry with the amount which it is putting into other industries, I think you

will see that the amount is ludicrous in the extreme. We have had a grant of
£13½ million over four years. There must be other contracts, but compared with
the total R. and D. spend of the country and compared with the vital importance
of this industry in the rest of the 1970s, we feel that the total R. and D. spend is
not enough.[45]

Indeed, compared to the £790 million invested in Concorde between
1962 and 1969, this was a very valid point. On the other hand, the
connotation of the term 'grant' was damaging to ICL's image, so that
what Wall really wanted was far more government orders, not just in ones
and twos, so that R&D could be funded out of revenues:

We feel that there is a need for the Government to encourage the use of
computers. That would give us more support than anything else. We want orders
and development contracts, not preference. . . . At the moment the Government
buys from us 'once offs'. If the Government buys machines that way, we are
worse off. It is well known that I.B.M. get orders for $320 million worth of
computers—there was an order for 110 computers for the American Air Force.
As long as the Government buys in penny packages we cannot be as efficient as
we ought to be.[46]

As to the actual scale of R&D funding that ICL needed, Wall stated
'our spend on R. and D., which is now about £14 million a year, could go
up to £20 million a year to meet our needs'.[47] This was in fact only a
modest understatement of ICL's true position. As Tables 13.3 and 13.4

Table 13.3   ICL R&D spend, 1968-73

	1969	1970	1971	1972	1973	Total
Total spend (£millions)	13.4	15.0	17.6	17.6	20.3	83.9
Percentage of revenues	11.7	11.5	11.7	11.4	12.0	

Source
'ICL: Five Year Forward Look, 1975/80', 20 January 1976, p. 5, ICL Board Papers.

show, ICL's R&D spend was not far out of line with its American competitors, although as a percentage of revenues it was considerably the
highest. Where ICL fell particularly short of American competitors in
terms of R&D, was in government support for advanced applications;
according to the OECD, some $250 million a year was spent on state-of-
the-art projects in the United States, whereas a negligible amount was
being spent in Britain.[48]

Throughout the hearings the generally low image of ICL's senior
management showed through time and again. One influential witness, the

Table 13.4   Comparative R&D spends of computer companies, 1969

Company	Turnover (£millions)	R&D (£millions)	Government contracts (£millions)	R&D-Turnover ratio (%)
IBM	3000	167	121	5.6
Burroughs	317	15	43	4.7
NCR	523	17	34	3.3
CDC	238	18	n/a	7.6
Honeywell/GE	766	42	42	5.5
ICL	115	13	n/a	11.7

Source
ICL sources.

American managing director of Leasco, Saul Steinberg, 'urged ICL to decide on which IBM executive it wanted and then to go out and pinch him'.[49] (This was a somewhat ironical comment coming from Steinberg, since in 1968 Leasco had poached ICL's Peter Hunt to head its new software subsidiary.) The effect of this type of statement was very damaging to the prestige of ICL, and, whether the criticism was valid or not, it meant that a change of ICL's top management would ultimately be necessary to secure further government funding.

Sub-Committee D heard its last evidence in May 1970, but before it could produce its report and recommendations a general election was called.*

The Heath Government and the Rothschild Report

The new Conservative Government of Edward Heath came into office on 18 June 1970, and it immediately changed the whole nature of the relationship between government and industry.[50] Its general policy for industry was to be one of disengagement, preferring the forces of the market-place, rather than direct government intervention, to achieve rationalization. The Heath Government had come to power pledged to repealing the Industrial Expansion Act, which had created ICL among others, and ultimately to dissolving the Industrial Reorganization Corporation. The Ministry of Technology was broken up, being replaced by the Department of Trade and Industry in late 1970, and its aviation role

* Although there was an unofficial minority report *British Computers and Industrial Innovation* (1971), edited by Eric Moonman, a member of Sub-Committee D who lost his seat in the June 1970 election, it was not particularly influential.

was taken over by the new Ministry of Aerospace. Open-ended support for industry, enjoyed by many companies during the Wilson era, was stopped in favour of what was to become known as the 'lame-duck' policy. Likewise, R&D subventions of the kind enjoyed by ICL were to be subjected to the special scrutiny of the Central Policy Review Staff (the 'Think Tank') headed by Lord Rothschild.

The Conservative Government did not, however, dismantle the Select Committee on Science and Technology established by the Labour Government, and in early 1971 the computer industry inquiry was reconstituted as Sub-Committee A, with Airey Neave as chairman again, but a largely different membership. ICL's evidence to Sub-Committee A was a good deal less sanguine than it had been at the Sub-Committee D hearings a year previously. As part of its economic policy to correct regional imbalances, the government had replaced investment grants by investment allowances from April 1971. By replacing front-end cash grants with retrospective tax allowances, the effect was to make computers more expensive. The impact of this measure on ICL was particularly acute; it came at the very moment that the computer industry was diving into recession, and UK inflation was touching 10 per cent.

ICL's evidence had to steer a course between a frank statement of its problems, in order to attract a measure of public support, and a bold front, to sustain shareholders' and customers' confidence. The depth of the recession in the computer industry was well known, however, and John Wall admitted that ICL's order books for industrial users had declined 20 per cent from the previous year. He stated that ICL had not asked the government for direct support of R&D, but he yet again pleaded for more orders: 'We get R and D money by selling things, not by having money given to us. If the Government were willing to place more orders for computers we would be able to do more R and D work'.[51]

In his evidence to the sub-committee, Sir John Eden, Minister for Trade and Industry, was somewhat ambivalent about ICL. On the one hand the DTI intended to maintain the various supports for ICL initiated by the Labour Government—the procurement policy, the final instalment of the £13.5 million subvention, and its shareholding and board representation—but on the other hand 'the Government sees no need for further support of these kinds'.[52] But the fact that *some* form of help for ICL would be needed was admitted by Eden: '. . . it is unrealistic to expect ICL to engage with IBM and the other main United States manufacturers who live in an economy which is eight times larger than that of the United Kingdom'.[53]

All the evidence suggests that the government at this time did not have a clear policy towards ICL, or indeed towards industry in general. In the very month, February 1971, that Eden gave his evidence to Sub-

Committee A, the financial collapse of Rolls Royce threw the lame-duck industrial policy into reverse, and the government announced its intention to take the aerospace assets of Rolls Royce into public ownership.

On the question of the new range, the ICL witnesses stonewalled. They admitted that Project 52 had been announced and was under active development, but refused to speak of the new range in public session. The facts of the matter, however, were that ICL did not itself know the prospects for the new range. In spring 1971 it received the last instalment of the government's £13.5 million subvention; the new range was a year behind schedule already; and it could not realistically be brought to the market without further government support. Unfortunately, there was little prospect of definite government action until the appearance of the report of Sub-Committee A, and the Rothschild Report, towards the end of 1971.

The crisis of 1971-72

In the meantime ICL's crisis deepened. In May 1971, IBM had cut its prices, ICL's order books collapsed further, and it had not only to survive the immediate future, but also to plan on the basis that government support might not ultimately be forthcoming. The stark choice facing ICL was whether to cut prices in line with IBM to maintain its market-share, and face certain losses; or to hold up prices, lose market-share, and become a slimmer but moderately profitable company. The latter course was taken, and 1600 direct workers were immediately laid off. In his June 1971 interim statement, John Wall announced optimistic results for 1970/71, but forecast an uncertain position for 1971/72. The City was well aware that current revenues were an indication of the previous year's order book; what mattered was this year's order book, and consequently the share price fell to 'ridiculously low levels', only just above par.[54] In July, another 1800 workers were dismissed, taking the total for the year to 3400. John Wall appealed directly to John Davis, Minister of Trade and Industry, and to Frederick Corfield, Minister for Aerospace, both for urgent R&D support and for more orders for computers. The government agreed that support of some kind would be provided, although they were unable to be specific on the kind or the amount. On 30 July 1971, Corfield read a statement to the House of Commons, couched in somewhat vague terms, about support for ICL in a European context.[55]

The statement did something to repair ICL's credibility, at least with the banks and finance houses who provided leasing finance; but the press reaction was sceptical. *The Economist*, in particular, ran a series of highly negative reports about 'propping up ICL', in which it stated that 'Hobbling a company with an unsuitable computer [that is, a 1900-series] can do real damage'.[56] The articles also added to the general grumbling about ICL's management:

ICL's top management is not over-endowed with the bright, energetic computer professionals who control most of the other major computer companies. . . . the Government should insist on a transfusion of new blood from outside the company. Britain's other computer companies are packed with talent; and there are all those British executives who work for ICL's powerful competitor, American-owned International Business Machines.[57]

These articles caused at least one overseas ICL customer to place its next order with IBM and to comment:

It doesn't do you any good, obviously ICL must have asked for money; they would not have said it if ICL had not asked for money. They did criticize your top management. In the USA the *Economist* carries a lot of weight.[58]

It would be difficult to overstate the damage negative press reporting of this kind caused ICL.

Morale within ICL sank to its lowest ebb, and it was clear that its restoration could not begin until Wall and Humphreys had been replaced; this was a necessity for the company's image, independent of their managerial capability; but it must be said that the Holdings board had lost confidence in the latter as well. The ICL operational board had also lost confidence in Wall and Humphreys, and it was a major flaw of the two-tier board structure that there was no channel of communication between the operational directors, who saw the need for change, and the Holdings board, that could have done something about it.[59] Arnold Weinstock also began to exert, through Lord Nelson, pressure for a management change.

During the autumn of 1971 no further progress was made with the government, and ICL made plans for two possible futures, with and without the new range. The first assumed government support of the order of £35 million over a four-year period, which would enable a phased announcement of all five new-range processors during 1973-75, deliveries commencing in mid-1974. The second plan assumed that no government support would be given, and that 'ICL must seek to remain in being by turning itself into an entirely different kind of company with more limited objectives'.[60]

The appearance of the report of Sub-Committee A and the Rothschild Report in late 1971 at last provided the basis for government action. The Sub-Committee A report, *The Prospects for the United Kingdom Computer Industry in the 1970's*, appeared in November 1971, and it made very good reading indeed so far as ICL was concerned. Besides generally recommending continuance of the procurement policy (with some reservations on single-tendering), the report was sharply critical of the government's role: 'We found it difficult to describe present Government action regarding computer research and development as a policy'.[61] It called for a much higher level of government support for the computer industry, citing the evidence supplied to the sub-committee by ICL on the much higher levels of support enjoyed by computer companies in the United States, France, Germany, and Japan:

We would not wish to put a figure on the scale of Government funded research and development expenditure which is likely to be required but we anticipate that the sum involved would be not less than ten times the average sum spent by the Government in recent years on computer research and development. We estimate this sum to be not less than £50 million per annum. Any delay in providing money will certainly mean that not only is the objective of independence delayed but also that larger sums will probably be needed to attain the objective at all. We therefore urge prompt action.[62]

This was widely interpreted as meaning £50 million per year for ICL, though this was not in fact the intention of the sub-committee. The Rothschild Report, *A Framework for Government Research and Development*, was also favourable to the kind of R&D support needed by ICL, maintaining that 'applied R and D, that is R and D with a practical application as its objective, must be done on a customer-contractor basis. The customer says what he wants; the contractor does it (if he can); and the customer pays'.[63] ICL's new range was the kind of specific and practical R&D project which the Central Policy Review Staff was willing to endorse.

In December 1971, ICL made a formal submission, 'ICL New Range Introduction Strategy', to the Department of Trade and Industry.[64] It estimated the overall R&D costs for the new range as being £85 million over a four-year period, 1971/72 to 1974/75, of which it asked the government to underwrite £35 million. The DTI was impressed by the quality of the technical and commercial arguments underlying the new-range strategy, but remained profoundly doubtful about ICL's higher management. The Holdings board decided that to make further progress it would be necessary for both Wall and Humphreys to step down in favour of a new chairman of the highest standing, and a managing director who would have the unquestioned support of the City and the government.[65] In the case of Wall, there was some justice in this decision, but it was a harsh judgement on Humphreys; Humphreys had only recently been honoured with a CBE, and in many respects the fact that there was a British computer industry at all was largely due to his decision to go for the 1900 series in 1964, and his marketing of it subsequently.

Lord Nelson approached Lord Kearton, recently freed from his duties as chairman of the now disbanded Industrial Reorganization Corporation.

Kearton agreed to accept the position as chairman of ICL, provided the future of the company was secured by a definite promise of government funding. Time was not unfortunately on the side of ICL, because the government's whole industrial and science policy was immobilized pending the reading of the Industry Act, and the formation of the Ministry of Industrial Development. The Kearton prospect gradually faded away, and Tom Hudson was elected to fill the breach. Sir John Wall stepped down in his favour on 24 February 1972. In fact, in Hudson, ICL could scarcely have found a better chairman. As the former managing director of IBM (UK), he probably knew more about the computer business than anyone at a comparative level in Britain; and as director of finance and corporate planning at Plessey, he had a financial and technical background that the majority of his predecessors had lacked.

Head-hunters had been engaged to help select a new managing director for ICL in January, and they brought up the name of Geoff Cross, a vice-president of Sperry Rand, and one-time head of the Univac European operation. Immediately after becoming chairman Hudson, with Humphreys, flew to Philadelphia to meet Cross and offered him the job, subject to board approval. Cross accepted, and on 2 May 1972 Arthur Humphreys was made deputy chairman, and Cross was appointed the new managing director. Geoff Cross, aged 37, had an outstanding track record, and he was exactly the kind of bright young managing director that ICL's critics had been prescribing for it for years.

ICL had made its case for new-range support, and it had changed its higher management; now it was up to the government.

14

Government launching aid for the New Range

1973-1975

A new dynamism in ICL
. . . Cross, who arrived at ICL, at a time of severe demoralisation, has changed the entire ethos of the company. For some months, even his close colleagues lived in some dread of his presence. He worked extraordinarily hard, with total dedication and expected others to do likewise.

—*Financial Times*, 26 October 1974.[1]

When Geoff Cross accepted the managing directorship of ICL in spring 1972, Tom Hudson and Arthur Humphreys did not over-emphasize ICL's problems. The magnitude of the immediate problems only became apparent to Cross on the first day he took up office in early May.[2] There were essentially four problems, which were interrelated; and all demanded immediate attention. First, ICL's half-year results, to be announced the following month, were catastrophic. Second, there was a crisis of confidence, both within ICL and without, dating from the *Economist* articles of February 1971. Third, ICL was almost in suspended animation, awaiting a government decision on launching aid for the New Range. Fourth, ICL was being pressured to merge with an American computer company. The only really bright spot was that the computer recession was coming to an end, and the order books were beginning to fill up again, so that once the first-half results were announced, the worst of the 1970-71 downturn would be over.

The Cross period: strategy, structure, and culture

Cross's appointment as managing director of ICL was a classic case of the company doctor brought in to restore an ailing firm back to health. Cross saw that he had essentially three tasks. First, to develop a coherent long-term strategy. Second, to overhaul the company structure to shorten lines of communication and to make the operating divisions more profit-conscious. Third, and perhaps most difficult, he saw a need to work on the company culture—to replace 'the home life of our own dear' ICL with dynamic American-style management.[3]

During his first ten days at ICL, Cross wrote a document, 'ICL Corporate Objectives and Strategy', both for presentation to the government (see next section), and to serve as a basis for action by ICL's internal business-planning organization. There was a portfolio of strategic objectives, but the three principal ones were:[4]

1. To double revenues over the next five years in real terms.
2. To become a credible multinational company, with at least fifty per cent of revenues derived from overseas business.
3. To successfully launch the New Range.

These objectives—and indeed ICL's survival as the UK flagship computer company—were all predicated on government support for R&D.

The first objective, doubling revenues over the next five years, would ensure that government support would not need to be sustained beyond 1977. It was estimated that ICL's long-term R&D requirements were of the order of £30 million a year. In 1971-72 this represented an unsustainable 20 per cent of ICL's annual revenues of about £150 million. By doubling revenues to £300 million by 1977, R&D would become 10 per cent of revenues, which was closer to the industry norm. Cross's second objective, of turning ICL into a true multinational company, was also aimed at long-term revenue growth, since overseas markets (excepting the United States) were generally growing faster than the domestic UK market. ICL's five-year plan projected overseas revenues increasing from a little over 30 per cent in 1971-72, to 50 per cent by 1977. The principal way of achieving this growth was to expand sales in Western Europe following Britain's entry into the European Economic Community (EEC) on 1 January 1973. In fact, although ICL made some progress in Europe, it was only with the acquisition of the international division of Singer Business Machines in 1976 that it established a serious European customer base (see Chapter 15).

The decision to base ICL's future on the New Range had effectively already passed the point of no return on Cross's arrival. However, the strategy of product differentiation, as opposed to IBM-compatibility, was one which Cross entirely endorsed, since it was also the policy successfully adopted by his *alma mater* Univac. So far as Cross was concerned, New Range was the only factor that could arrest IBM's otherwise inexorable progress from its current 40 per cent UK market share, to the 60 per cent or more it enjoyed in all its other territories.[5] On their own, however, mainframe sales would not give ICL the revenue growth it needed, since the mainframe sector was the slowest growing in the computer industry. To accelerate revenue growth, it was therefore decided to engage in high-growth sectors of the EDP business, such as key-edit and computer services, alongside the mainframe business. It was clear that New Range would strain all the technical, manufacturing, and marketing resources of the company. One of Cross's first decisions therefore was to husband resources by redefining ICL as 'a systems supplier' rather than an integrated manufacturer of the full spectrum of EDP equipment. This policy made explicit what had been a long-term trend, and in future ICL's peripherals would be increasingly bought in from OEM suppliers. For example discs would be exclusively bought from CDC, and in September 1972 ICL's disc-making subsidiary DRI was sold off.[6]

Cross's major restructuring of ICL took effect in October 1972,[7] as shown in Fig. 14.1. As well as shortening lines of communication, the restructuring was designed to expose the R&D function and to emphasize marketing. Prior to Cross's arrival, Hudson had already dismantled the cumbersome two-tier board structure, which had been replaced by a top-level main board to which the usual strategy, operating, and finance committees reported directly.

To co-ordinate and integrate New Range development, a new Product Development Group was formed, which took under its umbrella software development (formerly in the marketing group), hardware development (formerly in the manufacturing groups), and advanced research. The appointment of 'Ed' Mack as director of the Product Development Group was one of Cross's first cultural shockwaves. Mack was an abrasive character brought in from Univac; although he had technical ability of a high order, Cross made a fundamental error in giving him high-level strategic and managerial tasks.

The new Worldwide Marketing Group was headed by Peter Ellis, who was widely regarded as ICL's most able executive, and had been a strong contender for the position of managing director. One of the major changes made in the marketing group was to appoint local nationals to run the European sales operations: this was common practice with the American computer companies, but was new to ICL. (It is a source of surprise to Americans that, in spite of Britain's proximity to continental Europe, US firms have generally understood the European market better. This is perhaps a legacy of the much longer history of direct US investment in Europe—in the case of the office-machine industry, dating from the early 1900s.)[8] ICL's West European operations were transferred to a Paris-based headquarters, in order to exploit Britain's imminent entry into the EEC. ICL's participation in the spirit of Europe was to become a major factor in the government's attitude to the company.

The Data Entry Products Group was a new division formed to market 'key-edit' equipment in ICL territories, under an agreement with Consolidated Computers Limited (CCL) of Canada. Key-edit equipment was a

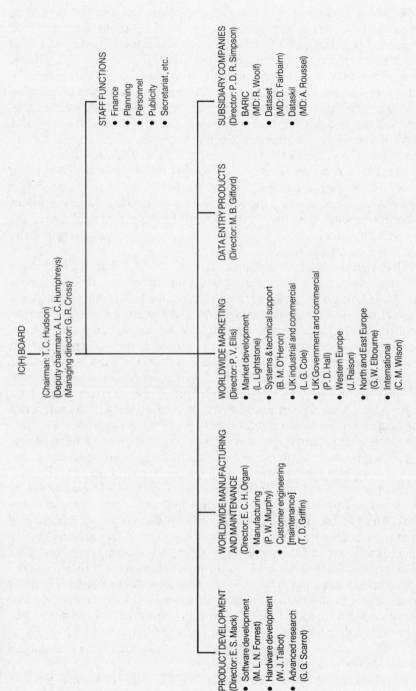

Fig. 14.1 ICL organization, autumn 1972

 IC(H) BOARD

(Chairman: T. C. Hudson)
(Deputy chairman: A. L. C. Humphreys)
(Managing director: G. R. Cross)

STAFF FUNCTIONS
- Finance
- Planning
- Personnel
- Publicity
- Secretariat, etc.

SUBSIDIARY COMPANIES
(Director: P. D. R. Simpson)
- BARIC
  (MD: R. Woolf)
- Dataset
  (MD: D. Fairbairn)
- Dataskil
  (MD: A. Roussel)

DATA ENTRY PRODUCTS
(Director: M. B. Gifford)

WORLDWIDE MARKETING
(Director: P. V. Ellis)
- Market development
  (L. Lightstone)
- Systems & technical support
  (B. M. O'Heron)
- UK industrial and commercial
  (L. G. Cole)
- UK Government and commercial
  (P. D. Hall)
- Western Europe
  (J. Raison)
- North and East Europe
  (G. W. Elbourne)
- International
  (C. M. Wilson)

WORLDWIDE MANUFACTURING
AND MAINTENANCE
(Director: E. C. H. Organ)
- Manufacturing
  (P. W. Murphy)
- Customer engineering
  [maintenance]
  (T. D. Griffin)

PRODUCT DEVELOPMENT
(Director: E. S. Mack)
- Software development
  (M. L. N. Forrest)
- Hardware development
  (W. J. Talbot)
- Advanced research
  (G. G. Scarrot)

fast-growing method of data input to computers that enabled data to be keyed directly on to a magnetic tape or disc, dispensing with the traditional punched card. Cross's objectives in raising the key-edit sales organization to divisional status were two-fold. First, to raise its visibility, since he had formed the impression that people in ICL generally seemed to think the punched card would go on forever.[9] Second, data-preparation costs accounted for 30 per cent of the cost of running a computer installation, and the key-edit business was growing at 40 per cent a year—more than twice as fast as the mainframe computer business. A successful entry into key-edit would make a major contribution to ICL's revenue growth. (In fact, ICL was not alone in over-estimating the key-edit business, and it never did produce the expected contribution to revenues.) For similar reasons of revenue growth, the ICL subsidiaries BARIC, Dataskil, and its computer-supplies company Dataset were brought more fully into the picture. They each had a higher growth rate and a higher profitability than the mainframe business.

When Cross arrived as managing director of ICL, he faced a formidable challenge in changing the culture of the company and raising its efficiency and spirits. According to Cross, the ICL he walked into seemed moribund, demoralized, and committee-minded.[10] There were a few clear lines of authority, no performance evaluation, and no concept of profit centres. Although the company had survived the computer recession of 1970–71, it was at a cost of nearly 5000 jobs, and morale was at a low ebb. The ICT and English Electric factions within ICL had never happily integrated, and perhaps they would not until they were forced to co-operate on the New Range. Cross took no part in the rights or wrongs of the 1968 merger: it was history and he was not interested.

A somewhat negative aspect of Cross's reign was that he filled several of the key posts with his former Univac colleagues, to the extent that there was a feeling that he and his cohorts had hijacked the firm. Perhaps the most controversial appointment was that of Brian O'Heron, whom he appointed to run Systems and Technical Support, a new division of the Marketing Group. The aim of this division was to act as a horizontal thread of management to raise customer satisfaction by ensuring that all the components of a system were delivered working and on time. O'Heron had learned his trade as a project manager at NASA, and he applied their technique of trouble-shooting sessions to resolve customer complaints.[11] O'Heron was a tireless and swashbuckling character, as he perhaps needed to be to fulfil his function. However, his 'fashion shoes and trendy shirts', and his motto that his staff 'would be tough as tigers' were not calculated to win over stolid ICL people, and he 'invoked both intense loyalty and outright hostility'.[12]

Cross's most revolutionary change in ICL was in forcing through financial accountability. Quite literally, he would sit down with senior colleagues and work through the numbers until he was satisfied; and his genius for landing on the single indefensible figure in a balance-sheet has become legendary. There was also positive reinforcement, in terms of regular performance evaluations, and bonus schemes for profit targets achieved.

Government launching aid: the first £14.2 million[13]

A number of events in 1971 had caused the Heath Government to weaken its lame-duck industrial policy. Foremost was the highly publicized formation of the state-owned Rolls Royce (1971) Ltd, rather than allowing Britain's most visible high-technology company to collapse. So far as the computer industry was concerned, the publication of the Report of the Select Committee on Science and Technology in October 1971 had recommended that the government should support 'market oriented' research at not less than £50 million a year.[14] This recommendation was said by Christopher Chataway, the Minister of Industrial Development, to 'harmonize exactly' with the government's adoption of the customer/contractor principle for applied R&D recommended by the Rothschild Report.[15]

In December 1971 ICL had made its first formal submission to the government for £35 million launching aid for the New Range, which the DTI was evaluating in early 1972.[16] When Hudson had become ICL chairman in February 1972, one of his first acts had been to initiate a review of the R&D and marketing costs of New Range.[17] As a result of this review, in a meeting with officials of the DTI on 10 March 1972, he announced that ICL now needed launching aid of £107 million instead of £35 million. This new estimate, which was a rough-and-ready one, had been arrived at 'on the basis of realism' in the light of ICL's declining rate of order-taking and reduced profit margins, and the 'requirement to continue to earn profits and pay dividends'.[18] The new estimate of £107 million came completely out of the blue to the DTI, which had been planning on the basis of the previous estimate of £35 million. Apart from casting doubts on the credibility of ICL's forecasting procedures, it meant that making a decision in the near future would be impossible. This sharp upward revision of costs also made the idea of a merger with a rich non-British computer firm attractive, and ICL was instructed to actively explore the possibilities of such a partnership.[19]

Of all the computer manufacturers, the closest in product philosophy to ICL was the American computer firm Burroughs. Like ICL, it had an advanced computer architecture that competed with IBM on the basis of technological excellence rather than compatibility. In April 1972 Hudson and Humphreys made a visit to Burroughs at the request of its President, Ray Macdonald. As a result of this meeting, Burroughs made a formal proposal for a complete merger with ICL, with Burroughs having control. The arrival of a firm bid from Burroughs presented the government with two clear alternatives. The first was to abandon the goal of an indigenous UK computer industry altogether, since, if the merger with Burroughs went ahead, it was likely that ICL's New Range would be dropped in favour of Burroughs American-designed computers; this in turn would be perceived as the beginning of the end for Britain's hardware and software design competence. The second alternative was to provide the £107 million support requested by ICL over a period of five years; but even then there was no certainty, or perhaps even likelihood, that ICL would be viable at the end of that period.

When Cross joined ICL, in early May 1972, he had been told little or nothing of the status of the negotiations with the government or of the Burroughs bid. Time was now not on ICL's side, but there was a feeling that the government would, in the end, come up with some form of financial support rather than allowing the industry to become controlled from America. In the meantime, Cross initiated his own review of the New Range development costs.

In fact, Christopher Chataway and the DTI had already decided to recommend to the Cabinet that ICL should be provided with the requested launching aid of £107 million; this price to maintain an indigenous computer industry was completely in line with the subventions being made by the French and German Governments to their computer industries. On 24 May, however, Hudson was summoned to the House of Commons by Christopher Chataway, who had to advise him that the proposal had been blocked on the grounds of cost by the Treasury, and that he had been told to explore further the possibility of a merger—without loss of control—with Burroughs.[20]

Following his own review of the New Range, Cross had formed the view that the figure of £107 million was somewhat arbitrary, and he judged that a sum of £50 million would suffice. In early June 1972 he gave a presentation to the DTI giving detailed financial forecasts and manufacturing cost breakdowns, justifying a subvention of £50 million. A formal request was left with the DTI for a definite commitment of £14.2 million to cover the period up to the end of the company's 1972/73 financial year, with the balance of the £50 million to be paid over the next three or four years.

During the next few days Chataway and the DTI explored merger possibilities with Burroughs' executives, and with Univac, which had also begun to take an interest. Both of these meetings were arranged without ICL's knowledge or participation. The DTI was still caught in the dilemma of two politically unacceptable alternatives: either allowing the control of

ICL to leave the UK, or a long-term commitment to financial support. Notwithstanding the reduced request of £50 million, the DTI still needed to find some middle course that it could sell to the Cabinet. The government's decision was of such importance to ICL's credibility in the City that it decided to delay the publication of the half-year results until 4 July —regarded by ICL's financial advisers as the last possible date. Indeed, the first half-year results were so bad that it was feared that there would be a major loss of investor confidence unless there was some promise of government support to report to shareholders, or some basis for a merger, or a realistic future strategy. While the DTI deliberated, City speculation grew: the Burroughs merger proposal leaked out, and the government's seeming ambivalence to ICL caused its share price to sink. ICL's major shareholders GEC and Plessey both bought in the market to support the share price, and Burroughs issued a press release saying it was talking to ICL with a view to acquiring a controlling interest.

By late June, the DTI had at last worked out a financial package which was accepted by the Cabinet. The DTI plan put off grasping the nettle by avoiding both a sell-out to an American company and a binding long-term financial commitment. In short, ICL was offered the £14.2 million requested by Cross for 1972/73, but no formal commitment beyond that was made; nor was any specific sum, £50 million or otherwise, guaranteed. Moreover, the monies advanced would eventually have to be repaid. On 3 July 1972, the day before ICL published its interim report, Christopher Chataway made the following statement to the House:

The Government have discussed with ICL, in the light of the report of the Select Committee on Science and Technology, the finance required for the company's R and D programme. The Government believe that the capability to develop, manufacture and market computer systems which ICL represents should be maintained in this country so that the company can play its part in a strong industry in Europe.

We have agreed, therefore, to provide the support of £14.2 million during the period up to September, 1973, for which the company has asked in order to maintain the momentum of its R and D programme. The Government are in touch with the new management about the company's long-term needs.[21]

The financial support was given the name 'launching aid' rather than 'grant'—a term that ICL found less damaging to its image, and which the government preferred, since it implied a loan, not a gift, for a specific project, and not merely a 'bailing out' operation.[22]

Towards a European computer industry

What the bland phrase 'The Government are in touch with the new management about the company's long-term needs' perhaps failed to convey adequately, was that the hard bargaining between ICL and the

DTI had only just begun. The impression given by the media—exemplified by the *Daily Telegraph* headline 'ICL to get unlimited State aid'—was very wide of the mark.[23] In essence the £14.2 million advance to ICL was a short-term holding operation while the company sought some way acceptable to itself and the government of finding an international partner to achieve the manufacturing scale and market-share that would make long-term support unnecessary.

Within the ICL board, there was a feeling that the company was the ball in a political football game between the DTI and the Treasury. ICL's position was that there were really only two alternatives: either the government provided £50 million of unconditional support over a period of four or five years, or ICL would have to sell itself to a foreign company. The government, however, was seeking a middle course between these alternatives: an arrangement with a foreign company that would not entail loss of sovereignty.

On 17 July 1972 the DTI produced a set of guidelines on the type of merger or association that would meet with government approval. The key guidelines were:

1. That control of the industry should remain in the UK.
2. That a substantial R&D, manufacturing and marketing capability should be maintained in the UK.
3. That design leadership in mainframe computer systems should be maintained either in New Range, or in an 'equally challenging programme'.
4. That any partnership should not preclude ICL's participation in a stronger European computer industry.[24]

The last of these conditions was very important from the government's viewpoint. With Britain's imminent entry into the EEC on 1 January 1973, there were hopes that ICL could be the nucleus around which a European industry would form.

The DTI instructed ICL to explore merger possibilities and to report back in the autumn. Within ICL, the prospects of any useful output from this exercise were considered negligible, and if the news that the company was talking to 'every Tom, Dick, and Harry' was leaked to the media it might seriously undermine the confidence of ICL customers.[25] To see why a satisfactory arrangement with a foreign firm seemed unlikely, one has only to explore the conflicting motives of ICL and the government, and those of a potential partner. What ICL and the government primarily wanted was to keep control of the industry, design leadership, and product policy in Britain, but to offset some of the cost of this by sharing R&D, manufacturing, and marketing costs with a foreign company. On the other hand, the only real attraction of ICL to a foreign manufacturer was its customer base. None the less, if ICL wanted the government's money it would have to jump through the hoops that had been set up.

There were three merger possibilities that were seriously explored at this time by ICL.[26] These possibilities were a link-up with one or other of the US firms Burroughs or Univac, or joining the European consortium of CII, Siemens and Philips—later known as Unidata. DTI representatives joined some of these discussions as observers, to ensure fair play.

Burroughs and ICL had been involved in merger discussions since spring 1972, and these had been on-going for about six months. The best deal ICL could make with Burroughs, however, would have broken most of the government guidelines. In particular, although there would be a management centre with considerable autonomy in the UK, control and product policy would remain in Detroit; this would be somewhat like the relationship between IBM and one of its overseas subsidiaries. Further, because Burroughs had its own computer range, it would drop ICL's New Range, and would not give written assurances on the maintenance of an R&D capability in the UK.

The best terms that could be got from Univac also broke most of the government guidelines, and moreover did not promise to reduce the need for government support. The arrangement proposed by Univac was that it would sell its UK and European organizations to ICL in exchange for a minority 40 per cent holding in the enlarged ICL. The balance of value, which would be considerable and in Univac's favour, would be met by 'UK Government cash in order to balance the assets and compensate for loss of earnings'.[27] Although Univac would be a minority shareholder, it would insist on appointing the managing director, the finance director, and the product planning director. The extent to which control could be said to remain in the UK under these circumstances was debatable; the situation was perhaps similar to the early years of IBM (UK), when the majority of the stock was nationally held, but control lay firmly in New York. So far as product development was concerned, the New Range would be dropped, and product evolution would be through Univac's 1100 and 9000 ranges.

The DTI accepted ICL's view that neither of the American possibilities should be pursued further. It insisted, however, that ICL should pursue the possibility of European collaboration much more actively than it had.

The French and German Governments were, in fact, already supporting their computer industries on a much more lavish scale than in Britain (Table 14.1a). Both France and Germany had completed four- or five-year support programmes in the second half of the 1960s, and had embarked on new five-year programmes for the 1970s. The majority of France's 'Plan Calcul' support went directly to CII: the programme had paid out over £44 million during the first five-year period, and was committed to

Table 14.1 Government computer R&D support programmes: Germany, France, and UK, 1966-75

	First programme		Second programme	
France	1966-70	44 263	1971-75	94 738
Germany	1967-70	37 216	1971-75	328 555

(a) *France and Germany (£000s)*

	ICL	Total
1969/70	4000	6404
1970/71	3250	6158
1971/72	2250	4922
1972/73	8800	13 377
Total	18 300	30 861

(b) *UK (£000s)*

Sources
Table (a): [HC 97-I], pp. 179-81.
Table (b): [HC473], p. 27 and [HC97-I], p. 181.

paying out £95 million in the second five-year period, 1971-75. In Germany, a modest £37 million programme in 1967-70 had been followed by a major programme of over £328 million for the five-year period 1971-75; of this 29 per cent (£93 million) was explicitly for the computer industry's R&D. The DTI statistics for computer support in Britain, which had at no time had a co-ordinated national plan, are shown in Table 14.1b. In contrast to the French and German commitments each of over £90 million for the computer industries during the period 1971-75, the UK Government had so far only supported ICL to the extent of less than £20 million, and was havering over its plans for on-going support. In November 1972, Hudson and Humphreys had round-table talks with CII and the Siemens computer division, but there were three major obstacles to any merger between the three. First, CII and Siemens were individually benefiting from R&D support from their governments of well over £10 million a year, whereas ICL had no government commitment at all beyond September 1973; this meant that ICL was negotiating from a fundamentally weak position. Second, the consortium was committed to bringing out an IBM-compatible range (evolved from the Siemens/RCA IBM-compatible series), and ICL's product philosophy and culture were totally opposed to this. Third, after the experience of the ICT–English Electric Computers merger, Hudson could not see any kind of real rationalization taking place in less than a time-frame of five to ten years.[28]

When ICL reported the outcome of these negotiations to the DTI, the message that came back was that the government was 'significantly unimpressed with ICL's lack of initiative in that the only solution ICL seemed capable of putting forward was that whereby HMG provided huge sums of money'.[29] Clearly, while the government felt there was a prospect of a merger that would save it having to part with money, the negotiations could drag on indefinitely. At this point ICL had to seriously evolve plans to become a slimmer, go-it-alone company, in case the worst should come to the worst.

In January 1973 the Select Committee on Science and Technology (Sub-Committee A) was reconvened for yet another inquiry into the UK computer industry. On this occasion the main focus of the sub-committee was on the prospects for the industry in the EEC. The first witnesses questioned were Christopher Chataway and his assistant secretary in the DTI, Ivor Manley. In his memorandum to the sub-committee, Chataway reiterated the DTI's policy—and that of his European ministerial counter-parts—to form a European-wide computer industry that would have at least a 10 per cent share of the world market, and hence would be capable of competing on equal terms with the American manufacturers, other than IBM. More than this, the DTI's European computer policy was vague; but that of a subsequent witness was much more explicit. This witness was Christopher Layton, who was formerly an academic researcher of European advanced-technology policy, and a consultant to ICL. Layton was now director of computer policy within the European Commission for Industry and Technology, an organization that carried a good deal of prestige though no political authority. The Commission's view was that there should be a gradual convergence of the European computer industry, perhaps involving two initial groupings:

No academic answer of principle can decide what form a re-grouped European industry should take. It has been argued that since the five leading European enterprises which currently aspire to be in the production of central processors, (I.C.L., Siemens, A.E.G./Nixdorf, C.I.I. and Philips) together have a turnover of less than a tenth of I.B.M.'s, most of them should be combined into one company. ... In practice, as you know, C.I.I. and Siemens, together with Philips, are already trying to form a nucleus of one European grouping with a common range. The Commission favours this and hopes they will succeed. I.C.L. is not in this group at present and as they have told you, have a rather different philosophy for competing with I.B.M.[30]

The second grouping would involve ICL:

... the I.C.L. philosophy, that of trying to go one better, rather than following I.B.M., tends to be shared by A.E.G./Nixdorf. Moreover this company appears to be complementary in its capabilities with I.C.L. It has strong marketing in Europe and sells large and small computers. I.C.L. has a strong technology and sells a range of medium sized machines. If these two companies were to form a second European group in the near future the Commission would warmly welcome such a move, as a further step towards the consolidation of the industry.[31]

Privately, most of the Commission's analysis made sense to the ICL board, but the public naming of Nixdorf as yet another potential bride for ICL was not welcomed. As Hudson put it in his evidence at the close of the sub-committee's hearings:

A question such as, 'Would you rather merge with UNIVAC or Nixdorf' is damaging because the question assumes we are going to do one or the other. . . . a man in Selby might be deciding whether to buy a computer or not and the selection is between ICL and IBM, and when he hears we might be merging with UNIVAC or Nixdorf he will say 'To hell with it, I will buy IBM'. That happens.[32]

Merger talks between ICL and Nixdorf had, in fact, been progressing quietly for many months. The mutual attraction of the companies was that Nixdorf had a customer base generating annual revenues of £80 million in Europe that would add at least 50 per cent to ICL's current annual revenues. For Nixdorf, the attraction was partly the scale and manufacturing economies that attracted ICL, but also access to ICL's New Range in the long term. And in the short run, Nixdorf would also have the opportunity to market a new small computer, the 2903, recently developed by ICL.

The 2903: a computer for Europe[33]

The 2903 was to become ICL's single biggest money-earning product in the 1970s, generating about 30 per cent of revenues at its peak. The project was very much a market-led and profit-oriented one, in which technology was secondary. (Like the decision to launch the 1900 series in 1964, ICL's most commercially successful products have not generally been ones that have stretched technology; and this is no doubt true of most other manufacturers.) The origin of the 2903 computer was a project known internally as PF73, which was ICL's response to the introduction of the IBM System/3 in 1969.

The IBM System/3 had proved an extraordinarily popular machine. Its power and simplicity of use, based on the RPG programming language, combined with low cost, opened up an entirely new market with small businesses that had previously been using visible-record computers or accounting machines. At that time, in order to compete with System/3, ICL had been forced to reduce the price of its smallest computer, the 1901A, by up to 40 per cent. To avoid losing money on 1901A sales, an attempt had been made to reduce selling costs, which were traditionally up to 40 per cent of the selling price. This was done by means of a new selling concept known as the 'customer centre'. The first five centres were established in the UK in mid-1971. Each centre was equipped with a 1901A and a staff of three sales people—usually women who, at the time, were considered less intimidating for computer-naïve customers. By bringing the customer to the sales team, instead of *vice versa*, sales costs were dramatically reduced, and customers gained confidence from the on-going relationship with the customer centres. ICL was probably the first computer manufacturer to introduce the customer-centre approach, which was later widely emulated.

Up to this point, ICL's response to System/3 had been largely reactive. It was the role of the Market Development Division of the Marketing Group to develop pro-active strategies to exploit new market opportunities. Hugh Macdonald, who was the Market Development Manager for small systems at this time, conceived the initial marketing plan for a new small computer.[34] The IBM System/3 had exposed two important new market opportunities, which ICL was not yet effectively exploiting. The first was the very large market of small and medium-sized businesses currently using visible-record computers and accounting machines; System/3 was satisfying this demand, in much the same way that the 1401 computer had displaced punched-card machines a decade earlier. The second market was for multiple small machines in large, decentralized companies. If ICL could develop a small machine and sell it cheaply in high volume, using the customer-centre concept, then it offered the opportunity for the rapid revenue growth, especially in Europe, that was its principal corporate objective. Macdonald's plan was accepted, and became known as PF73. The project, which was managed by John Freer, was one of a number of developments (including the CAFS—of which more later) that Humphreys allowed to keep running during the 1971–72 financial crisis.

The two main product-development priorities for PF73 were speed of implementation and low cost. These two requirements ruled out using the small P0 processor of the New Range, since that was not scheduled for completion until 1974 at the earliest. There was, however, a microcoded communications processor under development at Stevenage, known as MICOS 1, which could be rapidly brought into production. It was decided to use this processor to emulate the 1900-series instruction-set for PF73, since this would enable all the software developed for the small 1900-series machines to be used with minimal rewriting; and also to make use of the RPG compiler, which was then under development.* The MICOS 1 was a state-of-the-art processor, and actually a good deal more powerful than was strictly necessary. Again, to maximize speed of implementation and minimize development costs, all the peripherals were based on existing products. These included a disc store of 60 Mbytes, which was twice the maximum capacity then being offered on System/3. None of the processors or peripherals required an air-conditioned environment, so that the machine could be housed in any ordinary office.

The original PF73 announcement was planned for May 1973; but Cross decided in late January to bring the launch forward to catch the main European computer event, the Hanover Fair on 25 April. A task-force was established to ensure that a machine and software were available for the exhibition. At about the same time the model-number '2903' was selected for the new machine. This designation was chosen to create a conscious blurring of the distinction between the old and the new ranges, to give a sense that ICL's New Range would not entail an abandoning of the old. This was a subtle and almost self-contradictory objective, but it was achieved.[36] The high 2900s (2950, 2960, . . .) were used for the New Range, and the low 2900s (2903, 2904, . . .) were intended for the small machines. (The numbers below 2903 were not used.)

The 2903 launch at the Hanover Fair was an exceptionally slick affair. Glossy brochures were printed in nine languages, and a film presentation was given in the six principal West European languages. As always in computer fairs, the existence of a working machine running actual applications added to the credibility. The successful customer-centre concept was extended for the new machine, to a total of eighteen centres: five in the UK, five in Western Europe, and eight in the international division. Each centre gave training in RPG and the tailoring of applications packages, basic consultancy services, and program-testing facilities. Orders poured in, particularly from Western Europe, and within days the sales target was raised from 1000 to 2000 systems.

Government support and the Nixdorf negotiations

By spring 1973, the DTI had finally managed to reconcile ICL's request for £50 million launching aid for New Range and the Treasury's desire to

---

* The concept of microcoding was invented by M.V. Wilkes of Cambridge University, and was described in a paper in 1951; but it was first commercially exploited in the IBM System/360.[35] The technique enables a processor instruction-set to be defined by software 'microcode' instead of being 'hard-wired'. This allows a processor to emulate a different instruction-set simply by changing the microcode.

The view of some observers, that the 2903 was simply a re-engineered 1900, did not appreciate the sophistication of the microcoded processor. ICL had simply elected to use the 1900-series instruction-set for economy of software development. If the idea had been more widely applied in the New Range, its history might have been much less fraught.

part with no more money than was absolutely necessary. The terms offered by the government were: that the total launching aid provided would be £40 million, including the £14.2 million already advanced; that it would be repaid starting in 1977; and that the principal shareholders (GEC and Plessey) would undertake to provide an additional £15 million working capital should it prove necessary.

An additional condition attached to the offer was that ICL should 'make early and substantial progress in securing an arrangement with Nixdorf'.[37] In fact, both the DTI and ICL had by this time come to view an arrangement with Nixdorf as outstandingly the best chance for ICL to establish itself as a force in Europe. Talks between ICL and Nixdorf had begun early in 1972, predating Cross's arrival as managing director in May 1972, and had been going on in parallel with the talks with Burroughs and Univac. In the course of his first six months with ICL, Cross too became convinced that an arrangement with Nixdorf offered ICL an ideal entrée into the European market. He established an excellent personal rapport with Heinz Nixdorf, the founder and majority shareholder of the company, and he admired the Germanic engineering excellence of the Nixdorf products. Nixdorf's financial performance was also excellent, its revenues having quadrupled in the previous four years. Nixdorf made an evaluation of ICL products in March 1973, and estimated a potential market for 250–400 model 2903s in Western Germany, and foresaw a similar potential for ICL's key-edit equipment. Cross was convinced that ICL's own German marketing organization, ICL Deutschland, could never achieve these sales targets without a huge investment in human resources and sales offices. In the long term, both ICL and Nixdorf would expect to benefit from R&D support from their governments, which would enable them to jointly develop the New Range.

In June 1973, Cross proposed to the ICL board a two-phase convergence with Nixdorf.[38] The first phase, lasting approximately five years, would essentially be a dealership agreement: Nixdorf would sell the 2903 and key-edit equipment in Western Germany and Austria, and ICL would sell Nixdorf terminals in the UK and Ireland; ICL Deutschland would continue to sell ICL's mainframes. In the second phase, ICL and Nixdorf would co-ordinate their R&D for the New Range, with Nixdorf designing small processors and ICL designing the large machines. The ICL board authorized detailed negotiations for Phase I to go ahead.

While the Nixdorf negotiations were under way, on 4 July 1973, in a statement to the House of Commons, Christopher Chataway stated the terms of the Government's launching aid for ICL's New Range:

The Government have agreed to provide a further £25.8 million in support of the company's research and development programme from October this year until September 1976, making a total of £40 million in all. . . . As is normal with launching aid of this type, arrangements have been agreed with the company for the recovery of this £25.8 million, together with the £14.2 million I announced in July last year.[39]

The basis for the repayment had been the subject of some hard bargaining between Hudson and the DTI. The agreement finally reached was that during the seven-year period commencing September 1977, ICL would repay the government 25 per cent of its profits in excess of 7½ per cent of turnover, the total not to exceed the £40 million originally advanced.[40] (Of course, ICL never did make profits exceeding 7½ per cent of its turnover, and so nothing was ever repaid.) Neither the pledge for up to £15 million working capital from GEC and Plessey, nor the agreement to explore convergence with Nixdorf were announced to Parliament, so both had the status of gentleman's agreements. In the case of the former, the funds were never in fact called upon, and in the case of the latter, the convergence with Nixdorf was never proceeded with, although it came very close.

In November 1973, when the ICL–Nixdorf Phase I agreement was on the point of being signed, and Heinz Nixdorf had taken a personal 9.9 per cent holding in ICL, Hudson became convinced, after talking to Humphreys, that ICL was doing the wrong thing. The crux of the argument was that Nixdorf stood to gain more from selling the 2903 in Western Germany than ICL did. Hudson reminded the board of the agreement between ICT and Univac in 1963, whereby ICT sold Univac 1004 tabulators in territories where ICT was well-established and Univac was not. Although Univac gained marginally by increasing its manufacturing scale and making some short-term OEM profits, ICT gained far more in the long run, since the 1004 enabled it to add substantially to its customer base. Most of that customer base had remained with ICL, and virtually none had reverted to being Univac users. In the same way, Nixdorf would be creating a customer base at the expense of ICL Deutschland, while ICL would only be selling Nixdorf terminals, which were mere 'add-ons' that did nothing to extend ICL's customer base:

Why do we want to help Nixdorf to grow his customers in Germany with our products rather than plan to secure and grow the customers ourselves? If we have in mind taking him over or taking a share of his equity in the future, it is likely to be costly to do so, because we have helped him to be more prosperous.[41]

Coming at the eleventh hour, Hudson's change of heart was somewhat embarrassing. What had happened between June and November to make him change his mind? Simply that he had had time to reflect on the long-term implications, and that 'there is no logical reason for continuing on a course now thought to be wrong merely because some time ago there were thoughts that it might be right'.[42] And this was true, notwithstanding the gentleman's agreement with the government on ICL–Nixdorf convergence.

The logic of Hudson's argument was that if ICL wanted to expand, then it should do so by obtaining a customer base, in the same way that Honeywell had acquired the General Electric customer base in 1970 and Univac had taken over RCA's customers in 1971. There was no such opportunity in 1973, but when the opportunity did occur, in 1976, to acquire the Singer customer base, ICL leapt at it (see next chapter). In the meantime, the talks with Nixdorf were gradually wound down.

The New Range launch

With ICL's long-term R&D funding finally assured by the July 1973 government announcement, the New Range took centre place in ICL's five-year strategic plans for 1973-1978:

ICL's five-year plan essentially revolves around the success or otherwise of the New Range strategy. New Range, in all of its complexity, represents a fantastic challenge to ICL. No major computer manufacturer has announced, and successfully introduced, a new range of computers in the last six years. ICL's five year plan is based on the assumption that ICL will announce, develop, manufacture and install New Range systems with minimum difficulty. In achieving a smooth transition to New Range systems in customer environments, the total organisation of ICL will be called upon to meet tremendous challenges.[43]

At this time, New Range was planned as a range of processors, from small to large, P0 to P4, with small and large variants of the mid-range P2 processor (P2S and P2L). The concept of a 'top-down' introduction conceived in 1970, had been refined, and detailed marketing plans evolved. It was planned to announce the top two processors, the 2970 (P3) and the 2980 (P4) in October 1973, with deliveries in mid-1974. By introducing the two top-end processors first, ICL would strengthen its big-machine customer base (which was weak), hopefully without undermining its much larger medium-sized-machine base. Several steps were taken to protect the mid-range 1900 series: the models 1901T, 1902T and 1903T were announced in 1972-74, with enhanced transaction-processing facilities, and new peripherals sold by ICL were designed to be compatible with the New Range, in order to protect the users' investment. Developing and launching the biggest processors first was both a major technical advantage and disadvantage. The advantage was that by developing the largest processors first, developing the smaller processors later would be relatively easy, since it was essentially a sub-setting process. (By contrast, developing the large 1906 from the 1904 had been a formidable task, since it was necessary to enhance an architecture that was optimized for a mid-range

machine; IBM had similar problems with its large System/360 processors.)
The disadvantage was that all the most difficult development problems
had to be tackled immediately:

A characteristic of the large end of the computer market . . . is that the success or
failure of the first ten to twenty installations has a very significant effect on the
sales of these systems over their product life. Currently ICL's performance in this
area is largely unproven and therefore the success of the first New Range installations becomes doubly important.[44]

Early software performance would be especially important. The risk was
that the entire series would be judged for a long time on the early performance of the New Range operating system, and the experience of every
manufacturer had shown that a new operating system could take years to
settle down. Again, it was imperative that transition aids from the 1900
series and System 4 worked well, or there would be an adverse effect on
sales of the current ranges.

   To reduce the risk of an unsuccessful launch, Cross decided to postpone
the original target date of October 1973. This was partly the result of the
usual slippage in development. However, the economic indicators following the end of the 'Barber boom', the stock-market crash of 1973, and the
oil crisis later in the year, were ominous, and ICL had revised its revenue-
growth plans downwards to a more realistic 10 per cent. This in turn
reduced the available R&D funds, and Cross took the decision to put back
the launch a full year to October 1974. Fortunately ICL was under no
commercial (as opposed to Press) pressure to make an announcement of
the New Range. Now that the government had promised launching aid,
there was a resurgence of ICL current-range orders, which had been held
back by the uncertainty over ICL's future. Orders poured in for the new
1900 T-series and for the 1904S. The 2903 was also a major success, and
was later to receive the Institute of Marketing Award for 1976. The
decision to postpone the New Range also benefited from the fact that
ICL's image was completely transformed during 1974. The 1973 results
showed that a considerable recovery had been achieved, with profits of
£10.9 million on a turnover of £168 million. The first-half results in
June 1974 showed further improvements. Thus, when the New Range
was launched in October 1974, ICL already had a born-again glow.*

   The New Range launch turned out to be a considerable media event.
On 9 October 1974, the New Range was announced at an invitation-only
press conference at ICL's Putney head office. Two machines were
announced, the 2970 and the 2980, with powers of 0.8 and 3.0 mips

---

* ICL's share price stuck close to its low of 26p (it had been nearly £3 in 1968); but this
reflected in part its dividend-restraint policy, and perhaps a lingering doubt as to whether
the leopard could really change its spots.

respectively, putting them firmly in the range of IBM's two top-end machines, the 370/158 and the 370/168.* At the press launch, presentations were given by Ed Mack, head of the Product Development Group, and Bill Talbot and Mike Forrest, respectively heads of hardware and software development. Probably the software development was the most impressive: Forrest's group totalled some one thousand people, and in addition to a major operating system (System B, later known as VME/B), there was a raft of utilities, programming languages, and applications, in addition to the all-important software transition aids. Another presentation was given by Brian O'Heron—now styled 'Mr New Range'—whose task it was to head an action centre known as SPARC (System Program And Review Committee).

Because of the government's financial involvement in New Range, the launch was of interest to a general audience, as well as to computer professionals. The Press and TV reportage was wide, and almost universally favourable, especially of Cross. The Press was especially captivated by O'Heron's flamboyance, and journalists evoked the image of O'Heron's war-room probing into the deepest recesses of ICL, relays of secretaries and action telexes flying, noting 'it does, one has to admit, sound a far cry from the ICL we knew, loved, but despaired of'.[45] On 24 October product presentations on New Range were made simultaneously around the world to ICL customers. The 2900 series—'which looked as if it was never coming'—received orders valued at £21 million the same day.[46]

---

* mips: millions of instructions per second; a standard measure of processor power.

15

Rapid growth in a changing market
1975-1979

> High growth rates are tough to manage, particularly in our area of high technological change. To grow at 10 per cent a year is easy to manage; growth at 20 per cent—as we have done recently in real terms—is hard; but 25 per cent can be rough.
>
> —C.M. Wilson, February 1978.[1]

The New Range launch of October 1974 was, so to speak, only the end of the beginning. There remained the monumental R&D and manufacturing challenge of actually bringing the machines and software into the field. This task was to consume most of ICL's technical resources during 1975-78.

During this period, however, the market itself was undergoing changes as radical as the transition from punched-card machines to computers in the early 1960s. These changes were in terms of new products, notably small business systems and networks, and new competitors manufacturing IBM-compatible mainframes. The growth that Cross had built into his corporate plan was not, in the event, to prove adequate to sustain the escalating R&D costs. When he left, in December 1977, his successor Chris Wilson would be faced with the problem of how to cover the widening gap between earnings and R&D spending.

New Range: product strategy and development

ICL's product strategy for the second half of the 1970s was centred on the successful introduction of the New Range. Although by 1975 mini-computers and small business systems had come to account for about 50 per cent of the market (and the 2903 alone accounted for 20 per cent of ICL's despatches), ICL's major growth opportunity was perceived to be in large real-time mainframes, and this is where the bulk of R&D funds were allocated. The 'mainframe-minded' attitude within ICL was deeply entrenched, but it was reinforced by IBM's 'future series', the successor to System/370, which cast a shadow over the whole of the industry and was widely expected to be announced around 1978. Although the future series did not in the event materialize, the concern was no less real.[2]

At the time of the 2900 launch in October 1974, only the two largest models—the 2970 (processor P3) and the 2980 (processor P4)—were announced, the first deliveries being made in December 1974 and June 1975 respectively (Table 15.1). The top-down introduction strategy remained a cornerstone of the New Range launch. First, because the development task had to be phased over as long a period as possible, and the development schedules were in any case over-running by up to two years. Second, it was necessary to protect the 1900-series customer base, since the superior price/performance of the New Range would inevitably have caused a flood of rented machines to be returned from the field; moreover, it was necessary to secure a high volume of *new* orders for the 1900 series to maintain revenues.[3]

Table 15.1 New Range processors, 1974-80

Processor	Model	Announced	Delivered
P-series			
P4	2980	Oct 1974	Jun 1975
P3	2970	Oct 1974	Dec 1974
P2L	2960	Mar 1976	Dec 1975[a]
P2S	2950	Cancelled	
P1	2940	Cancelled	
P0	2930	Cancelled	
S-series			
S4		Cancelled	
S3	2966	Jun 1981	
S2	2956	Nov 1980	
S1	2950	Nov 1977	Jun 1978

Notes
Delivery dates are given for the first four principal processors in the New Range, the 2970, 2980, 2960, and 2950. The P-series and S-series used MSI and LSI technology respectively. Other models were derived from the S-series processors: from S1, model 2946; from S3, models 2955, 2977, 2988, and others.

[a] Sic; delivered early to fulfil a government contract.

The credibility of the top-down introduction strategy, however, did depend on regular and timely announcements of the remaining range. Any slippage of ICL's internal development schedules—which tended to leak to the trade press—cast credibility doubts. In fact, in 1975 ICL had only three 'modern' processors—the 2980, 2970, and 2903—which covered just 20 per cent of the market spectrum, so it was necessary to fill out the middle-range without any unnecessary delay. It had originally been planned to announce the mid-range 2900 series, the 2960 and the 2950 (both based on the P2 processor) in spring 1975, with the 2940 (P1) and the 2930 (P0) following in 1976 and 1977. As a result of development delays, ICL held back these announcements, so that by 1975 the trade press was running stories such as 'ICL's top-down policy misfires', and publicizing the loss of mid-range orders to other suppliers.[4]

The development delays were mainly due to the operating system software. During the six-year period of New Range development, 2900 software was to consume 35 per cent, or £56 million, of ICL's R&D expenditure, and the operating systems were to account for most of this. Two major operating systems were under development for the New Range: System B for the large processors, and System D for the mid-range machines; these were later renamed VME/B and VME/K. The introduction of the VME/K operating system was done on a whim of Ed Mack, and proved to be an unnecessary and costly development that was later abandoned. The large-scale operating system VME/B went the way of most major operating systems, and it was released with a low efficiency and a large number of bugs. During this period VME/B's under-performance started to cause a loss of confidence in the New Range. There were some lost orders, and in the case of some installations extra hardware or software maintenance had to be given to get the systems through their acceptance trials and to produce a flow of revenues. The fact that ICL's experience was not unique was not wholly mitigating:

It is true that other manufacturers' operating systems have taken an equivalent time to develop but prospective users are saying that this was the state of the art four years ago and we should have tested the products more fully before delivering to customer sites. Sales are tending to be very difficult because of this and there is a reluctance to introduce new prospects.[5]

Cross's displeasure was expressed by removing Mike Forrest as head of the Software Development Organization in 1975. (Forrest recalls that this was unpleasant at the time, but he later drew comfort from the fact that most large-scale operating systems had gone the same way—as had their managers.)[6] VME/B was a classic evolution-versus-revolution situation. American vendors were supplying mature, stable, and reliable operating systems aged seven or eight years, based on older computer architectures, though running on the latest processor technology. In moving to a new architecture, ICL had been forced to abandon its own acclaimed and fairly resilient GEORGE 3 operating system. The problems with VME/B had a knock-on effect on the resources available for the VME/K operating system for the mid-range machines. The 2960 and its VME/K operating system were only announced in March 1976, a full year later than anticipated. Even then, VME/K gave less than half the performance of the equivalent IBM operating system.

There were also problems with New Range hardware. One of the key problems was the rapid evolution of the scale of integration of semiconductor technology, which moved from MSI to LSI and then to VLSI in the course of the 1970s.* In order to keep pace with the change of semiconductor technology, it was decided in late 1975 to develop LSI-based S1 and S2 processors in place of the MSI-based P1 and P2; this further delayed deliveries of mid-range machines until 1977 and 1978. As realistic development and manufacturing costs became available for the S-series processors, it became clear that a true range-compatible processor (P0 or S0) for the small 2930 was not economically feasible, and it was cancelled. This left an uncomfortable void between the small 2903 (which was based on the 1900-series architecture), and the mid-range processors of the New Range. To bridge the gap, and provide a growth path for 2903 users, an enhanced processor—the 2904—was developed and announced in May 1976. This was a very necessary market introduction, but coming only two months after the 2960 announcement, it created some market confusion as to whether ICL was introducing a New Range top-down, or an Old Range bottom-up:[7] in fact it was doing both, and the success of the strategy, when the two ranges finally met, would depend on producing good software transition aids.

The changing market: minicomputers and small business systems

In 1972, the mainframe business had been beginning to show some signs of stability and maturity. After the shake-out of the 1970-71 computer recession, which had seen the withdrawals of General Electric and RCA from the computer business, the remaining computer manufacturers had settled back into their old relationships—although instead of being IBM and the seven dwarfs, it had now become IBM and the BUNCH.† Apart from the ill-fated Unidata, there had been no new major entrants into the mainframe business. The reason for this lack of new firms in the mainframe sector was simply that the capital requirements for entry were formidable—certainly in excess of $1 billion.[8] Even Unidata, sponsored by three nations, ceased operations in December 1975.

Although all the mainframe suppliers were supplying small business computers, of which the IBM System/3 was the best-selling, their main

* MSI: Medium-Scale Integration; LSI: Large-Scale Integration; VLSI: Very Large-Scale Integration. These terms describe increasing densities of integrated circuits: MSI, 10-100 gates/chip; LSI, 100-1000 gates/chip; VLSI, over 1000 gates/chip.

† BUNCH: Burroughs, Univac, NCR, CDC, and Honeywell.

product strategies were based on the model of large centralized computers with many—often hundreds—of geographically dispersed terminals. The airline reservations systems that were now in place with all of the major airlines epitomized this approach. The economic basis for the centralized-mainframe approach to computing had been encapsulated by the famous 'Grosch's Law'. This law, due to the computer pundit Herb Grosch, stated that the power of a processor varied as to the square of the cost.[9] Thus, in a given range of computers, a four-fold improvement in the power of a processor could be obtained for only double the cost. When processor costs dominated total installation costs, centralized mainframes were the most cost-effective way of organizing a computer centre. Grosch's Law had held good from its first statement in the mid-1950s up to the late 1960s. However, the rapid evolution of semiconductor technology in the 1970s, when price/performance was improving at an annual rate of about 25 per cent, meant that Grosch's Law no longer held, and a large processor was no longer significantly cheaper than multiple small computers. All the evidence suggests that the mainframe suppliers were slow to appreciate this trend to decentralization, and thus offered an opportunity for new competitors.

In the 1960s there had been four key barriers to entry into the computer business:

1. The R&D costs of producing a full range of computers and peripherals.
2. The cost of developing operating systems and applications software.
3. The need for a high volume of shipments to secure economies of scale in production.
4. The need for a sales force.

These four factors had effectively prevented the entry of any late arrivals into the mainframe business. The advent of low-cost integrated circuits, and the emergence of the peripheral and software sub-industries, caused a lowering of the first three of these barriers, permitting new entrants into the industry during the 1970s. These were the small-computer manufacturers, described here, and the plug-compatible mainframe manufacturers, described later in this chapter.

There were, broadly, two types of firm in the small-computer business: the technically-orientated manufacturer of minicomputers, and the supplier of small business systems. This structure had some parallels with the early computer industry of the 1950s, whose entrants had likewise been polarized between electronics/control manufacturers, and business-equipment manufacturers.

The capital requirements for entry into the minicomputer market were well under $5 million,[10] so that minicomputer manufacturers proliferated in the 1960s, much as mainframe manufacturers had proliferated in the 1950s. Pre-eminent among the minicomputer manufacturers was the American Digital Equipment Corporation (DEC). DEC had been established in 1957, and marketed its first computer, the PDP1, in 1961. By confining itself to a largely technical and scientific market, DEC was able to sell computers that did not belong to a range or family, that had very little software, and that did not require an extensive sales force to market. And by assembling systems largely from bought-in components, it could manufacture in low volume at low cost. DEC was well-established by the mid-1960s; but it was only when it launched the spectacularly successful low-cost PDP8 in 1965 that minicomputers became a well-defined industry sector. In the 1960s many new entrants were established in the United States: Scientific Data Systems (SDS) in 1961, Wang (1964), Interdata (1966), Data General (1968), and Prime (1971), and many others, including divisions of large companies such as Hewlett-Packard. In Britain there were also a number of minicomputer start-ups: Computer Technology Limited (CTL) in 1966, Digico (1966), and Arcturus Electronics (1968), as well as the minicomputer divisions established in Ferranti, GEC, and Plessey.[11]

Small business systems, although using the same processor technology as scientific minicomputers, were selling in a more demanding marketplace. For this reason they tended to come from either the ranks of the more successful minicomputer manufacturers seeking new markets, or from established business-equipment manufacturers seeking to diversify by acquisition into the EDP-computer business. Among the former DEC, Wang, and Hewlett-Packard all became formidable forces in the office-systems market in the 1970s. Among the latter, Singer Business Machines entered the market in 1963 by acquiring Friden, Honeywell acquired the Computer Control Corporation (CCC) in 1966, and Xerox acquired SDS in 1969. In Europe Nixdorf, Philips, and Olivetti all consolidated or established their positions as high-volume suppliers of small business computers in the early 1970s. The only British firm to enter the small business computer market was Business Computers Limited (BCL), which prospered surprisingly well for a number of years, but eventually went into receivership.

The small-computer business was growing very rapidly, at an annual rate of 40 per cent a year by value, compared with the computer business as a whole, which was growing at only 15 per cent. The British market rapidly came to be dominated by the United States suppliers, notably DEC, and, as in the 1960s, the public perception was that of Britain allowing a major industry to fall into the hands of the Americans. In June 1974, the Computer Industry Sub-Committee of the Select Committee of Science and Technology responded to the climate of opinion by recon-

vening for a one-day interrogation of the Department of Trade and Industry—now under the Ministership of Anthony Wedgwood Benn (the new
Labour Government had taken office in March 1974). A major criticism
made by the select committee was that the DTI's computer policy was too
mainframe-oriented and too ICL-oriented, and that it was ignoring the
needs of small-computer manufacturers. In response to the question 'But
it is a fact, is it not, that your policy is almost exclusively directed to
ICL?', the disingenuous reply of Benn's department was 'In terms of
sums of money, yes'.[12]

Much of the championing of the British minicomputer industry was
due to the charismatic leaders of CTL—its managing director, Ian Barron,
and his chairman, the former journalist Tom Margerison. In an influential
paper they presented a closely-argued case for a co-ordinated pan-
European minicomputer industry.[13] Barron and Margerison did not
advocate a physical concentration of European companies, of the kind that
led to Unidata, but rather a working federation of suppliers conforming to
common standards. This far-sighted concept has only recently begun to
happen with the arrival of 'open standards'—see the next chapter. In fact,
nothing significant came of the Barron–Margerison proposal. With the
benefit of hindsight, the concern over the *manufacturing* of small
computers in Britain was perhaps misplaced. Minicomputers—like micro-
computers later—would soon become a commodity item, with low profit
margins. The future much more certainly lay in 'value-added' technical
and business systems, which incorporated minicomputers from any source.
Suppliers who opted for this approach became known as 'turnkey' suppliers—they supplied a complete system, which the user merely switched
on, and for which he had no need of the normal EDP department.

The Singer acquisition: 'The merger we really wanted'[14]

IBM was the first of the mainframe suppliers to respond to the changing
market for small business systems. In 1973, an internal planning
document noted that:

The minicomputer has emerged from its traditional role as the small OEM processor and has developed into a full-function, low-price entry, general-purpose
computing system, spanning a variety of application areas . . . The distributive
and/or decentralized computing strategy underlying minicomputers is in direct
contrast with IBM's centralized systems approach.[15]

Although IBM had a strong presence in the small business computer
market through its System/3, this was—like the ICL 2903—spiritually a
mainframe, and very much at the top end of the market. In January 1975,
IBM launched its System/32, a much lower-cost computer which in-

cluded a wide variety of applications packages for specific industries, and a basic networking capability which provided distributed, as opposed to merely decentralized, computing for large-scale users. The other main-frame manufacturers quickly followed suit with their new small business systems. Honeywell introduced its Level 6 system in May 1975, developed from its CCC acquisition. The rest of the BUNCH manufacturers followed in the next year or two with small business systems, generally built afresh, rather than being derived from existing mainframe products. According to industry forecasters in 1975, small business systems sales were set to treble in the next few years. The market would be exceptionally competit-ive as the traditional mainframe manufacturers, the business-equipment manufacturers, and the turnkey suppliers battled for market-share.

In response to the market pressures, ICL announced a low-cost version of the 2903, the model 20, in October 1975. This was, however, not a particularly competitive machine, and there is little doubt that ICL's growth opportunities would have been limited because of its over-reliance on the mainframe market, had it not been for what amounted to a piece of good luck. This was the chance to acquire the international operations of Singer Business Machines (SBM).

The background of Singer Business Machines is as follows.[16] Singer diversified into the business-equipment market in the early 1960s, at a time when its sewing-machine business was rapidly losing market-share because of competition from the Japanese sewing-machine industry. With a sales force of 81 000 people in 96 countries, Singer made several acquisitions to broaden its product-range and absorb its manufacturing capacity. The most important of these acquisitions was the purchase of Friden Inc. in October 1963. Friden was a long-established manufacturer of electronic calculators and typewriters, and since the mid-1950s it had manufactured low-cost business computers. At that time, only 22 per cent of Friden's business was outside the United States, and the motive behind the Singer acquisition was to use its sales force to bring this pro-portion up to the order of 50 per cent.

During 1969-73, SBM introduced a very innovative and successful range of products.[17] These included the MDTS point-of-sale terminal in 1969, which rapidly became a market-leader, with over 65 000 units installed. The System Ten computer, announced in April 1970, was the first transaction-processing-oriented small business system to be intro-duced—by 1975 some 3500 had been sold, 1400 of them overseas. In 1973 SBM acquired the Cogar Corporation, which added the model 1500 intelligent-terminal system to its product portfolio. After this initially successful period, however, SBM began to lose money as the market became more competitive. In 1975, the United States operations were making a loss of $42 million on a turnover of $290 million. These losses were mainly due to development overspending on turnkey systems at a time of rapid inflation. The 'Sears deal', a large retail system for the Sears group, was also reported to be a particular problem.[18] The international division was much more profitable, however, since turnkey systems had generally been achieved through third-party vendors.

On 29 December 1975, Joseph Flavin, Singer's newly appointed president, announced his intention to sell the business-machines division of Singer. Immediately following the announcement that SBM was up for sale, talks were held between Singer and potential buyers, who included Univac, Honeywell, and Burroughs, and the computer press speculated on many more possibilities. ICL was not considered a likely buyer:

ICL cannot make a bid without the approval of its leading shareholders Plessey, GEC and the British government, and the time it took them to approve the much smaller investment in Computer Peripherals Inc proves the slow nature of their decision making processes.[19]

In fact, Flavin, who was well acquainted with Tom Hudson, approached ICL directly on 5 February 1976. Once the proposition was put to them, Hudson, Humphreys and Cross were all enthusiastic about taking on the international division of SBM, although they did not want the US business, which they considered non-viable—especially for ICL. Since no buyer for the entire operation had yet materialized, Flavin agreed to consider splitting the business along these lines. But ICL would have to act fast, since Univac was also interested in the international division. Moreover, after 31 March, Flavin stated that SBM would cease trading, and he would dispose of the assets piecemeal. During the second half of February, there were intense negotiations between ICL and Singer.

On 16 March 1976, Cross made the business case for acquiring the international division of SBM to the ICL board.[20] He argued the case on two grounds: financial and products. The financial case for acquiring the Singer operation was that it would greatly strengthen ICL's customer base, especially in Europe. For example, in Western Germany SBM had 200 System Tens installed compared with ICL's eighty or ninety 2903s; this would double the value of ICL's customer base. It also offered ICL an entrée into markets where it was not represented at all, such as Spain, Portugal, Finland, and certain South American territories. Singer was also very successful in some of ICL's strong territories, such as the UK and Australia, where it would add significantly to its customer base. Cross was encouraged by the experience of Honeywell, which had acquired the GE customer base in 1970, and Univac, which had acquired the RCA customer base in 1971; in both cases 60 per cent of the customer base had stayed with the acquiring firm. None the less, the true value of the customer base could only be guessed at, so that Cross shrewdly aimed 'to structure a financial deal with Singer that minimises ICL's exposure and financial commitment to a low level of expected results but lets Singer share in any excess revenue over this low level.' [21]

SBM's three key products fitted surprisingly well into ICL's portfolio. The System Ten computer, which was considerably smaller and cheaper than the 2903, would enable ICL to cover the small-business-system market much more effectively. It also happened that System Ten had a number of OEM peripherals in common with the 2903, so that the effect on inventory would be minimal. The Singer 1500 series of intelligent terminals, which had an installed base of 4800 units (2900 outside the United States), were superior to ICL's 7500 terminal system, and would eliminate its continued development. The Singer MDTS point-of-sale terminal, which had captured 50 per cent of the United States market, was recognized as the market-leader; ICL had no equivalent product, and it promised to improve an already strong position in retail systems.

The ICL board authorized Cross to make a deal along these lines with Singer, and on 18 March 1976 an agreement in principle was concluded, the terms being hammered out in detail over the next few weeks. The SBM international customer base in seventeen countries was acquired for $25 million, to be paid for by an initial 15 per cent cash (about £2 million), and the balance over the period up to 1980. The data-processing equipment on rental was acquired at valuation, for a further $26 million, to be paid not in cash, but by making over a proportion of the rental stream to Singer, up to 1980. SBM's international turnover in 1975 was $131 million, and Cross estimated it would generate profits of $40 million in 1976. To have acquired the entire operation for a front-end cost of £2 million was an extremely good deal. In August 1976 ICL also acquired the SBM Utica, New York, manufacturing plant, for $3.8 million. This was a conscious decision by Cross to ensure continuity of supply, and also to internationalize manufacturing operations, to make ICL less vulnerable to sterling exchange-rate fluctuations and labour unions. [22]

The integration of SBM into ICL was achieved in approximately six months, under the leadership of Doug Comish, director of small business systems. The logistics of integrating the operation into ICL were somewhat daunting, although ICL was perhaps well prepared for it by its long history of merger activity. And unlike the ICT–English Electric Computers merger, the products were complementary rather than over-lapping. In the first year of integrated operations, 1977, ICL's head count increased by approximately 2500, and its revenues by about £70 million. The SBM acquisition effectively doubled ICL's small-business-systems revenues.

The Cross period: an assessment

By spring 1977, Geoff Cross had been with ICL for five years. When he had become managing director, in May 1972, he had established a corporate plan with three principal objectives. First, to double revenues in real terms; second, to become a credible multinational company, with at least fifty per cent of revenues derived from overseas business; and third, to successfully launch the New Range.

Cross's first objective, of doubling revenues in five years, was decisively achieved. Revenues rose from £168.6 million in 1973 to £418.7 million in 1977. This represented a compound growth rate of 22 per cent a year, or 18 per cent in real terms. (The Singer acquisition had made a sizeable difference to the overall growth, which would otherwise have been 14 per cent in real terms.) While revenues grew, the ICL head count had been kept fairly static at around 28 000 (until the Singer acquisition), so that profits had grown nearly ten-fold, from £3.3 million in 1973 to £30.3 million in 1977. This latter figure was equivalent to 7 per cent of revenues, and a healthy 16 per cent on capital employed—a figure that had not been equalled since BTM's good years in the late 1950s. In global terms, ICL had matched or bettered the turnover growth of IBM and the BUNCH companies, although it fell well short of the fastest-growing company, DEC (Table 15.2).

Table 15.2   Turnover trends of major computer firms, 1973-78

$billions	ICL	IBM	Burroughs	Univac	NCR	CDC	Honeywell	DEC
1973	0.34	11.0	1.26	1.12	1.60	0.94	0.84	0.26
1978	1.02	21.1	2.42	2.05	2.61	1.85	1.29	1.44
Annual growth rate (%)	22.1	13.9	13.9	12.9	10.3	14.5	9.0	40.8

Sources
ICL sources.

Perhaps more impressive than ICL's turnover growth was the growth of its exports. The period 1973-78 saw the proportion of ICL's overseas revenues grow from under one-third to over a half (Table 15.3). Sales to Europe, largely from the 2903, had been a particular success, and ICL had grown from a 2½ per cent European market share in 1973, to 8½ per cent in 1978. When the government had provided launching aid for the

Table 15.3 Geographical breakdown of ICL turnover, 1973-78

	1973	1974	1975	1976	1977	1978	Annual growth (%)
UK (%)	68	64	61	59	50	49	18
Europe (%)	16	16	17	19	25	26	40
International (%)	16	20	23	22	25	25	36
Total (£millions)	163	192	258	311	431	509	26

Source
'Five Year Forward Look, 1978/83', February 1979, p. 28, ICL Board Papers.

New Range there had been two objectives: first, to maintain an indigenous computer manufacturing and design capability; and second, to prevent a deterioration in the balance of trade. In fact, the UK deficit had continued to deteriorate, from £94 million in 1973 to £198 million in 1978 (Table 15.4). The situation, however, would have been twice as bad had ICL not increased its overseas revenues five-fold in the same period. In April 1976 ICL received the Queen's Award for Export Achievement.

Table 15.4 UK balance of trade in IT, 1973-78

£ millions	1973	1974	1975	1976	1977	1978
Imports	257	346	383	553	692	827
Exports	162	209	242	318	498	629

Source
Business Monitor, passim.

By mid-1976, ICL was generally perceived to have turned the corner. The Queen's Award was followed by a favourably received interim report in June 1976, which showed operating profits up 35 per cent. By the end of 1976 ICL had become a recommended buy by brokers on both sides of the Atlantic. In March 1977, Cross was nominated *Guardian* Young Businessman of the Year. In a background article the *Guardian* stated:

International Computers is the prime example in British post-war history of the lame duck which has learned to walk again. It is the paradigm case for quotation by opponents of the doctrine of corporate euthanasia which argues that the weak should be left in the cold to die. . . . Today it is the only European large computer company which is enjoying healthy profits and growth without government support.[23]

ICL's own publicity department could hardly have done better.

Cross's third objective had been to achieve a successful launch of the New Range. Although Cross presided over the launch of the New Range, his energies were directed to financial strategies for product development, rather than product development *per se*. For example, an important contribution to containing R&D costs had been ICL's participation in Computer Peripherals Inc. (CPI), a company that had been proposed by Arthur Humphreys and William Norris, chairman of CDC, since 1972. This was a consortium of CDC, NCR, and ICL in peripheral developments. The cost of ICL's initial participation, in September 1975, was £4.2 million; but it enabled peripheral development costs to be kept at well under 10 per cent of R&D expenditure.

Cross's aim had been to become independent of government support by the end of 1976, when the last £8 million instalment of the New Range launching aid would be received. As Table 15.5 shows, while R&D expenditure remained approximately static in real terms, as a proportion of revenues it fell from 12 per cent to 7 per cent over the period 1973–78.

Table 15.5   ICL R&D spend, 1974–78

£ millions	1974	1975	1976	1977	1978	Total
Hardware	10.1	9.0	10.0	13.9	15.4	58.4
Software	8.9	11.7	12.2	13.0	17.5	63.3
Other	2.6	3.8	4.5	2.8	3.2	16.9
Total	21.6	24.5	26.7	29.8	36.1	138.7
Percentage of revenues	10.8	10.2	9.3	7.1	7.1	

Source
'Five Year Forward Look, 1978/83', February 1979, p. 34, ICL Board Papers.

At 7 per cent of turnover, ICL's R&D expenditure was only slightly higher than the average for the industry. However, while ICL remained one-third of the size of its American competitors, but offering a comparable range of machines, the relative under-spending on R&D should have been more apparent at the top levels of management than it was. As Peter Ellis put it, somewhat later:

Development under-achievement has been much greater than superficially apparent. Competitive levels of quality, reliability, diagnostics and maintainability have had to be sacrificed in the interest of reducing the development time slippage.

Design modifications after product introduction represent development incompleteness. A study during the last year showed 6,000 modifications per year for implementation by Manufacturing, thus increasing Manufacturing costs.[24]

For product strategy, Cross had been heavily dependent on Ed Mack, whom he had brought in from Univac. It was generally felt within ICL that Mack had a good deal more autonomy than was good for the company. Fundamentally, there was too much expenditure on the New Range at the expense of small business systems. Throughout 1973-77, mainframes declined as a percentage of turnover (from 87 per cent to 54 per cent), while small business systems rose from 9 per cent to 30 per cent.[25] Sales of the 2903 alone, in the mid-1970s, were growing at nearly 40 per cent a year. The actual development expenditure on the 2903 processor, however, accounted for only £3 million out of a total £49 million spent on all processor developments during the six-year period 1973-78.[26] In 1978, 2903 sales were to fall dramatically as its competitiveness was lost.

As for the New Range itself, there had been major problems in maintaining development schedules, which had generally slipped by up to two years. And the reliability of delivered hardware and software was generally below the standards of the rest of the industry. Mack's major technical blunder was the introduction of a second major operating system, VME/K, which added enormously to development costs. These development resources would have been far better spent on improving ICL's position in networking software. As the computer environment swung more and more to distributed computing in 1978-80, this lack of investment was to put the New Range at a competitive disadvantage.

In assessing Cross's five years at ICL, it is fair to say that he left the company in excellent financial health, but that its product development was weak. In November 1977, Cross decided to resign from ICL and return to the United States. The reason stated publicly at the time was that his children had bronchial problems and needed to live in a drier climate. This was true, although the reasons were also financial—caused by the combination of high UK tax rates and the declining value of the pound against the dollar—and in his letter of resignation Cross also complained that he was frustrated by the labour unions.*

Tom Hudson's opinion was that ICL had, in any case, had the best of Geoff Cross—he had brought the company back to financial health, but now it was time for a more product-minded insider to take the helm.[28]

---

* Other motives were speculated upon for Cross's departure—for example, that he had been frustrated by the government in his wish to acquire a minicomputer manufacturer,[27] or that he left before ICL was about to hit the financial rocks. The former suggestion is certainly groundless, and Cross denies the latter.

The person selected for the post of managing director was Chris Wilson, then head of the International Sales Division.

The changing market: plug-compatible mainframes

Unlike the small-business-systems sector of the computer market, which was highly volatile and competitive, the early 1970s had seen relative stability in the mainframe sector. IBM and the BUNCH manufacturers had continued to jockey for position, but the high barriers to entry had prevented the emergence of competitors. These barriers to entry, as out-lined earlier, were: the R&D costs of producing a full range of computers and peripherals; the cost of developing operating systems and applications software; the need for a high volume of shipments to secure economies of scale in production; and the need for a sales force.

Gene Amdahl is generally credited with devising, in 1970, the concept of the plug-compatible processor. Just as in the second half of the 1960s, plug-compatible peripheral manufacturers had evolved by attaching their peripherals to IBM processors, now Amdahl reversed the idea: by making a compatible processor, he could displace the IBM mainframe at the heart of a computer system. The plug-compatible processor concept overcame all the barriers to entry into the mainframe market at a stroke. It was not necessary to develop a range of computers, since the plug-compatible-processor manufacturer could initially target just one of the processors in the IBM range—in the case of Amdahl, the top of the range. Following IBM's decision to unbundle software in 1969, it was no longer necessary to develop any software whatever for a plug-compatible processor. Manu-facturing start-up costs were also modest, since the operation was con-fined to just the manufacture of a single processor, and not of a range of processors and peripherals. Finally, only the most modest sales force was needed, since the plug-compatible mainframe manufacturer was selling to an existing IBM customer. Altogether, the capital requirements for entry into the plug-compatible-mainframe business were perhaps only one-tenth of those needed for entry into full-scale mainframe manufacture.[29]

The Amdahl Computer Corporation was formed in 1970. Amdahl had been a principal IBM computer architect, and was the chief processor-designer of System/360. Of course, to ensure commercial success a plug-compatible mainframe (PCM) had to have a price/performance advantage of about a factor of two over the corresponding IBM processor; and this implied access to state-of-the-art semiconductor technology. This proved difficult for Amdahl to obtain in the climate of the 1970–71 computer recession; but in 1972 he made an agreement with the Japanese company Fujitsu, who took a minority shareholding in Amdahl. While the pro-cessors were designed in California, Fujitsu undertook their manufacture in Japan. (This was very similar to the relationship between ICL and Fujitsu ten years later for building the Estriel mainframe—see the next chapter.) In mid-1975, after a five-year gestation, Amdahl launched its first PCM, the Amdahl 470 V/6, which was sold as a one-for-one replacement for the IBM 370/168, IBM's most powerful processor. The Amdahl processor was more powerful and cheaper, and was an instant commercial success. By 1978 the turnover of the Amdahl Computer Corporation had reached $321 million, and it introduced several new processors.[30]

The success of the Amdahl PCM strategy was a turning point for the Japanese computer industry, for whom software had always been an insuperable barrier to entry. Although Honeywell had been using NEC technology for some years, it was the Amdahl-Fujitsu connection that effected the technology transfer of the IBM computer architecture to Japan. In the case of Hitachi, which developed the M-series of compatible mainframes, industrial espionage was also a factor.[31] In 1976, the American computer firm Itel began to market the Hitachi processors in the United States and other territories.

The early PCMs were generally aimed at IBM's largest processors. During 1970–78, IBM began to react to the PCM manufacturers by improving the price/performance of its top-end processors. In March 1977, it introduced the 370-3033 processor at the top of its range, with a price/performance improvement of a factor of 2½ over the existing 370/168; and it also made price-cuts on its existing mid-range models. To counter these moves, Amdahl introduced its model 470 V/5 and V/7 processors. In autumn 1977, IBM introduced two further 370 processors —the 3031 and 3032—to replace its mid-range models. And so it went on. This jockeying for price/performance in mainframes was to set the tone of the industry for the next five years. During 1977 and 1978, the plug-compatible-processor industry gathered momentum, with several new entrants, who included National Advanced Systems (NAS), Magnusson, Two Pi (a subsidiary of Philips in Holland), and CDC (marketing the Omega). These new entrants introduced mid-range machines, attacking IBM's complete System/370 range. IBM responded with price-cuts of up to 30 per cent. The other mainframe suppliers were soon forced to follow suit.

ICL's R&D portfolio

It was against this background of increasing competitiveness across the spectrum, from small business systems to mainframes, that during 1977 and 1978 the enormity of ICL's R&D commitment became increasingly apparent. The R&D programme fell into three broad areas: New Range fulfilment and enhancement; small business systems; and the differentiated products, 'DAP' and 'CAFS'. Inevitably, it was the New Range that accounted for the lion's share of the expenditure.

New Range fulfilment and enhancement

By early 1977, the New Range was beginning to show several serious competitive weaknesses. These included the non-availability of mid-range processors, the inadequate software transition aids between the old and new ranges, the ageing technology of the existing processors, and the lack of a communications architecture. These major problems were all in addition to the reliability problems of the machines already in the field.

Since the New Range launch in October 1974, only the top three members of the series—the 2960, 2970, and 2980—had been announced. This left a vacuum between ICL's small 2904 and the medium-sized 2960, which left the existing 1900-series customer base vulnerable to the competition. In November 1977, ICL finally announced the 2950, based on the S1 processor; and a new small machine, the 2905, was announced at the same time. These new products helped to close the gap, but a mid-range void still remained.

Although the smooth transition from the 1900 series and System 4 to the 2900 series had always been a key objective in the New Range strategy, it had been mostly honoured in the breach, and ICL was widely criticized for the 'tardiness with which it had introduced serious products'.[32] The initiative was eventually taken not by ICL, but by IBM, which began to aggressively market a 1900-series emulator for its System/370, in order to entice existing ICL users.* The UK divisions of Honeywell and Univac also announced software transition aids at about the same time. Although ICL had actually developed a 1900 emulator for the 2900 series, it had been restricted to in-house use and had not been marketed, since ICL preferred to sell the 2900 on its technical merits rather than as a 'hot tango 1900'. In response to the IBM emulator, however, ICL announced its 'Direct Machine Environment' (DME) emulators in April 1977, for both 1900 and System 4 users. This stopped some users defecting to the competition, and some installations continued to run their 1900 and System 4 programs in emulation-mode indefinitely. The move, however, added a further two operating systems to the two that ICL was already supplying.

An important impact of the emergence of the PCM manufacturers had been to make IBM assert its technological leadership, and to shorten the life-cycle of its processor technology, from perhaps four to three years.

---

* Emulator: a facility on one computer, for example, a System/370, which makes it obey the instruction code of another, for example, a 1900. An emulator, which uses special hardware techniques, is much more efficient than a simulator using only software techniques.

ICL now considered it was about three years behind IBM on key aspects of processor technology, and that progressive enhancement of all the P-series processors had become urgent. During 1978, plans were laid for replacement of the P3 and P4 processors by LSI processors (S3 and S4), and eventually by full VLSI processors (S3L and S4L) during 1982-84. This evolution would provide price/performance improvements of an order of magnitude over a period of about five years. Although ICL had established its own LSI facilities in 1976-77, to gain access to state-of-the-art semiconductor-design know-how an agreement was signed with Hitachi in May 1978 for the exchange of technical information.

The late 1970s saw a further acceleration of the trend towards distributed computing and computer networks, and the use of corporate-wide databases. Responding to the trend, IBM had announced its Systems Network Architecture (SNA) as early as 1972, and the other suppliers such as DEC, Burroughs, and Honeywell were also introducing networks by the mid-1970s. As one ICL user was to put it, as late as 1979, 'When, oh when, will ICL announce a data communications network architecture or at least a strategy?'[33] ICL only began to develop a coherent networking strategy in 1979; but for once its tardiness proved almost an advantage, since it was able to adopt the OSI international standards for networking. IBM and the other manufacturers, having started earlier, were locked into their own proprietary standards. ICL's Information Processing Architecture (IPA) was finally announced in 1980. The adoption of OSI standards was to become a major competitive weapon in the mid-1980s.

Small business systems

In the five years that the ICL 2903 had been on the market since its launch in April 1973, some 2600 systems had been sold, with sales growing at the rate of 39 per cent a year. In spite of this it had never had a corresponding R&D effort invested in it. In 1978, the 2903's age finally caught up with it, and sales actually fell 20 per cent over the previous year. This created an urgent need for a successor. During 1978 enhanced versions (the 2903 models 25, 40, and 50) were announced as a short-term response, but in the long term a completely new processor was needed. In a somewhat autocratic move, Ed Mack arranged to manufacture a little-known American design under licence. This was a universal emulator board, known as EMMY (for emulator), created by an American west-coast start-up, Palyn Associates.[34] Integration of this bare emulation logic in a full-scale system by ICL design staff led to the ME29 computer, launched in March 1980, which was to prove a highly successful product.

The System Ten inherited from Singer was also showing signs of age. As it happened, Singer had already developed a successor, the System Ten-220, that ICL was able to use with little development effort; but there was an acute need to introduce cost-effective LSI technology into the processor, though this was not approved by the board until July 1979. Finally, in the small-business-systems area, enhancements were also needed for the 1500-based and 7500-based systems, so that ICL could make an effective entry into the booming office-automation market.

DAP and CAFS exploitation

One of the consequences of the rise of the PCM manufacturers was that IBM-compatible mainframes were increasingly becoming a commodity, and the only way of achieving competitive advantage was in terms of price/performance. For the manufacturers of non-IBM-compatible mainframes, product differentiation, which had always been at least as strong a sales argument as price/performance, was now beginning to take on a new importance. Probably the three manufacturers with the best-differentiated mainframe products were ICL, Burroughs, and Honeywell, who all had architectures and operating software that were technically superior to IBM. With the most modern architecture and the VME operating systems, ICL was probably the best-placed of any of the mainframe manufacturers in this respect.

The falling cost of integrated circuits had also created another opportunity for entry into the computer business by the late 1970s. This was the design of processors with novel, or 'non-von Neumann', computer architectures, which would perform spectacularly well in certain narrow domains of application. In the United States a number of firms began to market products for matrix computation, vision processing, artificial intelligence, and so on.[35] ICL's Research and Advanced Development Centre, under Gordon Scarrott, a prominent figure in the UK computer research scene, had been working on two such projects for a number of years, DAP and CAFS. By the mid-1970s the time had come to exploit these innovations. A particular attraction of the flexibility of the New Range and the VME/B operating system was that special-purpose processors—'information engines' as they were coming to be called—could be incorporated into a regular 2900-series mainframe in a straightforward way, enabling users in quite ordinary environments to get a spectacular performance in certain applications.

The Distributed Array Processor (DAP) project had been started at ICL in 1972, with financial support from the government-funded Advanced Computer Technology Project.[36] The DAP consisted of an array of processors (initially 32×32) which enabled matrix calculations to proceed at several hundred million computations per second, about three orders of magnitude faster than a large conventional mainframe. The DAP was launched as a product in April 1978. The DAP was highly acclaimed as a technical innovation—it received the BCS/*Computing*

magazine award for technological achievement in 1979, which was
excellent for ICL's image; but the relatively narrow market meant that the
financial impact on ICL was not great.

The Content-Addressable File Store (CAFS) had the potential for a
much wider market. CAFS was actually conceived by Gordon Scarrott in
1962, but was not actively developed until 1969.[37] The CAFS is an
ingenious (and heavily patented) mechanism that enables a disc store to be
searched 'on-the-fly' independently of the main processor. This enables
the CAFS to do searching at speeds that otherwise could only be achieved
by a colossal mainframe. In 1972 a prototype was completed, and field
trials were conducted with the Post Office Directory Inquiries project.
The trials were so successful, giving a hundred-fold improvement on
conventional computer searching, that in 1975 a CAFS Exploitation
Review Committee was established to bring it into the ICL product line.
A product, CAFS 800, was announced in 1979.

The CAFS products have been showered with technical achievement
awards—the British Computer Society Award in 1980, *Computing*
magazine Product of the Decade in 1983, and the Queen's Award in
1985. A successor product, CAFS-ISP, was incorporated as standard in
1984 in ICL's Series 39 computers (the successor to the 2900 series). All
this, however, was very much in the future in 1978; the problem then
was paying for CAFS and all the other developments.

A high-growth, high-risk strategy

In May 1978, Cross's successor, Chris Wilson, presented his first five-
year plan to the ICL board.[38] The central issue, as in the past, was in
selecting an appropriate level of R&D expenditure and generating sufficient business to sustain it. The R&D programmes under way in 1978
(outlined in the previous section) indicated swiftly rising costs, increasing
from £36 million a year in 1978 to £89 million in 1983. During Cross's
five-year period 1973-77, total R&D expenditure had been £123 million;
and this was now set to more than double, to £266 million, in the next
five-year period, 1978-82. This increase was only partly accounted for by
inflation: most of it reflected ICL's broader spectrum of products, such as
DAP and CAFS, and its entry into networks and office systems; but the
dominant costs were those necessary to maintain the competitiveness of
the 2900 series by introducing LSI processors.

Wilson's five-year plan presented two possible scenarios. The first
assumed a modest but sustained 12-15 per cent growth in real terms—
that is, a doubling of revenues in the next five years. However, in the
absence of government support, it would be necessary to narrow the
product range in order to rein back R&D costs to about 7 per cent of

revenues. Under this plan ICL would be profitable, though a little un-adventurous. In effect, it would be the 'different kind of company' spoken of in 1972: profitable, competitive, successful, but not at the leading edge of technology, and in no sense a national flagship computer company.

The second scenario was that of a much more rapid growth, roughly tripling revenues over the five-year period by achieving an annual growth rate of 20-25 per cent. This would represent an organic growth rate considerably higher than Cross had achieved, and would give ICL a £1 billion turnover by 1982. The risks of the high-growth plan were considerable. First, the plan assumed that most growth would come from overseas business, with the proportion of exports rising from 50 per cent to 65 per cent of turnover; success of the plan was therefore contingent on the relative stability of sterling in the $1.80-$2.00 band to maintain price-competitiveness. Second, the plan assumed that the extremely competitive environment created by the competition between IBM and the PCM manufacturers would not worsen significantly. Finally, Wilson gambled that if an economic recession occurred during the five-year period, it would be like the one of 1973-74—when computer sales had held up—rather than the computer recession of 1970-71, when sales had fallen.[39]

The high-growth plan was accepted by the board, and during 1978 ICL in fact achieved a revenue growth of 22 per cent and a profit growth of 23 per cent. This was the highest growth rate of any company in the industry, excepting DEC and Fujitsu. Moreover, ICL was beginning to approach the size of its American BUNCH competitors in EDP revenues, and it had larger EDP revenues than any non-American manufacturer excepting Fujitsu. The City was ecstatic over ICL's transformation from lame duck to glamour stock, and the share price of ICL very nearly doubled, to 320p, between the beginning and end of 1978. In January 1979 Plessey shrewdly sold its shareholding, making a modest profit on its ten years as a principal shareholder. The offer was more than three times over-subscribed.*

In early 1979, encouraged by the high growth achieved in 1978, Wilson took the view that ICL now had a window of opportunity. Five more years of rapid growth would enable ICL to secure its long-term prosperity by achieving parity of scale with the American manufacturers, and keeping up with the growth of Japanese competitors. There was one final incentive to plough back profits for rapid growth. When the government had given its £40 million launching aid to ICL, it had been agreed that ICL would pay back 25 per cent of profits, in excess of 7½ per cent of turnover, during 1978-84. If ICL ploughed back its profits in excess of

---

* GEC had sold its shares to the National Enterprise Board in June 1976. The NEB took sufficient of the Plessey share sale to raise its holding to 25 per cent.

7½ per cent for the next five years, it would have to pay back the government nothing at all. In February 1979, Wilson advised the DTI, in a letter to Reay Atkinson, head of the computer division, that ICL had formally adopted a high-growth policy:

Our Board has now reviewed and approved the ICL Five Year Forward Look 1978/83 document, which I enclose. . . . The present Forward Look now takes 20% per annum growth as the Corporate aim. . . . ICL will, therefore, invest more than previously proposed in Research and Development, System Validation, Marketing and capital equipment in the Manufacturing process to support this growth. This choice makes it unlikely that the trading margins of 1978 will improve in the five year period of this Forward Look and thus no provision has been made for any payment under the £40 million Research and Development Support Agreement to HMG.[40]

Reay Atkinson endorsed ICL's high-growth strategy as being exactly the right thing to do. Moreover the Labour Government—now in its final months of office—was very supportive of ICL, and was not anxious for payment of the £40 million.[41]

The good news continued into the spring of 1979, with the half-year results showing turnover up 23 per cent, and orders up 30 per cent. Again the City was delighted: 'ICL cheers city with £18.6 million' (*London Evening News*), 'almost everything seems to be going ICL's way' (*Daily Telegraph*).[42] And the circulars of industry analysts were equally bullish: 'ICL's prospects are excellent . . . There is now every reason to be optimistic about ICL's future'.[43]

Meanwhile, however, IBM had responded to the increasing competition from the PCM manufacturers by making its most dramatic announcement of the decade. On 31 January 1979, it replaced its System/370 mid-range processors with the 4300 series. The new machines offered an unprecedented price/performance improvement over the machines they replaced. As Peter Ellis put it, 'The IBM price umbrella was now becoming rather leaky'.[44] ICL was about to get soaked.

The 4300 challenge

During the early months of 1979, ICL and the other mainframe manufacturers had begun to react to the launch of the IBM 4300 series. The 4300 series was initially announced as two processors—the models 4331 and 4341—which were intended as replacements for IBM's mid-range mainframes, with deliveries in the first half of 1979. In both cases, the machines offered a four-fold price/performance improvement over the existing System/370 models.

The 4300 series was IBM's considered strategic response to two major changes in the mainframe market since the mid-1970s. The first change was the emergence of the PCM suppliers, largely from Japan, but increasingly from the United States and Europe. The second factor was the year-upon-year improvement in the price/performance of semiconductors. These two factors had caused machines based on the IBM architecture to take on an increasingly commodity-like character. Although IBM had made a short-term response by price-cutting, this was a tactical step that could not be sustained indefinitely. The classic route out of a commodity-like market—product differentiation—was not of course available to IBM, since a radical change from its 15-year-old 360-based architecture could not be contemplated.

According to contemporary industry analysts, IBM had evolved a subtle two-point product strategy for the 4300 series.[45] First, users would be given approximately four times the processing and memory capacity at existing rental levels. Second, they would be motivated to use the increased power on new applications and software. In order to provide users with a four-fold price/performance improvement, IBM had made major investments in semiconductor technology, which enabled it to match the costs of Amdahl and its Japanese competitors. Under ordinary circumstances, a major price/performance improvement might have simply induced users to trade down to obtain the same power at a lower rental. The second part of the 4300 marketing strategy, however, was to simultaneously announce processor-hungry database, applications, and programmer-productivity software. IBM's market research had indicated the existence of an 'applications backlog' of about four years in the typical data-processing department. This backlog was largely due to the fact that programmers were spending perhaps 80 per cent of their time on the maintenance of existing programs. The new IBM software would enable users to develop applications more rapidly, requiring less maintenance, but consuming far more processor power. IBM judged that users would choose to maintain their data-processing budgets, and consume more processor power to use the new generation of software rather than trading down; this turned out to be the case, although the flood of rental returns of System/370 machines turned out to be a serious problem for IBM.[46]

For all the mainframe manufacturers the 4300 launch created the competitive environment of 1979. In effect, they were caught in the cross-fire between IBM and the Japanese, and during the early months of 1979 they all cut prices and announced new models. In February and March, Burroughs, NCR, and Honeywell announced new processors. These processors typically offered up to two or three times the power of existing models, for a somewhat lower rental. The PCM manufacturers also cut prices and announced new processors: the Japanese manufacturers, Fujitsu, Hitachi, and Mitsubishi, as well as Amdahl, Itel, and Siemens, all made major competitive product-announcements in the first half of 1979. Probably the first casualty of the 4300 launch was Itel, which came close to receivership after announcing heavy losses for the first half of 1979; and Amdahl suffered a drop in revenues of nearly a quarter.[47]

In July 1979, Wilson reported to ICL's top-level Operations Review Committee on the impact of the IBM announcements on the 2900 series:

For the first time, IBM has used its overwhelming investment capability to make a major advance in the state of the art of processor logic design, technology and implementation.[48]

The product strategy developed for ICL's five-year high-growth plan was now seen to be seriously underfunded:

The formal product strategy . . . was aimed at sustaining ICL's planned revenue growth over the next five years. The IBM posture, already visible by the time the strategy was issued in April 1979, has substantially endangered this objective. Furthermore, detailed examination of the costs and resource requirements to complete that programme in a timely and dependable manner has shown a short-fall of between 10 and 20% in available R and D budget for 1979/80.[49]

The major development problem was that the S3 and S4 LSI processors, for the 2970 and 2980 replacements, would be approaching obsolescence by the time that they were delivered. They either had to be expedited or dropped. It was therefore decided to cancel the largest processor, S4, and to allocate the resources to S3 to bring it out as rapidly as possible. At the same time the S3L and S4L programmes were accelerated to bring the VLSI processors out by 1983 or 1984. ICL was still overspending on R&D, however, and it seemed likely that it would eventually have to call on the government for some financial support. Wilson had tentatively approached Reay Atkinson at the DTI, and received some encouraging words.[50]

In fact, when government assistance became necessary, it would not prove so straightforward as Wilson and Atkinson had supposed. On 3 May 1979 Margaret Thatcher's Conservative Government had been elected into power. Like the Heath Government of 1971, the Thatcher administration was pledged to a disengagement from direct involvement in industry; and one of its first acts was to disband the National Enterprise Board, and sell off its shareholdings in the computer companies Inmos, Nexos, and ICL. The new government was not uninterested in information technology—indeed, its manifesto pledged the formation of a Department of Information Technology; but its policy was directed towards the diffusion of computing to make British industry more competitive, rather than towards the sectional interests of computer manufacturers. When ICL ran into difficulties in mid-1980, this policy would determine the very limited help the government would be willing to consider.

But in any case it would have been premature to make a direct approach to the government at this stage. The fact was that the ICL balance-sheet had never looked better. The 1979 results showed that turnover was up 23 per cent, and profits up 22 per cent. At the annual general meeting in December, Tom Hudson announced his retirement on the grounds of age, and the appointment of his successor, E.P. Chappell. Philip Chappell was a non-executive director of ICL, and vice-chairman of Morgan Grenfell Holdings. Interestingly, there had been a search for a successor to Hudson for several months, and Sir Kenneth Corfield, the chairman and chief executive of STC, had been approached to take the job; but in the event the board settled for a devil-they-knew. If Corfield had taken the job, ICL's future would no doubt have been very different.[51]

The City reaction to the 1979 results was enthusiastic, and shortly afterwards the government sold its 25 per cent shareholding at 455 pence per share—the highest that ICL's shares had stood since its creation in 1968. In February 1980, ICL made a 4:1 share split, reflecting the improved stock-market valuation. They shortly peaked at 137p. Hudson had chosen a good moment to retire.

16

Convergence

the 1980s

ICL occupies only a narrow position within the information processing industry, the boundaries of which are widening. This creates the risk of a declining market share and competitiveness within this wider market. The threat and the scale of the challenge in converting to the wider information storage and processing industry is comparable to that which faced BTM/Powers-Samas/ICT in managing the transition to computing.

—ICL Five Year Forward Look, February 1979.[1]

In 1980, ICL and all the other mainframe manufacturers were faced with two major challenges, one short-term and one medium-term. The short-term problem was to come to terms with the lower profit margins caused by the price-war between IBM and the Japanese plug-compatible main-frame manufacturers. The medium-term problem was to respond to the coming convergence of computers and communications: this convergence implied not merely developing networked computer systems, but also achieving strategic alliances or mergers with telecommunications firms. In the United States, following de-regulation of the telecommunications industry, new competitors such as AT&T had begun to offer computer and information services, and several computer companies had already made alliances with communications suppliers. Before ICL could respond to these larger issues, however, it had to deal with its short-term problems.

An approach to the government

By spring 1980 the competitive pressures caused by the launch of the IBM 4300 had begun to seriously affect order-taking, and ICL was forced to revise its forward plans. The situation had been made worse by a rise in the sterling exchange rate. ICL's high-growth plan, formalized a year earlier, had been based on a sterling exchange rate in the $1.80-$2.00 band. During 1979 sterling had crept up to $2.20, and by May 1980 was standing at $2.35, close to its peak. This had a marked effect on ICL's overseas revenues. The UK was now in an economic downturn of comparable severity to the one that had brought on the computer recession of the early 1970s. ICL was faced with a £100-million order-shortfall, and turnover could only be maintained by reducing profit margins and giving generous leasing terms. To avoid cutting R&D expenditure, borrowings were increased. This was only acceptable on a short-term basis, since uncontrolled borrowing would make the company vulnerable to any small downturn in orders.[2]

Throughout the summer of 1980, ICL's trading position continued to deteriorate. In September 1980, the board approved a restructuring to improve competitiveness and to reduce the cash outflow. An immediate recruitment ban was imposed, and offers of employment were withdrawn from 140 new graduates. This was the first public indication that ICL was in trouble. In December, ICL published its 1980 results, which showed that although turnover was up 15 per cent, profits had been reduced by 46 per cent to £25 million. By the new year, ICL's internal forecasts were predicting a £25 million loss for the half-year, and £50 million for the whole year. Moreover, borrowing would have reached £100 million by the spring, representing a gearing of nearly 70 per cent—ICL would then be in danger of exceeding its legal borrowing powers. It was at this point that it was decided to approach the government for aid.[3]

ICL's approach to the government coincided with the formation of the new Department of Information Technology under Kenneth Baker, who was to prove very supportive. On 15 January 1981, ICL gave a frank account of its problems in a formal meeting with Sir Peter Carey, Permanent Secretary of the Department of Trade and Industry, and his officials. As a result of this meeting the DTI agreed that it would give ICL what support it could. There were three major reasons for this positive attitude. First, the government needed to protect its massive investment in ICL computers. Second, if ICL failed, then it would damage the entire UK information technology industry, many of whose products were ICL-related. Third, if ICL failed, then it would undermine the credibility of the newly formed Ministry of Information Technology.[4]

At this time, ICL's major problem was the widening gap between its earnings and the R&D expenditure necessary to keep its products competitive. While previous governments had provided direct R&D support, this was not the route chosen by the new Thatcher administration. Rather, the view was taken that ICL should explore the possibility of merging with another mainframe company in order to achieve a larger market-share to fund its R&D. During the early months of 1981, a great deal of management time was taken up in talking to several American companies, including Univac and NCR, as well as Fujitsu in Japan. In fact the American companies were primarily interested in ICL's customer base rather than in sharing R&D costs, so that a merger would have been unacceptable both politically and from a business viewpoint. In any case, a merger with another mainframe company did not address the longer-term issues of the convergence of computers and communications. Nonetheless, the press rumours of the possibility of an ICL merger—many of which were entirely speculative, even from a journal of the standing of *The Economist*—had an unsettling effect on ICL customers; and this in turn affected order-taking.

At ICL's annual general meeting on 3 February 1981, Chappell disclosed a pre-tax half-year loss of £20 million, and forecast a full-year loss of £50 million. By this time, ICL had effectively exhausted its borrowing facilities. ICL's bankers were understandably nervous at extending credit further, even though Chris Wilson had begun to plan for a large-scale redundancy programme and other retrenchment measures that would stem the cash outflow. In March 1981, in a meeting between ICL, its bankers, and the government, a highly imaginative solution to ICL's cash problems was put forward in the form of a loan guarantee. Provided ICL's bankers would extend it the £200 million it needed, the government would guarantee the loans against ICL's defaulting. In fact a total of £270 million was provided, of which the government guaranteed £200 million for a period of two years. Since ICL subsequently repaid the loans, and the guarantees never had to be called, the assistance given to ICL cost the government not a penny-piece.

In reaching the decision to provide the loan guarantees, the government had concluded—on the advice of management consultants—that ICL's problems were in large part managerial. The loan guarantees were therefore made conditional upon ICL's accepting a new management team, and the government's nominating three main-board directors.

The new management team

During the next few weeks, the DTI persuaded Robb Wilmot, an *enfant terrible* of the electronics industry, and Christophor Laidlaw, who was a major industrial figure, to take over the running of ICL. Wilmot, aged 36, was the managing director of Texas Instruments in Britain, and both he and his company were well known to the DTI. Wilmot was asked by Reay Atkinson of the DTI if he would be interested in the managing directorship of ICL, and he was given the management consultant's report on the company to read over the weekend. A few days later, Wilmot made a presentation on ICL to Sir Peter Carey and Treasury officials. The presentation was so effective that they were convinced they need look no further for a new managing director for ICL.[5] Christophor Laidlaw, aged 59, was deputy chairman of BP, and had just missed, on age grounds, becoming chairman. He was a director of Barclays Bank, one of ICL's major bankers, and he was well known in the DTI and the Treasury.

Laidlaw was initially hesitant about taking on ICL, since he knew nothing about computers; but after two meetings with Wilmot they agreed to bring their different backgrounds to ICL. None of these plans were known to ICL at the time.

On 8 May 1981, Kenneth Baker advised ICL that the government was ready to exercise its prerogative of changing the top management of ICL by nominating Robb Wilmot as managing director, Christophor Laidlaw as chairman, and John Gardiner—chief executive of the Laird Group—to be a non-executive director. The following Sunday, 10 May 1981, at a special meeting of the ICL board, the new board members were installed, and Chappell and Wilson tendered their letters of resignation.

Laidlaw and Wilmot had complementary talents, and they achieved an almost classical split of the chairman's and managing director's roles. Laidlaw was an establishment figure, with strong City connections and a formidable reputation as an industrialist. By contrast, Wilmot, although well known in the electronics industry, was little known in the computer industry, and still less known in the City. Laidlaw saw it as an important part of his role to act as a mediator between the brash Wilmot and the conservative financial institutions whose money he was spending.[6]

Within ICL, however, Wilmot was firmly in charge. Immediately upon taking office he began to publicize a recovery plan for ICL. At the corporate level, Wilmot was an exceptionally effective communicator (although at the personal level he had a well-deserved reputation for abrasiveness). He was given to crisp slogans, and he summarized the recovery plan in a typical three-point formula. First: survival. Second: return to profit. Third: profitable growth. The survival phase would be a short one, about twelve to eighteen months, during which the aim would be to stem the losses, and to restore customer confidence and employee morale. With no immediate end to the recession in sight, and consequently no significant increase in turnover, the second phase of the recovery would be simply to return the company to profit on a turnover of around £700 million. This phase, again, would take about twelve to eighteen months, and would effectively restore ICL to its 1979 position. Finally, after a total of 2-3 years, ICL would enter phase three—profitable growth.

The recovery plan was based on financial, product, and marketing strategies. The financial strategy was initially one of survival, which meant reducing the cash outflow. Within eighteen days of taking office in May 1981, Wilmot began to implement the plans laid down by Wilson for a major cost-cutting exercise. The measures taken were all very standard, very unpleasant, but unavoidable if ICL was to become viable again: several plants were closed and workers were laid off; short-time working and early retirement were introduced; and inventories were slashed. The cutting of the work-force continued throughout the ICL recovery, the total head count reducing from a peak of 33 000 in 1980 to about 20 000 by 1985.

Laidlaw's most pressing financial problem was to bring ICL's borrowing under control. To reduce the financial gearing, it was decided to make an urgent £50 million issue of preference shares to convert some of the borrowings into equity. Behind the scenes, Laidlaw cajoled the banks into accepting the issue, which they did only on the basis that the shares were covered by the government guarantee, and were therefore redeemable in March 1983. This was achieved by the end of the 1981 financial year, enabling the gearing to be brought down to an acceptable, though still very high, 70 per cent. The high costs of the redundancy programme resulted in a £50 million loss for the year.[7]

During his first few months of office, Laidlaw brought in two new key members of the management team—Peter Bonfield and Robin Biggam. Bonfield was in fact an associate of Wilmot's from Texas Instruments, and had at one time been director of their European marketing operations, although he was now based in the United States. At Texas Instruments, while Wilmot had a reputation as a technical strategist, Bonfield was known for operations and marketing. Wilmot had been using Bonfield as an informal consultant ever since he took on the ICL managing directorship, and he eventually agreed to join ICL in October 1981 as director of marketing—not least because he was unable to resist the persuasive powers of Laidlaw. Laidlaw also persuaded Robin Biggam, then a rising star with ICI, to join ICL as finance director in December 1981. Laidlaw, Wilmot, Bonfield, and Biggam were to be the principal architects of ICL's recovery. Laidlaw also strengthened the non-executive membership of the board, eventually bringing in Sir John Hoskyns and Robert Horton, chief executive of BP.

Without any doubt, Wilmot's most important individual contribution to the ICL recovery was his firm grasp of the technical strategy. This ability was unique in a managing director of ICL at any time. Within six months of his arrival, Wilmot had re-oriented ICL's product strategy around two themes: mainframe rationalization, and a new 'Networked Product Line'.

Mainframe rationalization: DM/1 and Estriel

Immediately on joining ICL in May 1981, Wilmot called for a review of ICL's mainframe products, the unprofitable core of its business. The review disclosed some alarming trends.[8] First, the 2900 series accounted for a disproportionate fraction of ICL's R&D spend: mainframes which produced about one-third of turnover, consumed two-thirds of overall R&D costs. This R&D burden was inhibiting ICL's participation in the market for small and micro-computers and for office systems. Second, market projections showed that mainframe sales were virtually static, and there was no real prospect of greater volume to offset the rising R&D costs. Further, as semiconductor technology moved towards VLSI in the mid-1980s, ICL would not have the volume to justify in-house semiconductor fabrication. Third, the forward plans for the 2900 series were unrealistically ambitious for the market size. In 1981, ICL was supporting five distinct 2900-series processors and two major operating systems. Although there were plans for some degree of rationalization, the mainframe hardware and software commitments were essentially unsupportable—particularly with the shortening product life-cycles, and the need for networking software.

Wilmot's short-term strategy for the 2900 series was therefore aimed at reducing the on-going R&D commitment, and diverting some of the released resources to small systems. On the hardware side, the entire 2900 range was reduced to two processors—ME29-based small systems, and S3-based medium-sized systems. Both the ME29 and the S3 were, of course, fruits of the Wilson period, and would not have existed if the R&D momentum had not been sustained in 1979-80. The S3 processor was launched as the 2966 in June 1981, and derivative versions were launched later in the year. Both the ME29 and the 2966 were major product successes which generated the revenues that sustained ICL during the recovery period. On the software side, the VME/K operating system was dropped entirely in favour of VME/B, which was relaunched as VME 2900 in July 1981.

When Wilmot had been made managing director, there was considerable surprise in the press at the selection of a 'chip man', who knew nothing about the mainframe industry. As it turned out, however, it was chip technology that was at the heart of the problems of the 2900 series. Both the VME architecture and operating system were well-proven and competitive; but ICL lacked the semiconductor technology to manufacture systems price-competitive with IBM.

In October 1981, Wilmot—assisted by some behind-the-scenes activity from the government and the tactical advice of Bonfield—succeeded in obtaining an agreement with Fujitsu to obtain access to its semiconductor technology. A key feature of the Fujitsu collaboration was what Wilmot was to call 'technology intercept'. ICL would obtain access to Fujitsu's emerging technologies, typically one year before general availability. Fujitsu's technology was considered the best in the world, and certainly better than IBM's—which was what mattered. By designing products based on the best emerging technology, rather than current technology, it was hoped to extend the product life-cycle from three to perhaps five years.[9] The technology-intercept concept was relatively risky, however, since if the technology did not emerge then neither would the product.[10]

The ICL-Fujitsu agreement fell into three broad areas, corresponding to three main product lines: the small DM/1 distributed mainframe, the medium-sized Estriel processor, and the large Atlas 10 IBM-compatible mainframe (Table 16.1).* The DM/1 processor would be the replacement for ME29 users and small/medium 2900s. All the architecture, design, software, and manufacturing would remain in Britain, with Fujitsu supplying semiconductor-design tools and components. DM/1 was to be based on Fujitsu's state-of-the-art 8000-gate CMOS technology.† By exploiting the flexibility of the VME nodal architecture, DM/1 would be

Table 16.1 ICL–Fujitsu agreement, October 1981

Processor	Mips	Architecture	Design	Software	Manufacture	Technology
DM/1[a]	0.8–2.6	ICL	ICL	ICL	ICL	Fujitsu
Estriel[b]	7–20	ICL	ICL	ICL	Fujitsu	Fujitsu
Atlas 10[c]	15–25	Fujitsu	Fujitsu	Fujitsu	Fujitsu	Fujitsu

Notes
[a] Announced as Series 39 level 30, April 1985.
[b] Announced as Series 39 level 80, April 1985.
[c] Announced as Atlas 10, models 15 and 25, May 1982.

Sources
'ICL and Fujitsu Announce Major Collaboration in Mainframe Computers', ICL Press Announcement, 7 October 1981 (ICL Historical Collection). R.W. Wilmot, 'ICL Mainframe Strategy', 16 September 1981, ICL Board Papers.

capable of multi-processor configurations giving a performance range of 0.8 to 2.6 mips, which was a substantial portion of the lower-mainframe spectrum. The Estriel processor was to be a VLSI replacement for the existing S3 processor. Again, all architecture and design control would remain with ICL, with Fujitsu being responsible for the semiconductor technology. Estriel was to be based on very fast ECL technology using Fujitsu's 'top hat' air-cooled technology, which had been proven on its own mainframes. To minimize production costs and lead-times, and to increase Fujitsu's own production volume, the heart of the processor would be manufactured in Japan. Again, by using the VME nodal architecture, Estriel could be configured to give models with a performance in the range of 7 to 20 mips. It was this flexibility of the VME architecture that enabled an entire mainframe range to be based on just two processors —a major advantage over ICL's competitors.

* DM/1 and Estriel were new names for the S1L and S3L processors. The name Estriel arose because the Japanese had difficulty in getting their tongues around 'ess-three-el'.

† CMOS: Complementary Metal Oxide Semiconductor. ECL: Emitter-Coupled Logic. The technical distinction between these two semiconductor technologies is unimportant here, except that CMOS is cheap and moderately fast, while ECL is expensive and very fast.

The third part of the ICL–Fujitsu agreement was for ICL to market Fujitsu's largest M380 and M382 IBM-compatible mainframes as the ICL Atlas 10 series. This agreement did not really harmonize with ICL's mainframe range, but it was part of the give-and-take between Fujitsu and ICL. It was never anticipated that ICL would sell more than about two dozen machines, but it did offer a 'top cover' for ICL's largest users, and there was a business opportunity for sales in mixed ICL/IBM sites. As was noticed by press commentators, Atlas 10 left the option open for an eventual move to IBM-compatible mainframes, although this was too far in the future to be an explicit strategy. In fact, the Atlas 10 was a marketing failure, and ICL withdrew in 1984. This effectively closed any future likelihood of ICL becoming IBM-compatible.

On 7 October 1981, Wilmot gave one of his frequent press conferences to announce the Fujitsu collaboration, which was to extend over a term of twelve to fifteen years, ensuring life for the VME mainframes until well into the 1990s.[11] The Press and City reactions were both highly favourable. The ICL–Fujitsu agreement was perceived as an exceptionally innovative solution to ICL's mainframe challenge, and has since come to be regarded as a classic example of technology transfer in the 1980s.[12]

NPL: the Networked Product Line

The Networked Product Line was ICL's strategy both to address the technical deficiencies of its product line, and to seize a new marketing opportunity in office systems. The NPL concept is encapsulated in Fig. 16.1, which was first used for publicity purposes in autumn 1981. At this time only a few of the products illustrated had become a reality. An entry into the office-systems market had, of course, been a key feature of ICL's product strategy since the late 1970s, but it had been overshadowed by mainframes. Wilmot's essential contribution was to shift resources away from mainframes and towards distributed systems based on small and micro-computers.

The first product announcements were made in the second half of 1981 (Table 16.2). In June, System Ten was relaunched as System 25, and provided with networking capabilities so that it could be linked to either ICL or IBM mainframes. In September, the small 7500/1500 computers were relaunched as a fully networked 'Distributed Resource System', DRS 20. Both System 25 and DRS 20 were developments that had been initiated during the 1979-80 period, although Wilmot increased their resources and priorities. System 25 and the DRS line were to become major new earners for ICL during the 1980s.

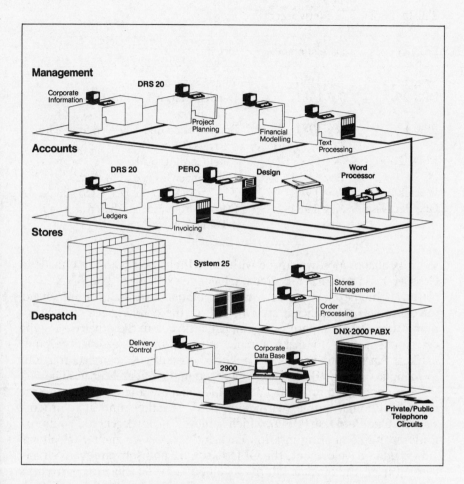

Fig. 16.1   The Networked Product Line, October 1981

Although Wilmot's mainframe rationalization had effectively doubled the resources available for the NPL, it was still necessary both for reasons of development cost and of lead-times to make collaborative or licensing deals to fill out the product range. The first of these collaborations, announced in September 1981, was with the Three Rivers Computer Corporation, an American manufacturer of scientific/engineering work-stations. This agreement gave ICL the manufacturing and marketing rights (excluding the United States and Japan) to the PERQ work-station, which at the time was far in advance of anything being made in Britain. A

Table 16.2   ICL Networked Product Line

Product	Date announced	Origin
System 25	Jun 1981	Singer System Ten
DRS 20	Sep 1981	Derived from ICL 7500/1500 small computers
PERQ	Sep 1981	Bought/made under licence from Three Rivers Computer Corp., USA
DNX-2000	Oct 1981	Mitel Corp., Canada
PC	Apr 1982	Made under licence from Rair, UK
Wordskil	Apr 1982	ICL 7500/1500, Logica VTS, and Nexos
One-Per-Desk	Nov 1984	Derived from Sinclair (hardware) and Psion (software)

second collaboration was made with the Mitel Corporation of Canada in October 1981 to market its digital telephone exchanges. The DNX 2000 private branch-exchange was a major component in the NPL infrastructure, and was a significant step for ICL in the convergence of telecommunications and computing. Again, ICL lacked both the expertise and the development time to make a rapid entry into the personal-computer market. An agreement was made with the small UK manufacturer Rair to manufacture its 'Black Box' microcomputer under licence. The ICL PC was announced in April 1982, which made it a late entrant into the market, although only a year behind IBM. Another innovative product was the One-Per-Desk (OPD), which achieved a convergence of communications and computing in a low-cost, full-function computer/telephone. To expedite development, the OPD hardware and software were largely derived from the Sinclair QL microcomputer (which in turn derived its software from the British software house Psion).

To achieve the networking of the entire ICL product range called for further internal development and external collaboration. The software resources released by the cancellation of VME/K in September 1981 were immediately put to work on the accelerated development of IPA, the Information Processing Architecture for VME mainframes. A key aspect of ICL's networking strategy was to help establish and implement international 'open networking standards' through the OSI standards organization with other, mainly European, manufacturers. This was in sharp distinction to the American manufacturers—such as IBM, DEC, and Wang—who all had proprietary network architectures, designed in part to lock-in existing customers. By conforming to international standards, ICL would be able to have its products and terminals 'surrounding enemy machines',[13] and would also be able to use the products of other manufacturers to fill the gaps in its own product range. Writing in the late 1980s, the development of OSI IT standards, in which ICL has been a major force, seems to have been one of the most important developments of the decade.[14] The OSI standards will enable European suppliers to compete with the American and Japanese giants, not by physical concentration of the kind that led to Unidata, but by a loose and informal federation. Individual members of the federation will be able to gain economies of scale by achieving high volumes on a limited number of products which, by adhering to OSI standards, they will be able to integrate with the products of other suppliers.

The creation of new products was a major part of the NPL strategy, but not the whole of it. The NPL was a product-plus-marketing response to the increasingly commodity-like IT market of the early 1980s. On their own, new products would not be sufficient to differentiate ICL from other manufacturers. A key component of the NPL strategy was therefore to sell complete networked systems, rather than specific items of hardware. The two key ways of achieving this were to sell into generic EDP markets, and to focus on specific industries. The two key generic EDP markets of the early 1980s were 'office automation' and 'decision support'. To enter the office-automation market, a major need was for specialized word-processing software and workstations—these were both acquired through a collaboration with Logica, and by acquiring the Nexos office-automation company. Decision support—the use of computers to facilitate management decisions—was a smaller, though highly fashionable, opportunity. The CAFS search engine was a particularly potent component for decision-support systems, and it was relaunched as the CAFS-ISP in late 1982, and fitted as standard on VME mainframes. Industry specialization was, of course, a long-standing marketing strategy for ICL, dating from the mid-1960s; but under Peter Bonfield new strategies and structures evolved to reinforce the concept.

The reshaping of ICL

While ICL's product and marketing strategies were evolving, the structure and culture of the company were redirected, and many of the existing line directors left or took early retirement. The organizational structure changed almost constantly to keep pace with the evolving technical and marketing strategies. The new structures owed a good deal to Wilmot's and Bonfield's backgrounds at Texas Instruments. The organization they took over in 1981 was essentially the functional structure established by Cross in the early 1970s. Although Cross had achieved a measure of decentralization, moving away from a centralized functional structure was always difficult for ICL, since it had been essentially a one-product company. Under the new management team, over a three-year period ICL's organization evolved into a more matrix-like structure. The first spate of reorganization occurred in July 1981, when the old Product Development Group was broken up into three separate divisions for mainframes, distributed systems, and networks. The purpose of this reorganization was to give small systems and networks their proper emphasis in the Networked Product Line, instead of being overshadowed by mainframes. To co-ordinate product and technical strategy across the separate divisions, a staff organization known as the Technical Directorate was created. During the next two to three years, the ICL organization saw many more changes. New development divisions were created, and others folded in response to the developing strategies.

The most radical change to ICL's marketing organization occurred with the formation of business centres. A business centre was a cross-divisional organization, rapidly created to exploit a specific business opportunity. The business centre would create a product and marketing strategy for the business opportunity, and would act as a broker between the development and manufacturing divisions and the sales division. The first business centre, for retail, was created in June 1983, and others for major sectors were quickly established—manufacturing, public administration, financial systems, etc. Further business centres were set up for generic applications, such as decision-support and knowledge engineering. The effect of these changes was to make ICL a much more reactive company.[15]

At least as important as the organizational changes in ICL were the cultural changes, and the image that ICL projected to the outside world. As in the Cross period of the early 1970s, there was culture-shock, as well as culture-change. The shock came from the youth of the new management team, the speed of events, and the decisiveness with which the workforce was reduced by one-third. And not everyone was comfortable with Wilmot's American-style slogans—'one plus one equals three synergy', etc. More seriously, however, Wilmot's collaborative agreements with other companies were seen as masterly, both outside and inside the company. It cannot be said that all of the collaborations were successful—for example the Atlas 10 and the PC were failures; but it was always realized that not all of Wilmot's geese would turn out to be swans. The collaborations achieved a major cultural change, by turning ICL from an inward-looking company to an outward-looking one. In February 1983 ICL initiated a major in-house campaign 'The ICL Way', with the aim 'of a commitment to change and evolvement of the new ICL culture'. The campaign was backed up with the machinery of quality circles, and awards for excellence. The same month, ICL embarked upon a £2 million advertising campaign devised by J. Walter Thompson to restore its public image, and to promote itself as 'a total systems supplier' through its Networked Product Line, with the slogan 'We should be talking to each other'. The campaign was memorable and expensive, and marked a turning point for ICL's renaissance in the market place.

Simultaneously with the revitalization of ICL's products, marketing strategies, and corporate spirit, Laidlaw and Biggam steadily achieved its financial rehabilitation. The 1981 results published in December 1981 confirmed the £50 million loss that the City had been expecting; but on the strength of the rationalization measures set in train, the successful autumn preference-share issue, and the signing of the Fujitsu agreement, the share price rose to 45p (it had been 22p at its low point). Laidlaw was now able to proceed with a one-for-one rights issue at 25p a share in order to further reduce borrowings. The shares were eagerly taken up and, as the share price continued to rise through 1982 to the 70-80p level, they turned out to be a bargain. The 1982 results, published the following year, showed that ICL had at last moved into profit, a modest £24 million. At this point ICL's survival period was over, and the return to profit had begun. It was now possible to make a second rights issue to reduce borrowing still further. The 1983 results showed that ICL had now made a complete recovery: gearing had been reduced to 27 per cent, and revenues and profits were fully restored to the levels of 1979-80.[16]

On 1 April 1984, Laidlaw—who had become Sir Christophor Laidlaw in the 1982 Birthday Honours—retired as chairman of ICL, having served three years instead of the two originally planned. He was immediately succeeded by Sir Michael Edwardes, the former chairman and chief executive of British Leyland.

Convergence: STC ICL

Edwardes had been in office just a little under four months when on 26 July 1984, entirely out of the blue, a take-over bid was received from Sir Kenneth Corfield, the chairman and chief executive of STC.* Corfield's

---

* STC—Standard Telephones and Cables—was formed in 1883 as the British subsidiary of Western Electric. Over the years it had operated increasingly independently of its American parent, and at the time of the ICL bid it was only 35 per cent US-owned—by ITT. Its principal businesses were in telecommunications (especially telephone exchanges and submarine cables), electronic components, and defence systems. It had a turnover of about £1 billion and about 30 000 employees, which made it 40-50 per cent larger than ICL. A company history of STC, *Power of Speech*, was published in 1983.[17]

rationale for the take-over bid was the coming convergence of telecommunications and computers. This was exactly the logic that had lain behind Plessey's attempted takeover bid of ICT in 1967; but while in 1967 the convergence arguments had seemed less than convincing, in 1984 they were much stronger, and had been for some years. Indeed, with its agreement with Mitel, ICL was already well down the convergence road. Moreover, during his period as chairman, Laidlaw had initiated talks with a number of telecommunications companies to try to achieve both a long-term technological convergence and the benefits of greater scale through a merger.[18] Consequently, although the STC bid came as a surprise, it was not altogether unwelcome, and meshed well with the long-term direction of the information business.

When STC made its bid, it had already built up a 9.8 per cent stake in ICL, at a cost of £34 million. The STC offer valued ICL's shares at 87p a share, or a 77p cash alternative. (The shares had stood at 61p on the last trading day before the STC bid.) This was, of course, just the opening bid, and Edwardes immediately released a statement recommending that shareholders take no action, as the STC offer was 'totally inadequate'. After negotiation between Edwardes and Corfield, and their merchant bankers, a revised offer valuing ICL's shares at 95p was made, with a cash alternative of 90p. In a message to shareholders on 16 August 1984, ICL recommended acceptance of the offer, and gave a detailed rationale:

The technology of computers and telecommunications is converging rapidly. Many of the components, manufacturing techniques, research and development programmes and human skills are now shared by both technologies. At the same time, customers are seeking integrated networks of computers and telecommunications equipment.

The merger will combine the strengths of ICL in computer systems and software and of STC in network and transmission systems, thus providing an exciting opportunity to create a group capable of offering a broad range of information technology products and services, including integrated voice and data communication systems.

The combination of STC and ICL will create a strong British group with the resources to meet the challenge of international competition and strongly placed to take advantage of many growth opportunities in the converging computer and telecommunications markets.[19]

During the next three weeks, three important hurdles had to be cleared. First, the American company ITT reduced its shareholding in STC to 24 per cent, so that the new STC Group would have an amount of British sovereignty acceptable to the British Government. Second, Fujitsu—which had the right to terminate the collaboration with ICL if ICL was taken over—agreed to continue its partnership with the STC Group.

Third, the Secretary of State for Trade and Industry agreed not to refer the bid to the Monopolies and Mergers Commission.[20]

On Monday 10 September 1984, STC had acquired 81.4 per cent of ICL ordinary shares, and the take-over was declared unconditional. On 30 September, Edwardes and all the non-executive directors resigned from the board, and were replaced by executive directors for what was now to be the operating board of a wholly-owned subsidiary of the STC Group. Wilmot became chairman, and Peter Bonfield managing director. Edwardes resigned, having been in office just six months, making his chairmanship one of the briefest in the history of the company.

On 15 April 1985, the name of the company was changed to STC International Computers Limited. Before any real progress towards integration had been made, however, STC was itself caught up in a financial crisis. Like ICL's difficulties of 1981, the problems were essentially managerial, and were caused by the company's growing too fast; the remedies were also the same: a change of management, and a recovery based on new product strategies and rationalization. On 2 August 1985, Corfield was forced to resign, and a new chairman, Lord Keith, was appointed. Keith, a merchant banker and industrialist, had been a non-executive director of STC since 1977. Two months later Arthur Walsh, formerly managing director of Marconi, was appointed chief executive of the STC Group. At the end of 1985 Peter Bonfield was appointed chairman and managing director of ICL, following the resignation of Wilmot, and he was subsequently also made deputy chief executive of the STC Group. STC's recovery was very rapid, and within eighteen months profit levels were fully restored to the levels of 1984. No small part in the recovery was played by ICL, which has contributed approximately 60 per cent to the turnover and profits since it joined the STC Group (Table 16.3). Today the STC Group is Britain's second largest electronics group, specializing in communications and information systems.

Table 16.3 STC-ICL turnover and profits, 1985-88

£ millions	1985	1986	1987	1988
STC-ICL				
Turnover	1035.8	1171.2	1299.0	1362.9
Operating profit	71.1	89.1	109.9	128.8
STC Group				
Turnover	1997.2	1933.4	2066.6	2356.8
Profit (loss)	(11.4)	134.2	188.0	230.0

Source STC Group Annual Reports, 1985-88.

This is as far as the history of ICL can reasonably be taken; and no doubt a decade's hindsight will provide a clearer view of the 1980s. In the final chapter of this book an attempt it made to trace some more general patterns from the evolution of ICL in the information business.

17

Summing up

ICL and the evolving information business

The concept of an 'information business' is a relatively new one. Thus, if we consider the period prior to the Second World War, BTM and Powers-Samas, the forebears of ICL, were considered to be members of the 'office-appliance trade': they were viewed as manufacturers of office machines, and that is certainly how they saw themselves. With the merger of the punched-card companies to form ICT in 1959, ICT and its competitors were seen by industrial commentators as being in the 'computer business' —it was only within the companies themselves that the broader vision of information systems was beginning to emerge. By the 1970s, however, ICL and the other mainstream computer companies were clearly seen as being in the information business: the computer was now regarded as a means to an end, and not an end in itself.

During the 1980s the structure of the information business has become much more clearly understood. An appreciation of this structure gives a broader view of the information business, and helps to reveal the inter-relationship of many apparently disparate activities. One way of viewing this structure is shown in the information-business 'maps' of Fig. 17.1.* Information-business maps of this kind have been used within the IT industry as an aid to strategic thinking, and they help to get a perspective both of the development of the industry and its present structure. Although the maps are an analytical tool of the 1980s, they are a useful aid for visualizing long-term trends in the information business. The three maps shown in Fig. 17.1 can be regarded as three snapshots of ICL and its ancestor companies, taken at three points in time: the 1930s, the 1960s, and the 1980s.

The axes of the information business map are Products/Services in the vertical direction, and Channel/Content in the horizontal direction. The Product/Services axis shows pure products at one extreme, and pure services at the other. The particular choice of this axis is useful because it enables us to plot 'system activities', which are part product and part service. This distinction also mirrors the economist's traditional view of

---

* The information-business maps given here are based on a scheme published by J.F. McLaughlin and A.E. Birini of the Center for Information Policy Research, Harvard University.[1] The maps have been modified to emphasize ICL's specific businesses, and for British terminology.

vertical integration within the firm. The horizontal axis, Channel/Content, enables us to distinguish between companies that provide products for information-handling, and those that produce information *per se*. The position along the Channel/Content axis gives a measure of the informational content of a particular activity. The four corners of the map, in

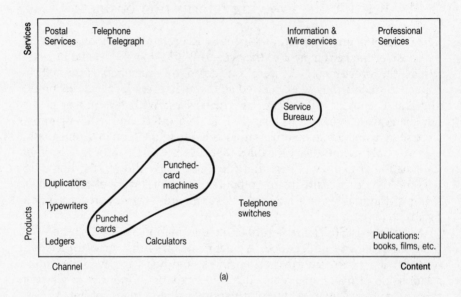

(a)

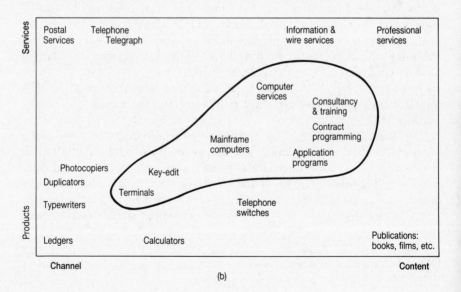

(b)

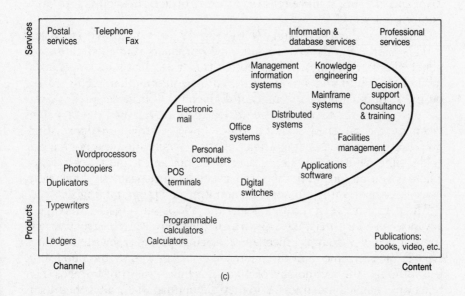

Fig. 17.1 Evolution of the information business
(a) The 1930s: punched-card business (b) The 1960s: computer business
(c) The 1980s: information-systems business

effect, define the limits of the information business. Thus in the bottom
left we have artefacts such as accounting ledgers and dumb office-
machines: these are products devoid of an informational or service
content. In the top left, we have postal and telephone services: these are
pure services with no physical or informational content. In the bottom
right we have publications such as magazines, books, and films: these are
pure information products (the physical medium being irrelevant).
Finally, in the top right-hand corner we have professional services, such
as writing, accounting, financial services, government and corporate
planning, scientific research, and so on. These represent the highest
evolution of the provision of information-plus-service.

If we were to construct an information-business map for the nineteenth
century, we would find that it was populous at the four corners, but
relatively sparse in the central region. The sparseness of this central region
highlights the fact that there were very few information technologies that
could act as an interface between the provider of a professional service and
the crude office technologies of the day. This interfacing was of course
achieved not by machines, but by a huge clerical labour force. Information
systems have evolved to fill the central void of the information-business

map, and in doing so have released an army of clerical labourers for more fulfilling roles.

Turning to the 1920s and 1930s (Fig. 17.1a) we see that BTM and Powers-Samas were then providing two products: punched cards and punched-card machines. Thus both firms were integrated operations located well into the product-oriented, low-information sector of the business. In retrospect, a significant development of the early 1930s was the opening of the first service bureaux; these represented the first steps taken by the punched-card companies towards providing information-processing services. The importance of this diversification was not realized at the time, and the service bureaux were not an integrated part of the whole operation, nor were they seen as being a core business. They were, however, important precursors of computing and programming services.

The period between the 1930s and the 1960s saw great technological advances in office machines, by which their physical construction was transformed. For example, mechanical calculators and typewriters became electric or electronic, and the photocopier began to oust the duplicator. But although the technology of office machines was transformed, their functions changed much less, and they did not materially alter their locus on the information-business map. A far more important development was the emergence of the mainframe computer, which came to occupy the largely empty centre of the information business map (Fig. 17.1b). For some industries, the advent of the computer was seen as an important and totally new phenomenon—this was true, for example, of the electronics manufacturers that entered the booming computer industry in the 1950s and 1960s. But to the office-machine companies, the computer was seen as a natural development of the older office-machine technologies. For example, the punched-card machine companies saw the computer as evolutionary: the tabulator was seen to give way to the electronic punched-card calculator, and this in turn gave way to the computer. In fact, both of these views were valid, and this accounts for much of the disparity between the strategic approaches of the traditional office-machine firms and the electronics firms towards the computer.

During the 1960s, ICT—and later ICL—became much more than just office-equipment manufacturers. For example, punched cards were phased out in favour of more intelligent key-edit equipment and terminals. Service bureaux, instead of being an isolated operation, blossomed into computer services, and eventually into a subsidiary company BARIC. Consultancy and training services became an integrated part of the operation, and a significant earner of revenues. The 'systems investigation department' of the punched-card period likewise evolved to become contract-programming services and applications-software development. In the early 1970s, with the formation of Dataskil, programming began to make an important contribution to total revenues. These events signified a change of emphasis away from office machines and towards the information-systems business: this is indicated by the much larger 'footprint' of ICL on the information-business map, and its migration towards the top right.

The 1970s and 1980s saw a far more rapid evolution of information systems than had been seen in the previous half-century. As Fig. 17.1c reveals, dumb office products were replaced by much more intelligent and information-rich devices: for example, the typewriter gave way to the word-processor; electronic calculators became much more functional; and the ledger gave way to computerized accounting and spreadsheets. Indeed, the entire administration of the modern office was altered out of all recognition, and people began to talk of office systems rather than office machines. These trends in large part came about because of the semiconductor revolution, which enabled the computer to vary in size and price from very small to very large, so occupying a far larger area of the information-business map.

There were also dramatic advances in communications technologies. In information transmission, telephone exchanges became digital and electronic, and telegraph and telex gave way to fax and electronic mail. In information services, ticker-tape and wire services gave way to the interactive database. A particularly important development was the trend towards the full-scale networking of information systems, which was the result of the convergence of computing and communications technologies. This convergence was widely forecast in the late 1960s, but because of a short-lived trend towards decentralized computing, the convergence did not really occur until the late 1970s. At that time there was a rash of strategic alliances and mergers between computer and communications firms, and with conglomerates that were not yet in the information business but were seeking to diversify into it. Although ICL shared this vision of convergence, the British recession of the early 1980s prevented a response at that time. Hence, when the new management team of Wilmot, Laidlaw, and Bonfield was established in ICL, one of its first actions was to establish an agreement with Mitel to use its digital switch, and to launch the Networked Product Line in October 1981. During 1982–84, there were further efforts to establish a strategic alliance with a firm in the communications business. This was finally achieved by the incorporation of ICL into the STC Group in September 1984.

As well as a broadening of the technological base of computers and communications, the 1970s and 1980s also saw a change in all the main-stream computer companies from being primarily suppliers of hardware and software to becoming true system-builders. ICL responded to this wider information-systems market by establishing several new products and services in the 1980s, such as knowledge engineering, financial services, retail systems, management-information systems, and decision-support systems. These new businesses are very close to the spirit of professional services. It is this important strategic shift that distinguishes the true information-systems firms from those which are merely supplying 'boxes', whether they be personal computers or plug-compatible mainframes. Yet, paradoxically, in the commodity-like computer market of the 1980s and 1990s, in which the user has become less and less concerned with the physical realization of information-systems products, success in the business will depend crucially on access to the best emerging technologies. With the possible exception of the one biggest company, none of the mainstream information-systems companies can afford to develop all of these technologies. Without any doubt, one of the key achievements of the new ICL management team was to establish a licensing agreement with Fujitsu, which has given the company long-term access to the very best semiconductor technologies. And now, within the STC Group, ICL also has access to major evolving communications technologies.

These, then have been some of the trends of the last half-century of the information business. From today's perspective, the most noticeable long-term trend has been the move away from the manufacture of pure hardware, towards value-added information systems and professional services. Competitive computer and communications products are still important; but they are not enough for long-term survival. It is quite certain that in the coming years Japanese competition and open standards will have the effect of lowering profit margins, while R&D costs will continue to escalate. To prosper in the next decade, a world-class information-systems company needs to have a much broader vision than in the past. Today, ICL sees itself not as being primarily a hardware manufacturer, but as a creator and distributor of complex information-systems and professional services. This is an appropriate stance for the 1990s.

Notes

N.B.: Books, articles, interviews, and documents which are referred to repeatedly in the following notes are cited with the full available details (for a book, for example, the author, title, publisher, and place and date of publication) at their first citation in the notes for *each chapter*. In later notes, the citation includes only the author's or interviewed person's name, or a short title in the case of anonymous items.

A note on sources

The principal sources used in writing the history of ICL can be classified as follows: closed ICL sources, open ICL sources, interviews, non-ICL sources, and government reports.

The closed ICL sources are those located in the ICL Archives, Putney, London. For reasons of commercial sensitivity, as well as practical access, the ICL Archives are not normally open to researchers. There are upwards of 1000 shelf-feet of material, of which about one-third was of direct value in writing this history. Documents include the board minutes and papers of ICL and its ancestor companies (The Tabulator Ltd, BTM, Acc and Tab, Powers Accounting Machines, Powers-Samas, ICT, English Electric Computers, IC (Holdings), ICL, and ICL plc). In addition, there are the papers and minutes of operating, finance, and research committees, statutory annual and interim reports, internal planning reports, reports produced by consultants for ICL, and reports prepared by ICL for the government. A particularly rich source of information was David Marwood's Informal Notes, made in his capacity as company secretary over a period of twenty years; these notes consist largely of reports of meetings with government officials, and reports of special board meetings concerning mergers, financial crises, or management changes, that were too sensitive for distribution with the normal board papers. The ICL Archives are the principal source on which this history is based, and, although the Archives are not generally open to scholars, I have given many references to them in the Notes below, on the grounds that most scholars prefer inclusion to omission.

The open ICL sources are those in the ICL Historical Collection, Stevenage, Hertfordshire. The manager, Gordon Collinson, actively encourages scholars to use the collection. The ICL Historical Collection is of a similar size to the Putney archives, and consists mainly of company publications. The material includes brochures and other publicity material, operating and maintenance manuals for equipment, and company magazines. The collection houses the only known complete runs of the following magazines: *The Tabulator* (mid-1930s to 1958), *Tabacus* (1946–58), *Powers-Samas Magazine* (1935–58), *Powers-Samas Gazette*

(1949–58), *ICT House Magazine* (1959–68), *ICT Data Processing Journal* (1959–67), *Dataline* (1967–68), and *ICL News* (1968–present). The collection also contains a small number of unpublished research and marketing reports.

Because the internal documentation for the history of ICL is substantial and of high quality, research has been document-led, and interviews have been used mainly to obtain evidence that does not appear in the written record, to confirm hypotheses, and to resolve ambiguities. Interviews have mainly been conducted with former chief executives, senior managers, and research personnel. The people interviewed included:

W.R. Atkinson (ex-DTI), A.G. Bagshaw, B. Bassett, R.L. Bird, P.L. Bonfield, J. Bull, G.R. Cross, P.V. Ellis, M.L.N. Forrest, C. Gardner (ex-LFE), T.D. Griffin, A.C.D. Haley, N.F. Hedges, T.C. Hudson, A.L.C. Humphreys, P.M. Hunt, L. Knight, L. Lightstone, C.C.F. Laidlaw, K.H. Macdonald, N. Marshall (ex-RCA), A.T. Maxwell, E.C.H. Organ, V.V. Pasquali, J.M.M. Pinkerton, B.C. Warboys, C.M. Wilson.

In most cases, where practical, interviews were tape-recorded. These interviews are not immediately available to researchers, but some of them will be transcribed and made available through the Charles Babbage Institute (University of Minnesota) and the National Archive for the History of Computing (University of Manchester).

The most important sources on the history of the British information technology industry, outside ICL, are the various trade journals: *International Export Review* (1921–39), *Office Equipment Industry* (1940–60), and *Computer Weekly* (1965–present); all of these are located in the Newspaper Library, Colindale, London. Other background information, especially statistical data, appears in *Datamation* and *Computer Survey*.

There are now quite a number of economic and business histories of the computer industry. The most useful were: G.W. Brock, *The U.S. Computer Industry: A Study of Market Power* (Ballinger, Cambridge, MA, 1975); F.M. Fisher *et al.*, *IBM and the U.S. Data Processing Industry* (Praeger, New York, 1983); and K. Flamm, *Creating the Computer* (Brookings Institution, Washington DC, 1988). Of the many histories of IBM, the two most authoritative are: S. Englebourg, *International Business Machines: A Business History* (Arno Press, New York, 1976; originally published as a Harvard University Ph.D. thesis, 1954), and J. Connolly, *A History of Computing in Europe* (IBM World Trade Corp., New York, 1967). Less reliable historically, but excellent in terms of the analysis of strategic issues is: R. Sobel, *IBM: Colossus in Transition* (Times Books, New York, 1981). A valuable book on technical issues affecting IBM is C. Bashe *et al.*, *IBM's Early Computers* (MIT Press, Cambridge MA, 1985). Like all the current generation of business historians, I acknowledge my debt to A.D. Chandler's seminal works: *Strategy and Structure* (MIT Press, Cambridge MA, 1962), and *The Visible Hand* (MIT Press, Cambridge MA, 1971).

I have consulted the following sources of unpublished material: the Hollerith Papers (Library of Congress), the NRDC Papers (IEE, London), The Public Record Office (Kew, London), the Unisys Archives (Hagley Museum and Library, Wilmington, Delaware), the National Archive for the History of Computing, and the Charles Babbage Institute Archives. These all provided some useful nuggets of information, but none approached the ICL Archives and ICL Historical Collection in importance.

Finally, without any question the most important open sources on the British computer industry in the late 1960s and early 1970s are the reports of the Parliamentary Select Committees on Science and Technology (1969–74). The complete list of reports is as follows:

[HC137] Select Committee on Science and Technology (Sub-Committee D), Session 1969–70, *Vol. 1: Minutes of Evidence*, HMSO, London, 1970.

[HC272] Select Committee on Science and Technology (Sub-Committee D), Session 1969–70, *Vol. 2: Appendices*, HMSO, London, 1970.

[HC621-I] Select Committee on Science and Technology (Sub-Committee A), Session 1970–71, *The Prospects for the United Kingdom Computer Industry in the 1970's, Vol. 1: Report*, HMSO, London, 1971.

[HC621-II] Select Committee on Science and Technology (Sub-Committee A), Session 1970–71, *The Prospects for the United Kingdom Computer Industry in the 1970's, Vol. 2: Minutes of Evidence*, HMSO, London, 1971.

[HC621-III] Select Committee on Science and Technology (Sub-Committee A), Session 1970–71, *The Prospects for the United Kingdom Computer Industry in the 1970's, Vol. 3: Appendices*, HMSO, London, 1971.

[HC473] Select Committee on Science and Technology (Sub-Committee A), Session 1970–71, *The Prospects for the United Kingdom Computer Industry in the 1970's: Reply by the Department of Trade and Industry [and] Minutes of Evidence*, HMSO, London, 1972.

[HC309] Select Committee on Science and Technology (Sub-Committee A), Session 1972–73, *Second Report on the U.K. Computer Industry (First Part)*, HMSO, London, 1973.

[HC97-I] Select Committee on Science and Technology (Sub-Committee A), Session 1972–73, *Second Report on the U.K. Computer Industry (First Part): Minutes of Evidence [and] Appendices*, HMSO, London, 1973.

[HC199] Select Committee on Science and Technology (U.K. Computer Industry Sub-Committee), Session 1974, *Minutes of Evidence*, HMSO, London, 1974.

Notes to Chapter 1

1 T.C. Martin, 'Counting a Nation by Electricity', *Electrical Engineer*, 12, 1891, pp. 521–30; p. 522.

2 Although catalogues of typewriters and calculating machines exist, and there were contemporary textbooks on office mechanization, almost nothing has been written on the economic history of office machinery. Some excellent recent work has been published on the typewriter as a social phenomenon and its impact on women's work, but this belongs to a different genre.

3 These statistics are cited in A.D. Chandler, *The Visible Hand*, MIT Press, Cambridge MA, 1971, p. 546, n. 41.

4 *A History of the Sperry Rand Corporation*, Recording and Statistical Company Division of Sperry Rand Corporation, USA, September 1964, p. 5.

5 J.W. Oliver, *A History of American Technology*, Ronald Press, New York, 1956, pp. 440-2. 'A Condensed History of the Writing Machine', *Typewriter Topics, the International Business Equipment Magazine*, October 1923, reprinted in D.R. Post, *Collector's Guide to Antique Typewriters*, Post-Era Books, Arcadia CA, 1981. G. Tilghman Richards, *The History and Development of Typewriters*, Science Museum/HMSO, London, 1964.

6 The advertisement is reproduced in D.R. Post, op. cit., p. 80.

7 M.R. Williams, *A History of Computing Technology*, Prentice-Hall, Englewood Cliffs NJ, 1985, chapter 3. J.A.V. Turck, *Origin of Modern Calculating Machines*, Western Society of Engineers, Chicago, 1921.

8 A.D. Chandler, op. cit., p. 565, n. 51. William Seward Burroughs (1855-1898), *Dictionary of American Biography*.

9 This data and the slogan appear in a 1908 Burroughs advertisement reproduced in J.A.V. Turck, op. cit., p. 142.

10 R.W. Barnard, *A Century of Service: The Story of the Prudential, 1848-1948*, London, 1949, p. 82.

11 As quoted in L. Hannah, *The Rise of the Corporate Economy*, Methuen, London, 1983, p. 86.

12 J.W. Oliver, op. cit., p. 453. The superiority of the American manufacturing goes back to well before the arrival of office machinery, and first became a burning issue at the time of the Great Exhibition in 1851 (see D.L. Burn, 'The Genesis of American Engineering Competition, 1850-1870', *Economic History*, **2**, 1931, pp. 292-311.

13 H.C. Livesay and P.G. Porter, 'Vertical Integration in American Manufacturing, 1899-1948', *Journal of Economic History*, **29**, 1969, pp. 494-500.

14 A.D. Chandler, op. cit., p. 313.

15 *A History of the Sperry Rand Corporation*, p. 25.

16 W.R. Merriman, 'The Evolution of Modern Census Taking', *Century Magazine*, April 1903, pp. 831-42. L.E. Truesdell, *The Development of Punched Card Tabulation in the Bureau of the Census 1890-1940*, GPO, Washington DC, 1965.

17 G. Austrian, *Herman Hollerith: Forgotten Giant of Data Processing*, Columbia University Press, New York, 1982.

18 T.C. Martin, op. cit.

19 'Data Processing—1890 Style', *Datamation*, July 1966, p. 44.

20 H. Hollerith, 'The Electrical Tabulating Machine', *Journal of the Royal Statistical Society*, **57**, 1894, pp. 678-82.

21 G. Austrian, op. cit. L.E. Truesdell, op. cit.

22 Tables of early revenue figures may be found in the business correspondence in the Hollerith Papers.

23 Robert Percival Porter (1852-1917), *Dictionary of American Biography*. 'Death of Mr. R.P. Porter', *The Times*, 1 March 1917, p. 10d.

24 C.A. Everard Greene, *The Beginnings*, British Tabulating Machine Company, London, c.1959 (ICL Historical Collection).

25 Sir Ralegh Buller Phillpotts (1871-1950), *Who Was Who*. L.S. Amery, 'Obituary: Sir Ralegh Buller Phillpotts', *The Times*, 7 October 1950, p. 8.

26 G. Austrian, op. cit., p. 213.
27 'Passing of a Punched-Card Pioneer' [obituary of C.A. Everard Greene], *ICT House Magazine*, November 1963, p. 1.
28 C.A. Everard Greene, op. cit., p. 3.
29 The Tabulator Board Minutes, 28 July 1904.
30 C.A. Everard Greene, op. cit., p. 17. The Tabulator Share Register (ICL Archives).
31 C.A. Everard Greene, op. cit., p. 17.
32 The Tabulator Board Minutes, 5 April 1906.
33 As quoted in G. Austrian, op. cit., p. 178.
34 Ibid., p. 243.
35 'Machine Records', *c*.1940, p. 3/14 (ICL Historical Collection). This loose-leaf book is a catalogue of almost every machine ever rented or sold by BTM.
36 G. Austrian, op. cit., p. 244.

Notes to Chapter 2

1 R.B. Phillpotts, letter to T.J. Watson, 28 August 1918 (ICL Archives).
2 L. Hannah, *The Rise of the Corporate Economy*, Methuen, London, 1983.
3 BTM Annual Report, 1918.
4 C.A. Everard Greene, *The Beginnings*, British Tabulating Machine Company, London, *c*.1959, p. 12 (ICL Historical Collection).
5 C.A. Everard Greene, letter to R. Bailey, 15 November 1910 (Public Record Office, STAT 12 10/9).
6 R. Bailey, memorandum, 29 November 1910 (Public Record Office, STAT 12 10/9).
7 'The Tabulator', *The Engineer*, 1911, pp. 96-7, 146-8, 196-7, 279-80.
8 BTM Annual Report, 1913.
9 S. Englebourg, *International Business Machines: A Business History*, Arno Press, New York, 1976, p. 56.
10 S.G. Koon, 'Hollerith Tabulating Machinery in the Business Office', *Machinery*, **20**, 1913, pp. 25-6; p. 25.
11 J. Connolly, *A History of Computing in Europe*, IBM World Trade Corp., New York, 1967.
12 G. Austrian, *Herman Hollerith: Forgotten Giant of Data Processing*, Columbia University Press, New York, 1982.
13 S. Englebourg, op. cit., p. 59.
14 C.R. Flint, *Memories of an Active Life*, Putnam, New York, 1925.
15 G. Smith, letter to BTM, 20 January 1913 (ICL Archives).
16 R.B. Phillpotts, letter to TMC, 8 February 1913 (ICL Archives).
17 'Subject: James Powers', National Personnel Records Center, U.S.A., 11 August 1969 (ICL Historical Collection).
18 'Handling the Census Returns for the Whole United States', *American Machinist*, 5 May 1910, pp. 809-11. L.E. Truesdell, *The Development of Punched Card Tabulation in the Bureau of the Census 1890-1940*, GPO, Washington DC, 1965.
19 By far the best contemporary account of the Powers machines is W. Freeman, 'Improvements and Advantages Offered by Powers . . . Machines', *National*

Electric Light Association's 38th Convention, San Francisco, June 1915, pp. 16–33.

20 T.J. Watson, letter to H. Hollerith, 6 August 1914 (Hollerith Papers).

21 'Report on the "Powers" Accounting and Tabulating Machines', *c.*1914 (Public Record Office, STAT 12 25/5).

22 'British Tabulating Machine Company (Limited)', *The Times*, 11 March 1914, p. 18.

23 BTM Annual Report, 1918.

24 British Patent No. 23566, 1914.

25 C.A. Everard Greene, letter to Gershom Smith 18 June 1915; H. Hollerith, letter to S.G. Metcalf, 6 August 1915 (Hollerith Papers).

26 'Documentary Evidence BTM' (ICL Historical Collection).

27 R.B. Phillpotts, letter to T.J. Watson, 28 August 1918 (ICL Archives).

28 S.C. Downes, 'Progress of Powers Machines During the Past 17 Years', typescript précis of a lecture, 22 October 1930 (ICL Historical Collection).

29 'Accounting in the States', *The Accountant*, September 1914, p. 337.

30 'The Office Machinery Users Association', *The Accountant*, December 1918, p. 328.

31 L.R. Dicksee, *Office Machinery and Appliances* (1st edn), Gee and Co., London, 1917.

32 The figure of £20 000 appears in Acc and Tab Board Minutes, 3 June 1919.

33 R.W. Barnard, op. cit.

34 Untitled report on the Prudential Powers operation, 13 December 1923 (ICL Historical Collection).

35 British Patent No. 108942, 1916.

36 BTM Annual Report, 1919.

37 Acc and Tab Board Minutes, 13 March 1919.

Notes to Chapter 3

1 E.B.P. Jackson, 'Office Appliance Trades Association . . .', *International Export Review*, January 1927, pp. 8–9; p. 8.

2 A.J. Youngson, *The British Economy, 1920–1957*, Allen and Unwin, London, 1960, pp. 24–5. W.J. Reader, *Metal Box*, Heinemann, London, 1974, p. 137. P. Jones, 'Office Appliance Trades Association . . .', *International Export Review*, January 1926, p. 9.

3 Acc and Tab Board Minutes, 22 January 1919.

4 Almost nothing is known of Pailthorpe's background, except that he was a small-scale entrepreneur mechanical engineering manufacturer. There appear to be no obituaries.

5 A. Thomas, *Powers-Samas Accounting Machines: Thirty Years of Progress*, 1952, p. 5 (ICL Historical Collection).

6 'For Services Rendered' [profile of C. Foster], *Powers-Samas Magazine*, August 1955, pp. 13–14.

7 The film 'The Factory, Aurelia Road, Croydon' has recently been restored by the National Film Archive. 'Powers Accounting Machine Manufacturing

System', *American Machinist*, European edition, 67, 1927, pp. 171E–174E, 182E–184E.

8 Ibid., p. 172E.
9 'The Hollerith Tabulating System', *The Engineer*, January 1934, pp. 101–5 and supplement; p. 101.
10 £150 000 capitalization was generally considered the minimum for a public quotation: F.W. Paish, *Business Finance*, Pitman, London, 1953.
11 'Acquisition of tabulating machinery for the 1921 census', n.d. (Public Record Office, STAT 12 28/2).
12 BTM Annual Report, 1920.
13 B. Bassett, interview with M. Campbell-Kelly, 22 May 1985.
14 'Supply of Cards and Tabulating Machines for Use in Census Work, Scotland', n.d. (Public Record Office, STAT 12 35/20).
15 'Wales Interests Control Powers Accounting Machines', *Business Equipment*, New York, 15 April 1923, p. 1.
16 Acc and Tab Board Minutes, 3 September 1924 and 17 September 1924.
17 L.E. Brougham, transcript of interview with B. Bellringer, 19 July 1977.
18 IBM correspondence (ICL Archives).
19 C.A. Everard Greene, letter to R.B. Phillpotts, 12 January 1923 (ICL Archives).
20 L.E. Brougham, op. cit.
21 'International Business Machines', *Fortune*, January 1932, pp. 34–50; p. 39.
22 R. Sobel, *IBM: Colossus in Transition*, Times Books, New York, 1981, p. 84.
23 'Powers Accounting Machine Manufacturing System', p. 183E.
24 BTM Annual Report, 1926.
25 For a history of the OATA see: 'Mr J. Halsby', *International Export Review*, February 1927, p. 7.
26 See *International Export Review*, May 1926, p. 16.
27 L.E. Brougham, 'Report on Visit to U.S.A. October 1929', n.d. (ICL Historical Collection).
28 The ICL Historical Collection has a reference for Foster on the letterhead of 'British Calculators Limited', dated 11 September 1914.
29 E.A. Ford, letter to T.J. Watson, 9 December 1916 (Hollerith Papers).
30 C. and R. Eames, *A Computer Perspective*, Harvard University Press, Cambridge MA, 1973, p. 92.
31 The British patents for the elimination of stop and total cards are: J. Powers, No. 104703, 1916, and H. Hollerith, No. 117985, 1917. An excellent description of the BTM/IBM automatic control tabulator appears in 'A New Type of Tabulating Machine', *The Engineer*, 14 March 1924, pp. 274–6.
32 L.E. Brougham, op. cit.
33 Ibid.
34 See chapter 5 for a description of the Enigma. The Hole machine, incidentally, had a rather better specification since it printed the encrypted text, unlike the Enigma, which required manual transcription.

35 Acc and Tab Board Minutes, 30 March 1927.
36 BTM Annual Report, 1928.
37 'S.A.M.A.S.', Powers-Samas Board Papers, 9 April 1951.
38 James Henry Rand (1859-1944), *Dictionary of American Biography*.
39 'Remington Rand, Inc., New York', *International Export Review*, April 1927, p. 6.
40 'Finest for Forty Years', *Remington Rand World*, June 1948, pp. 4-5; 'Mr. Powers Went to Washington', *Sales Whys*, April 1948, pp. 10-12 (Unisys Archives).
41 Acc and Tab Board Minutes, 22 June 1927.
42 L.E. Brougham, op. cit.
43 Ibid. The 1932 Fortune article 'International Business Machines', states that IBM had 80-90 per cent of the market.

Notes to Chapter 4

1 As quoted in 'Private Exhibition of Powers-Samas Accounting Machines', *International Export Review*, May 1932, pp. 6-10.
2 A.J. Youngson, *The British Economy, 1920-1957*, Allen and Unwin, London, 1960, pp. 96-115. See also B.R. Michell and P. Deane, *Abstract of British Historical Statistics*, Cambridge University Press, 1962.
3 'Mr. H.R. Russell', *International Export Review*, April 1930, p. 1. 'Mr. Russell Resumes Activity in the United States', *International Export Review*, January 1932, p. 34.
4 L.E. Brougham, transcript of interview with B. Bellringer, 19 July 77.
5 H.R. Russell, 'General Report', 18 November 1931 (ICL Archives).
6 Only a single issue survives: Vol. 2, No. 1, May 1931 (ICL Historical Collection).
7 See ICL Historical Collection catalogue for several similar examples.
8 H.R. Russell, op. cit.
9 J. Connolly, *A History of Computing in Europe*, IBM World Trade Corp., New York, 1967, pp. 28ff.
10 See articles on David Gestetner (1854-1930) and Augustus David Klaber (1861-1915)—founder of Roneo—in D.J. Jeremy (ed.), *Dictionary of Business Biography*, Butterworths, London, 1984-86; **2**, pp. 519-24; **3**, pp. 602-4.
11 G. Nerheim and H.W. Nordvik, *IBM: Not Only Machines*, IBM A/S, Oslo, 1987.
12 'Mr. W. Desborough O.B.E.', *International Export Review*, October 1933, p. 1. 'Retirement of Mr. W. Desborough O.B.E.', *Powers-Samas Gazette*, July/August 1952. W. Desborough, *Office Machines, Appliances and Methods*, Pitman, London, 1921.
13 R. Whelan, letter to M. Campbell-Kelly, 26 February 1985.
14 *International Export Review*, *passim*.
15 'International Business Machines', *Fortune*, January 1932, pp. 34-50; p. 39.

16 S. Englebourg, *International Business Machines: A Business History*, Arno Press, New York, 1976.
17 A.J. Youngson, op. cit.
18 BTM Annual Report, 1932.
19 G.E. May (1871–1946), *Dictionary of National Biography*.
20 'Review of Trade Conditions', *International Export Review*, January 1932, p. 6.
21 *Powers-Samas Punch*, May 1931, p. 1.
22 L.C.M.S. Amery (1873–1955), *Dictionary of National Biography*.
23 BTM Annual Report, 1932.
24 'The Hollerith Tabulator', *The Engineer*, January 1934, pp. 101–5 and supplement.
25 Ibid., p. 101.
26 J. Connolly, op. cit., p. 25.
27 'The Bull Statistical Machine', *International Export Review*, October 1930, p. 50. L. Heide, 'From Invention to Production: the Development of Punched Card Machines 1918–1930 by Frederik Rosing Bull and Knut Andreas Knutsen', unpublished typescript, Odense University, January 1988.
28 J. Connolly, op. cit., p. 34.
29 R. Beulow, 'Francisco Campos', unpublished typescript, 1987.
30 Remington Rand Director's Minutes, 3 March 1931 (Unisys Archives).
31 L. Couffignal (1933) 'Calculating Machines: Their Principles and Evolution', translated in B. Randell, *The Origins of Digital Computers*, Springer Verlag, Berlin, 1982, pp. 145–54; pp. 147–8. There are other accounts of the Campos machine in the literature, for example in C.R. Curtis, *Mechanised Accountancy*, Griffin, London, 1932.
32 L.E. Brougham, 'Re. CAMPOS', 11 November 1935, Powers Development Committee Papers (ICL Archives).
33 See *Office Equipment Industry*, March 1947, p. 11, for an advertisement for the Logabax Campos machine.
34 S. Englebourg, op. cit., p. 291.
35 A. Thomas, *Powers-Samas Accounting Machines: Thirty Years of Progress*, 1952 (ICL Historical Collection).
36 S. Englebourg, op. cit., p. 336. J. Connolly, op. cit., p. 34.
37 J. Connolly, op. cit., p. 29.
38 A. Thomas, 'Major and Minor ATA', c.1930 (ICL Historical Collection).
39 'Rolling Total Machines', October 1935 (ICL Historical Collection). 'The Hollerith Tabulator', [see note 24].
40 'H.H. Keen O.B.E.', *Tabacus*, June 1952, p. 1. 'Retirement of Mr. H.H. Keen', *ICT House Magazine*, August 1959, p. 4.
41 J. Bull, interview with M. Campbell-Kelly, 10 December 1984.
42 S. Englebourg, op. cit., p. 257.
43 The Keen RTT patents are: rolling totals, No. 422135, 7 July 1933; alphabetic printing mechanism, No. 446104, 23 October 1934; statement device, No. 446521, 30 October 1934.

44 BTM Board Minutes, *passim*.
45 T.J. Watson, letter to Sir G.E. Chadwyck-Healey, 21 January 1936, BTM Board Papers.
46 Sir G.E. Chadwyck-Healey, draft letter to T.J. Watson, *c*.February 1936, BTM Board Papers.
47 J. Connolly, op. cit., p. 37.
48 A brief obituary of C.E. Hunter appeared in *International Export Review*, April 1937, p. 46.
49 'Editorial', *Powers-Samas Magazine*, March 1938, p. 1.
50 'Retirement of Mr. H.V. Stammers', *ICT House Magazine*, September 1961, p. 4. 'Obituary: C.G. Holland-Martin', *The Times*, 29 April 1983, p. 14.
51 BTM Annual Reports, *passim*.
52 Statistics cited in 'Importation of Office Machines', *Powers-Samas Magazine*, March 1939, pp. 7–8.
53 B. Bassett, interview with M. Campbell-Kelly, 22 May 85.
54 As note 52; p. 8.
55 W. Desborough, 'Import Duties into Great Britain on Punched Card Machines', 25 September 1947, Powers-Samas Deputy Chairman's Conference Papers.
56 As note 52, and 'Importation of Office Machines', *Powers-Samas Magazine*, April 1939, p. 1.

Notes to Chapter 5

1 G. Welchman, *The Hut Six Story*, Allen Lane, London, 1982, p. 140.
2 A.J. Youngson, *The British Economy, 1920–1957*, Allen and Unwin, London, 1960, p. 142.
3 The economic and administrative background to this chapter is mainly drawn from the Civil Histories of the Second World War (HMSO, London). M.M. Postan, *British War Production*, 1952. E.L. Hargreaves and M.M. Gowing, *Civil Industry and Trade*, 1952. J.D. Scott and R. Hughes, *The Administration of War Production*, 1955. W. Hornby, *Factories and Plant*, 1958. M.M. Postan, D. Hay, and J.D. Scott, *Design and Development of Weapons*, 1964.
4 BTM Board Minutes, 31 January 1939.
5 L.E. Brougham, transcript of interview with B. Bellringer, 19 July 1977, p. 10.
6 'Friends Across the Sea', *The Tabulator*, No. 52, *c*.early 1942. The ICL Historical Collection has a number of Watson's Christmas messages, on 78 rpm gramophone records.
7 T.G. and M.R. Belden, *The Lengthening Shadow: The Life of Thomas J. Watson*, Little, Brown and Co., Boston, 1962.
8 'The British Tabulating Machine Company 1907–1957', unpublished typescript, *c*.1957 (ICL Historical Collection).
9 Powers Accounting Machines Board Minutes, 8 April 1940.
10 Hargreaves and Gowing, op. cit., p. 550.

11 Ibid., p. 44.
12 Ibid., p. 540.
13 BTM Board Minutes, 14 October 1941.
14 As note 8.
15 *Powers-Samas Magazine*, January 1940, p. 1.
16 'No. 1 Statistics Unit RAOC MELF' (ICL Historical Collection).
17 BTM Board Minutes, 9 September 1941.
18 N.F. Hedges, interview with M. Campbell-Kelly, 10 September 1985.
19 Hargreaves and Gowing, op. cit., 551.
20 Ibid.
21 *Office Equipment Industry*, May 1942, p. 1.
22 Statutory Rules and Orders 1942, No. 29.
23 Hargreaves and Gowing, op. cit., p. 550.
24 Postan, op. cit., pp. 484–5.
25 Hornby, op. cit., p. 166.
26 BTM Board Minutes, 7 November 1939.
27 Powers Accounting Machines Board Minutes, 20 November 1939.
28 Postan, op. cit., p. 299.
29 Powers Accounting Machines Development Committee Minutes, 11 June 1942.
30 Powers Accounting Machines Board Minutes, 15 July 1940.
31 Postan, Hay, and Scott, op. cit., pp. 116ff.
32 Powers Accounting Machines Development Committee, 11 June 1942.
33 There appears to be no open technical literature on the Mark XIV bombsight other than the British patent: No. 16816/41, filed 12 December 1941, by P.M.S. Blackett and H.J.J. Braddick.
34 Powers Accounting Machines Development Committee, 8 July 1943.
35 [Profile of A. Thomas], *Powers-Samas Gazette*, November–December 1952, p. 1.
36 The official history is F.H. Hinsley *et al.*, *British Intelligence in the Second World War*, 3 vols, HMSO, 1979, 1981, 1983. Less authoritative but more readable accounts are as follows. F.W. Winterbotham, *The ULTRA Secret*, Weidenfeld and Nicolson, London, 1974. R. Lewin, *Ultra Goes to War: The Secret Story*, Hutchinson, London, 1978. B. Johnson, *The Secret War*, BBC, London, 1978. *After the Battle*, No. 37, London, 1982. The best technical accounts are as follows. G. Welchman, *The Hut Six Story*, Allen Lane, London, 1981. A Hodges, *Alan Turing: The Enigma*, Burnett Books, London, 1983. B. Randell, 'The Colossus', in N. Metropolis *et al.*, *A History of Computing in the Twentieth Century*, Academic Press, New York, 1980.
37 'The [Powers-Samas] Cryptograph Machine', *International Export Review*, April 1927, p. 46. 'Swedish Damm System Cryptograph', *International Export Review*, December 1929, p. 60.
38 A. Hodges, op. cit., p. 170.
39 G. Welchman, op. cit., pp. 295–309.
40 N.F. Hedges, interview with M. Campbell-Kelly, 10 September 1985. I am indebted to Mr Hedges, who was a member of the maintenance team, for some of the details that follow.

41 BTM Annual Report, 1942.
42 BTM Board Minutes, 4 February 1943.
43 D. Payne, 'My Secret Life with Ultra', *After the Battle*, **No.** 37, 1982, pp. 9–16.
44 The American bombes are described in R.I. Atha, 'Bombe! I could hardly believe it!', *Cryptologia*, 9, 1985, pp. 332–6.
45 N.F. Hedges, interview.
46 Ibid.
47 R.W. Whelan, letter to M. Campbell-Kelly, 29 March 1985.
48 Ibid.
49 A.M. Turing, G. Welchman, C.H.O'D. Alexander, and P.S. Milner-Barry, letter to Winston Churchill, 21 October 1941. As quoted in A. Hodges, op. cit., pp. 219–21.
50 Ibid.
51 'Awarded OBE for His Services' [retirement of F.V. Freeborn], *ICT House Magazine*, May 1963.
52 BTM Annual Report, 1945.
53 Powers Accounting Machines Development Committee Minutes, 15 November 1943.
54 A. Thomas, 'Powers-Samas Accounting Machines: Thirty Years of Progress', 1952 (ICL Historical Collection).
55 Powers Accounting Machines Development Committee Minutes, 24 February 1944.
56 Powers Accounting Machines Research Board Minutes, 7 December 1944.

Notes to Chapter 6

1 Lord Halsbury, 'Ten Years of Computer Development', *Computer Journal*, 1, 1959, pp. 153–9; p. 155.
2 A.J. Youngson, *The British Economy*, 1920–1957, Allen and Unwin, London, 1960, p. 159.
3 J. Connolly, *History of Computing in Europe*, IBM World Trade Corp., New York, pp. 45ff.
4 'Histoire d'I.C.T. (France)', *ICT House Magazine*, February 1961, p. 1.
5 A.T. Maxwell, transcript of interview with A.L.C. Humphreys, 9 January 1980, p. 3 (Charles Babbage Institute Archives).
6 J.D. Scott, *Vickers: A History*, Weidenfeld and Nicolson, London, 1963, chapter 26.
7 Ibid., p. 323.
8 'Editorial', *Powers-Samas Magazine*, Sept-October 1945, p. 1.
9 'Obituary: Colonel J.A. Davies', *The Times*, 13 August 1987, p. 12.
10 A.E. Impey, 'Unexecuted Orders', 28 August 1946, Powers-Samas Board Papers.
11 See, for example, F.R.M. de Paula, *Developments in Accounting*, Pitman, London, 1948.
12 A.E. Impey, 'Fuel Crisis', 14 March 1947, Powers-Samas Board Papers.

13 C.G. Holland-Martin, 'Activities of the Technical Division', 3 June 1948, BTM Board Papers.

14 A.E. Impey, 'Rental and Outright Sales Margins', 10 February 1950, p. 3, Powers-Samas Board Papers.

15 L.E. Brougham, 'Production Division', 2 October 1947, Powers-Samas Deputy Chairman's Conference Papers.

16 A.E. Impey, 'Organisation', 21 May 1948, Powers-Samas Board Papers.

17 W.E. Hutchins, 'Hard Thinking for the Export Executive', *Office Equipment Industry*, July 1944, p. 1.

18 As cited in *Office Equipment Industry*, August 1951, p. 18.

19 J. Connolly, op. cit., p. 45.

20 For a detailed account of the fuel crisis see A. Cairncross, *Years of Recovery: British Economic Policy 1945–51*, Methuen, London, 1985.

21 'Office Machinery Shares' [re. Powers-Samas share offer], *The Times*, 6 July 1948, p. 7.

22 'Powers and Hollerith Prices', 23 June 1948, Powers-Samas Deputy Chairman's Conference Papers.

23 As quoted in W. Desborough, 'Report on Visit to Sweden', 4 October 1948, Powers-Samas Deputy Chairman's Conference Papers.

24 As quoted in a dramatic report by A.E. Impey, 'Devaluation of the £ Sterling as it Affects Powers-Samas', 20 September 1949, Powers-Samas Board Papers.

25 W. Desborough, 'Report on Visit to America, October 1949', 4 November 1949, Powers-Samas Deputy Chairman's Conference Papers.

26 W. Desborough, 'Remington Rand Tabulating Machines Division: General Impressions', 7 June 1949, Powers-Samas Board Papers.

27 J. Connolly, op. cit., p. 47. Connolly's *History of Computing in Europe* was in fact suppressed by IBM, and few copies exist outside the company.

28 BTM Board Minutes, 18 September 1947.

29 Linklaters and Paines, letter to BTM, 15 March 1949, BTM Board Papers.

30 Ibid.

31 Ibid.

32 BTM Board Minutes, 15 September 1949.

33 *Tabacus*, October 1949, p. 2; and elsewhere.

34 T.J. Watson Jr, transcript of interview with A.L.C. Humphreys, 25 April 1985 (Charles Babbage Institute Archives).

Notes to Chapter 7

1 W.B. Woods, 'A Healthy Industry', *Office Equipment Industry*, November 1949, p. 6.

2 A.L.C. Humphreys, transcript of interview with E. Tomash, 28 February 1981, p. 2 (Charles Babbage Institute Archives). BTM was not untypical of British companies that were run by ageing boards of country gentlemen; see M. Weiner, *English Culture and the Decline of the Industrial Spirit, 1850–1980*, Penguin, Harmondsworth, 1981.

3 G.H. Baillie wrote several books on the history of clocks and watches: *Watch and Clockmakers of the World*, 3 editions, 1929, 1947, and 1951; *Watches: Their History, Decoration and Mechanisms*, 1929; *Clocks and Watches*, 1951; and several others. His books are still regarded as definitive.

4 L.S. Amery, 'Obituary: Sir Ralegh Buller Phillpotts', *The Times*, 7 October 1950, p. 8.

5 Sir Cecil McAlpine Weir (1890–1960), *Dictionary of National Biography*. 'Obituary: Sir Cecil McAlpine Weir', *The Times*, 31 October 1960, p. 20; supplementary note by A.T. Maxwell, 2 November 1960, p. 15.

6 Sir Cecil McAlpine Weir (1890–1960), *Dictionary of National Biography*.

7 'Interim Report on Committee of Organisation', *c*.May 1953, BTM Board Papers.

8 For a discussion of the organizational structure of British firms see D.F. Channon, *The Strategy and Structure of British Enterprise*, Macmillan, London, 1973.

9 A.D. Chandler, *Strategy and Structure*, MIT Press, Cambridge MA, 1962, pp. 362–70. R. Sobel, *IBM: Colossus in Transition*, Times Books, New York, 1981, pp. 160–2. R. Sheehan, 'Tom Jr.'s I.B.M.', *Fortune*, September 1956, pp. 112–19, 198, 203–4.

10 J.D. Scott, *Vickers: A History*, Weidenfeld and Nicolson, London, 1963, p. 261.

11 A.T. Maxwell, transcript of interview with A.L.C. Humphreys, 9 January 1980, p. 4 (Charles Babbage Institute Archives).

12 J.D. Scott, op. cit., p. 368.

13 Untitled article on IBM, *The Times*, 31 August 1954, p. 3.

14 T.C. Hudson, interview with M. Campbell-Kelly, 3 August 1988.

15 A.E. Impey, 'Exploitation by Powers-Samas of the World Market', 14 November 1949, Powers-Samas Deputy Chairman's Conference Papers.

16 A.E. Impey, 'Rental and Outright Sales Margins', 10 February 1950, p. 3, Powers-Samas Board Papers.

17 F.J. Nash, 'Overseas Visit', *Powers-Samas Gazette*, July-August 1954, p. 1–2.

18 R. Wonfor, 'American Venture', 8 January 1952, p. 7, Powers-Samas Board Papers.

19 The Samas-Forty machines were enthusiastically described in several American office-machinery books. For example, B.D. Friedman, *A Punched Card Primer*, Public Administration Service, USA, 1955.

20 *Twenty Five Years of Achievement: 1930–1955*, Hollerith Machines (S.A.) (Pty.) Limited, 1955 (ICL Historical Collection).

21 As cited in S. Englebourg, *International Business Machines: A Business History*, Arno Press, New York, 1976, p. 135.

22 'Office Robots', *Fortune*, January 1952, pp. 82–87, 112, 114, 116, 118; p. 114.

23 L. Knight, interview with M. Campbell-Kelly, 12 November 1984. J. Bull, interview with M. Campbell-Kelly, 10 December 1984.

24 Powers Accounting Machines Research Board Minutes, 13 November 1944.

25 R. Wonfor, 'Research and Development', 22 July 1953, p. 6, Powers-Samas Board Papers.
26 'New Tabulator', 17 October 1950, BTM Board Papers.
27 J. Bull, 'Technical Division Report', 18 June 1951, BTM Board Papers.
28 W. Desborough, 'Trends in Accounting Machines', *Office Equipment Industry*, October 1949, p. 12.
29 'A Balanced Policy: Evolutionary rather than Revolutionary', *The Tabulator*, September 1956, pp. 3–4.
30 B.E. Phelps, 'Early Electronic Computer Developments at IBM', *Annals of the History of Computing*, 2, 1980, pp. 253–67; p. 253.
31 Ibid., p. 261.
32 L. Knight, 'An Electronic Calculator for Punch-Card Accountancy', *Proc. IEE*, 103, Part B, Supplement 2, 1956, pp. 228–41.
33 N. Stern, *From ENIAC to UNIVAC*, Digital Press, Bedford MA, 1981.
34 M. Campbell-Kelly and M.R. Williams (ed.), *The Moore School Lectures*, MIT Press and Tomash Publishers, Cambridge MA and Los Angeles, 1985.
35 S.H. Lavington, *A History of Manchester Computers*, NCC, Manchester, 1975.
36 M.V. Wilkes, *Memoirs of a Computer Pioneer*, MIT Press, Cambridge MA, 1985.
37 M. Campbell-Kelly, 'Programming the Pilot ACE: Early Programming Activity at the National Physical Laboratory', *Annals of the History of Computing*, 3, 1981, pp. 133–68.
38 B.V. Bowden, 'The Language of Computers', First Richard Goodman Memorial Lecture, unpublished typescript, May 1969, p. 4.
39 J.R.M. Simmons, *LEO and the Managers*, Macdonald, London, 1962.
40 M.G. Croarken, 'The Centralization of Scientific Computation in Britain, 1925–1955', Ph.D. thesis, Warwick University, 1986. To be published by Oxford University Press.
41 M.V. Wilkes, op. cit., pp. 140–1.
42 G.E. Haigh *et al.*, 'NRDC and the Environment for Innovation', *Nature*, 232, 1971, pp. 527–31.
43 H.J. Crawley, 'NRDC Computer Project', February 1957, p. 4, NRDC Paper 132 (NRDC Papers).
44 Ibid., p. 4.
45 As quoted in J. Hendry, *NDRC and the Early British Computer Industry*, to be published by MIT Press, Cambridge MA.
46 Lord Halsbury, draft of a letter to C.G. Holland-Martin, *c*.March 1950, (NRDC Papers, 86/6/11).
47 J.A. Davies, 'Electronic Computers', 27 April 1950, BTM Board Papers.
48 Lord Halsbury, 'Ten Years of Computer Development', *Computer Journal*, 1, 1959, pp. 153–9.
49 File entitled 'Computers. BTM and Ferranti. Development', *passim* (NRDC Papers, 86/6/11). B.B. Swann, 'The Ferranti Computer Department', unpublished typescript, 1975 (National Archive for the History of Computing).
50 H.J. Crawley, 'Note on Discussion with Mr. Holland-Martin of British

Tabulating Machine Company, on November 15th 1950', 16 November 1950 (NRDC Papers, 86/6/11).

51 A.D. Booth, 'Computers in the University of London, 1945-1962', *The Radio and Electronic Engineer*, 45, 1975, pp. 341-5.

52 R. Bird, 'The HEC Computer', *Proc. IEE*, **103**, Part B, Supplement 2, 1956, pp. 207-16. R. Bird, interview with M. Campbell-Kelly, 23 March 1989.

53 R.L. Michaelson, letter to M. Campbell-Kelly, 19 September 1977.

54 Powers-Samas Electronic Advisory Panel Minutes, 13 January 1954.

55 A.T. Maxwell, interview with M. Campbell-Kelly, 27 October 1987.

56 Gabor's report appears to be lost.

57 'Agreement', *Powers-Samas Gazette*, November-December 1954, p. 1.

Notes to Chapter 8

1 C. Mead, 'Managing Director's Report', 11 November 1955, p. 2, BTM Board Papers.

2 M. Stewart, *Keynes and After*, Penguin, Harmondsworth, 1969, p. 166.

3 Powers-Samas Board Minutes, 7 February 1955.

4 For a large firm, maximum borrowings were traditionally permitted such that interest payments did not exceed one-third of profits on domestic operations. F.W. Paish, *Business Finance*, Pitman, London, 1953.

5 BTM Board Minutes, 21 July 1955.

6 M. Stewart, op. cit., p. 156.

7 C. Mead, 'Managing Director's Report', 25 January 1956, BTM Board Papers.

8 C.M. Weir, 'Report by Chairman on a Visit to South Africa', 30 November 1955, p. 11, BTM Board Papers.

9 F.T. Ross, 'The Story Behind the Samastronic', *Powers-Samas Gazette*, July-August 1957, pp. 8-10. C.T.A. Jones, 'Diary of Events on Samastronic', 5 March 1959 (ICL Historical Collection).

10 'Large Card Tabulators', 31 March 1955, Powers-Samas Board Papers.

11 BTM Annual Report, 1955, p. 4.

12 H.V. Stammers, 'A Note on . . . Mechanisation of British Banks', 10 September 1956, p. 1, BTM Board Papers.

13 A.T. Maxwell, letter to M. Campbell-Kelly, 26 January 1989.

14 Powers-Samas Board Minutes, 19 September 1955.

15 W.E. Johnson, 'Powers-Samas/Ferranti Collaboration', 20 July 1955, Powers-Samas Board Papers.

16 R. Bird, 'In the Beginning . . . HEC Cut the Cost of Commercial Computing', *Computer Weekly*, 3 June 1969, pp. 10-11.

17 *The DIANA Data Processing System*, Laboratory for Electronics, Boston, November 1956 (ICL Historical Collection).

18 L. Knight, interview with M. Campbell-Kelly, 12 November 1984.

19 *The Scope for Electronic Computers in the Office*, Office Management Association, London, 1955.

20 H.V. Stammers, 'Report', 12 November 1955, BTM Board Papers.

21 'Formation of New Companies', *Tabacus*, July 1956, p. 3.
22 CDL Board Minutes, 13 November 1956.
23 K.B. Elbourne, 'Computer Development Plans', 21 January 1957, BTM Board Papers.
24 Lord Halsbury, 'Ten Years of Computer Development', *Computer Journal*, 1, 1959, pp. 153–9; p. 157.
25 L. Knight and M. Circuit, 'A High-Density File Drum as a Computer Store', *J. British IRE*, January 1960, pp. 41–5.
26 W.E. Johnson, 'Samastronic Machines', 9 October 1957, Powers-Samas Managing Director's Committee Papers.
27 Powers-Samas Managing Director's Committee Minutes, 12 August 1957 and 16 September 1957.
28 'ICT', *ICT Data Processing Journal*, No. 1, 1959, p. 7.
29 C.M. Weir, *The First Steps in European Integration*, Federal Educational and Research Trust, London, 1957.
30 C. Mead, 'General Marketing and Production Position', 4 October 1957, p. 3, BTM Board Papers.
31 J.A. Davies, 'Report by the Managing Director (Engineering)', 6 September 1957, BTM Board Papers.
32 'Memorandum by Deloitte and Co, Dated 13th May 1958, on Proposed Merger' (ICL Archives).

Notes to Chapter 9

1 H.V. Stammers, 'Visit to America, January/February 1960', *c*.March 1960, ICT Board Papers.
2 A.D. Chandler, *Strategy and Structure*, MIT Press, Cambridge MA, 1962, pp. 362–70. R. Sobel, *IBM: Colossus in Transition*, Times Books, New York, 1981, pp. 160–2.
3 D.F. Channon, *The Strategy and Structure of British Enterprise*, Macmillan London, 1973, pp. 123–5.
4 Policy Planning Group Minutes and Reports (ICL Archives).
5 Summarized from a statement of ICT policy in J.A. Davies, 'Report on Tour of USA . . . 1960', 29 February 1960, ICT Board Papers.
6 T.J. Watson, *Meeting the Challenge of Growth*, as quoted (p. 60) in C. Freeman, C.J.E. Harlow, J.K. Fuller, and R.C. Curnow, 'Research and Development in Electronic Capital Goods', *National Institute Economic Review*, 34, 1965, pp. 40–91.
7 ICT Planning Division, 'High Speed Tabulators', 13 April 1959, ICT Board Papers.
8 A.L.C. Humphreys, interviewed with M. Campbell-Kelly, 28 October 1987.
9 This estimate appears in 'Note of a Meeting between Viscount Knollys, Chairman of Vickers and Sir Cecil Weir and Colonel A.T. Maxwell on Monday, 5 October, 1959', C.M. Weir Papers (ICL Archives).
10 'IBM Computers—the Story of Their Development', *Data Processing*, 2, April–June 1960, pp. 90–101.

11 A.L.C. Humphreys, interview. P.V. Ellis, interview with M. Campbell-Kelly, 30 October 1987.

12 A.T. Maxwell, interview with M. Campbell-Kelly, 27 October 1987.

13 Policy Planning Group Minutes, 14 October 1958 (ICL Archives).

14 L.D. Stevens 'The Evolution of Magnetic Storage', *IBM Systems Journal*, 25, 1981, pp. 663–75.

15 F.M. Fisher, J.W. McKie, and R.B. Mancke, *IBM and the U.S. Data Processing Industry*, Praeger, New York, 1983.

16 B.O. Evans 'System/360: A Retrospective View', *Annals of the History of Computing*, 8, 1986, pp. 155–79. Other estimates or 1401 sales go as high as 14 000, or even 20 000.

17 A.L.C. Humphreys, personal communication.

18 C. Bashe *et al.*, *IBM's Early Computers*, MIT Press, Cambridge MA, 1985.

19 R. Sheehan, 'Q. What Grows Faster Than I.B.M.? A. I.B.M. Abroad', *Fortune*, November 1960, pp. 166–70, 236, 241–4.

20 H.V. Stammers, 'Acting Chairman's Survey', 9 December 1960, ICT Board Papers.

21 R. Sheehan, op. cit., p. 241.

22 ICT Annual Report, 1961, p. 9. E.C.H. Organ, interview with M. Campbell-Kelly, 26 November 1987. R.L. Bird, interview with M. Campbell-Kelly, 23 March 1989.

23 R. Sheehan, op. cit., p. 242.

24 C. Mead, 'Design Programme 1960/61, 1961/62, 1962/63', 17 February 1961, ICT Board Papers.

25 J. Bull, 'Managing Director's Report', 6 November 1962, ICT Board Papers.

26 'Planning Committee' in 'Report by Mr. C. Mead, Deputy Chairman', 28 February 1962, ICL Board Papers.

27 A.L.C. Humphreys, interview.

28 A. Sampson, *The New Anatomy of Britain*, Hodder and Stoughton, London, 1971, p. 266.

Notes to Chapter 10

1 A. Robertson, 'ICT—Born of the Age We Live In!', *The Manager*, March 1965, pp. 52–4; p. 52.

2 M.H. Weik, *A Third Survey of Domestic Electronic Digital Computing Systems*, BRL, Aberdeen MA, 1961. S. Rosen 'Electronic Computers: A Historical Survey', *Computing Surveys*, 1, 1969, pp. 7–36.

3 OECD, *Gaps in Technology: Electronic Computers*, Paris, 1969. C.W. Layton, *European Advanced Technology*, Allen and Unwin, London, 1969.

4 J.A. Davies, 'Report on Tour of USA . . . 1960', 29 August 1960, ICT Board Papers. Many quotations in a similar vein, from other British industrialists, appear in J.E. Sawyer, 'The Social Basis of the American System of Manufacturing', *Journal of Economic History*, 14, 1954, pp. 361–79.

5 B.M. Murphy, 'The Development of the British, French and German Native Computer Industries, 1960–1978', in S.H. Lavington (ed.), *Information*

Processing 80, North-Holland, Amsterdam, 1980, pp. 873–8.

6 Comparative IBM, ICT and European statistics appear in R. Sheehan, '*Ç*. What Grows Faster Than I.B.M.? A. I.B.M. Abroad.' *Fortune*, November 1960, pp. 166–70, 236, 241–4.

7 Table 10 in C. Freeman, C.J.E. Harlow, J.K. Fuller and R.C. Curnow, 'Research and Development in Electronic Capital Goods', *National Institute Economic Review*, 34, 1965, pp. 40–91.

8 Ibid, Table 9.

9 See *Annals of the History of Computing*, 5, No. 3, 1983—a special issue on SAGE.

10 W. Buchholz, *Planning a Computer System: Project Stretch*, McGraw-Hill, New York, 1962. H. Lukoff, *From Dits to Bits*, Robotics Press, Portland ORE, 1979.

11 J. Hendry, 'Prolonged Negotiations: The British Fast Computer Project and the Early History of the British Computer Industry', *Business History*, 26, 1984, pp. 280–306.

12 *A History of the Sperry Rand Corporation*, Recording and Statistical Company Division of Sperry Rand Corporation, USA, September 1964.

13 F.M. Fisher, J.W. McKie, and R.B. Mancke, *IBM and the U.S. Data Processing Industry*, Praeger, New York, 1983, p. 46.

14 A.L.C. Humphreys, interview with M. Campbell-Kelly, 28 October 1987.

15 See *Annals of the History of Computing*, 9, No. 1, 1987—a special issue on the B5000.

16 A.T. Maxwell, interview with A.L.C. Humphreys, 18 February 1980 (Charles Babbage Institute Archives). A.T. Maxwell, interview with M. Campbell-Kelly, 27 October 1987, and letter, 26 January 1989.

17 T.R. Bransten and S.H. Brown, 'Machines Bull's Computer Crisis', *Fortune*, July 1964, pp. 154–5, 242, 244. G.H. Wierzyuski, 'G.E.'s $200-Million Ticket to France', *Fortune*, 1 June 1967, pp. 92–5, 159–60, 162.

18 K.D. Fishman, *The Computer Establishment*, McGraw-Hill, New York, 1982.

19 R. Jones and O. Marriot, *Anatomy of a Merger: A History of GEC, AEI and English Electric*, Cape, London, 1970, pp. 183–4.

20 A.L.C. Humphreys, interview. A.T. Maxwell, interviews.

21 'Report by Messrs. Lightstone and Humphreys on Fact Finding and Feasibility Studies Conducted with RCA and EE', 26 January 1961 (ICL Archives, Box 399).

22 A.L.C. Humphreys, interview.

23 Ibid.

24 'Elliott-Automation: Bread But No Butter', *Economist*, 3 June 1967, p. 1054. Elliott-Automation Annual Reports.

25 J. Hendry, 'The Teashop Computer Manufacturer: J. Lyons and the Potential and Limits of High-Tech Diversifications', *Business History*, 29, 1987, pp. 73–102.

26 A.L.C. Humphreys, interview.

27 K. Crook, 'In the Beginning . . . EMIDEC 2400s are Still Giving Sterling Service', *Computer Weekly*, 1 May 1969.

28 K. Crook interview with M. Campbell-Kelly, 29 September 1983. J. Hendry, *NRDC and the Early British Computer Industry*, 1987, to be published by MIT Press, Cambridge MA.

29 E.W. Playfair, 'Electric and Music Industries Limited: Memorandum by Chairman', 26 June 1962, ICT Board Papers.

30 A.T. Maxwell, interviews.

31 G.G. Scarrot, 'Significance of Orion', unpublished typescript, 1973.

32 G. Burck, 'The Assault on Fortress I.B.M.', *Fortune*, June 1964, pp. 112–6, 196, 198, 200, 202, 207. F.M. Fisher *et al.*, op. cit., pp. 308–16.

33 A.T. Maxwell, interviews. Diary of B.F. Clarke, 10 September 1962 (Midland Bank Group Archives).

34 M.J. Marcotty, F.M. Longstaff, and A.M. Williams, 'Time Sharing on the FP6000 Computer System', *Proc. AFIPS SJCC*, April 1963.

35 'FP6000: Report on Visit to Ferranti-Packard by Mr C.H. Devonald, Mr D. Eldridge, Mr Arthur Jackson and Mr M.J. Wingstedt', 4 April 1963, p. 44 (ICL Historical Collection).

36 A.L.C. Humphreys, interview.

37 M.L.N. Forrest, interview with M. Campbell-Kelly, 4 August 1988.

38 All interviewees asked have expressed much the same opinion of Basil de Ferranti. See also 'Obituary: Basil de Ferranti [1930–88]', *The Times*, 26 September 1988, p. 16.

Notes to Chapter 11

1 T.A. Wise, 'I.B.M.'s $5,000,000,000 Gamble', *Fortune*, September 1966, pp. 118–23, 224, 226, 228; p. 119.

2 P.V. Ellis, interview with M. Campbell-Kelly, 30 October 1987.

3 See for example R. Malik, *And Tomorrow the World: Inside I.B.M.*, Millington, London, 1975.

4 T.A. Wise, op. cit., September 1966. T.A. Wise, 'The Rocky Road to the Market Place', *Fortune*, October 1966, pp. 138–43, 199, 201, 205–6, 211–12.

5 [SPREAD Report], 'Processor Products—Final Report of SPREAD Task Group, December 28, 1961', reprinted in *Annals of the History of Computing*, 5, 1983, pp. 6–26.

6 B.O. Evans, 'System/360: A Retrospective View', *Annals of the History of Computing*, 8, 1986, pp. 155–79.

7 F.L. Westwater, 'The Interface Concept', *Data Processing*, November-December 1964, p. 326. R. Bird, interview with M. Campbell-Kelly, 23 March 1989.

8 P.V. Ellis, interview.

9 E.W. Pugh, *Memories that Shaped an Industry: Decisions Leading to System/360*, MIT Press, Cambridge MA, 1984.

10 [SPREAD Report], p. 6.

11 T.A. Wise, op. cit., September 1966, p. 118.

12 J.D. Aron *et al.*, 'Discussion of the SPREAD Report, June 23, 1982', *Annals of the History of Computing*, 5, 1983, pp. 27–44; p. 44.

13 B.O. Evans, op. cit., p. 170.
14 As quoted (p. 202) in G. Burck, 'The Assault on Fortress I.B.M.', *Fortune*, June 1964, pp. 112–16, 196, 198, 200, 202, 207.
15 OECD, *Gaps in Technology: Electronic Computers*, Paris, 1969.
16 F.M. Fisher, J.W. McKie, and R.B. Mancke, *IBM and the U.S. Data Processing Industry*, Praeger, New York, 1983, chapter 6.
17 As quoted (p. 128) in G.H. Wierzynski, 'Control Data's Newest Cliffhanger', *Fortune*, February 1968, pp. 126, 128–9, 176, 179.
18 K.B. Elbourne, 'Computer Development Plans', 21 January 1957, BTM Board Papers.
19 C. Mead, 'Visit of Colonel A.T. Maxwell and Mr. C. Mead to the United States of America', 25 March 1964, ICT Board Papers.
20 Ibid., p. 2.
21 A.L.C. Humphreys, interview with M. Campbell-Kelly, 28 October 1987. P.V. Ellis, interview. R.L. Bird, interview.
22 N. Marshall, interview with M. Campbell-Kelly, 4 July 1988.
23 A.L.C. Humphreys, interview. E.C.H. Organ, interview with M. Campbell-Kelly, 26 November 1987.
24 P.V. Ellis, interview.
25 Ibid.
26 'ICT 1900 Presentation', 16mm film, 1964 (ICL Historical Collection).
27 Ibid.
28 Ibid.
29 'ICT 1900 Series', 16mm film, 1964 (ICL Historical Collection).
30 ICT Board Minutes, 13 January 1965, minute 8b.
31 'ICT 1900 Presentation', 16mm film, 1964 (ICL Historical Collection).
32 A. Robertson, 'ICT—Born of the Age We Live In!', *The Manager*, March 1965, pp. 52–4. 'Pattern for the Mid-Sixties . . . I.C.T. Reorganization', *ICT Data Processing Journal*, No. 24, 1965, pp. 9–10.
33 Ibid., p. 9.
34 As quoted in A. Robertson, op. cit., p. 54.
35 'Mr. Cousins, Minister of Technology, Opens I.C.T.'s New R. and D. Laboratories', *Computer Bulletin*, 9, 1965, pp. 63–4. 'The Future Came Yesterday', 16mm film, 1967 (ICL Historical Collection).
36 B.Z. de Ferranti, 'Managing Director's Report', 26 May 1967, ICT Board Papers.
37 'ICT 1900 Software Development Organisation', 16mm film, c.1966 (ICL Historical Collection).
38 ICT Annual Report, 1965, p. 9.
39 P. Stoneman, 'Merger and Technological Progressiveness: The Case of the British Computer Industry', *Applied Economics*, 10, 1978, pp. 125–40.
40 F.M. Fisher et al., op. cit., p. 151.
41 P.M. Hunt, interview with M. Campbell-Kelly, 8 December 1987.
42 F.P. Brooks, *The Mythical Man-Month: Essays on Software Engineering*, Addison-Wesley, Reading MA, 1975.
43 J.M.M. Pinkerton, interview with M. Campbell-Kelly, 25 November 1987.

44 D.T. Caminer, D.J. Blackwell, and A.C.D. Haley, 'Report and Recommendations Following Visit to RCA, November 23rd–December 10th 1964', English Electric Leo internal report (J.M.M. Pinkerton, personal papers).

45 'RCA's New Spectra 70 Series', *Datamation*, December 1964, pp. 34-6.

46 D.T. Caminer *et al.*, op. cit., para. 3.3.3.3.

47 Ibid., para. 3.3.3.4.

48 R. Jones and O. Marriot, *Anatomy of a Merger: A History of GEC, AEI and English Electric*, Cape, London, 1970.

49 'English Electric's Leapfrog', *Fortune*, March 1966, pp. 65, 68.

50 'Troubles for English Electric Small Machines', *Computer Weekly*, 31 August 1967, p. 1.

Notes to Chapter 12

1 J.-J. Servan-Schreiber, *The American Challenge*, Hamish Hamilton, London, 1968, p. 99.

2 As quoted (p. 875) in B.M. Murphy, 'The Development of the British, French and German Native Computer Industries, 1960–1978', in S.H. Lavington (ed.), *Information Processing 80*, North-Holland, Amsterdam, 1980, pp. 873-8.

3 As quoted (p. 25) in R. Clarke, 'Mintech in Retrospect', *Omega*, 1, 1973, pp. 26-38 and 137-63 (2 parts).

4 As quoted (p. 1) in *The Ministry of Technology*, Ministry of Technology, London, August 1967.

5 H. Wilson, *The Labour Government 1964-1970*, Weidenfeld and Nicolson and Michael Joseph, London, 1971, p. 8.

6 Ibid., p. 9.

7 As quoted (p. 29) in *The Ministry of Technology*, August 1967.

8 This statistic appears (p. 3) in the ICT submission to the government 'The Role of Government vis-a-vis the United Kingdom Computer Industry', *c*.autumn 1964 (ICL Archives).

9 *The Ministry of Technology*, August 1967, p. 3.

10 *Computers for Research*, Cmnd. 2883, HMSO, London, 1966.

11 J.K. Iliffe, *Basic Machine Principles*, Macdonald, London, 1968.

12 'Large Computer Project', 20 July 1965, ICT Board Papers.

13 C. Mead, 'Anglo/French Negotiations', 22 July 1965, ICT Board Papers.

14 *ICL, EELM: Large Computer Project: Presentation to the Government*, September 1965 (NRDC Papers, 86/35/5).

15 'Report of the Large Computer Technology Working Party', 29 December 1965, (ICL Archives). See also papers on the working party in the Stanley Gill Papers, D34, Science Museum Library.

16 ICT Interim Report, 23 June 1965.

17 'Report by the Chairman', 6 August 1965, ICT Board Papers.

18 A.G. Burney, 'Preliminary Report to the Board', 31 August 1965, ICT Board Papers.

19 OECD, *Gaps in Technology: Electronic Computers*, Paris, 1969, p. 157.

20 Ibid., Tables 3, 5, and 7 in statistical appendix.
21 There is a great deal of detail on the progress of the merger negotiations in the ICL Archives, both in the board papers and in the contemporary 'Informal Notes' of D.C.L. Marwood, ICT Company Secretary. Only documents directly quoted from have been cited here. Additional detail is based on interviews with A.T. Maxwell, A.L.C. Humphreys, and others.
22 As quoted (p. 189) in A. Graham, 'Industrial Policy', in W. Beckerman (ed.), *The Labour Government's Economic Record: 1964–1970*, Duckworth, London, 1972, pp. 178–217.
23 [Pears Report], S.J. Pears, 'Rationalisation of Certain Companies in the British Computer Industry', 27 September 1966. There is an extant copy of the Pears Report in the ICL Archives. ICT submitted a major report on its history and present circumstances at the request of the Pears inquiry, 'International Computers and Tabulators Limited', 30 June 1966, also in the ICL Archives. English Electric Computers also presumably submitted a report to the Pears inquiry, but it has not been located.
24 [Pears Report], para. 39.
25 Ibid., para. 42.
26 'I.C.T.'s Submission to Government on the Future of the British Computer Industry', 6 May 1966 (ICL Archives).
27 As quoted (p. 114) in R. Jenkins, *Tony Benn: A Political Biography*, Writers and Readers, London, 1980. See also, J. Bloor, 'Interview: Why Benn Still Backs British Computing', *Computing* (Europe), 18 January 1973, pp. 14–15.
28 'Elliott-Automation: Butter But No Bread', *Economist*, 3 June 1967, p. 1054.
29 *Notes on Science and Technology in Britain: Electronic Computers*, Central Office of Information, HMSO, London, 1971.
30 D.C.L. Marwood, Informal Notes, 3 May 1967.
31 J.M.M. Pinkerton, interview with M. Campbell-Kelly, 25 November 1987.
32 'Report of the Working Party on a New Range of Computing Systems', July 1967, para. 20 (ICL Archives).
33 A.T. Maxwell, 'Harvard and Yale', 12 September 1967, ICT Board Papers. ('Harvard' and 'Yale' were codenames for English Electric and Plessey, to maintain security.)
34 T.C. Hudson, interview with M. Campbell-Kelly, 3 August 1988.
35 'Link-up of UK Industry Moves Nearer', *Computer Weekly*, 21 December 1967, p. 1.
36 D.C.L. Marwood, Informal Notes, 30 January 1968.
37 D.C.L. Marwood, Informal Notes, 7 February 1968.
38 *Industrial Expansion*, Cmnd. 3509, HMSO, London, 1968. *Industrial Expansion Act*, HMSO, London, 1968.
39 *Industrial Investment: The Computer Mergers Project*, Cmnd. 3660, HMSO, London, 1968.
40 A.L.C. Humphreys, transcript of interview with E. Tomash, 28 February 1981, p. 17 (Charles Babbage Institute Archives).
41 E.C.H. Organ, interview with M. Campbell-Kelly, 26 November 1987.

42 A.L.C. Humphreys, interview with M. Campbell-Kelly, 28 October 1987.
43 'Benn's Former Adviser Lashes Out', *Computing* (Europe), 1 February 1973, p. 1.

Notes to Chapter 13

1 As quoted (p. 87) in P. Siekman, 'Now it's the Europeans versus I.B.M.', *Fortune*, 15 August 1969, pp. 86–91, 174, 176, 178.
2 'Growth and Improvement Plan', 10 September 1970, IC(H) Board Papers.
3 A.T. Maxwell, interview with M. Campbell-Kelly, 27 October 1987.
4 G. Turner, *Business in Britain*, Eyre and Spottiswoode, London, 1969, p. 338.
5 'The Marketing Award 1967: Mr A.L.C. Humphreys', ICT, n.d. (ICL Historical Collection).
6 'ICL Corporate 5-year Business Plan, 1968/69-1972/73', 5 October 1968, ICL Board Papers.
7 G. Turner, op. cit., p. 327.
8 As quoted in P. Siekman, op. cit., p. 91.
9 *Industrial Investment: The Computer Merger Project*, Cmnd. 3660, HMSO, London, 1968, para. 4.
10 A.L.C. Humphreys, interview with M. Campbell-Kelly, 28 October 1987.
11 [S. J. Pears], 'Report on . . . English Electric Computers Ltd, 15 May 1969' (ICL Archives).
12 M.L.N. Forrest, interview with M. Campbell-Kelly, 4 August 1988.
13 Dozens of reports were prepared in the course of new range planning. The two most important summary documents in the ICL Archives are [NPRO1], 'Introduction and Summary Documents', Book 1, 30 April 1969; [NPRO2], 'Phase II: Situation Report', 20 October 1969. In the public domain, an excellent account appears in J.K. Buckle, *The ICL 2900 Series*, Macmillan, London, 1978. There are many more reports in the ICL Historical Collection.
14 'New Range Planning: Notes on a Meeting . . . 28th January 1969', ICL Board Papers.
15 'An Evaluation of the ICL 1900 Series Architecture', Auerbach Corp., Philadelphia PA, 15 April 1969 (Charles Babbage Institute Archives).
16 V.V. Pasquali, interview with M. Campbell-Kelly, 21 September 1988.
17 M.L.N. Forrest, interview. V.V. Pasquali, interview.
18 A.L.C. Humphreys, interview.
19 'ICL's Super Computer Cancelled', *Computer Weekly*, 11 September 1969, p. 1.
20 A.G. Bagshaw, interview with M. Campbell-Kelly, 21 September 1988.
21 M.L.N. Forrest, interview. V.V. Pasquali, interview.
22 There was a *lot* of paper, however. For example, an enormous tome, 'Project 52' ['strictly confidential, and distribution is on a limited basis'], ICL, May 1971 (J.M.M. Pinkerton, personal papers).
23 C.M. Wilson, interview with M. Campbell-Kelly, 6 September 1988.
24 [ICL submission to DTI], 'ICL New Range Introduction Strategy', 1 December 1971, p. 28. ICL Archives Box 3.

25 'ICL: Five Year Forward Look, 1975/76 to 1979/80', 20 January 1976, p. 5, ICL Board Papers.

26 P.V. Ellis, 'ICL and CII Status Report', 2 August 1971, IC(H) Board Papers.

27 A.L.C. Humphreys, 'ICL and CDC', 23 October 1970, IC(H) Board Papers.

28 'Operating Plan 1971/72', 21 October 1971, IC(H) Board Papers.

29 B.M. Murphy, 'European Strategy in the World Computer Market', 3 December 1968, ICL Board Papers.

30 [HC621-I], p. xi, para. 22.

31 [HC137], p. 30, para. 56.

32 F.M. Fisher, J.W. McKie, and R.B. Mancke, *IBM and the U.S. Data Processing Industry*, Praeger, New York, 1983, p. 342. K.D. Fishman, *The Computer Establishment*, McGraw-Hill, New York, 1981, p. 139.

33 L. Lightstone, 'Sales Group Report . . .', 8 October 1969, ICL Board Papers.

34 F.M. Fisher *et al.*, op. cit., p. 367.

35 Ibid., p. 217.

36 As quoted in [HC621-I], p. xxiv, para. 86.

37 G.W. Brock, *The U.S. Computer Industry*, Ballinger, Cambridge MA, 1975, p. 113.

38 P.V. Ellis, interview with M. Campbell-Kelly, 30 October 1987.

39 [HC621-I], p. vii, para. 2.

40 In E. Moonman (ed.), *British Computers and Industrial Innovation*, Allen and Unwin, London, 1971, p. xviii.

41 E. Moonman, op. cit., p. 4.

42 [HC137], 'The Procurement of Computers for Central Government', pp. 445-6, para. 15.

43 [HC137], p. 416, para. 2036.

44 As quoted (p. 157) in J. Hills, *Information Technology and Industrial Policy*, Croom Helm, London, 1984.

45 [HC137], p. 422, para. 2070.

46 [HC137], pp. 406-7, paras 2036 and 2037.

47 [HC137], p. 423, para. 2074.

48 OECD, *Gaps in Technology: Electronic Computers*, Paris, 1969, p. 133.

49 E. Moonman, op. cit., p. 71.

50 See, for example, P. Mottershead 'Industrial Policy' in F.T. Blackaby (ed.), *British Economic Policy, 1960-74*, Duckworth, London, 1978.

51 [621-II], p. 155.

52 [621-II], p. 140.

53 [621-I], p. xxxvi, para. 137.

54 J.E. Wall, 'The Company's Current Share Price', 30 June 1971, IC(H) Board Papers.

55 *Hansard*, written answers, 30 July 1971, pp. 196-7.

56 'How Should ICL Be Helped?', *The Economist*, 7 August 1971, p. 74.

57 'To the Rescue of ICL, Again', *The Economist*, 24 July 1971, p. 70.

58 Transcript of a phone conversation with an ICL customer in Jamaica in 'Operating Plan 1971/72', 21 October 1971, pp. 41-3, IC(H) Board Papers.

59 P.V. Ellis, interview.

60 IC(H) Board Minutes, minute 117, 26 October 1971.

61 [HC621-I], p. lx, para. 255.

62 [HC621-I], p. lx, para. 258.
63 *A Framework for Government Research and Development*, Cmnd. 4814, HMSO, London, 1971, para. 6.
64 [ICL submission to DTI], 'ICL New Range Introduction Strategy', 1 December 1971 (ICL Archives).
65 D.C.L. Marwood, Informal Notes, February 1972.

Notes to Chapter 14

1 J. Ensor, 'Man of the Week: A New Dynamism in ICL', *Financial Times*, 26 October 1974.
2 G.R. Cross, interview with M. Campbell-Kelly, 14 March 1988.
3 The quotation comes from K. Owen, 'Management: Mr New Range at ICL', *The Times*, 28 October 1974, p. 18.
4 'Corporate Business Plan 1972/73 to 1976/77', 2 vol, April–May 1973 (ICL Archives). This document subsumes G.R. Cross's 'ICL Corporate Objectives and Strategy', 1972, the only known copy of which is in the personal possession of Cross.
5 G.R. Cross, interview.
6 ICL Annual Report, 1972, p. 5.
7 Ibid., p. 21.
8 See M. Wilkins, *The Emergence of Multinational Enterprise*, Harvard University Press, Cambridge MA, 1970; chapter 5, particularly.
9 G.R. Cross, interview.
10 Ibid.
11 T.D. Griffin, interview with M. Campbell-Kelly, 3 August 1988.
12 The quotations come from K. Owen, op. cit.
13 Many of the details and dates in this section come from Informal Notes made by the Company Secretary, D.C.L. Marwood.
14 [HC621-I], p. lx, paras 257-8.
15 [HC473], p. 2, para. 7.
16 [ICL submission to DTI], 'ICL New Range Introduction Strategy', 1 December 1971 (ICL Archives).
17 T.C. Hudson, interview with M. Campbell-Kelly, 3 August 1988.
18 A.L.C. Humphreys, 'Notes of a Meeting with the Department of Trade and Industry . . . Friday, 10th March 1972', 13 March 1972, IC(H) Board Papers.
19 D.C.L. Marwood, Informal Notes, 15 March 1972.
20 Ibid., 6 June 1972.
21 *Hansard*, 3 July 1972, col. 34.
22 [HC473], p. 10, paras 32-3 [Christopher Chataway's evidence].
23 M. Becket, 'ICL to Get Unlimited State Aid', *Daily Telegraph*, 4 August 1972.
24 [DTI], 'Guidelines which HMG would wish ICL to adopt in considering potential partners', *c*.July 1972, ICL Board Papers.
25 D.C.L. Marwood, Informal Notes, 3 August 1972.

26 'International Computers (Holdings) Limited: Report to the Minister on Possible Partnerships', October 1972 (ICL Archives).

27 Ibid., p. 3.

28 T.C. Hudson, interview. D.C.L. Marwood, Informal Notes, 8 November 1972.

29 Ibid.

30 [HC97-I], p. 57, paras 10–11.

31 Ibid.

32 [HC97-I], p. 139, paras 822–3.

33 A detailed history of the ICL 2903 is given in a report entitled 'International Computers Limited', April 1976, submitted for the 1976 Award of the Institute of Marketing. There is a copy of the report in the ICL Historical Collection.

34 K.H. Macdonald, interview with M. Campbell-Kelly, 28 June 1988.

35 M.V. Wilkes, 'The Genesis of Microprogramming', *Annals of the History of Computing*, 8, 1986, pp. 116–26.

36 A.C.D. Haley, interview with M. Campbell-Kelly, 11 December 1987.

37 T.C. Hudson, 'Government Support', 1 June 1973, IC(H) Board Papers.

38 G.R. Cross, 'ICL and Nixdorf', 7 November 1973, p. 2, IC(H) Board Papers.

39 *Hansard*, 4 July 1973, col. 530.

40 ICL Annual Report 1973, pp. 7 and 15.

41 T.C. Hudson, 'ICL/Nixdorf', November 1973, p. 2, IC(H) Board Papers.

42 Ibid., p. 5. T.C. Hudson, interview.

43 'Five Year Strategic Plan, 1973/4 to 1977/8', 30 August 1973, p. 11 (ICL Archives).

44 Ibid., p. 42.

45 Judith Bloor, 'ICL at the Crossroads', *Computing* (Europe), 24 October 1974, pp. 12–13.

46 'Viewpoint: Great Expectations?', *Data Processing*, November-December 1974, p. 361.

Notes to Chapter 15

1 C.M. Wilson, interview with M. Peltu, *Computer Weekly*, 16 February 1978, p. 12.

2 'ICL Five Year Forward Look, 1975/76 to 1979/80', 20 January 1976, p. 20, IC(H) Board Papers.

3 C.M. Wilson, interview with M. Campbell-Kelly, 6 September 1988.

4 'ICL's Top-Down Policy Misfires', *Computer Weekly*, 12 June 1975, p. 1.

5 G.R. Cross, '2900 Status Report', 5 May 1976, IC(H) Board Papers.

6 M.L.N. Forrest, interview with M. Campbell-Kelly, 4 August 1988.

7 [Editorial], 'Time ICL Answered Some Questions', *Computer Weekly*, 2 October 1975, p. 2.

8 See 'Capital Requirements as a Barrier to Entry', chapter 5 of G.W. Brock, *The U.S. Computer Industry: A Study of Market Power*, Ballinger, Cambridge MA, 1975, pp. 55–67.

9 'Grosch's Law', *Encyclopedia of Computer Science and Engineering* (2nd edn), Van Nostrand Reinhold, New York, 1983.

10 G.W. Brock, op. cit., p. 56.

11 G. Frazer, 'Britain's Electronic Davids', *Management Today*, September 1973, pp. 91–3, 174, 180, 186.

12 [HC199], p. 12, para. 44.

13 I.M. Barron and T. Margerison, 'Proposal for the Development of the Mini-computer Industry in Europe', 26 March 1974. Reprinted in [HC199], pp. 35–43.

14 G.R. Cross, 'The Merger We Really Wanted', *ICL News*, May 1976, p. 1.

15 As quoted (p. 436) in F.M. Fisher, J.W. McKie, and R.B. Mancke, *IBM and the U.S. Data Processing Industry*, Praeger, New York, 1983.

16 E.K. Faltermayer, 'Its a Spryer Singer', *Fortune*, December 1963, pp. 145–8, 154–68; reprinted as chapter 18 of H.I. Ansoff, *Business Strategies: Selected Readings*, Penguin, Harmondsworth, 1969.

17 Singer Friden Division, 'News Release', 1 April 1970 (Charles Babbage Institute Archives).

18 'The Decision to Sell Singer Computers', *Computer Weekly*, 3 June 1976, pp. 8, 27.

19 F. Lamond, 'Market View: Cash and Courage to Take on Singer', *Computer Weekly*, 11 March 1976, pp. 26–7.

20 G.R. Cross, 'Singer Business Machines Division', 1 March 1976, IC(H) Board Papers.

21 Ibid., p. 6.

22 G.R. Cross, interview with M. Campbell-Kelly, 14 March 1988.

23 'How the Cross Road Avoided Corporate Euthanasia', *Guardian*, 2 March 1977, p. 18.

24 P.V. Ellis, 'Five Year Forward Look, 1978/83: An Appreciation', February 1979, ICL Board Papers.

25 P.V. Ellis, 'ICL Five Year Forward Look, 1978/83', February 1979, p. 29, ICL Board Papers.

26 Ibid., p. 35.

27 'Did the Government Cause Cross to Quit ICL?', *Computer Weekly*, 10 November 1977, pp. 1, 5.

28 T.C. Hudson, interview with M. Campbell-Kelly, 3 August 1988.

29 G.W. Brock, op. cit., p. 60.

30 G. Amdahl, 'The Early Chapters of the PCM Story', *Datamation*, February 1979, pp. 113–14. K. Flamm, *Creating the Computer*, Brookings Institution, Washington DC, 1988, chapter 6.

31 K. Flamm, op. cit., p. 195. R. Sobel, *IBM vs. Japan*, Stein and Day, New York, 1986, pp. 160–5.

32 G. Newell, 'Bridging from the 1900 to the 2900', *Computer Weekly*, 9 September 1976, p. 17.

33 As quoted (p. 35) in F. Lamond, 'The IBM 4300 Series . . .', unpublished consultancy report for ICL, *c*.spring 1979 (ICL Archives).

34 A.C.D. Haley, interview with M. Campbell-Kelly, 11 December 1987.

35 An excellent exposition of the ICL view of non-von Neumann architectures is given in M.D. Godfrey, 'Innovation in Computational Architecture and Design', *ICL Technical Journal*, 4, 1985, pp. 18–31.

36 A brief history of DAP appears in: 'ICL Takes World Lead', *ICL News*, April 1978, pp. 1–2. See also many papers on DAP exploitation in the *ICL Technical Journal*.

37 J.W.S. Carmichael, 'History of the ICL Content-Addressable File Store (CAFS)', *ICL Technical Journal*, 4, 1985, pp. 352–7.

38 'ICL Five Year Forward Look, 1977/8 to 1982/3', May 1978, ICL Board Papers.

39 C.M. Wilson, interview.

40 C.M. Wilson, letter to Reay Atkinson, 21 February 1980, ICL Board Papers.

41 R. Atkinson, interview with M. Campbell-Kelly, 12 September 1988.

42 'A Half-Year of Progress', *ICL News*, June 1979, p. 1.

43 J. Tysoe and P. Hickey, 'ICL and the Computer Industry', 8 August 1979, Laurie, Milbank and Co., Electronic Industry Analysts, pp. 1–2 (National Archive for the History of Computing).

44 D.C.L. Marwood, Informal Notes, 9 July 1980, p. 4.

45 F. Lamond, op. cit.

46 R. Sobel, op. cit., pp. 160–5.

47 Ibid. J. Tysoe and P. Hickey, op. cit., p. 25.

48 C.M. Wilson, 'ICL Processor Strategy: Funding Considerations', 12 July 1979, Operations Review Committee Papers (ICL Archives).

49 Ibid., p. 1.

50 Ibid., p. 1. C.M. Wilson, interview. R. Atkinson, interview.

51 T.C. Hudson, interview. A.L.C. Humphreys, interview with M. Campbell-Kelly, 28 October 1981.

Notes to Chapter 16

1 'ICL Five Year Forward Look, 1978/79 to 1982/83', February 1979, pp. 17–18, ICL Board Papers.

2 D.C.L. Marwood, Informal Notes, 9 July 1980, p. 8.

3 D.C.L. Marwood, Informal Notes, 14 January 1981, p. 6.

4 R. Atkinson, interview with M. Campbell-Kelly, 12 September 1988.

5 Ibid.

6 C.C.F. Laidlaw, interview with M. Campbell-Kelly, 27 January 1989.

7 A fuller analysis of ICL's financial strategy is given in: D.C.L. Marwood, 'ICL: Crisis and Swift Recovery', *Long Range Planning*, 18, 1985, pp. 10–21.

8 [R.W. Wilmot], 'Notes: Presentation on Mainframe Strategy', c.September 1981, ICL Board Papers.

9 R.W. Wilmot, 'Cooperation with Fujitsu', 17 August 1981, ICL Board Papers.

10 V.V. Pasquali, interview.

11 'ICL and Fujitsu Announce Major Collaboration in Mainframe Computers', ICL Press Announcement, 7 October 1981 (ICL Historical Collection).

12 M. Pastalos-Fox, 'How to Buy Technology', *Management Today*, December 1983, pp. 78–81. A. Cane, 'State of the Art at ICL', *Financial Times*, 25 April 1985, p. 40.

13 'Surrounding enemy machines'—another Wilmot slogan.

14 For a discussion on standards see: K. Flamm, *Creating the Computer*, Brookings Institution, Washington DC, 1988, pp. 242-6.

15 P.L. Bonfield, interview with M. Campbell-Kelly, 3 February, 1989.

16 D.C.L. Marwood, op. cit. Share prices: Datastream.

17 Peter Young, *Power of Speech: A History of Standard Telephones and Cables, 1883-1983*, Allen and Unwin, London, 1983.

18 C.C.F. Laidlaw, interview.

19 'STC Bid for ICL', ICL Press Announcement, 16 August 1984 (ICL Archives).

20 'STC/ICL Merger Confirmed', *ICL News*, September 1984, p. 1.

Note to Chapter 17

1 J.F. McLaughlin and A.E. Birini, 'Mapping the Information Business', Report of the Program on Information Resources Policy, Center for Information Policy Research, Harvard University, Cambridge MA, 1980.

Appendices

Appendix 1: the TMC–BTM agreements

The 1908 agreement

THIS AGREEMENT made this thirty-first day of March One thousand nine hundred and eight BETWEEN THE TABULATING MACHINE COMPANY a Corporation organized and existing under the laws of New Jersey U.S.A. party of the first part and THE BRITISH TABULATING MACHINE COMPANY LIMITED a Company formed under the Companies Acts 1862 to 1900 of Great Britain and Ireland whose registered office is situate at No. 2 Norfolk Street Strand London England party of the second part WITNESSETH

WHEREAS the party of the second part is desirous of developing in the United Kingdom of Great Britain and its Colonies (excluding Canada) hereinafter called the "Territory" a business similar to that now being conducted by the party of the first part in the United States that is to say the rental of tabulating and sorting machines and the sale of punches and cards employed in the Hollerith Tabulating System and

WHEREAS the party of the first part has agreed in consideration of the payments to be made to it as hereinafter set forth to transfer and assign to the party of the second part certain Letters Patent of Great Britain and certain inventions embodied in the present type of tabulating and sorting machines for which applications for Letters Patent of Great Britain have been made and are about to be made as hereinafter specifically set forth and

WHEREAS the party of the second part has paid to the party of the first part the sum of Two thousand one hundred pounds sterling as an advance payment on account of the royalties hereinafter specified the receipt of which is hereby acknowledged said payment having been made as follows to wit: One hundred pounds in May One thousand nine hundred and seven and Two thousand pounds on or about January First One thousand nine hundred and eight.

NOW THEREFORE this agreement is as follows:

The party of the second part hereby agrees to pay to the party of the first part the further sum of Two thousand pounds sterling on or before January First One thousand nine hundred and nine and the further sum of Two thousand pounds sterling on or before January First One thousand nine hundred and ten as advance payments on account of the royalties hereinafter specified making with the first mentioned sum of Two thousand one hundred pounds heretofore paid the sum of Six thousand one hundred pounds sterling to be paid to the party of the first part as advance payments on account of the royalties hereinafter specified.

The party of the first part in consideration of the premises and the covenants herein contain [sic] agrees that it will when the said sum of Six thousand one hundred pounds sterling has been fully paid to it provided it is paid as and within the times above provided make execute and deliver to the party of the second part its successors and assigns assignments in due form of the following Letters Patent of Great Britain, to wit:

No. 10,502 of 1901 dated May 21, 1901.

No. 19,372 of 1901 dated September 28, 1901.

No. 27,072 of 1904 dated December 12, 1904.

No. 4,898 of 1906 dated February 28, 1906.

and also of any Letters Patent of Great Britain that may be granted upon an application filed in the British Patent Office on or about December Seventh One thousand nine hundred and seven No. 27,067 of 1907, and also any Letters Patent of Great Britain that may be granted upon an application about to be filed in the British Patent Office for the transfer mechanism employed in the present type of automatic tabulating machine the number of the United States application covering said transfer mechanism being No. 300,007.

The party of the second part further agrees that in consideration of the premises it will proceed to introduce and develop the said business within the Territory and will use its best efforts to make the business of renting the said tabulating and sorting machines and of selling the said cards and punches extensive and profitable and further agrees that the hand tabulating machines automatic tabulating machines and automatic sorting machines shall be only rented to customers and shall not be sold and that the key punches and gang punches shall be only sold to its customers and shall not be rented.

The party of the second part shall have the right to rent said tabulating and sorting machines and to sell said punches cards and other materials to its customers for such rentals and prices and on such terms as it may desire provided however that the aggregate rentals and prices which it shall charge to any customer shall in no case exceed the rentals and prices which the party of the first part would regularly charge one of its customers for the same machines cards and materials for a like period.

The party of the second part further agrees that it will not operate or do business directly or indirectly outside of the Territory and will make and will use every lawful and proper effort to enforce the condition that none of the machines or apparatus supplied by it to its customers shall be taken or used outside the Territory without the written consent of the party of the first part.

The party of the second part further agrees that it will pay to the party of the first part in consideration of the premises and as royalties quarter-yearly hereafter for the machines rented by it as follows:

For each and every automatic tabulating machine of the present type and construction in use by or in possession of the customers of the party of the second part during the three preceding calendar months a sum which shall equal twenty-five (25) per centum of the amount that the party of the first part and [sic] shall then regularly charge its customers in the United States for a similar machine of like capacity and for a like period.

For each and every hand tabulating machine in use by or in possession of the

customers of the party of the second part during the three preceding calendar
months a sum which shall equal forty (40) per centum of the amount that the
party of the first part shall then regularly charge its customers in the United States
for a similar machine of like capacity and for a like period.

For each and every automatic sorting machine of the present type and
construction in use by or in possession of the customers of the party of the second
part during the three preceding calendar months a sum which shall equal twenty-
five (25) per centum of the amount that the party of the first part shall then
regularly charge its customers for a similar machine of like capacity and for a like
period but the sum of Two thousand one hundred pounds heretofore paid to the
party of the first part and the further sum of Four thousand pounds to be paid in
two instalments of Two thousand pounds each if duly paid as and when hereinbefore provided are to be credited to the party of the second part on account of the
royalties first accruing to the party of the first part under the provision of this and
the three preceding paragraphs and after the royalties computed as above on the
machines which have been or are in use by its customers amount to Six thousand
one hundred pounds then and thereafter all the royalties in excess of the amounts
theretofore paid on·account of royalties shall be paid quarter-yearly in cash as
aforesaid to the party of the first part at its office in New York or Washington in
current funds at such place of payment.

The aforesaid royalties are to be paid as above during the months of January
April July and October and for the purpose of facilitating their computation it is
agreed that one shilling shall be considered as the equivalent of twenty-five cents.

The term "customers of the party of the second part" shall include all users of
the machines supplied by the party of the second part whether supplied directly or
through any intermediary or agent.

The charges now regularly made by the party of the first part to its customers in
the United States for machines and apparatus of the present type form and
construction are set forth in the annexed Schedule. The party of the first part shall
have the right to change such charges from time to time as it may desire. Said
charges however as a basis for the determination of the royalties to be paid as
hereinbefore provided shall not for machines and apparatus of the present type
form and construction exceed the prices in said Schedule but this covenant the
purpose of which is only to fix the maximum royalty rate for machines and
apparatus of the present type form and construction shall not apply to any
machines or apparatus of new or different type form or construction or to any
improved machines or apparatus.

In case the party of the first part shall make develop or acquire any improvements in the present machines or apparatus or any new types of tabulating or
sorting machines or apparatus such improvements (whether consisting of modifications in the present forms or of new types and forms) shall from time to time be
promptly communicated to the party of the second part to enable it to patent them
in the Territory. The party of the second part shall have the right to elect whether
it will patent them or not. If it elects to patent them it shall so notify the party of
the first part within sixty days after the date of such communication and shall
forthwith at its own expense file and properly prosecute applications for Letters
Patent therefor in the Territory. If the party of the second part shall elect not to

patent such improvements or if it shall fail to notify the party of the first part of its election within said sixty days or if it shall fail to promptly apply for patents as aforesaid the party of the first part shall have the right to apply for patents in the Territory for its own use and benefit and the party of the second part shall have no right to or interest in the patents therefor and no right to use such improvements.

The party of the first part shall have the right to determine and fix the charges which it shall make for any new different or improved machines and in case the party of the second part shall acquire the right to use such improvements in the Territory by patenting the same as required by the preceding paragraph it agrees to pay to the party of the first part as hereinbefore provided a royalty for their use which shall equal in amount twenty-five (25) per centum of the price fixed and regularly charged by the party of the first part to its customers in the United States for such new or improved machines.

The party of the first part agrees to promptly notify the party of the second part of the prices fixed and charged by it for new or improved machines and apparatus and also to promptly notify the party of the second part of any changes in such prices as well as any changes in its charges for machines and apparatus of the present type and construction.

The party of the second part agrees to furnish to the party of the first part during each of said months hereafter a full and accurate written statement of the number of machines of each description rented the number of punches sold and the number of cards sold to each customer during the three preceding calendar months the name and address of each customer the place where the machines were used and the amount received from each customer for the rental of machines for the sale of punches for the sale of cards and for the sale of other materials connected with the use of tabulating or sorting machines; and the total amount of such receipts from each customer during said three months which statement shall be signed by an officer of the party of the second part and shall be sworn to if required. And the party of the second part agrees to keep full and accurate books of account showing clearly the above facts, which books of account and the records of its business shall be open at reasonable times to a representative of the party of the first part for examination and for the verification of the aforesaid statements.

If so desired (but only to such extent as will not, under the laws of the Territory, affect the validity of said patents or impair the exclusive privileges thereby granted) the party of the first part will furnish to the party of the second part the machines and apparatus above referred to and parts of same and duplicates of tools used by the party of the first part in their manufacture, for the actual cost of same, plus ten per cent (10%) f.o.b. at the place of manufacture.

The party of the second part agrees that it will from and after the date hereof duly pay all taxes and annuities on the above enumerated patents and on any patents taken out by it on the inventions hereinafter communicated by the party of the first part as above provided; and will pay and bear the expense of prosecuting or defending all infringement suits and all actions or proceedings relating to said patents for revocation or otherwise and further that it will at its own expense do all acts and things requisite or necessary to duly comply with the requirements of the law relating to the working or manufacturing of the patented inventions within the Territory and to maintain said patents and the exclusive privileges thereby granted in full force and effect; and the party of the second part further agrees that it will not do or suffer to be done anything that will invalidate any of said patents or impair the exclusive rights thereby granted.

In case the party of the second part fails to fully keep and perform any of the covenants or conditions on its part herein contained this contract shall thereupon terminate and all payments made by it to the party of the first part as advance royalties or otherwise shall be forfeited to the party of the first part and the party of the first part shall have the right to make use and sell the machines and apparatus above referred to in the Territory.

This agreement shall not be affected by the expiration of the term or terms for which any Letters Patent have been or may be granted, but, subject to the provisions of the preceding paragraph, is to continue in full force and effect until terminated or abrogated by mutual agreement of the parties hereto.

Until the above enumerated patents shall be assigned to the party of the second part as hereinbefore provided the party of the second part is hereby granted an exclusive license to make use and let out on hire within the Territory the inventions covered by the said patents which license however shall terminate in case of party of the second part fails to keep and perform any of the covenants or conditions on its part herein contained.

The foregoing provisions are to be construed as conditions as well as covenants.

Nothing herein contained shall be construed as constituting or tending to create an agency or copartnership between the parties hereto or make either party hereto liable for the acts or omissions of the other party.

The successors and assigns of the parties hereto are included in the terms and provisions of this contract.

IN WITNESS WHEREOF the parties hereto have caused these presents to be duly signed sealed executed acknowledged and delivered by the party of the second part on the day and year first above written and by the party of the first part on the 18th day of April 1908.

THE TABULATING MACHINE COMPANY.
(Sgd). A.L. Salt, Vice President.
(Sgd). S.G. Metcalfe, Secretary.

THE BRITISH TABULATING MACHINE COMPANY.
(Sgd). Ralegh B. Phillpotts, Director. (Chairman).
(Sgd). W.G. Dunstall, Secretary.

SCHEDULE.

Of charges now being made by the party of the first part to its customers in the United States for machines and apparatus of the present type form and construction.

KEY PUNCHES are sold at $75.00 each.
GANG PUNCHES are sold at $75.00 each.

HAND TABULATING MACHINES are rented at $15.00 per month, each.
AUTOMATIC SORTING MACHINES are rented at $20.00 per month, each.
AUTOMATIC TABULATING MACHINES are rented, the rental being based upon the number of counters or adding mechanisms in the machine and the number of magnets in such counters, as follows:

For the base of the machine, $25.00 per month
For each counter,   3.00   "   "
For each magnet,   .50   "   "

CARDS are sold at the following prices:
Manilla cards 5.5/8" long, $ .85 per thousand
Manilla cards 7.3/8" long, 1.00   "   "
Coloured cards 5¢ per thousand extra.

The supplementary agreement, 1923

Heads of AGREEMENT between THE TABULATING MACHINE COMPANY of America represented by Mr. O.E. Braitmayer Vice-President and THE BRITISH TABULATING MACHINE COMPANY LIMITED represented by Mr. W.G. Dunstall Director intended to be read as supplemental to the Agreement between the said Companies dated 31st March 1908:-

The British Company admit the violation of the Agreement between the American Company and the British Company and agrees that the American Company is entitled to damages.

The Representative of the American Company agrees that there were certain extenuating circumstances and in recognition of the same is willing to waive a part of its claim for damages and accept in settlement of the above damages the following:-

A payment of Four Thousand Pounds in cash; One thousand Pounds to be paid immediately to the Representative of the American Company; One Thousand to be paid within six months from date and the remaining Two Thousand Pounds to be paid within one year from date. Any further amount claimed for damages by the American Company up to the end of 1923 will be waived in view of the agreement of the British Company to assign any patents they may have secured and to communicate and assign to the American Company all applications for Letters Patent upon any inventions it has or may have in the future outside the territory controlled by the British Company.

In view of the desire of the British Company to secure freedom of action in the fixing of its charges for apparatus and cards the Representative of the American Company will agree to the following:-

1. From and after 1st January 1924 the British Company may charge whatever rental it wishes to its users for tabulating apparatus paying the American Company as royalty twenty-five per cent. of the total rental collected or received for the same (except as noted in clause 4) the amount of such royalty in no event to be less than twenty five per cent. of what the American Company regularly charges its customers for similar equipment as at the date of installation of the machines.

2. The British Company agrees that it will put no attachments or improvements on the machines as furnished under the American Company's patents without the consent of the American Company, which consent shall not be unreasonably withheld.

3. If any extra rental charge is made by the British Company for any such improvement or attachment patented by themselves in their territory and not communicated to them by or through the American Company the bill to the customer of the British Company shall show separately the amount of such extra charge.

4. The British Company may charge additional rental for such improvements or attachments referred to in Clause 3 such charge however not to exceed that proportion of the total rental that the capital cost of manufacturing such improvements shall bear to the total capital cost to the British Company of the machine with the improvement and the American Company is not to receive royalty on such additional rental charge. The capital cost of the American apparatus shall be as billed in New York to the British Company.

The foregoing clause is not to be taken as precluding that a separate agreement may be made at some future time in case the British Company should develop improvements that indicate a higher commercial value than indicated by the Capital Cost.

5. All applications for patents in territory outside that controlled by the British Company shall be communicated promptly to the American Company so that they may patent the same at their expense in such outside territory the American Company to pay no royalty to the British Company for such inventions.

6. From and after 1st January 1924 the British Company to be at liberty to charge more than the American Company's price for cards with the understanding they shall pay the American Company one halfpenny for each threepence charged above the following schedule:-

	Printed one side.	Printed two sides.
Manilla Cards:	six shillings per thousand.	nine shillings per thousand.
Coloured or coloured strip cards.	six shillings and three pence per thousand.	nine shillings and three pence per thousand.

Signed for THE TABULATING MACHINE COMPANY of America
(Sgd.) O.E. Braitmayer.

and for THE BRITISH TABULATING MACHINE COMPANY LIMITED.
(Sgd.) W.G. Dunstall.

Dated The Twenty-fifth Day of September One Thousand Nine Hundred and Twenty-three.

Appendix 2a

Directors of The Tabulator (1904-1907)
British Tabulating Machine Co. (1907-1959)

(Sir) Ralegh B. Phillpotts	1904-50
R.B. Porter	1905-15
J.L. Hunter	1904-41
M. Cradock	1904-06
G.H. Baillie	1910-30; 1940-47
(Sir) G.E. Chadwyck-Healey	1921-51
W.G. Dunstall	1916-55
The Hon. O.H. Stanley	1920-52
H.P. Chadwyck-Healey	1921-49
The Rt. Hon. L.C.M.S. Amery	1931-39
C.A. Everard Greene	1937-51
H.V. Stammers	1945-*
H.S. Briggs	1945-46
J.A. Davies	1946-*
E. Holland-Martin	1948-*
A. Cranfield	1948-59
(Sir) Cecil Mead	1948-*
Sir Cecil M. Weir	1951-*
C.G. Holland-Martin	1951-*
A.H. Haworth	1951-59
(Sir) Walter E. Puckey	1952-*
Sir John Whitworth-Jones	1955-59

Note

   * asterisked names remained on the board when the name of the company was changed to ICT on 1 October 1959.

Appendix 2b

Directors of Accounting & Tabulating Corp. of Great Britain (1915-1936)
Powers Accounting Machines (1936-1948)
Powers-Samas Accounting Machines (1949-1959)

J.E. Evans-Jackson	1915-18
Various non-British directors and alternates until acquired by Prudential	1915-18
A.C. Thompson	1919-28
(Sir) Joseph Burn	1919-45
W.C. Sharman	1919-21
H.R. Gray	1919-40
E. Dewey	1919-45

F.P. Symmons	1921-45
Sir Gerald E. May	1921-32
E.J.W. Borrajo	1921-59
Sir Alexander Aikman	1945-51
A.E. Impey	1945-50
L.E. Brougham	1945-47
(Sir) James Reid-Young	1945-52
A.J. Palmer	1945-52
S.D. Parker †	1945-49
F.R.M. de Paula	1945-53
F.P. Laurens	1947-49; 1955-*
A.T. Maxwell	1949-*
W. Desborough	1949-52
R. Wonfor	1950-55
S.S. Rae	1949-56
F.G.S. English	1952-53
F.J. Nash	1952-*
W.D. Opher	1952-53
J.R. Kelly	1953-55
W.E. Johnson	1953-59
E.J. Waddington	1954-59
T.R. Swift	1955
F.T. Davies	1956-*
F.W. Hutchins	1956-59
A.H. Hird	1957-*
A. Le M. Scott	1957-*

Notes

* asterisked names joined the board of ICT on 1 October 1959.
† Remington Rand nominee.

Appendix 2c

Directors of International Computers and Tabulators (1959-1968)

Sir Cecil M. Weir	1959-60
A.T. Maxwell	1959-68
H.V. Stammers	1959-61
A.H. Hird	1959-61
(Sir) Cecil Mead	1959-67
J.A. Davies	1959-64
F.P. Laurens	1959-62
J. Bull	1959-68
F.J. Nash	1959-61
C.G. Holland-Martin	1959-64
A. Le M. Scott	1959-68

F.T. Davies	1959-*
E. Holland-Martin	1959-65
W.E. Ogden	1959-64
Sir Walter E. Puckey	1959-68
Sir John H. Woods	1959-62
Sir Edward Playfair	1961-66
Sir Alan Wilson FRS	1962-68
A.L.C. Humphreys	1963-*
M. McCrea	1963-68
E.C.H. Organ	1963-*
H.R. Prytz	1963-68
B.Z. de Ferranti	1963-*
E. Grundy	1963-68
(Sir) Anthony Burney	1965-*
P.D. Hall	1965-*

Secretaries

W.W. Baker	1959-61
D.C.L. Marwood	1961-68

Note

    * asterisked names remained on the board when the name of the company was changed to ICL on 1 October 1968.

Appendix 2d

Directors of International Computers (Holdings) Limited (1968-1976)
ICL Limited (1977-81)
ICL Public Limited Company (1981-84)

Sir John Wall[e]	1968-72
A.T. Maxwell[v]	1968-69
(Sir) Anthony Burney[n]	1968-72
(Sir) John Clark[p]	1968-79
F.T. Davies[v]	1968-69
J.C. Duckworth[g]	1968-76
B.Z. de Ferranti[f]	1968-69
T.C. Hudson[p/e]	1968-80
A.L.C. Humphreys[e]	1968-82
Lord Nelson of Stafford[x]	1968-74
G.A. Riddell[x]	1968-74
Sir Alan Wilson FRS[n]	1968-72
G.R. Cross[e]	1972-77
E.P. Chappell[n/e]	1973-81
R.H. Grierson[x]	1974-76
J.T. Wiltshire[x]	1974-76

G. Black[n]	1976-84
P.V. Ellis[e]	1976-81
J.R. Hendin[v]	1976-82
T.G.P. Rogers[p]	1976-79
C.M. Stuart[e]	1976-81
C.M. Wilson[e]	1977-81
J.A. Ritmeester van de Kamp[n]	1979-84
(Sir) Christophor Laidlaw[e]	1981-84
R.W. Wilmot[e]	1981-*
R.A. Biggam[e]	1981-*
P.L. Bonfield[e]	1981-*
J.A. Gardiner[n]	1981-84
R.B. Horton[n]	1982-84
Sir John Hoskyns[n]	1982-84
Sir Michael Edwardes[e]	1983-84
M.S. Scott Morton[n]	1983-84

Secretaries

D.C.L. Marwood	1968-84
others	
J.G. Bates	1985-*

Notes

[e] Executive director   [n] Non-executive director   [f] Ferranti nominee
[g] Government nominee   [p] Plessey nominee   [v] Vickers nominee
[x] English Electric/GEC nominee
* asterisked names remained on the board of ICL following the STC take-over, 1 October 1984.

Index